A Conductor's Guide to Nineteenth-Century Choral–Orchestral Works

Jonathan D. Green

The Scarecrow Press, Inc.
Lanham, Maryland • Toronto • Plymouth, UK
2008

SCARECROW PRESS, INC.

Published in the United States of America
by Scarecrow Press, Inc.
A wholly owned subsidiary of
The Rowman & Littlefield Publishing Group, Inc.
4501 Forbes Boulevard, Suite 200, Lanham, Maryland 20706
www.scarecrowpress.com

Estover Road
Plymouth PL6 7PY
United Kingdom

Copyright © 2008 by Jonathan D. Green

All rights reserved. No part of this publication may be reproduced, stored in a retrieval system, or transmitted in any form or by any means, electronic, mechanical, photocopying, recording, or otherwise, without the prior permission of the publisher.

British Library Cataloguing in Publication Information Available

Library of Congress Cataloging-in-Publication Data

Green, Jonathan D., 1964–
  A conductor's guide to nineteenth-century choral-orchestral works / Jonathan D. Green.
    p. cm.
  Includes bibliographical references (p.).
  ISBN-13: 978-0-8108-6046-9 (hardcover : alk. paper)
  ISBN-10: 0-8108-6046-5 (hardcover : alk. paper)
  1. Choruses with orchestra—19th century—Bibliography. 2. Choruses with orchestra—19th century—Analysis, appreciation. I. Title. II. Title: Conductor's guide to 19th-century choral-orchestral works.

ML128.C48G73 2008
016.7825—dc22   2007032406

∞™ The paper used in this publication meets the minimum requirements of American National Standard for Information Sciences—Permanence of Paper for Printed Library Materials, ANSI/NISO Z39.48-1992.
Manufactured in the United States of America.

This book is dedicated to David F. Evans;
singer, conductor, teacher, and friend.

CONTENTS

Preface   xi

The Works   1
Beach, Mrs. H. H. A.   1
   Grand Mass in E^b 2
   The Sea-fairies   4
   The Minstrel and the King: Rudolph von Hapsburg   6
   Festival Jubilate   6
   The Rose of Avon-town   8
   The Chambered Nautilus   8
   The Canticle of the Sun   8
Beethoven, Ludwig van   10
   Christus am Oelberge   12
   Mass in C   15
   Fantasia in C minor   17
   Die Ruinen von Athen   19
   König Stephan   21
   Der glorreiche Augenblick   23
   Meerestille und glückliche Fahrt   25
   Missa Solemnis   27
   Symphony No. 9   31
Berlioz, Hector   37
   Messe solennelle   39
   Requiem: Grande messe des morts   41
   Romeo et Juliette   46
   La Damnation de Faust, légende dramatique   50
   Te Deum   55
   L'Enfance du Christ   59
   La révolution grecque, scène héroïque   63
   Huit scènes du Faust   65

Lélio ou le Retour à la vie	67
Le Cinq Mai: Chant sur la mort de l'empereur Napoléon	70
Tristia	71
Méditation religieuse	
La Mort d'Ophélie	
Marche funébre pour dernière scène d'"Hamlet"	
Vox populi	74
Hymne à la France	
La Menace des Francs	
L'Impériale	76
Brahms, Johannes	79
Ave Maria	81
Begräbnisgesang	82
Psalm 13	84
Ein deutsches Requiem	85
Rinaldo	90
Alto Rhapsodie	92
Schicksalslied	94
Triumphlied	96
Nänie	98
Gesang der Parzen	100
Bruch, Max	102
Arminius	103
Frithjof	107
Schön Ellen	108
Salamis	109
Odysseus	109
Das Lied von der Glocke	111
Achilleus	112
Das Feuerkreuz	114
Moses	115
Gustav Adolf	117
Bruckner, Anton	119
Requiem in D minor	120
Missa Solemnis in B^b minor	122
Psalm 146	124
Psalm 112	125
Mass No. 1 in D minor	127

Contents

Mass No. 2 in E minor	129
Mass No. 3 in F minor	132
Te Deum	134
Psalm 150	137
Helgoland	138
Cherubini, Luigi	141
Requiem Mass in D minor	142
Coleridge-Taylor, Samuel	144
The Song of Hiawatha	144
Hiawatha's Wedding Feast	
The Death of Minnehaha	
The Departure of Hiawatha	
Delibes, Léo	148
Messe Brève	148
Dvořák, Antonin	150
Stabat Mater	151
Psalm 149	153
Svatební kosile (The Spectre's Bride)	155
Svata Ludmila (St. Ludmila)	158
Requiem Mass	160
Te Deum	162
Elgar, Edward	165
The Light of Life	167
Caractacus	169
Fauré, Gabriel	172
Pavane	173
Messe de Requiem	174
Messe des pêcheurs de Villerville	177
Gounod, Charles François	180
Requiem	181
Liszt, Franz	183
Die Legende von der heiligen Elisabeth	185
Christus	187
Mendelssohn-Bartholdy, Felix	192
Christus	194
Elijah	196
Die erste Walpurgisnacht	201
Hymn	204
Lauda Sion	206
St. Paul	208

Psalm 42, Wie der Hirsch schreit	213
Psalm 95, Kommt, laßt uns anbeten	215
Psalm 98, Singet dem Herrn ein neues Lied	217
Psalm 114, Da Israel aus Aegypten zog	218
Psalm 115, Non nobis Domine [Nicht unserm namen, Herr]	220
Symphony No. 2, Lobgesang	222
Tu es Petrus	225
Messager, André	227
Paine, John Knowles	228
The Nativity	228
Parker, Horatio	231
Hora Novissima	232
Puccini, Giacomo	235
Messa a 4 Voci (Messa di Gloria)	236
Rimsky-Korsakov, Nikolai	238
Alexey, the Man of God	239
Slava	240
Rossini, Gioachino	242
Petite Messe Solennelle	243
Stabat Mater	245
Saint-Saëns, Camille	249
Oratorio de Noël	250
Schubert, Franz	253
Deutsche Messe	254
Graduale: Benedictus es, Domino	256
Kyrie in D, D. 31	257
Kyrie in D, D. 49	258
Kyrie in F, D. 66	259
Magnificat	260
Mass No. 1 in F	262
Mass No. 2 in G	264
Mass No. 3 in B^b	265
Mass No. 4 in C	267
Mass No. 5 in A^b, "Missa Solemnis"	268
Mass No. 6 in E^b	271
Offertorium: Intende voci in B^b	273
Offertorium: Tres sunt	274
Stabat Mater in G minor ["The Little"]	275

Stabat Mater in F	277
Tantum Ergo in C, D. 460	279
Tantum Ergo in C, D. 739	280
Tantum Ergo in D, D. 750	281
Tantum Ergo in E^b, D. 962	282
Schumann, Robert	284
Das Paradies und die Peri	285
Szenen aus Goethes Faust	289
Requiem für Mignon	292
Nachtlied	294
Mass	295
Requiem	297
Scriabin, Alexander	299
Symphony No. 1	300
Symphony No. 5, Prométhée, le poème du feu	301
Strauss, Richard	304
Wanderers Sturmlied	305
Taillefer	307
Tchaikovsky, Piotr Ilyich	310
K radosti	312
Cantata for the Opening of the Polytechnic Exhibition	314
Cantata in Celebration of the Golden Jubilee of Osip Petrov	316
Moskva	317
Verdi, Giuseppe	320
Messa da Requiem	321
Stabat Mater	325
Te Deum	327
Appendix: Text Sources	329
About the Author	337

PREFACE

This is the fifth conductor's guide to choral-orchestral music that I have written for Scarecrow Press. This volume addresses works of the Romantic era from Beethoven through Scriabin.

The works for choir and orchestra of this period are remarkably diverse and surprisingly uneven in quality. A number of excellent composers of the era produced some remarkably insipid works, often as fodder for the large choral festivals that became so popular during this time. I have elected to include here only works that I believe deserve a permanent place in the repertory. Among these are a number of compositions by Beach and Bruch for which complete performing materials are not readily available. It is my hope that these and many other neglected gems of the period will find their way back into our contemporary publishing houses and concert halls.

A brief biographical sketch is included for each composer. Dates, places, and names were culled from *The Oxford Dictionary of Music*, *Baker's Biographical Dictionary of Music and Musicians*, and *The New Grove Dictionary of Music and Musicians*. For each work the approximate duration, text sources, performing forces, currently available editions, locations of manuscript materials, notes, performance issues, evaluation of solo roles, evaluation of difficulty, and a discography and bibliography are presented when available. Durations are taken from many sources, but primarily actual recording times of performances are used. The purpose of this book is to aid conductors in selecting repertoire appropriate to their needs and the abilities of their ensembles. The discographies and bibliographies are not exhaustive, but should be helpful in further research.

Much of the information for each work was culled directly from the scores. Many materials were secured through the Sweet Briar College Library, where I received kind assistance from L. Joseph Malloy, Lisa Johnston, John Jaffe, and Shirley Reid. Additional materials were provided by the libraries of the University of Virginia, the University of

North Carolina at Chapel Hill, and the University of North Carolina, Greensboro, where Sarah Dorsey, Ted Hunter, and M. K. Amos were most helpful. I am also grateful to Sweet Briar College for its continued support.

Most of all, I must thank my beautiful wife, Lynn Buck, for her continued patience and constant encouragement.

THE WORKS

Beach, Mrs. H. H. A. (b. [Amy Marcy Cheney] Henniker, New Hampshire, 5 September 1867; d. New York, 27 December 1944)

Life: The daughter of a prominent New England family, she made her debut as a pianist in Boston at age 16, and two years later, she married a surgeon who was considerably older than she. From that point on she used the name Mrs. H.H.A. Beach. She began composing soon afterward. The premiere of her Grand Mass in E^b (see below) marked the first time a work of a female composer was performed by the Handel and Haydn Society. Her *Gaelic Symphony* was premiered by the Boston Symphony in 1896, and in 1900 she appeared as soloist with that orchestra in the first performance of her Piano Concerto. Dr. H.H.A. Beach died in 1910, and soon thereafter, Mrs. Beach embarked on a concert tour of Europe where she received great acclaim as the first American woman to compose works on the level expected in top-tier concert halls.

Mrs. Beach's songs and piano music have seen a revival in recent decades. A number of her works for choir have been edited, often as graduate research projects, and published in high-quality performing editions. The remaining works remain available in piano-vocal editions in many choral libraries. There are substantial collections of manuscripts and archived published scores in the libraries of the University of New Hampshire (http://www.izaak.unh.edu/specoll/mancoll/beach.htm#mus) and the University of Missouri at Kansas City (http://www.umkc.edu/lib/spec-col/amy-b.htm) that would allow the precocious conductor to prepare materials for revival performances of a number of fine out-of-print compositions by Mrs. Beach. Incomplete commentaries on those works appear at the end of her entry to provide a starting point for research in the hope that her entire choral oeuvre may return to the performance repertoire.

Teacher: Junius W. Hill

Other Principal Works: *Gaelic Symphony* (1896), Violin Sonata (1896), Piano Concerto (1900), Piano Quintet (1908), String Quartet (1929), numerous choral works: see below.

Selected Composer Bibliography

Tuthill, Burnet C.: "Mrs. H. H. A. Beach," *The Musical Quarterly* (1940), volume 26, number 3, 297-310.
Merrill, E. Lindsey: *Mrs. H.H.A. Beach: Her Life and Music.* Eastman School of Music: dissertation, 1963.
Eden, Myrna G.: *Energy and Individuality in the Art of Anna Huntingtin, Sculptor, and Amy Beach, Composer.* Metuchen, NJ: Scarecrow Press, 1987.
Reigles, B. Jean: *The Choral Music of Amy Beach.* Texas Tech University: dissertation, 1996.
Block, Adrienne Fried: *Amy Beach, Passionate Victorian: The Life and Work of an American composer, 1867-1944.* New York: Oxford University Press, 1998.

Grand Mass in E^b (1890)

Duration: ca. 65 minutes

Text: The text is from the Roman Catholic communion liturgy.

Performing Forces: voices: soprano, alto, tenor, and bass soloists; SATB choir; **orchestra:** 2 flutes, 2 oboes, 2 clarinets (B^b), 2 bassoons, 4 horns (F), 3 trumpets (F), 3 trombones (alto, tenor, and bass), timpani (2 drums), harp, organ, and strings.

First Performance: 18 February 1892; Boston; Handel and Haydn Society

Editions: Full scores and parts for Grand Mass in E^b are available from Edwin F. Kalmus (A8805). The piano-vocal score was originally published in Boston in 1890 by Arthur P. Schmidt. This score is now available in reprint from Recital Publications in Huntsville, Texas.

Notes: The Kalmus score, which is reproduced from manuscript in two different hands, indicates an intermission before the "Graduale." This reproduction is quite legible with some odd changes of score order, but many labels of instruments are cut off. Most of this is self-evident, but determining solo quartet versus choir requires some divining. Also some pages of the "Graduale" are out of order in the full score. The page numbers are in correct sequence, but the measures are not. It should read pages 94, 96, 95, 97.

Performance Issues: The choral writing combines homophonic and imitative writing. Virtually all of the choral parts are doubled by the orchestra. The vocal writing for the choir and the soloists is fairly athletic. A large choir is demanded to balance the orchestration. There is an a cappella section for the solo quartet in the "Sanctus." Much of the solo material is interspersed with choral passages. Each soloist, with the exception of the bass, has an extended aria. The English horn solo in the "Qui tollis" movement is assigned its own line below the bassoons, but it can be navigated best by the oboe I player. There is a cello solo in the "Gloria" [63] that requires significant facility. The orchestral writing is fairly inconsistent. Some of the wind and violin passages are high for the spirit of the music. The individual parts are generally very difficult. The balancing of parts and harmonies may prove challenging in certain sections. The composer's youth and orchestrational naïveté are evidenced by the haphazard use of the orchestra. It is clearly derivative of a number of scores she had studied. This aside, it is an attractive and effective piece despite its idiosyncracies, and deserves to remain in the repertory beyond the role of "poster child" for Victorian women's compositions. **Soloists:** soprano - range: d'-$b^{b''}$, tessitura: f'-f'', this is a sustained and dramatic solo requiring a strong voice; alto - range: a-$f\#''$, tessitura: d'-$b^{b'}$, this is a lyric and sustained solo with a few high passages, it is best suited to a mezzo-soprano; tenor - range: e-$a\#'$, tessitura: f-f', this is a sustained solo that must be able to carry over the entire ensemble; bass - range: G^b-$e^{b'}$, tessitura: c-c', this is the easiest of the solos with only occasionally exposed lyric passages; **choir:** medium difficult; **orchestra:** medium difficult.

Selected Discography

Barbara Schramm, Daniel Beckwith, Paul Rogers; Michael May Festival Chorus; conducted by Michael May, recorded in 1989. Newport Classic: NCD 6008. This is a version transcribed for organ, harp, and percussion.

Margot Law, Martha Remington, Ray Bauwens, Joel Schneider; Stow Festival Chorus; conducted by Barbara Jones, recorded 22 January 1995 in the Cathedral of St. Paul in Boston. Albany Records: Troy 179.

Selected Bibliography

Hale, Philip: "Amy Beach: A Review of Mass in E-flat," Boston Evening Transcript (8 February 1892), 5. Reprinted in *Source Readings in American Choral Music: Composers' Writings, Interviews, and Reviews*, edited by David P. DeVenney; *Monographs and Bibliographies in American Music*, number 15, 74-76. Missoula, MT: College Music Society, 1995.

Ochs, Ruth Amelia: *Amy Beach's Mass in E^b, op. 5: A Study of its Style and Sources*. Harvard College: Honors thesis (A.B.), 1997.

Zerkle, Paula Ring: *A Study of Amy Beach's Grand Mass in E flat major, op. 5*. Indiana University: dissertation, 1998.

The Sea-fairies, op. 59 (1904)

Duration: ca. 15 minutes

Text: The text is by Alfred Lord Tennyson.

Performing Forces: voices: 2 soprano and one alto soloist; SSAA choir; **orchestra:** 2 flutes, 2 clarinets (A), 2 horns (F), harp, and strings.

First Performance: February 1905; Philadelphia; Eurydice Chorus conducted by Walter Damrosch

Editions: The original piano-vocal score of *The Sea-fairies* was published by A.P. Schmidt in 1904. A modern performing piano-vocal edition, prepared by Adrienne Fried Block in 1996, is available from Hildegard Publishing Company. A scholarly edition of the full score has been prepared by Andrew Thomas Kuster, was published by A-R Editions in 1999 as *Recent Researches in American Music*, volume 32.

Autograph: The holograph full score is in the Spaulding Library of the New England Conservatory of Music in Boston (Vault ML96 B38 op. 59). The composer's manuscript is in the Beach Archive in the Special Collection of the University of New Hampshire Library (box 5, f. 18).

Notes: *The Sea-fairies* was commissioned by the Thursday Morning Musical Club of Boston.

Performance Issues: The choir has significant unaccompanied passages in four parts. The choral writing is mostly homophonic, but has a number of extended melismas, which curiously exceed any melismatic writing for the soloists. The solos are appropriate for strong choristers. There are only a few places where a solo appears concurrently with the choir. The harp part is an integral element of the score. The wind and string parts are conservatively written. The scoring allows for effective performances using a solo string quintet and a small choir. There were performances during the composer's lifetime with a choir of 12 singers. **Soloists:** soprano I - range: $f\#'-b''$, tessitura: $g'-f''$, this is a sustained solo with some long phrases; soprano II - range: $e^{b'}-f''$, tessitura: $e^{b'}-e^{b''}$, this is a simple solo; alto - range: $g-e^{b''}$, tessitura: $c'-c''$, this is a lyric solo; **choir:** medium easy; **orchestra:** medium easy.

Selected Discography

At the time of this writing, no recordings were available.

Selected Bibliography

Kuster, Andrew Thomas: "Introduction" and "Critical Report" from *Recent Researches in American Music*, volume 32, Amy Beach: The Sea-Fairies, Opus 59. Madison, WI: A-R Editions, Inc., 1999.

Additional Works by Amy Beach

The following works are not yet available in modern performing editions.

The Minstrel and the King: Rudolph von Hapsburg, op. 16 (1892)

Duration: ca. 25 minutes

Text: The text, in German and a singing English translation, is by Friedrich Schiller.

Performing Forces: voices: tenor and baritone soloists; TTBB choir; **orchestra:** 2 flutes, 2 oboes, 2 clarinets, 2 bassoons, 4 horns, 2 trumpets, 3 trombones, timpani, and strings.

Editions: The piano-vocal score of *The Minstrel and the King* was originally published in Boston in 1894 by Arthur P. Schmidt. This score is now available in reprint from Recital Publications in Huntsville, Texas.

Autograph: The autograph full score of *The Minstrel and the King* is in the Spalding Library of the New England Conservatory in Boston.

Festival Jubilate, op. 17 (1891)

Duration: ca. 12 minutes

Text: The text is the 100th Psalm in English.

A Conductor's Guide to 19th-Century Choral-Orchestra Works 7

Performing Forces: voices: SATB choir; **orchestra.**

First Performance: 1 May 1893; World's Columbian Exposition, in Chicago; Exposition Orchestra, choristers from William Tomlin's Apollo Club of Chicago, conducted by Theodore Thomas.[1]

Editions: The piano-vocal score was originally published in Boston in 1892 by Arthur P. Schmidt. This score is now available in reprint from Recital Publications in Huntsville, Texas. A modern performing edition, prepared by Randy C. Brittain, is available from Hildegard Publishing Company.

Autograph: The autograph full score of *Festival Jubilate* is in the Spalding Library of the New England Conservatory in Boston.

Notes: This work was selected to be included in the opening ceremonies of the World's Columbian Exposition in Chicago in 1892, but was withdrawn by the Bureau of Music due to apparent gender prejudice. The work was performed for the dedication of the Woman's Building at the same exposition.

Performance Issues: The choral writing nicely balances passages of homophonic writing often including two-part divisi in all sections with extended passages in pervasive imitation. Some of the intervals of imitation (3rd and 6th) are cleverly incorporated. Many of the imitative procedures betray a keen familiarity with the choral works of Brahms. All of the choral material is well supported by the accompaniment. This work was first performed by an ensemble of approximately 300 singers. It is an effective and celebratory work that will be most successful with a large symphonic choir; **choir:** medium easy.

Selected Discography

At the time of this writing, no recordings were available.

---

[1] Randy Brittain, from the introduction to the 1995 edition of the piano-vocal score.

Selected Bibliography

Brittain, Randy Charles: *Festival jubilate, op. 17 by Amy Cheney Beach (1867-1944): A Performing Edition.* University of North Carolina at Greensboro: dissertation, 1994. This includes nine pages of bibliographic references. The score is published commercially by Hildegard, see above.

The Rose of Avon-town, op. 30 (1896)

Text: The text is by Caroline Mischka.

Performing Forces: voices: soprano soloist, SSAA choir; **orchestra.**

Editions: *The Rose of Avon-town* was originally published in Boston by Arthur P. Schmidt. This piano-vocal score is now available in reprint from Recital Publications in Huntsville, Texas.

The Chambered Nautilus, op. 66 (1907)

Text: The text is by Oliver Wendell Holmes.

Performing Forces: voices: soprano and alto soloists, SSAA choir; **orchestra.**

Autograph: The composer's manuscript in the Beach Archive in the Special Collection of the University of Missouri at Kansas City Library (box 1, manuscript 9).

Editions: A modern performing piano-vocal edition, prepared by Adrienne Fried Block in 1994, is available from Hildegard Publishing Company.

The Canticle of the Sun, op. 123 (1924)

Duration: ca. 22 minutes

Text: The text is by St. Francis of Assisi.

Performing Forces: voices: soprano, alto, tenor, and bass soloists; SATB choir; **orchestra.**

First Performance: with organ: 8 December 1928; St. Bartholomew's Episcopal Church, New York

With orchestra: 13 May 1930; Toledo Choral Society; Chicago Symphony

Notes: "The origin of The Canticle of the Sun is interesting. In 1924, she went to the MacDowell Colony. Here, she came across the text of St. Francis of Assisi's *Canticle of the Sun*. In a 1943 interview published in *The Etude*, she told this story. 'I took it up and read it over - and the only way I can describe what happened is that it jumped at me and struck me, most forcibly! As if from dictation, I jotted down the notes of my Canticle. In less than five days the entire work was done.'"[2]

Selected Discography

Capitol Hill Choral Society and Orchestra; conducted by Barbara Buchanan. It was released in July 1998. Albany Records: Troy 295.

---

[2] From the Albany Records website promoting their recording of the work. No author was attributed.

Beethoven, Ludwig van (b. Bonn, 15 or 16 December 1770; d. Vienna, 26 March 1827)

Life: Beethoven is not only one of the supreme geniuses of Western art music, but his is one of the best-documented lives of the 19th century. He left behind a significant collection of letters and what is possibly the richest repository of sketchbooks to survive any composer in history. Because of his deafness, we have many conversation books documenting half of the discussions he had with many of his visitors over the course of two decades. While he did not publish prose documents during his lifetime, many have been collected, annotated, and published. They provide a remarkable insight into one of the greatest creative lives in history.

Born into a musical family—his grandfather and abusive father were both singers in the court in Bonn—he received his early training from his father who wished to exploit his precocious son in the model of Leopold Mozart. He attracted patronage from Count Waldstein when he was 16. He soon attracted the attention of Haydn whose composition lessons with Beethoven are reputed to have been exasperating for teacher and pupil. We do know that Haydn emphasized counterpoint in this tutelage, and that J.J, Fux's *Gradus ad Parnassum* provided many of the exercises, which prepared him for study with Albrechtsberger and surely cultivated his future contrapuntally oriented compositional style.

Beethoven enjoyed the Patronage of Prince Lichnowsky in Vienna, living in his home (1794-1796). In the following 30 years he lived in as many apartments in Vienna, producing numerous masterpieces and literally transforming every musical genre in which he worked.

Beethoven's deafness has been the subject of much discussion, as have his relationships with women, his politics, and his religious views. All of these had profound influences upon his works and his choices of texts for his vocal works. While it is true that working in his imagination he explored simultaneities a hearing composer might not have considered, arguments that his choral writing would not have been as vocally taxing had he been able to hear rehearsals clearly are entirely specious. Beethoven's challenging tessituras are the result of counterpoint, not disability. His choral works are vocally demanding, but the countless excellent performances of the Ninth Symphony and *Missa Solemnis* mitigate such discussions.

Teachers: Johann Georg Albrechtsberger, Franz Joseph Haydn, Christian Gottlob Neefe, Antonio Salieri
Students: Carl Czerny

Other Principal Works: opera: *Fidelio* (1804-1805); **orchestral:** Symphony No. 1 (1800), Symphony No. 2 (1801-1802), Symphony No. 3 (1803-1804), Symphony No. 4 (1806), Symphony No. 5 (1807-1808), Symphony No. 6 (1808), Symphony No. 7 (1811-1812), Symphony No. 8 (1812), Symphony No. 9 (1815-1818, 1822-1824), Violin Concerto (1806), Piano Concerto No. 1 (1795, 1800), Piano Concerto No. 2 (1795), Piano Concerto No. 3 (1800?), Piano Concerto No. 4 (1805-1806), Piano Concerto No. 5 (1809), Triple Concerto (1803-1804), *Die Geschöpfe des Prometheus* (1800-1801), *Coriolan Overture* (1807), *Leonora Overture* No. 1 (1806-1807), *Leonora Overture* No. 2 (1804-1805), *Leonora Overture* No. 3 (1805-1806), *Egmont* (1809-1810), *Die Ruinen von Athen* (1811), *König Stephan* (1811), *Die Weihe des Hauses* (1822); **chamber music:** 32 pianos sonatas, 3 piano quartets, numerous variations for piano, 16 string quartets, Die Grosse Fugue; **songs:** *Adelaide* (1794-1795), *An die Hoffnung* (1811), *An die ferne Geliebte* (1815-1816), etc., and numerous folksong arrangements.

Selected Composer Bibliography

Beethoven, Ludwig van: *The Letters of Beethoven*, translated and edited by Emily Anderson. London: Macmillan, 1961.
MacArdle, Donald: *An Index to Beethoven's Conversation Books.* Detroit: Information Service, 1962.
Thayer, Alexander Wheelock: *Thayer's Life of Beethoven*, revised and edited by Elliot Forbes, second edition. Princeton, NJ: Princeton University Press, 1967.
Cooper, Martin: *Beethoven: The Last Decade 1817-1827.* London: Oxford University Press, 1970.
The Beethoven Companion, edited by Thomas K. Sherman and Louis Biancolli. Garden City, NY: Doubleday, 1972.
Solomon, Maynard: *Beethoven.* New York: W. W. Norton, 1977.

Kerman, Joseph, and Alan Tyson: *The New Grove Beethoven.* New York: W. W. Norton, 1983.
Johnson, Douglas, Alan Tyson, and Robert Winter: *The Beethoven Sketchbooks.* Berkley, CA: University of California Press, 1985.
Mellers, Wilfrid: *Beethoven and the Voice of God.* London: Oxford University Press, 1985.
Dahlhaus, Carl: *Ludwig van Beethoven und seine Zeit.* Laaber: Laaber-Verlag, 1987.
Beethoven and His World, edited by Scott Burnham and Michael P. Steinberg. Princeton: Princeton University Press, 2000.
Fuchs, Ingrid: *Ludwig van Beethoven: Die Musikautographe in öffentlichen Wiener Sammlungen.* Tutzing, Germany: Hans Schneider, 2004.

Christus am Oelberge, op. 85 (1803)

Duration: ca. 54 minutes

Text: The text is by Franz Xavier Huber.

Performing Forces: voices: soprano (Seraph), tenor (Jesus), and bass (Peter) soloists; SATB choir; **orchestra:** 2 flutes, 2 clarinets (A, B^b, and C), 2 bassoons, 2 horns (B^b, C, D, E^b, and G), 2 trumpets (C, D, and E^b), 3 trombones (alto, tenor, and bass), timpani (2 drums), and strings.

First Performance: 5 April 1803, Theater an der Wien, Vienna[3]

Editions: Full scores and parts for *Christus am Oelberge* were published in a critical edition, *Ludwig van Beethoven's Werke: Vollständige kritisch durchgesehene überall berichtigte Ausgabe*, series 19, by Breitkopf and Härtel. It is also available for purchase in other editions from: Breitkopf and Härtel, H. W. Gray, and Kalmus.

Autograph: The full score is in the Deutsche Staatsbibliothek in Berlin. There are manuscript studies for this work in the Wielhorsky

---

[3] This concert included a performance of Beethoven's Symphony No. 2 and C minor Piano Concerto with the composer as soloist.

Sketch book, which is in the Beethoven-Haus in Bonn Germany (HCB Mh 69).

Notes: In 1803, Beethoven assumed a post at the Theater an der Wien, which put an orchestra and choir at his disposal. This work was his firt appearance in Vienna as a composer of dramatic vocal works.[4] The score was first published in Leipzig in 1811. It is organized as follows:

1. Introduction, recitative and aria	Jesus
2. Aria and angel choir	Seraph and SATB choir
3. Recitative and duet	Seraph, Jesus
4. Recitative and soldier choir	Jesus, TTB choir
5. Recitative, youth and soldier choirs	Jesus, (A)TTB choir
6. Recitative and trio	Seraph, Jesus, Peter
Soldier and youth choirs	(A)TTB
Angel choir	SATB

Performance Issues: The choral writing is generally syllabic and well reinforced by the orchestra. Although in homophonic passages there is little direct doubling of parts, fugal sections are clearly doubled throughout by the instruments. The choral parts are quite sustained and have fairly high tessituras. In movement 5, the "Choir of Youths" is in two parts with a tenor clef; however, the tessitura suggests that altos should be used for the upper part. In movement 6, the orchestra has double-dotted figures concurrent with single-dotted choral parts. This should be reconciled in favor of the double-dotted rhythm. There are exposed passages for all of the instruments, including prominent melodic passages for all of the winds; however, the string parts are particularly difficult, including rapid figurations and some challenging syncopations. This is a rhythmically complex score with many passages that will require care to integrate the parts. The choral material is all quite accessible, and scored to accommodate less secure choral ensembles. This is a good work for larger choirs of moderate skill when paired with a strong orchestra. The tenor soloist has the largest role, but the soprano part demands a highly skilled singer with flexibility at the top of the range. **Soloists:** soprano - range: e'-

---

[4] Kerman, Joseph, and Alan Tyson: *The New Grove Beethoven*, 36. New York: W. W. Norton, 1983.

14   The Works

d'''(e'''), tessitura: g'-a'', this is a difficult lyric solo with some ornate coloratura figures and very long phrases; tenor - range: d-a$^{b'}$, tessitura: f-g', this is a declamatory and lyric role with some broad melodic leaps; bass - range: B^b-e$^{b'}$, tessitura: c-c', this is a declamatory and simple solo role; **choir:** medium difficult; **orchestra:** difficult.

Selected Discography

Erna Spoorenberg, Fritz Wunderlich, Hermann Schey; Groot Symphony Orchestra; conducted by Henk Spruit, recorded in 1957. Re-released on CD by Bella Voce.
Cristina Deutekom, Nicolai Gedda, Hans Sotin; Philharmonic Chor der Stadt Bonn, Chor des Theaters der Stadt Bonn; Orchester der Beethoven-Halle; conducted by Volker Wangenheim, recorded in 1970 for the Beethoven centennial. Re-released on CD as EMI Classics: 7243 85687.
Maria Venuti, Keith Lewis, Michael Brodard; Gächinger Kantorei Stuttgart; Stuttgart Bach Collegium; conducted by Helmut Rilling, recorded in 1993 in Hegelsaal, Stuttgart. Hänssler Classics: 98422. Re-released on Brilliant Classics: 92825.
Luba Orgonasova, Placido Domingo, Andreas Schmidt; Rundfunkchor Berlin; Deutsches Symphonie-Orchester Berlin; conducted by Kent Nagano, released in 2004. Harmonia Mundi: HMC 901802.

Selected Bibliography

Upton, George: *The Standard Oratorios*, 53-59. Chicago: A. C. McClurg and Company, 1893.
Tyson, Alan: "The 1803 Version of Beethoven's Christus am Oelberge," in *Musical Quarterly* (1970), volume 56, 551-584.
Weinstock, Herbert: "Christus am Ölberge," in *The Beethoven Companion*, edited by Thomas K. Sherman and Louis Biancolli, 775-778. Garden City, NY: Doubleday, 1972.
Smither, Howard E.: *A History of the Oratorio*, volume 3, 513-535. Chapel Hill, NC: University of North Carolina Press, 1987.
Berger, Melvin: *Guide to Choral Masterpieces: A Listener's Guide*, 41-42. New York: Anchor Books, 1993.

Mass in C, op. 86 (1807)

Duration: ca. 47 minutes

Text: The text is from the Roman Catholic communion liturgy.

Performing Forces: voices: soprano, alto, tenor, and bass soloists; SATB choir; **orchestra:** 2 flutes, 2 oboes, 2 clarinets (C), 2 bassoons, 2 horns (C), 2 trumpets (C), timpani (2 drums), organ, and strings.

First Performance: 13 September 1807; Eisenstadt Palace

Editions: Full scores and parts for Mass were published in a critical edition, *Ludwig van Beethoven's Werke: Vollständige kritisch durchgesehene überall berichtige Ausgabe*, series 21, by Breitkopf and Härtel. It is also available for purchase in other editions from: Breitkopf and Härtel, H. W. Gray, C. F. Peters, and Kalmus.

Autograph: The composer's manuscript of the Kyrie and Gloria are in the Beethoven-Haus in Bonn.

Notes: This mass was commissioned by Prince Nikolaus Esterhazy, Haydn's final patron, for the Name Day of his wife, Princess Maria von Lichtenstein. The score bears a dedication to Prince Ferdinand Kinsky. It was first published in Leipzig in 1812.

Performance Issues: The choral parts are texturally complex, incorporating homophonic, fugal, and freely contrapuntal passages. Some of these passages include rapid ensemble melismas. Much of the choral material is clearly supported by the orchestra, but this is harmonically more evident than it is is rhythmically. The choir must be quite independent in its parts as the accompanimental reinforcement is sometimes subtle. Some of the choral soprano and alto parts sit high in the voice, and there are considerable sustained passages for the entire choir. The score features dramatic dynamic contrasts and melodic leaps for the singers. In fact the choristers have more vocally demanding parts than the soloists. Most of the solo work is in a quartet context. The scoring and treatment of the orchestra and choir suggest the use of a large choral ensemble and a full complement of strings. There are demanding passages for all of the instruments with particular technical challenges in the strings. The organ is a continuo part, which includes figures. Although the score is functional without the organ it should be used if at all possible. There are rapid melismatic passages for all of the soloists. This is a remarkably beautiful and expressive score requiring a skilled choir and expert orchestra. The vocal writing is more idiomatic than most of Beethoven's other concerted choral works. This mass is woefully under-performed, perhaps having been eclipsed by the *Missa Solemnis*. It is most deserving of greater attention from good ensembles. **Soloists:** soprano - range: $e'-a^{b''}$, tessitura: $g'-f''$, this is a lyric solo with some sustained singing; alto - range: $d'-e''$, tessitura: $f\#'-c\#''$, this is a declamatory solo best suited to a mezzo-soprano; tenor - range: $e-g'$, tessitura: $a-f'$, this is a very sustained and lyric role; bass - range: (F) $G-d'$, tessitura: B^b-c', this is a declamatory solo role for whom the lowest indicated pitch is exposed; **choir:** difficult; **orchestra:** difficult.

Selected Discography

Elly Ameling, Janet Baker, Theo Altmeyer, Marius Rintzler; New Philharmonia Chorus and Orchestra; conducted by Carlo Maria Giulini. Re-released on Brilliant Classics: 92825.

Henriette Schellenberg, Marietta Simpson, Jon Humphrey, Myron Meyers; Atlanta Symphony Orchestra and Chorus; conducted by Robert Shaw, recorded 6-7 November 1989 in Symphony Hall, Atlanta. Telarc: CD-80248.

Charlotte Margiono, Catherine Robbin, William Kendall, Alastair Miles; The Monteverdi Choir, Orchestre Révolutionnaire et Romantique; conducted by John eliot Gardiner, recorded in 1992. Deutsche Grammophone: D 101485.

Selected Bibliography

Pahlen, Kurt: *The World of the Oratorio*, translated by Judith Schaefer with additional English-language material by Thurston Dox, 48-49. Portland, OR: Amadeus Press, 1990.

Berger, Melvin: *Guide to Choral Masterpieces: A Listener's Guide*, 42-44. New York: Anchor Books, 1993.

Fantasia in C minor for Piano, Chorus, and Orchestra, op. 80 (1808)

Duration: ca. 19 minutes

Text: The author of the text is unknown, but some sources, including Carl Czerny, attribute it to Christoph Kuffner

Performing Forces: voices: 2 soprano, alto,[5] 2 tenor, and bass soloists; SATB choir;[6] **orchestra:** 2 flutes, 2 oboes, 2 clarinets (C, A), 2 bassoons, 2 horns (C, F), 2 trumpets (C), timpani (2 drums), strings, and solo piano.

First Performance: 22 December 1808; Theater an der Wien; Beethoven as piano soloist

Editions: Full scores and parts for *Fantasia* were published in a critical edition, *Ludwig van Beethoven's Werke: Vollständige kritisch durchgesehene überall berichtige Ausgabe*, series 9, by Breitkopf and Härtel in the 19th century. The full score is reprinted by Dover. It is also available for purchase in other editions from: Breitkopf and Härtel, H. W. Gray, G. Schirmer, and Kalmus.

Autograph: The composer's manuscript of the vocal score is in the Beethoven-Haus in Bonn.

Notes: The Choral Fantasy is dedicated to Maximilian Joseph, King of Bavaria. This work was composed to serve as a finale to the concert upon which it was premiered, which also included the first performances of the fith and sixth symphonies, the Vienna premiere of the fourth piano concerto, and portions of the Mass in C and the scene and aria "Ah! Perfido." At the premiere, which was clearly over-programmed, and apparently under-rehearsed, Beethoven improvised the opening piano solos. The final piano part

---

[5] There is a two-note divisi in the solo alto passage, which is not labeled as an "ossia," but there are no other indications for two voices.

[6] Some editions label the chorus as SSATTB; however, the only divisi of the soprano and tenor parts occur in passages labeled "solo."

was written out in 1809, and the score was first published in London in 1810 and Leipzig in 1811.

Performance Issues: The choral writing is virtually all homophonic. The choral parts are well supported by the accompaniment, and none of them is vocally demanding. The tessitura of the choral soprano part is fairly high and narrow, but not nearly as challenging as Beethoven's other choral works. The choral material is also fairly concise and should be quickly and easily learned by most choirs. The piano part requires a skilled soloist, but the remaining orchestral parts are all quite easy. This is an excellent work for youth orchestras wishing to combine with amateur choirs if an able pianist is available. The opening portion of the solo vocal portion contains the divisi. The singers assigned to soprano I and tenor I should be those utilized for the pure quartet passages that follow. While all of the solo parts are well within the abilities of good choristers, the soprano II and tenor II solos should logically be assigned to choristers even if a true solo quartet is used. All of the solo material is written as trio and quartet textures. **Soloists:** soprano I - range: a'-a'', tessitura: b'-g'', this is a simple declamatory solo; soprano II - range: g'-c'', tessitura: g'-c'', this is a simple ensemble solo; alto - range: g-c'', tessitura: c'-c'', this is a simple declamatory solo; tenor I - range: a-f', tessitura: a-f', this is a simple declamatory solo; tenor II - range: e-c', tessitura: g-c', this is a simple ensemble solo; bass - range: G-c', tessitura: c-c', this is a simple declamatory solo; **choir:** medium easy; **orchestra:** medium easy.

Selected Discography

Sviatoslav Richter, piano; Russian State Academy Chorus; conducted by Kurt Sanderling, recorded between 1948 and 1952. Re-released as a CD as Urania: SP4219.
Daniel Barenboim, piano; John Alldis Choir; New Philharmonia Orchestra; conducted by Otto Klemperer. Re-released on CD as EMI: 0077776336922.
Maurizio Pollini, piano; Vienna State Opera Chorus; Vienna Philharmonic Orchestra; conducted by Claudio Abbado. Deutsche Grammophon: 469549-2.
Alfred Brendel Piano; London Philharmonic Choir and Orchestra; conducted by Bernard Haitink. Philips: 434148-2.

Aldo Ciccolini, piano; I Pomeriggi Musicali; conducted by Aldo Ceccato. Frame: FR0137-2.
Chor der Deutschen Staatsoper; Berlin Philharmonic; Daniel Barenboim as pianist and conductor. EMI Classics: 0724355551627. Also released as a DVD.
Hélène Grimaud, piano; Swedish Radio Symphony Orchestra and Choir; conducted by Esa-Pekka Salonen. Deutsche Grammophon: 471769-2.
Yefim Bronfman, piano; Schweizer Kammerchor; Tonhalle Orchestra; conducted by David Zinman. Arte Nova: 82876825852.

Selected Bibliography

Pahlen, Kurt: *The World of the Oratorio*, translated by Judith Schaefer with additional English-language material by Thurston Dox, 46-48. Portland, OR: Amadeus Press, 1990.

Berger, Melvin: *Guide to Choral Masterpieces: A Listener's Guide*, 38-40. New York: Anchor Books, 1993.

Die Ruinen von Athen [The Ruins of Athens], op. 113 (1811)

Duration: ca. 40 minutes

Text: The text is by August von Kotzebue.

Performing Forces: voices: soprano and 2 bass soloists; SATB choir; **orchestra:** 2 flutes (flute II doubling piccolo),[7] 2 oboes, 2 clarinets (C, B♭), 2 bassoons, 4 horns (C, D, E♭, G, B♭), 2 trumpets (C, B♭, D, E♭), 3 trombones (alto, tenor, and bass), timpani (2 drums), percussion (3 players — triangle, cymbals, and bass drum), and strings.

First Performance: 10 February 1812, Pest (now Budapest)

Editions: Full scores and parts for *Die Ruinen von Athen* were published in a critical edition, *Ludwig van Beethoven's Werke: Vollständige kritisch durchgesehene überall berichtige Ausgabe*, series

---

[7] The piccolo part is presented as a discrete line; however, it never appears concurrently with the flute II.

20, by Breitkopf and Härtel. Selections are also available for purchase in other editions from: Breitkopf and Härtel and Kalmus.

Autograph: The composer's manuscript is in the Deutsches Staatsbibliothek in Berlin.

Notes: During the summer of 1811, Beethoven composed incidental music for two plays by Kotzebue, *Die Ruinen von Athen* and *König Stephan*, which had been written for the opening of a new theater in Pest. The musical numbers of *Die Ruinen von Athen* are as follows:

	Overture	orchestra
1.	Tochter des Mächtigen Zeus	chorus
2.	Ohne Verschulden	soprano and bass duet
3.	Du hast in deines Ärmels Falten	chorus of dervishes
4.	Turkish March	orchestra
5.	Music under the scene	windband
6.	Schmückt die Altäre	march and chorus
	Mit reger Freude	bass recitative
7.	Wir tragen empfängliche Herzen	bass aria and chorus
8.	Heil unserm König, heil!	chorus

The overture was first published in 1823, but the complete score did not appear until 1846. The publisher dedicated this edition to Kaiser Wilhelm IV of Prussia.

Performance Issues: The score includes indications for the choir to be "invisible" relevant to a staged production. There are also dialogues between some of the movements, which could be effective in a concert settting if presented in the language of the audience. The choral writing is declamatory and generally scalar or triadic. The vocal material is well supported by the orchestra and includes brief a cappella passages. There are two passages with peculiar part crossings between the sopranos and altos in the final movement that appear to be for dramatic effect, but reversing these may be advised. The choral parts are vocally reasonable and musically very accessible. There are important exposed solo passages for the flute I, oboe I, and bassoon I. The remaining instrumental parts are all quite practical. The critical edition includes an appendix version of movement 6 for concert use, which includes no overlay of spo-

A Conductor's Guide to 19th-Century Choral-Orchestra Works 21

ken text and uses a traditional seated orchestra. In movement 6, the score calls for a full section of winds to be "off-stage" alternating with a matching group "in the orchestra." The "Greek man and woman" appear only in the duet of movement 2. The "High Priest. **Soloists:** soprano (a Greek woman) - range: f'-a'', tessitura: f'-f'', this is a simple lyric solo appropriate for a chorister; bass (high priest) - range: C-e', tessitura: G-c', this is a declamatory solo requiring projection throughout the range, there are ossias provided for the lowest passage; bass (a Greek man) - range: d-d', tessitura: d-a, this is a simple lyric solo appropriate for a chorister; **choir:** medium easy; **orchestra:** medium difficult.

Selected Discography

Berlin Philharmonic; conducted by Bernhard Klee. Volume 3 of the Complete Beethoven Edition, Orchestral Works: Music for the Stage. Deutsche Grammophon:

Selected Bibliography

Upton, George P.: *The Standard Cantatas*, seventh edition, 49-52. Chicago: A. C. McClurg and Company, 1899.

König Stephan [King Stephen], op. 117 (1811)

Duration: ca. 37 minutes

Text: The text is by August von Kotzebue.

Performing Forces: voices: SATB choir; **orchestra:** 2 flutes, 2 oboes, 2 clarinets (C, A, B^b), 2 bassoons, contrabassoon, 4 horns (C, D, E^b, G, B^b), 2 trumpets (C, E^b), 3 trombones (alto, tenor, and bass), timpani (2 drums), and strings.

First Performance: 10 February 1812, Pest (now Budapest)

Editions: Full scores and parts for *König Stephan* were published in a critical edition, *Ludwig van Beethoven's Werke: Vollständige kritisch durchgesehene überall berichtige Ausgabe*, series 20, by Breitkopf and Härtel.

Autograph: The composer's manuscript is in the Deutsches Staatsbibliothek in Berlin.

Notes: During the summer of 1811, Beethoven composed incidental music for two plays by Kotzebue, *Die Ruinen von Athen* and *König Stephan*, which had been written for the opening of a new theater in Pest. The musical numbers of *König Stephan* are as follows:

	Overture	orchestra
1.	Ruhend von seinem Taten	men's chorus
2.	Auf dunklem Irrweg	men's chorus
3.	Sieges marsch	orchestra
4.	Wo die Unschuld Blumen streute	women's chorus
5.	Melodrama	speakers and orchestra
6.	Eine neue strahlende Sonne	mixed chorus
7.	Melodrama	speakers and orchestra
8.	Heil unserm Könige!	march, chorus, and melodrama
9.	Heil unsern Enkeln	mixed chorus

The overture was first published in 1826, but the complete score did not appear until it was published in the first collected works by Breitkopf and Härtel.

Performance Issues: There are four-part divisi for the tenors. The choral writing is declamatory and generally homophonic. It is well conceived for the voices and presents few vocal challenges. The vocal material is well supported by the orchestra. There is intricate passagework in all of the principal wind parts. The score includes dialogue between most of the movements, which should be in the language of the audience, if used. The melodramas are very brief. The orchestral writing is energetic and may provide some challenges for balance within the orchestra, particularly in the final movement. This is a rarely performed work that is well within the abilities of any large choral society. The orchestral accompaniment should be playable by a reasonable pick-up ensemble; **choir:** medium easy; **orchestra:** medium difficult.

Selected Discography

Ulrike Jackwerth, Dietrich Fischer-Dieskau; Roma Orchestra dell'Accademia Nazionale di Santa Cecilia; conducted by Myung-Whun Chung. Deutsche Grammophon 431778.

Selected Bibliography

Nothing of substance related specifically to this work is currently available.

Der glorreiche Augenblick, op. 136 (1814)

Duration: ca. 34 minutes

Text: The text is by Alois Weissenbach, a deaf surgeon and admirer of Beethoven from Salzburg, whom Beethoven met in Vienna while Weissenbach was there to attend the festivities surrounding the Congress of Vienna. This new friendship led them to collaborate on this work.[8]

Performing Forces: voices: 2 sopranos,[9] tenor, and bass soloists; SATB choir; SA children's choir; **orchestra:** 2 flutes, 2 oboes, 2 clarinets in B^b and A, 2 bassoons, contrabassoon, 4 horns (C, D, F, G, A), 2 trumpets (C, D, F), 3 trombones (alto, tenor, and bass), percussion (3 players — triangle, bass drum, and cymbals), timpani, and strings.

First Performance: 29 November 1814; Vienna

Editions: Full scores and parts for *Der glorreiche Augenblick* were published in a critical edition, *Ludwig van Beethoven's Werke: Vollständige kritisch durchgesehene überall berichtige Ausgabe*, series 21, by Breitkopf and Härtel.

---

[8] Kerman, Joseph, and Alan Tyson: *The New Grove Beethoven*, 61. New York: W. W. Norton, 1983.

[9] This is often listed as a soprano and an alto part, but Beethoven used soprano clef for each, and the ranges are virtually identical.

Autograph: The composer's manuscript is in the Deutsches Staatsbibliothek in Berlin.

Notes: This work was composed for the Congress of Vienna in 1814 using the Weissenbach text. It was published in Vienna in 1837 with the new text, "Preis der Tonkunst," by Friedrich Rochlitz.[10] Most sources agree that the text is the cause for this work falling out of the repertoire. Other figures have also attempted to revive the piece with new lyrics, but none has been particularly successful. Each of the soloists portrays an allegorical figure. The work is organized as follows:

1. Chorus
2. Recitative (Genius and Führer des Volkes) and Chorus
3. Aria (Vienna) and Chorus
4. Recitative (Seherinn) and Chorus
5. Recitative (Quartet) and Quartet
6. Chorus (adults and children)

Performance Issues: Most listings of the performing forces of this work do not include the children's choir, but the final movement divides the choral forces into three groups: women's choir, children's choir, and men's choir. There are occasional divisi for the choir. Most of the choral material is clearly doubled by the orchestra. There are dramatic alternations of dynamics, but the overall effect of the choir is bombastic. A large choral component is desirable. Some of the soprano material stays in the upper range, but not as mercilessly as in some other more-performed works of Beethoven. There are a few unaccompanied passages that are fairly static and clearly prepared. The choral parts are principally syllabic and homophonic with some contrapuntal writing that is less conspicuously doubled by the accompaniment. The orchestral parts are well conceived for the respective instruments, but many have challenging passagework, and some of the integration of parts, particularly in movement 5, will require attentive rehearsal. Rhythmic clarity in the strings may present challenges as well. There is an exposed and challenging violin solo throughout movement 4. There is another solo for cello in movement 2 that is exposed, but significantly

---

[10] As stated in the works list of *The New Grove Beethoven*; however, Kurt Pahlen states that it was Ludwig Rellstab.

shorter. The timpanist can be used as one of the percussionists as these parts are not concurrent. **Soloists:** soprano I (*Vienna*) - range: c#'-c''', tessitura: a'-a'', this is a lyric solo with some sustained high singing; soprano II (*Seherinn*) - range: e'-a'' (b'' optional), tessitura: a'-f#'', this is a lyric solo with some declamatory passages; tenor (*Genius*) - range: db-g#', tessitura: f#-f#', this is a lyric solo with some broad melodic leaps; bass (*Führer des Volkes*) - range: A-e', tessitura: d-d', this is an articulate and declamatory role; **choir:** medium difficult; **orchestra:** difficult.

Selected Discography

Deborah Voigt, Elizabeth Futral, Collegiate Chorale; Orchestra of St. Luke's; conducted by Robert Bass. Koch Classics: 7377.

Luba Orgonasova, Iris Vermillion, Vincenzo Bolognese, Timothy Robinson, Franz Hamlata; Roma Orchestra dell'Accademia Nazionale di Santa Cecilia; conducted by Myung-Whun Chung. Deutsche Grammophon 453798.

Selected Bibliography

Schünemann, G.: "Beethovens Skizzen zur Kantate 'Der glorreiche Augenblick,'" in *Die Musik* (1909-1910), volume 9, 22, 93.

Pahlen, Kurt: *The World of the Oratorio*, translated by Judith Schaefer with additional English-language material by Thurston Dox, 50-51. Portland, OR: Amadeus Press, 1990.

Meerestille und glückliche Fahrt, op. 112 (1814-1815)

Duration: ca. 7-8 minutes

Text: The text is by Johann Wolfgang von Goethe, to whom Beethoven dedicated the score.

Performing Forces: voices: SATB choir;[11] **orchestra:** 2 flutes, 2 oboes, 2 clarinets in A, 2 bassoons, contrabassoon, 4 horns (D, G), 2 trumpets (D), timpani (2 drums), and strings.

First Performance: 25 December 1815; Akademie zum Besten des Bürgerspitalfonds, Vienna

Editions: Full scores and parts for *Meerestille und glückliche Fahrt* were published in a critical edition, *Ludwig van Beethoven's Werke: Vollständige kritisch durchgesehene überall berichtige Ausgabe*, series 21, by Breitkopf and Härtel. It is also available for purchase in other editions from: Breitkopf and Härtel and Kalmus.

Autograph: The location of the manuscript is unknown.

Notes: The score was first published in Vienna in 1822. It is divided into two sections, the former sustained and reserved, the latter quick, articulate, and joyful.

Performance Issues: The choral writing is sustained and requires significant control in the first half of the work. The second half presents some passages that will require significant attention, as they become tongue twisters at performance tempo. The orchestral material is very idiomatic. There is some challenging passagework for the strings, and much of the horn material is exposed and set fairly high. This is a brief and effective work that serves best as a concert opener; **choir:** medium difficult; **orchestra:** medium difficult.

Selected Discography

Vienna State Opera Chorus; Vienna Philharmonic Orchestra; conducted by Claudio Abbado. Deutsche Grammophon: 469549-2.
Atlanta Symphony Orchestra and Chorus; conducted by Robert Shaw, recorded 7-8 May 1990 in Symphony Hall, Atlanta. Telarc: CD-80248.

---

[11] Some sources indicate a solo quartet, but this is misleading as there are only occasional brief passages within the choral material for which the composer indicates a solo voice. These should be assigned to member of the choir.

The Monteverdi Choir, Orchestre Révolutionnaire et Romantique; conducted by John eliot Gardiner. Recorded in 1992. Deutsche Grammophone: D 101485.

Schweizer Kammerchor; Tonhalle Orchestra; conducted by David Zinman. Arte Nova: 82876825852.

Selected Bibliography

Tovey, Francis: "Beethoven: Cantata, 'Becalmed Sea and Prosperous Voyage,' Op. 112 (Dedicated to Goethe)," in *Essays in Musical Analysis*, volume 5, 193-194. London: Oxford University Press, 1937.

Downes, Edward: "Meerestille und Glückliche Fahrt," in *The Beethoven Companion*, edited by Thomas K. Sherman and Louis Biancolli, 960-961 [originally program notes for the New York Philharmonic in 1966]. Garden City, NY: Doubleday, 1972.

Missa Solemnis, op. 123 (1819-1823)

Duration: ca. 81 minutes

Text: The text is from the Roman Catholic communion liturgy.

Performing Forces: voices: soprano, alto, tenor, and bass soloists; SATB choir; **orchestra:** 2 flutes, 2 oboes, 2 clarinets (A, C, B^b), 2 bassoons, contrabassoon, 4 horns (D, E^b, B^b basso, E, G), 2 trumpets (D, B^b, C), 3 trombones (alto, tenor, and bass), timpani, organ, and strings.

First Performance: 6 April 1824; St. Petersburg, Russia, in a benefit concert sponsored by Prince Nikolaus von Galitzin[12]

May 1824; Vienna; three movements were performed on the same program as the premiere of the Ninth Symphony.

---

[12] Kurt Pahlen uses this date and 26 March, which may be a reflection in the disparity between eastern and western European calendars at that time, but this is not clarified. Other sources also indicate 6 April.

Editions: Full scores and parts for *Missa Solemnis* were published in a critical edition, *Ludwig van Beethoven's Werke: Vollständige kritisch durchgesehene überall berichtige Ausgabe*, series 21, by Breitkopf and Härtel. It is also available for purchase in other editions from: Breitkopf and Härtel, C. F. Peters, G. Schirmer, and Kalmus. Eulenburg published a miniature score edited by Willy Hess (1964) from the original manuscript source materials.

A facsimile of the autograph score of the first movement is published as *Ludwig van Beethoven: Missa Solemnis, op. 123*. Tutzing: Schneider, 1965. An accompanying booklet was written by Wilhelm Virneisel [see below].

Sketch materials are published as

Ludwig van Beethoven: Drei Skizzenbücher zur Missa Solemnis, facsimile and transcription with commentary by Joseph Schmidt-Görg in two volumes. Bonn: Beethovenhaus, 1970-1972.

Ludwig van Beethoven: Ein Skizzenbuchr zu den Diabelli-Variationen und zur Missa Solemnis, facsimile and transcription with commentary by Joseph Schmidt-Görg in six volumes. Bonn: Beethovenhaus, 1952-1970.

Autograph: The composer's manuscript is in the Deutsches Staatsbibliothek in Berlin.

Notes: Beethoven had intended this work for the enthronement of Archduke Rudoph, to whom the score is dedicated; however, the score was completed well after the fact. Rudoph had been a pupil of Beethoven's.

Performance Issues: This is a remarkable work in its breadth of expressive gestures and colorful orchestration. It is an exceptionally demanding work for the choir and orchestra alike. The choral parts have considerably sustained passages at times on static pitches at the top of their respective ranges. This is a work well suited to a large opera chorus, as it demands athletic and articulate singing and control of a broad dynamic palette at extremes of range. It will present endurance concerns for most choirs. The choral alto part has an unusually high tessitura. There are many noteworthy con-

A Conductor's Guide to 19th-Century Choral-Orchestra Works   29

trapuntal sections for the singers. All of these passages are clearly supported by the orchestra. All of the orchestral parts are demanding, but idiomatic. There are significant unison passages that may present pitch issues between instrumental families. Likewise, the virtuosity of the string writing will present some ensemble issues for the strings. The wind parts are sometimes densely orchestrated; at these points particular attention will need to be directed toward balance. There is a difficult and exposed violin solo throughout the "Benedictus." The sostenuto passages and wind and brass writing necessitate the use of a large string section and large choir. Thoughtful planning is needed for the registrations of the organ part. The composer has provided a bare minimum of annotations in the organ part. Many performances use the organ to punctuate specific passages in the score through changes in registration. The composer provides no assistance in these decisions, and great consideration should be made about whether there is musical justification for these traditions. **Soloists:** soprano - range: $e^{b\prime}$-$b\prime\prime$ (there is one optional $c\prime\prime\prime$), tessitura: $b\prime$-$g\prime\prime$, this is a sustained and dramatic role requiring a powerful voice; alto - range: b^b-$e\prime\prime$, tessitura: $f\prime$-$d\prime\prime$, this is a true mezzo-soprano part with several exposed passages at the upper range; tenor - range: c-$a\prime$, tessitura: g-$g\prime$, this role remains within a narrow pitch compass most of the time, it does require some very sustained singing; bass - range: F-$e\prime$, tessitura: c-$c\prime$, this is a dramatic role requiring clarity at the bottom of the range; **choir:** very difficult; **orchestra:** very difficult.

Selected Discography

Heather Harper, Janet Baker, Robert Tear, Hans Sotin; London Philharmonic Orchestra and Chorus; conducted by Carol Maria Giulini, recorded 10 May 1975 in Kingsway Hall, London. EMI Classics. Re-released on Brilliant Classics: 92825.
Lella Cuberli, Trudeliese Schmidt, Vinson Cole, José van Dam; Wiener Singverein, Berlin Philharmonic; conducted by Herbert von Karajan (recorded in September 1985). Deutsche Grammophon: 419 166-1/2/4.

Selected Bibliography

Tovey, Francis: "Beethoven: *Missa Solemnis*, Op. 123," in *Essays in Musical Analysis*, volume 5, 161-184. London: Oxford University Press, 1937.

Adorno, Bruno: "Verfremdes Hauptwerk: zur *Missa Solemnis*" (1959) in *Moments musicaux*. Frankfurt am Main: Suhrkamp, 1964. Published in English as, "Alienated Masterpiece: the *Missa Solemnis*," translated by Duncan Smith, *Telos*, volume 28 (1976), 113-124.

Virneisel, Wilhelm: "Zur Handschrift der *Missa Solemnis* von Beethoven," *Österreichische Musikzeitschrift*, volume 21 (1966), 261-268.

Kirkendale, Warren: "New Roads to Old Ideas in Beethoven's *Missa Solemnis*," *The Musical Quarterly*, volume 56 (1970), 665-701.

Lester, Joel: "Revisions in the Autograph of the *Missa Solemnis* Kyrie,' *Journal of the American Musicological Society*, volume 23 (1970), 420-238.

Fiske, Roger: *Beethoven's Missa Solemnis*. London: Elek, 1979.

Ohl, John F.: "Beethoven: *Missa Solemnis*" in *The Choral Journal* (February 1981), 9-17.

Winter, Robert: "Reconstructing Riddles: The Sources for Beethoven's *Missa Solemnis*," *Beethoven Essays: Studies in Honor of Elliot Forbes*, edited by Lewis Lockwood and Phyllis Benjamin, 217-250. Cambridge, MA: Harvard University Press, 1984.

Kinderman, William: "Beethoven's Symbol for the Deity in the *Missa Solemnis* and the Ninth Symphony," *19th-Century Music*, volume 9 (1985-1986), 102-118.

Pahlen, Kurt: *The World of the Oratorio*, translated by Judith Schaefer with additional English-language material by Thurston Dox, 51-55. Portland, OR: Amadeus Press, 1990.

Drabkin, William: "The Agnus Dei of Beethoven's *Missa Solemnis*: the Growth of its Form," *Beethoven Studies*, edited by William Kindermann. Lincoln, NE: University of Nebraska Press, 1991.

_____: *Beethoven: Missa Solemnis* [from the series, *Cambridge Music Handbooks*]. Cambridge: Cambridge University Press, 1991.

Berger, Melvin: *Guide to Choral Masterpieces: A Listener's Guide*, 44-47. New York: Anchor Books, 1993.

Del Mar, Norman: *Conducting Beethoven: Volume II — Overtures, Concertos, Missa Solemnis*, 139-173. Oxford: Clarendon Press, 1993.

Symphony No. 9, op. 125 (1824)

Duration: ca. 65 minutes[13]

Text: The text is "An die Freude" by Friedrich von Schiller excerpted and edited by the composer.

Performing Forces: voices: soprano, alto, tenor, and bass soloists; SATB choir; **orchestra:** piccolo, 2 flutes, 2 oboes, 2 clarinets (B^b, C), 2 bassoons, contrabassoon, 4 horns (B^b basso, D, E^b, B^b), 2 trumpets (B^b, D), 3 trombones, timpani, percussion (2 or 3 players: triangle, cymbals, bass drum), and strings.

First Performance: 7 May 1824; Hoftheater, Vienna; soloists: Henriette Sontag, Caroline Unger, Anton Haitzinger, Joseph Seipelt

Editions: Full scores and parts for Symphony No. 9 were published in a critical edition, *Ludwig van Beethoven's Werke: Vollständige kritisch durchgesehene überall berichtige Ausgabe*, series 1, by Breitkopf and Härtel. It is also available for purchase in other editions from: Breitkopf and Härtel and Kalmus.

Autograph: The composer's manuscript is in the Deutsches Staatsbibliothek in Berlin.

Notes: The score, which was first published in Mainz in 1826, is dedicated to Friedrich Wilhelm III of Prussia. The principal tune of the finale, often referred to as the "Ode to Joy" theme, was explored in WoO 118, no. 1, "Seufzer eines Ungeliebten" (1794-1795), and op. 80, the Choral Fantasy (1808).

The structure of the final movement has been the subject of much speculation, and arguments in support of traditional musical forms are far from convincing. One scenario that this author has comfortably embraced is a dramatic narrative in which the composer comes to terms with his frustration about the expressive limitations of music without text. In the introduction of this movement, the or-

---

[13] David Daniels: *Orchestral Music: A Handbook*, third edition, 371. Lanham, MD: Scarecrow Press, 1996.

chestra reviews each of the major themes of the previous movements followed by a discordant expression of frustration. The doublebasses and cellos introduce a new theme, which is taken up by the rest of the instruments with great optimisim only to be cut off by the same frustrated cry. At this point, the bass soloist stands and sings the composer's words, "O friends, not these sounds! Let's strike up more pleasing and joyful ones." This leads into the Schiller text using the tune previously introduced by the lower strings.

Performance Issues: This is one of the true monuments of Western art music. Although this work is competently performed by regional ensembles with great frequency, the challenges in mounting a truly good performance should not be underestimated. The range of expressive gestures and colors requires a disciplined and mature ensemble. The choral parts are musically quite accessible and clearly supported by the orchestra; however, they are vocally difficult. All parts have extended powerful passages at extremes of range. The choral soprano part is particularly troublesome due to its high tessitura and the composer's merciless persistence within a narrow pitch band near the top of the range. This is almost more problematic in rehearsal than performance. Repetition in rehearsal should be carefully planned to avoid undue fatigue. The choir must be capable of rapid and expressive changes in dynamic as well as rhythmic and textual clarity. The scoring of the winds requires a full complement of strings and a choral ensemble capable of balancing with an orchestra accompanying some passages in full orchestration and a forte dynamic. Likewise, the soloists must be able to clearly penetrate the full ensemble. The string writing presents a number of challenges to accurate ensemble playing. There are also significant balance issues, particularly in the final movement. If a cymbal is mounted on the bass drum, 2 percussionists may be used. The overall architecture of the piece not only explores sophisticated cyclic ideas, but is dependent upon complex internal tempo relationships that should be well established prior to rehearsal. There is some controversy regarding the metronome marking of the Alla Marcia section of the final movement, which is marked dotted-quarter = 84 in the standard scores. Manscript letters from the composer include reference to this tempo being dotted-half = 84. Outside of this single tempo issue, for which the latter indication is an effective solution, the metronome markings are highly recommended.[14] **Soloists:** soprano - range: e′-b″, tessitura: a′-a″, this is a high and sustained solo that requires both power and soft singing at the top of the indicated range; alto - range: d′-e″, tessitura: e′-d″, this is the least demanding solo, but must be able to balance within the quartet, it is ideally a mezzo-soprano part; tenor - range: f-b♭′, tessitura: g-g′, this is a heroic solo with some sustained singing; bass - range: F#-f#′, tessitura: A-e′, this is a declamatory and powerful solo role; **choir:** difficult; **orchestra:** difficult.

Selected Discography

Tilla Briem, Elisabeth Hongen, Peter Anders, Rudolf Watzke; Chorus Brno Kittel; Berlin Philharmonic; conducted by Wilhelm Furtwängler, recorded live on 22 March 1942 in Berlin. Russian Compact Disc: RCD25006.

Eileen Farrell, Nan Merriman, Jan Peerce, Norman Scott; Robert Shaw Chorale; NBC Symphony Orchestra; conducted by Arturo Toscanini, recorded 31 March and 1 April 1952 in Carnegie Hall. Re-released as CD on RCA: D 217018C.

Hilde Gueden, Sieglinde Wagner, Anton Dermota, Ludwig Weber; Singverein der Gesellschaft der Musikfreunde; Vienna Philharmonic; conducted by Erich Kleiber, recorded between 1949 and 1955. Re-released as CD on Decca: 4756080.

Elisabeth Schwarzkopf, Elisabeth Hongen, Hans Hopf, Otto Edelmann; Choir and Orchestra of the Bayreauth Festspiele; conducted by Wilhelm Furtwängler, recorded 22 August 1954. EMI: 0724356695320.

Irmgaard Seefried, Maureen Forrester, Ernst Haefliger, Dietrich Fischer-Dieskau; Chorus of St. Hedwig's Cathedral; Berlin Philharmonic; conducted by Ferenc Fricsay. Deutsche Grammophon: 463626-2.

Emilia Cundari, Nell Rankin, Albert Da Costa, William Wildermann; Columbia Symphony Orchestra and Chorus; conducted by Bruno

---

[14] See: Rudolf, Max: The Metronome Indications in Beethoven's Symphonies" and "A Question of Tempo in Beethoven's Ninth Symphony," in *Max Rudolf: A Musical Life Writings and Letters*, 241-260 and 261-264. Hillsdale, NY: Pendragon Press, 2001.

Walter, recorded 26 January 1959 in th American Legion Hall, Hollywood. Sony: SMK 64464.[15]

Aase Nordmo-Lövber, Christa Ludwig, Waldemar Kmentt, Hans Hotter; Philharmonia Chorus and Orchestra; conducted by Otto Klemperer. EMI: 0724356679726.

Gundula Janowitz, Hildegard Rossel-Majdan, Waldemar Kmentt, Walter Berry; Vienna Singverein; Berlin Philharmonic; conducted by Herbert von Karajan, recorded in 1962. Deutsche Grammophon: 447401-2.

Sheila Armstrong, Anna Reynolds, Robert Tear, John Shirley-Quirk; London Symphony Orchestra and Chorus; conducted by Carlo Maria Giulini. EMI: 0724358549027.

Helen Donath, Teresa Berganza, Wieslaw Ochman, Thomas Stewart; Bavarian Radio Orchestra and Chorus; conducted by Rafael Kubelik. Deutsche Grammophon: 459463-2.

Margaret Price, Marianna Lipovsek, Peter Seiffert, Youri Egorov; Stadtischer Musikverein zu Dusseldorf; Royal Concertgebouw Orchestra; conducted by Wolfgang Sawallisch. EMI: 0724357332927.

Janet Perry, Agnes Baltsa, Vinson Cole, José van Dam; Vienna Singverein; Berlin Philharmonic; conducted by Herbert von Karajan, recorded in 1983. Deutsche Grammophon: 439006-2.

Pilar Lorengar, Yvonne Minton, Stuart Burrows, Martti Talvela; Chicago Symphony Orchestra and Chorus; conducted by Georg Solti. Decca: 430792-2.

Gwyneth Jones, Hanna Schwarz, René Kollo, Kurt Moll; Vienna State Opera Chorus; Vienna Philharmonic; conducted by Leonard Bernstein. Deutsche Grammophon: 457910-2.

Helen Donath, Doris Soffel, Siegfried Jerusalem, Peter Lika; Munich Philharmonic Chorus and Orchestra; conducted by Sergiu Celibidache. EMI: 0724355684226.

Arleen Auger, Catherine Robbin, Anthony Rolfe Johnson, Gregory Reinhart; London Symphony Chorus; Academy of Ancient Music; conducted by Christopher Hogwood. Decca: 452551-2.

Birgit Remmert, Charlotte Margiono, Robert Holl, Rudolf Schasching; Arnold Schoenberg Choir; Chamber Orchestra of Europe; conducted by Nikolaus Harnoncourt. Teldec: 2292-46452-2.

---

[15] An excerpt of the rehearsal for this recording has been released on a companion disc of Walter's rehearsal of Beethoven Symphonies 4, 5, 7, and 9. It is on Sony: SMK 64465.

Luba Orgonasova, Anne Sophie von Otter, Anthony Rolfe Johnson, Gilles Cachemaille; Monteverdi Choir; Orchestre Revolutionnaire et Romantique; conducted by John Eliot Gardiner. Deutsche Grammophon: 447074-2.

Karita Mattila, Violetta Urmana, Thomas Moser, Thomas Quasthoff; Eric-Ericson Chamber Choir, Swedish Radio Chorus; Berlin Philharmonic; conducted by Claudio Abbado. Deutsche Grammophon: 471491-2.

Soile Isokoski, Rosemary Lang, Robert Gambill, René Pape; Chorus of the Deutsche Oper Berlin; Staatskapelle Berlin; conducted by Daniel Barenboim. Teldec: 8573-83063-2.

Selected Bibliography

Grove, George: *Beethoven and His Nine Symphonies*, third edition, 309-400. London: Novello and Ewer, 1898. Reprinted: New York: Dover, 1962.

Weingartner, Felix: *On the Performance of Beethoven's Symphonies*, translated by Jessie Crossland. London: C. H. Ditson, 1907. Reprinted: New York: Dover, 2004.

Schenker, Heinrich: *Beethoven's Ninth Symphony: A Portrayal of Its Musical Content, with Running Commentary on Performance and Literature As Well*, translated and edited by John Rothgeb. New Haven, CT: Yale University Press, 1992. Originally published in German in 1912.

Tovey, Donald: *Beethoven's Ninth Symphony*. London: Oxford University Press, 1928.

Vaughan Williams, Ralph: *Some Thoughts on Beethoven's Choral Symphony, with Other Musical Subjects*. London: Oxford University Press, 1953.

Treitler, Leo: "History, Criticism, and Beethoven's Ninth Symphony," in *19th-Century Music* (1979-1980) volume 3, 193.

Winter, Robert: "The Sketches for the 'Ode to Joy,'" in Beethoven, Performers, and Critics, edited by Robert Winter and Bruce Carr, 176-214. Detroit: Papers given during the International Beethoven Congress of 1977, 1980.

Kinderman, William: "Beethoven's Symbol for the Deity in the *Missa Solemnis* and the Ninth Symphony," *19th-Century Music*, volume 9 (1985-1986), 102-118.

Cook, Nicholas: *Beethoven: Symphony No. 9* [from the series, *Cambridge Music Handbooks*]. Cambridge: Cambridge University Press, 1993.

Del Mar, Norman: *Conducting Beethoven: Volume I — The Symphonies*, 169-217. Oxford: Clarendon Press, 1992.

Berger, Melvin: *Guide to Choral Masterpieces: A Listener's Guide*, 47-51. New York: Anchor Books, 1993.

Schwaegermann, Ingrid: *Joy: How the Ode to It Was Written.* http://raptusassociation.org/creation2_e.html.

A Conductor's Guide to 19th-Century Choral-Orchestra Works 37

Berlioz, Hector (b. La Côte-Saint-André, Isère, 11 December 1803; d. Paris, 8 March 1869)

Life: The son of a musically predisposed physician, Berlioz learned the guitar and recorder from his father. He moved to Paris to study medicine, but he began to compose choral works and soon entered the studio of LeSueur at the Paris Conservatory, eschewing medicine for a career in music.

In 1827, Berlioz attended a touring production of *Hamlet*. He immediately became obsessed with Shakespeare and the Irish actress Harriet Smithson, who portrayed Ophelia. His obsession led to the composition of *Symphonie fantastique* and ultimately to his marriage to Smithson. The ensuing decade saw the production of a number of masterpieces.

Berlioz supplemented his income as a composer through conducting and writing. His *Memoirs* are still regarded as great literature and his criticism remains an important window into the musical world of the 19th century. His *Grande Traité d'Instrumentation et d'orchestration modernes* became the standard for orchestration manuals. In it, Berlioz described his ideal orchestra, which was a gargantuan ensemble utilizing quint bassoons, "full-sized" basses, and forces so large that sub-conductors connected electronically with the music director to lead players too distant to see the principal podium. An appendix, "On Conducting" in the *Grande Traité* was the first to propose the current pattern for conducting in 3, and it was the first to provide a method for conducting in 5. It is also the first publication to state that the conductor's responsibility was to determine an interpretation of a score for the ensemble.

Although Berlioz exercised more influence on the excesses of 19th-century music, he did so with great artistry and conviction. While a number of his works rarely receive performances because of their length and the forces required, when they are performed it is an important musical event.

Teachers: Jean François LeSueur, Anton Reicha
Students: Louis Moreau Gottschalk, Gustav Roguski

Selected Writings

Grande Traité d'Instrumentation et d'orchestration modernes. Paris: Schonenberger, 1843; second edition 1855. Published in English as: *A Treatise Upon Modern Instrumentation and Orchestration,* translated by M. Cowden Clarke. London: Novello, 1856.

Les Soirées de l'orchestre. Paris: Michel Lévy, 1852. Published in English as: *Evenings with the Orchestra,* translated by Jacques Barzun. Chicago: University of Chicago Press, 1959, reprinted in 1999.

A travers chants. Études musicales, adorations, boutades, et critiques. Paris: Michel Lévy, 1870. Published in English as: *The Art of Music and Other Essays,* translated by Elisabeth Csicsery-Rónay. Bloomington, IN: University of Indiana Press, 1994.

Mémoires d'Hector Berlioz. Paris: Michel Lévy, 1870. Published in English as: *The Memoirs of Hector Berlioz,* translated by Rachel and Eleanor Holmes, annotated and revised by Ernest Newman. New York: Knopf, 1932. Reprinted, New York: Dover 1966.

Correspondance générale d'Hector Berlioz, six volumes, edited by Pierre Citron, Yves Gérard, and Hugh Macdonald. Paris: Flammarion, 1972-1995.

Other Principal Works: opera: *Benvenuto Cellini* (1834-1837), *Les Troyens* (1856-1858), *Béatrice et Bénedict* (1860-1862); **orchestral:** *Symphonie fantastique* (1830), *Harold en Italie* for viola and orchestra (1834), *Grande symphonie funèbre et triomphale* (1840), *Le Carnaval romain* (1844), *Le Corsaire* (1844); **songs:** *Les Nuit d'été* (1840).

Selected Composer Bibliography

Barzun, Jacques: *Berlioz and the Romantic Century,* two volumes, second edition. New York: Columbia University Press, 1969.

Dickinson, Alan E. F.: *The Music of Berlioz.* New York: St. Martin's Press, 1972.

Primmer, Brian: *The Berlioz Style.* London: Oxford University Press, 1973.

Crabbe, John: *Hector Berlioz, Rational Romantic.* London: Kahn and Averill, 1980.

Holoman, D. Kern: *The Creative Process in the Autograph Documents of Hector Berlioz, c. 1818-1840.* Ann Arbor: UMI Research Press, 1980.

Rushton, Julian: *The Musical Language of Berlioz*. Cambridge: Cambridge University Press, 1983.
Holoman, D. Kern: *Catalogue of the Works of Hector Berlioz*. Kassel: Bärenreiter, 1987.
_____: *Berlioz*. Cambridge, MA: Harvard University Press, 1989. Simultaneously published in London by Faber.
Cairns, David: *Berlioz: The Making of an Artist*. London: Deutsch, 1989.
Langford, Jeffrey A., and Jane Denker Graves: *Hector Berlioz: A Guide to Research*. New York: Garland, 1989.
Macdonald, Hugh: *Berlioz*, second edition. [from *The Master Musicians* series], London: Dent, 1991.
Bloom, Peter A.: *Berlioz Studies*. Cambridge: Cambridge University Press, 1992.
Del Mar, Norman: *Conducting Berlioz*. Oxford: Clarendon Press, 1997.
Bloom, Peter A.: *The Life of Berlioz*. Cambridge: Cambridge University Press, 1998.
_____, editor: *The Cambridge Companion to Berlioz*. Cambridge: Cambridge University Press, 2000.
Rushton, Julian: *The Music of Berlioz*. Oxford: Oxford University Press, 2001.

Messe solennelle, H. 20A (1824)

Duration: ca. 60 minutes

Text: The text is from the Roman Catholic communion liturgy.

Performing Forces: voices: soprano, tenor, and bass soloists; SSAATTB choir; **orchestra:** piccolo (optional), 2 flutes, 2 oboes, 2 clarinets (C), 2 bassoons, 4 horns (C, D, E^b, E, F, G), 2 trumpets (D, E^b, F), 3 trombones, serpent, Buccin[16] (or ophicléide), timpani (2 drums), percussion (2 players — cymbals, tam-tam), 2 harps (optional), and strings.

---

[16] The buccin was a short-lived instrument of great power developed at the end of the French Revolution. It had already fallen from use before Berlioz included in this score. In this case, a Sousaphone might be an ideal substitute.

Every modern conductor surely rejoices to see that piccolo is an optional instrument, but serpent is not. A tuba is an ideal substitute.

First Performance: 10 July 1825; Church of St. Roch, Paris

Editions: *Messe solennelle* is published in a critical edition in *The New Berlioz Edition*, volume 23, edited by Hugh MacDonald, by Bärenreiter (BA 5463). Orchestral parts, a piano-vocal score, and a study score are also available.

Autograph: The autograph score is in the library of St. Carolus Borromenskerke in Antwerp.

Notes: Berlioz had indicated in his *Memoirs* that he had burned the score of the *Messe solennelle*; however, a manuscript was discovered in the Church of St. Carolus-Borromeus in Antwerp in Belgium in 1991.

Performance Issues: This is a contrapuntally conceived work. The choral parts are quite simple and accessible to most choral singers. The vocal material is well supported by the orchestra. There are some passages, particularly in the "Gloria," where one section of the choir sings in quarter notes while another sings in eighths with eighth rests in between. Extra care must be taken to guarantee that it is an intriguing effect rather than sloppy preparation. This is an early work, and there are a number of quirky notations like this that soon disappear from Berlioz's compositional palette. Some of the writing is not yet idiomatic for the singers or instrumentalists. Sometimes repetitions in the score may promote early fatigue for the performers. There is a passage in the "Resurrexit" movement labeled for a choral bass solo. There is no reason not to use the soloist here. Although the harps are optional, they should be used if at all possible. The orchestral parts are not difficult, and with the exception of a brief fanfare in the "Resurrexit" movement, there is little bombast. In fact, this is a delicate and transparent work. It is probably Berlioz's most accessible choral-orchestral work for less experienced ensembles. With a little creativity, the obsolete instruments can be substituted. **Soloists:** soprano - range: d'-g'', tessitura: g'-e'', this is a lyric solo role with some odd melodic figures; tenor - range: f-g', tessitura: g-f', this is a simple, lyric solo role; bass - range: G-e' (f'), tessitura: f-d', this is a lyric and simple solo role; **choir:** medium easy; **orchestra:** medium easy.

Selected Discography

Donna Brown, Jean-Luc Viala, Gilles Cachemaille; Monteverdi Choir; Orchestre Révolutionnaire; conducted by John Eliot Gardiner, recorded in 1993. Philips: 442 137-2.

Selected Bibliography

Berlioz, Hector: *The Memoirs of Hector Berlioz*, translated by Rachel and Eleanor Holmes, annotated and revised by Ernest Newman, 23, 74. New York: Knopf, 1932. Reprinted, New York: Dover, 1966.

Barzun, Jacques: *Berlioz and the Romantic Century*, second edition, I: 58, 63, 64, 65-66, 74, 83, 87, 92, 204, 212, 274, 559; II: 56, 104. New York: Columbia University Press, 1969.

Dickinson, Alan E. F.: *The Music of Berlioz*, 39-41. New York: St. Martin's Press, 1972.

Macdonald, Hugh: "Berlioz's Messe solennelle," *19th-Century Music*, volume 16 (Spring 1993), 267-285.

Rushton, Julian: "Ecstacy of Emulation: Berlioz's Messe solennelle and his debt to Lesueur," *Musical Times*, volume 140, issue 1868 (Autumn 1999), 11-18.

Locke, Ralph P.: "The Religious Works," in *The Cambridge Companion to Berlioz*, edited by Peter A. Bloom, 96-107. Cambridge: Cambridge University Press, 2000.

Rushton, Julian: *The Music of Berlioz*, 10-11, 107-112, 192-202. Oxford: Oxford University Press, 2001.

Requiem: Grande Messe des Morts ["Grand Mass of the Dead"], op. 5 (1837), H. 75

Duration: ca. 82 minutes

Text: The text is from the Roman Catholic liturgy of the Mass for the Dead.

Performing Forces: voices: tenor soloist; STB choir; **orchestra:** 4 flutes, 2 oboes, 2 English horns, 4 clarinets (A, B^b), 8 bassoons, 12 horns (B^b basso, C, D, E^b, E, F, G, A), timpani (10 players and 8 pairs of drums), percussion (14 players — 2 bass drums, 4 tam-tams, 10 pairs of cymbals), strings.

Four brass bands:
Band I: 4 cornets (A, B^b), 4 trombones, 2 tubas
Band II: 4 trumpets (D, E), 4 trombones
Band III: 4 trumpets (D), 4 trombones
Band IV: 4 trumpets (C), 4 trombones, 4 ophicléides[17]

Berlioz indicates that the choir should consist of 80 sopranos, 60 tenors, and 70 basses. Likewise, he calls for 50 violins, 20 violas, 20 cellos, and 18 doublebasses. He adds that the choral numbers are only relative, and that double or triple these number would be welcome if space permits, suggesting that the instrumental forces might be expanded slightly as well. He does state that when using a choir of 700 to 800, the entire ensemble should probably only sing in the *Dies Irae, Rex tremendae*,[18] and *Lacrimosa*, using only 400 in the other movements.

First Performance: 5 December 1837; Cathedral of St. Louis des Invalides in Paris; conducted by François Antoine Habeneck.

Editions: *Grande messe des morts* is published in a critical editions in *The New Berlioz Edition*, volume 9, edited by Jürgen Kindermann, by Bärenreiter (BA 5449). Orchestral parts, a piano-vocal score (BA 5449a), and a study score (TP 332) are also available. It was published by Breitkopf and Härtel in the previous critical edition, *Hector Berlioz: Werke*, volume 7, edited by C. Malherbe and Felix Weingartner. Other editions which are available for purchase include: Breitkopf and Härtel and Kalmus.

Autograph: The composer's manuscript of the full score and the original set of parts are in the Paris Conservatory.

---

[17] Tubas may be substituted for the ophicléide parts.

[18] The score actually states *Tuba mirum*, which is part of the *Dies irae*. *Rex tremendae* is the intention.

A Conductor's Guide to 19th-Century Choral-Orchestra Works

Notes: Requiem was commissioned by the French government to be presented in a memorial service for the victims of the 1830 July Revolution. The score is organized into 10 movements as follows:

1. Requiem et Kyrie
2. Dies irae. Prose.
3. Quid sum miser
4. Rex tremendae
5. Quaerens me   a cappella SSTTBB choir
6. Lacrimosa
7. Offertoire   labeled "Choir of souls in purgatory"
8. Hostias
9. Sanctus   tenor soloist and choir
10. Agnus Dei

Performance Issues: Berlioz placed the brass ensembles at the extreme points of the cathedral and the principal orchestra and choir at the crossing. Halls will dictate the placement of these groups, but every effort should be made to surround the audience with these brass bands so the sounds of entrances around the listeners is palpable. The timpani are tuned to all 12 discrete pitches of an octave (F-f); however, the tunings change between movements. They are used to create a visceral rumble; therefore, it may also be advantageous to place them in the hall so the audience can feel their part being played. There are divisi in all of the choral parts. The vocal material is clearly reinforced by the accompaniment most of the time, although there are a cappella passages throughout the work. There are extended passages wherein the tessitura of the choral basses is relatively high. Although there are frequent divisi for the sopranos, the lower part does not provide a functional alto part. A traditional mixed SATB choir will find it difficult to utilize the altos consistently in this piece; however, there is an independent "contralto" part in movement 9, which is the only movement in which the soloist appears. The score indicates that the choral tenor section may be substituted for the soloist; however this would greatly diminish the contrast between the solo part and the choir. There are some soli passages for the choir in movement 6. In spite of the enormous forces called for in this score, much of it is orchestrated delicately and transparently, which makes the bombastic passages all the more effective. The orchestral writing is idiomatic and colorful. The effect of the brass bands and percussion is one of the great tours de force in the symphonic repertoire, but it also requires the most attention in rehearsal because of the articulate figurations of the fanfares and the obvious challenge of acoustic distance and timing. There are dramatic dynamic shifts and quick gestural diminuendi that are included for dramatic effect. Sometimes secondary conductors are employed, the practicality of which may be determined by the space. The individual orchestra parts are not particularly difficult, although the antiphonal brass groups and the orchestral horns have the most challenging parts. The diversity of scoring and the ensemble challenges presented by the distribution of players throughout the performance space make this an exceedingly difficult piece to perform well. Of equal limitation for most presenters is the enormous roster of players and the sheer quantity of percussion equipment. **Soloists:** tenor - range: a^b-$b^{b\prime}$, tessitura: b^b-$b^{b\prime}$, this is a high lyric solo with long sustained phrases; **choir:** difficult; **orchestra:** very difficult.

Selected Discography

Léopold Simoneau; Vienna State Opera Chorus; Vienna Philharmonic Orchestra; conducted by Dmitri Mitropoulos, recorded in 1956. Reisued on CD in 1997 - Orfeo: C 457 971 B [mono].
Richard Lewis; Royal Philharmonic Chorus and Orchestra; conducted by Thomas Beecham, recorded in 1957. Reissued on CD in 1999 – BBC Music: BBCL 4011-2.
Ronald Dowd; Wandsworth School Boys' Choir, London Symphony Orchestra and Chorus; conducted by Colin Davis, recorded in 1969. Philips: 416 283-2.
John Aler; Atlanta Symphony Orchestra and Chorus; conducted by Robert Shaw, recorded in 1985. Reissued on Telarc: CD 801109.
Luciano Pavarotti; Ernst-Senff-Chor; Berlin Philharmonic; conducted by James Levine, recorded in 1992. Deutsche Grammophon: DG 429 724-2.
John Mark Ainsley; Montréal Symphony Orchestra and Chorus; conducted by Charles Dutoit, recorded in 1999. Decca: 289 458 921-2.
Frank Lopardo; Atlanta Symphony Orchestra and Chorus; conducted by Robert Spano, recorded 2004. Telarc: CD-80627 and SACD-60627,

Selected Bibliography

Berlioz, Hector: *The Memoirs of Hector Berlioz*, translated by Rachel and Eleanor Holmes, annotated and revised by Ernest Newman, 204-213, 232, 235, 239, 241, 285, 287, 288, 299-301, 328-333, 362, 458, 488-489. New York: Knopf, 1932. Reprinted, New York: Dover, 1966.

Upton, George: *The Standard Oratorios*, 70-77. Chicago: A. C. McClurg and Company, 1893.

Robertson, Alec: *Requiem: Music of Mourning and Consolation*, 85-95. New York: Frederick A. Praeger, 1967.

Barzun, Jacques: *Berlioz and the Romantic Century*, second edition, I: 204, 219, 228, 232, 262, 272, 273, 275-277, 279-289, 447, 525; II: 105, 148, 208, 281, 289, 297. New York: Columbia University Press, 1969.

Dickinson, Alan E. F.: *The Music of Berlioz*, 91-106. New York: St. Martin's Press, 1972.

McDonald, Hugh: "Preface" to Hector Berlioz: *Grande messe des morts "Requiem,"* edited by Jürgen Kinder. Kassel: Bärenreiter, 1978.

Pahlen, Kurt: *The World of the Oratorio*, translated by Judith Schaefer with additional English-language material by Thurston Dox, 58-61. Portland, OR: Amadeus Press, 1990.

Berger, Melvin: *Guide to Choral Masterpieces: A Listener's Guide*, 53-55. New York: Anchor Books, 1993.

Locke, Ralph P.: "The Religious Works," in *The Cambridge Companion to Berlioz*, edited by Peter A. Bloom, 96-107. Cambridge: Cambridge University Press, 2000.

Rushton, Julian: *The Music of Berlioz*, 40-41, 203-215. Oxford: Oxford University Press, 2001.

Romeo et Juliette, op. 17 (1839), H. 79

Duration: ca. 95 minutes

Text: The text is by Emile Deschamps, based upon the David Garrick adaptation of Shakespeare's play.

Performing Forces: voices: alto, tenor, and bass soloists; chamber ATB choir (14 to 20 members); two SATB choirs; **orchestra:** piccolo, 2 flutes, 2 oboes (oboe II doubling English horn), 2 clarinets, 4 bassoons, 4 horns, 2 trumpets, 2 cornets, 3 trombones, tuba, timpani (4), percussion (bass drum, cymbals, 2 triangles, 2 tambourines, 2 crotales [F, B^b]), 2 harps, and strings.

First Performances: 24 November, 1 and 15 December 1839; Paris Conservatoire; Emily Widemann, Alexis Dupont, Louis Alizard; a pick-up choir and orchestra; conducted by the composer

Editions: *Roméo et Juliette* is published in a critical editions in *The New Berlioz Edition*, volume 18, edited by D. Kern Holoman, by Bärenreiter (BA 5458). Orchestral parts, a piano-vocal score (BA 5458a), and a study score (TP 334) are also available. It was published by Breitkopf and Härtel in the previous critical edition, *Hector Berlioz: Werke*, volume 3, edited by C. Malherbe and Felix Weingartner. Other editions, which are available for purchase include: Breitkopf and Härtel, G. Schirmer, and Kalmus.

Autograph: The autograph score is in the library of the Paris Conservatory (Ms. 1165).

Notes: Berlioz composed *Roméo et Juliette* as a tribute to Paganini. The soloists portray three characters from the play: alto - Juliet, tenor - Romeo, and bass - Friar Laurence. The two large choirs represent the Montague and Capulet families, and the chamber choir serves a narrating capacity. The score is organized around the sequence of the drama in three subdivided sections as follows:

Part One
   1. Introduction
      Combat

A Conductor's Guide to 19th-Century Choral-Orchestra Works 47

      Tumulte
      Intervention du Prince
  2. Prologue
     a. Récitatif choral: *D'anciennes haines endormies*
     b. Strophes: *Premiers transports que nul n'oublie*
     c. Recitative and Scherzetto: *Bientôt de Roméo la pâle rêverie*

Part Two
1. Roméo seul
   Tristesse
   Bruits lointains de Concert de Bal
   Grande Fête chez Capulet
2. Nuit sereine
   Le Jardin de Capolet, silencieux et désert
   Les jeunes Capulets, sortant de la fête...
   Scène d'amour
3. La Reine Mab ou la Fée des Songes (Scherzo)

Part Three
1. Convoi Funèbre de Juliette: Jetez des fleurs pour la vierge expirée
2. Roméo au tombeau des Capulets
   Invocation
   Joie délirante
   Dernières angoisses et mort des deux amants
3. Finale: La foule accourt au Cimitière
   a. Choeurs et Récitatif du Père Laurence
   b. Air: *Pauvres enfants que je pleure*
   c. Serment: *Jurez donc par l'auguste symbole*

Performance Issues: Berlioz indicates the physical arrangement of the singers and orchestra in the score, which may not be practical in some halls, but will aid in the clarity of the storytelling. The two choirs represent the feuding Montague and Capulet families, and should be placed on opposite sides of the stage with the chamber choir and soloists in the middle. The score calls for two off-stage four-part men's choirs in II/2. The choral writing is practical, and not particularly vocally demanding. Most of the choral material is well supported by the accompaniment. The aforementioned off-stage men's choirs are the exception to this. Here, an offstage chorus-master is necessary. The principal conductor needs to follow the chorus in this section as the orchestra provides a transparent accompaniment under the more rhythmic choral parts. Here the choir and orchestra seem almost oblivious of each other. The choirs sing in about one-third of the score. All of the orchestral writing is fairly virtuosic. Two harps are needed to effect a reasonable balance with the rest of the ensemble. They should be placed near the front of the stage. The wind and string sections have some particularly complex passagework. The brass is fanfare-like with some sustained playing. As is typical in Berlioz's music, the choirs of the orchestra are often given contrasting strata of musical material. A sectional rehearsal is well advised. Sections II/1 and II/3 will require the most attention from the orchestra. The finale will present the greatest difficulties in coordinating the choirs and orchestra. This is a very expressive score that has been expertly orchestrated to allow the singers to be heard throughout the work. The score builds conflicting rhythmic layers upon each other that require clear direction, and may at times provide challenges to cohesive ensemble playing. This is an ideal work for a professional orchestra wishing to feature a large semi-skilled choral group. **Soloists:** alto - range: c'-e'', tessitura: d'-$c\#''$, this is a simple, lyric, and declamatory solo; tenor - range: e-g', tessitura: f-e', this is a simple, declamatory solo; bass - range: G-e', tessitura: c-$e^{b'}$, this is a sustained solo requiring a strong lyric voice; **choir:** medium difficult; **orchestra:** difficult.

Selected Discography

Regina Resnik, André Turp, David Ward; London Symphony Orchestra and Chorus; conducted by Pierre Monteux. Recorded in London, June 1962. Released on the Westminster label, re-released on CD as MCA Classics: MCAD2-9805-A.

Patricia Kern, Robert Tear, John Shirley-Quirk; John Alldis Choir; Londonson Symphony Orchestra and Chorus; conducted by Colin Davis, recorded in 1968. Philips: 416 962-2.

Catherine Robbin, Jean-Paul Fouchécourt, Gilles Cachemaille; Monteverdi Choir; Orchestre Révolutionnaire et Romantique; conducted by John Eliot Gardiner, recorded in October 1995 in the Colosseum in Watford, England. Philips: 454 454-2.

Melanie Diener, Kenneth Tarver, Denis Sedov; Cleveland Symphony Orchestra and Chorus; conducted by Pierre Boulez, recorded in

May 2000 in the Masonic Auditorium in Cleveland. Deutsche-Grammophon: 474 2372.

Selected Bibliography

Berlioz, Hector: *The Memoirs of Hector Berlioz*, translated by Rachel and Eleanor Holmes, annotated and revised by Ernest Newman, 230-232, 239-240, 283, 285, 291, 294, 298-301, 327-328, 332, 333, 336-337, 342, 377, 414-415, 419-420, 427-428, 438-440, 477, 479, 481, 482, 486, 489-490, 503, 504. New York: Knopf, 1932. Reprinted, New York: Dover, 1966.

Upton, George P.: *The Standard Cantatas*, seventh edition, 70-74. Chicago: A. C. McClurg and Company, 1899.

Bass, Edward C.: *Thematic Procedures in the Symphonies of Berlioz*. Doctoral dissertation: University of North Carolina Chapel Hill, 1964.

Barzun, Jacques: *Berlioz and the Romantic Century*, second edition, I: 156, 318-329, 330-335, 337, 430, 567; II: 185, 289. New York: Columbia University Press, 1969.

Chailley, Jacques: "Roméo et Juliette," *Revue de Musicologie*, volume 63 (1977), 115-122.

Cockrell, William Dale: *Hector Berlioz and "Le Système Shakespearien."* Doctoral dissertation: University of Illinois, 1978.

Elliott, John R., Jr.: "The Shakespeare Berlioz Saw," *Music and Letters*, volume 57 (1976), 292-308.

Friedheim, Philip: "Berlioz's Roméo Symphony and the Romantic Temperament," *Current Musicology*, volume 63 (1983), 101-111.

Langford, Jeffrey A.: "The 'Dramatic Symphonies' of Berlioz as an Outgrowth of the French Operatic Tradition," *The Musical Quarterly*, volume 69 (1983), 85-103.

Shamgar, Beth: "Program and Sonority: An Essay in Analysis of the 'Queen Mab' Scherzo from Berlioz's Roméo and Juliet'," *College Music Symposium* (1988), 40-52.

Holoman, D. Kern: foreword to *Berlioz: Roméo et Juliette* in *The New Berlioz Edition*. Kassel: Bärenreiter, 1990.

Kemp, Ian: "*Romeo and Juliet* and *Roméo et Juliette*," 37-79, *Berlioz Studies*, edited by Peter A. Bloom. Cambridge: Cambridge University Press, 1992.

Rushton, Julian: *Berlioz: Romeo et Juliette* [from the series, *Cambridge Music Handbooks*]. Cambridge: Cambridge University Press, 1994.

Langford, Jeffrey: "The Symphonies," in *The Cambridge Companion to Berlioz*, edited by Peter A. Bloom, 53-68. Cambridge: Cambridge University Press, 2000.

Rushton, Julian: *The Music of Berlioz*, 41-44, 149-151, 269-275, 289-291. Oxford: Oxford University Press, 2001.

La Damnation de Faust, légende dramatique
["The Damnation of Faust, a dramatic legend"], op. 24 (1845-1846), H. 111

Duration: ca. 120 minutes

Text: The text is by Berlioz, Almire Gandonnière, and Gérard de Nerval.

Performing Forces: voices: Marguerite (mezzo-soprano), Faust (tenor), Méphistophélès (baritone or bass),[19] and Brander (bass) soloists; SATB choir and SA children's choir; **orchestra:** 3 flutes (all doubling piccolo), 2 oboes (oboe II doubling English horn), 2 clarinets (A, B^b), bass clarinet (B^b), 4 bassoons, 4 horns (C, D^b, D, E^b, F, A, B^b, B), 2 trumpets (B^b, B, C, D, F), 2 cornets (B^b, A), 3 trombones, tuba, timpani (4 drums),[20] percussion (4 players — a bell (c, d, f#, or a), triangle, snare drum, bass drum, cymbals,[21] tam-tam), 2 harps, and strings.

First Performance: 6 December 1846; Salle Favart of the Opéra Comique in Paris; conducted by the composer

The first staged performance was given in Monte Carlo on 18 February 1893.

---

[19] The score includes ossia passages to accommodate either voice type.

[20] Throughout most of the score a single player and two drums are required. In scenes 9 and 15, Berlioz calls for four timpanists each playing a single drum. At this point, the other percussionists are unoccupied and can cover those parts. There is an additional section for four drums with two players in scenes 12 and 19; here a single percussionist can join the timpanist to effect the part.

[21] Berlioz uses the words *piatti* and *cinelli* for cymbals without indicating an intended difference.

A Conductor's Guide to 19th-Century Choral-Orchestra Works   51

Editions: *La Damnation de Faust* is published in a critical edition in *The New Berlioz Edition*, volume 8, edited by Julian Rushton, by Bärenreiter (BA 5448). Orchestral parts, and a piano-vocal score (BA 5448a) are also available. It was published Breitkopf and Härtel in the previous critical edition, *Hector Berlioz: Werke*, volumes 11 and 12, edited by C. Malherbe and Felix Weingartner, which includes an English singing translation by John Bernhoff. Other editions, which are available for purchase include: Breitkopf and Härtel, G. Schirmer, and Kalmus.

The "Rakoczy March," "Ballet des sylphs," and "Menuet de follets" movements are published independently by Breitkopf and Härtel and Kalmus.

Autograph: The composer's manuscript of the full score is in the library of the Paris Conservatory (ms. 1190).

Notes: This work is organized as a concert drama with each singer assigned a role within the story. It is freely adapted from selected scenes in Goethe's telling of the Faust legend. The "Rakoczy March" is Berlioz's arrangement of what he calls "The Hungarian War-Song." The composer has organized the work into four acts comprising twenty scenes as follows:

Part One: *The Plains of Hungary*

    1. Introduction
    2. Ronde des Paysans
    3. March Hongroise

Part Two: *In northern Germany*

    4. Faust seul dans son cabinet de travail
       Chant de la Fête de Pâques
    5. Faust
       Méphistophélès

    Auerbach's cellar in Leipzig

    6. Chœur de Buveurs
       Chanson de Brander

Fugue sur le theme de la Chanson de Brander
Chanson de Méphistophélès

Forest and meadows on the banks of the Elb

7. Air de Méphistophélès
   Chœur de Gnomes et de Sylphes
   Ballet des Sylphes
8. Chœur de Soldats
   Chanson d'Etudiants

Part Three: In Marguerite's room

9. Tambours et Trompettes sonant la retraite
   Air de Faust
10. Faust
    Méphistophélès
11. Marguerite
    Le Roi de Thulé
12. Evocation
    Menuet des Follets
    Sérénade de Méphistophélès avec Chœur de Follets
13. Duo
14. Trio et Chœur

Part Four

15. Romance de Marguerite
16. Invocationá la nature
17. Récitatif et Chasse
18. La Course á l'Abîme
19. Pandœmonium
20. Dans le Ciel

Performance Issues: There are a number of descriptive passages within the score that identify what the music represents. Likewise there are many stage directions for the singers that would be lost in a pure concert performance. These should be incorporated into the program, or projected as super titles during the performance. The Breitkopf and Härtel edition includes singing translations in German (using Goethe's original text) and English. Slight alterations are given in the score to accommodate minor syllabic deviations from the French. There are divisi in all of choral parts, although more predominantly for the men. The tessitura for the tenor I part is quite high and will demand secure and mature singers for proper effect. The choral writing is conservatively conceived focusing upon evident triadic and scalar relationships, and the parts are clearly doubled by the orchestra throughout much of the work. There are a few complex fugal sections for the choir, but these are quite directly doubled and fairly diatonic. There are some unaccompanied choral passages. The choral material is more vocally demanding than it is challenging to learn. Also some sections, particularly in scene 7, present a great amount of text quite quickly, which may require special attention in rehearsal. This is a large symphonic work requiring a sizable choir and expansive string section. The children's choir appears in only the final scene, which may pose some logistical issues. From the choir, a group of 4 boys is assigned a unison solo, which may be given to a single child if he has a sufficient voice to carry the part. Berlioz indicates that their placement should be dictated by the size of the group. He indicates that a group of "2 to 300 children" may be used. The composer also calls for 8 soloists within each violin section, which should be an indication of the scale he intended. The editor has indicated that with a smaller ensemble, single players could provide the necessary contrast. There are exposed passages for most of the wind and brass players. There are rapid melodic and accompanimental figurations throughout the winds and strings. There is an important and prolonged viola solo in scene 11. There are also some extended brass-choir passages accompanying very soft solo singing, which will require skilled players able to maintain a reduced dynamic. These passages may also shape seating decisions for the orchestra. Likewise, scene 9 calls for the trumpets and two horns to be behind the scenes. This is one of many indications that this work is best if treated as a concert opera. The score implies significant action, some of which is not evident in the lyrics and scoring alone. Every effort should be made to clearly present the drama in a pseudo-theatrical fashion. **Soloists:** Marguerite (mezzo-soprano) - range: c'-a'', tessitura: d'-d'', this is a sustained and lyric solo role; Faust (tenor) - range: $d\#$-$c\#''$, tessitura: g-g', this is a demanding, sustained, and heroic solo role; Méphistofélès (baritone or bass) - range: (A) B^b-f' (g'), tessitura: d-d', this is a lyric role that is probably more effective as a baritone, which provides greater contrast between the three male soloists, it is also the variant that provides the fewer melodic compromises; Brander (bass) - range: A-d', tessitura: c-c', this is a simple lyric role; **choir:** difficult; **orchestra:** difficult.

Selected Discography

Nicolai Gedda, Janet Baker, Gabriel Bacquier, Maria Peronne, Pierre Thau; Choeurs de l'Opéra de Paris; Orchestre de Paris; conducted by Georges Prêtre, recorded in 1969. EMI: 7243-5 68 583-2 (CD).

Nicolai Gedda, Jules Bastin, Josephine Veasey, Richard Van Allan, Gillian Knight; London Symphony Orchestra and Chorus; conducted by Colin Davis, recorded in 1973. Philips: 416 395-2.

Placido Domingo, Dietrich Fischer-Dieskau, Yvonne Minton, Jules Bastin; Choeurs de l' Orchestre de Paris, Choeur d'Enfants de Paris; Orchestre de Paris; conducted by Daniel Barenboim, recorded 1978. Reissued as a CD in 2003. Deutsche Grammophon: DG 474 440 2.

Anne Sofie von Otter, Fiona Wright, Michael Myers, Jean-Philippe Lafont, René Schirrer; Edinburgh Festival Chorus, Orchestre de l'Opéra de Lyon; conducted by John Eliot Gardiner, recorded in the Auditorium Ravel in Lyon on 27 September and 2 October 1987. Philips: 426 199-2.

Selected Bibliography

Berlioz, Hector: *The Memoirs of Hector Berlioz*, translated by Rachel and Eleanor Holmes, annotated and revised by Ernest Newman, 97, 386, 418-420, 427, 428, 436-437, 440, 445-447, 474, 476, 481-483, 486, 488, 528, 532. New York: Knopf, 1932. Reprinted, New York: Dover, 1966.

Upton, George P.: *The Standard Cantatas*, seventh edition, 74-81. Chicago: A. C. McClurg and Company, 1899.

Bass, Eddie C.: *Thematic Procedures in the Symphonies of Berlioz*. Doctoral dissertation: University of North Carolina Chapel Hill, 1964.

Barzun, Jacques: *Berlioz and the Romantic Century*, second edition, I: 108, 118, 378, 483-503, 508, 509, 511, 556, 567, 569; II: 44, 47, 51, 71, 72, 105. New York: Columbia University Press, 1969.

Dickinson, Alan E. F.: *The Music of Berlioz*, 63-80. New York: St. Martin's Press, 1972.

Rushton, Julian: "The Genesis of Berlioz's 'La Damnation de Faust,'" *Music and Letters*, volume 56 (1975), 129-146.

_____: "The figure and the background: Faust in *La damnation*," in *The Musical Language of Hector Berlioz*, 228-256. Cambridge: Cambridge University Press, 1983.

Pahlen, Kurt: *The World of the Oratorio*, translated by Judith Schaefer with additional English-language material by Thurston Dox, 61-64. Portland, OR: Amadeus Press, 1990.

Werth, Kent: "'Nature Immense,' A Sketch from Berlioz's *La Damnation de Faust*: A New View of the Composer at Work," *The Musical Quarterly*, volume 74, number 1 (1990), 74-82.

Reeve [Kolb], Katherine: "*The Damnation of Faust*: The Perils of Heroism in Music," in *Berlioz Studies*, edited by Peter A. Bloom, 148-188. Cambridge: Cambridge University Press, 1992.

Berger, Melvin: *Guide to Choral Masterpieces: A Listener's Guide*, 57-59. New York: Anchor Books, 1993.

Haar, James: "The Operas and the Dramatic Legend," in *The Cambridge Companion to Berlioz*, edited by Peter A. Bloom, 81-95. Cambridge: Cambridge University Press, 2000.

Rushton, Julian: *The Music of Berlioz*, 50-53, 303-315. Oxford: Oxford University Press, 2001.

Te Deum, op. 22 (1849), H. 118

Duration: ca. 52 minutes

Text: This is an anonymous hymn of thanksgiving in church use since the sixth century. It is usually sung during the Matins service. The apocryphal source of its genesis is that it was spontaneously sung by Ss. Ambrose and Augustine on the evening when Augustine was baptized.[22]

Performing Forces: voices: tenor soloist; 2 STB choirs, children's choir;[23] **orchestra:** 4 flutes, 4 oboes, 4 clarinets (in A, B^b, C), 4

---

[22] Jeffers, Ron: *Translations and Annotations of Choral Repertoire, Volume I: Sacred Latin Texts*, 218. Corvallis, OR: Earthsongs, 1988.

[23] Berlioz states in the score that the children's choir should be as large as possible. The score is labeled SA, but it is virtually in unison with a few octave divisi.

bassoons, soprano saxophone (in B♭), 4 horns (D♭, D, E♭, E, F, B♭, B), 4 trumpets (in D♭, D, E♭, E, B), 4 cornets (in A, B♭), 6 trombones, 2 tubas, timpani (2 drums), percussion (6 players — 4 tenor drums [tuned to F], 6 snare drums, bass drum, 4 or 5 pairs of cymbals), organ, 12 harps, and strings.

First Performance: 30 April 1855; St. Eustache Church, Paris; conducted by the composer

Editions: *Te Deum* is published in a critical edition in *The New Berlioz Edition*, volume 10, edited by Denis McCaldin, by Bärenreiter (BA 5782). Orchestral parts, a piano-vocal score (BA 5782a) are also available. It was published by Breitkopf and Härtel in the previous critical edition, *Hector Berlioz: Werke*, volume 8, edited by C. Malherbe and Felix Weingartner. Other editions that are available for purchase include: Breitkopf and Härtel, G. Schirmer, and Kalmus.

Autograph: A copy of the composer's manuscript of the full score is in the public library in St. Petersburg, Russia.

Notes: This score is dedicated to Prince Albert. In the hope that the *Te Deum* might be premiered at the coronation of Napoleon III in 1853, Berlioz added the Prélude and March; however, the work would not be performed until the Universal Exhibition of 1855. It was performed to open the Badinguet Agricultural Show. The composer states that if the work is not to be performed for a thanksgiving or military service, the two instrumental movements should be deleted. It is organized in eight movements as follows:

1. Te Deum	Hymn
2. Tibi Omnes	Hymn
3. Prélude	orchestra only
4. Dignare Domine	Prayer
5. Christe, rex gloriæ	Hymn
6. Te ego quæsumus	Prayer
7. Judex crederis	Hymn and Prayer
8. March for the presentation of the colors	orchestra and organ

Performance Issues: In the score, Berlioz indicates that the choirs and orchestra should be at the opposite end of the church from the organ. He includes recommendations for assistant conductors or his electric metronome, which was a device that flashed in synchrony with the beat of the conductor. The choral writing is contrapuntally conceived with some very elegant fugal sections and clever interplay between the choirs. There are divisi for all of the choral parts. The bass II parts of both mixed choirs have many pedal Ds. The choral parts are well written for the singers, and there is considerable support of the vocal parts within the accompaniment. There is a brief section of movement 5 that calls for a solo quartet from the choirs. The end of movement 6 is a cappella. The choral material is challenging; however, the children's choir is quite accessible and simple. The composer's demand for as large a group as possible is warranted given the context in which they appear. The orchestration is obviously large, but there are significant passages that are delicately transparent. The brass section is used to great effect. A large pipe organ is ideal. The harps only appear in the finale. Their quantity is certainly negotiable. Berlioz indicates that a harmonium may be substituted, but this is an unlikely complement to the forces of the orchestra. The antiphonal effects between the orchestra and the organ are quite dramatic. The composer also indicates the preferred placement of the choirs. The sonic space is an important consideration for the composer's decision making, so this must not be trivialized. There are rapid and challenging passages throughout the orchestra most of which are idiomatically written. The composer's desired ensemble contains approximately 900 singers and instrumentalists for which this is an ideal score. A more mortal-sized group may be used, but this work does demand as large a complement of performers as can be conscripted. **Soloist:** tenor - range: f#-g', tessitura: g-f', this is a lyric solo that is not threatened by heavy accompaniment; **choir:** difficult; **orchestra:** difficult.

Selected Discography

Alexander Young; London Philharmonic Choir, Dulwich College Boys' Choir; Royal Philharmonic Orchestra; conducted by Thomas Beecham, recorded in 1953. Reissued on CD in 2003 – Sony Classics: SMK 87964.

Keith Lewis; Matthias Eisenberg, organ; Vokalensemble Frankfurt, Bachchor und Currende der Christuskirche Mainz, Kinder und Jugendchor des Hessischen Rundfunks; Radio-Sinfonie-Orchester; conducted by Eliahu Inbal, recorded 25-26 February 1988 in the Old Opera House in Frankfurt. Denon: CO-76142.

Stuart Neill; Dresden Philharmonic Chorus and Children's Chorus, Dresden Singakademie, Dresden State Opera Chorus; Dresden Staatskapelle; conducted by Colin Davis, recorded in 1998. Profil Medien: PH06039.

Roberto Alagna; Choeurs de l' Orchestre de Paris, Choeur d'Enfants de l'Union Européenne; Orchestre de Paris; conducted by John Nelson, recorded in 2001. Virgin Classics: 5 45449 2.

Selected Bibliography

Berlioz, Hector: *The Memoirs of Hector Berlioz*, translated by Rachel and Eleanor Holmes, annotated and revised by Ernest Newman, 482, 489, 493, 508. New York: Knopf, 1932. Reprinted, New York: Dover, 1966.

Dickinson, Alan E. F.: *The Music of Berlioz*, 91-106. New York: St. Martin's Press, 1972.

Barzun, Jacques: *Berlioz and the Romantic Century*, second edition, I: 228, 266, 357, 401, 550, 554, 561-573; II: 70, 125, 289. New York: Columbia University Press, 1969.

Pahlen, Kurt: *The World of the Oratorio*, translated by Judith Schaefer with additional English-language material by Thurston Dox, 64-66. Portland, OR: Amadeus Press, 1990.

Berger, Melvin: *Guide to Choral Masterpieces: A Listener's Guide*, 55-57. New York: Anchor Books, 1993.

Locke, Ralph P.: "The Religious Works," in *The Cambridge Companion to Berlioz*, edited by Peter A. Bloom, 96-107. Cambridge: Cambridge University Press, 2000.

Rushton, Julian: *The Music of Berlioz*, 55-57, 220-236. Oxford: Oxford University Press, 2001.

L'Enfance du Christ ["The Childhood of Christ"], op. 25 (1850-1854), H.130

Duration: ca. 93 minutes

Text: The text, which is in French, is by the composer.

Performing Forces: voices: Marie (mezzo-soprano), Récitant (tenor), Centurion (tenor), Joseph (baritone), Hérode (bass), Père de famille (bass), Polydorus (bass) soloists; SATB choir; **orchestra:** 2 flutes (flute II doubling piccolo), oboes (oboe II doubling English horn), 2 clarinets (A, B^b), 2 bassoons, 2 horns (E^b), 3 trombones, organ or harmonium (offstage), harp, timpani (2 drums), and strings.

First Performance: The first section[24] was premiered 12 November 1850 in Paris. The entire oratorio received its premiere 10 December 1854 in Paris.

Editions: *L'Enfance du Christ* is published in a critical edition in *The New Berlioz Edition*, volume 11, edited by David Lloyd-Jones, by Bärenreiter (BA 5451). Orchestral parts, a piano-vocal score (BA 5451a – French/German, 5451b — French/English) are also available. It was published by Breitkopf and Härtel in the previous critical edition, *Hector Berlioz: Werke*, volume 9, edited by C. Malherbe and Felix Weingartner. Other editions, which are available for purchase include: Breitkopf and Härtel, G. Schirmer, H. W. Gray, and Kalmus.

Autograph: The composer's manuscript is in the Bibliothèque Nationale in Paris.

Notes: The Breitkopf edition includes singing translations in German by Peter Cornelius and Felix Weingartner and in English by John Bernhoff. The score is divided ito three larges sections: Part One — *Le Songe d'Hérode*, which is dedicated to the composer's

---

[24] This sectional premiere was presented under the pseudonym Pierre Ducré, whom Berlioz had fabricated as an unknown 17th-century composer whose work he had recently discovered.

nieces, Josephine and Nanci Suat; Part Two — *La Fuite en Egypte*, which is dedicated to Mr. Ella, the Director of the London Musical Union; and Part Three — *L'Arrivée à Saïs*, which is dedicated to the Singakademie and Universitäts-Sängerverein "Paulus" in Leipzig. It is organized as follows:

Part One: *Le Songe d'Hérode*
1. Introduction — Récitant
2. Marche nocturne — Centurion and Polydorus
3. Air d'Hérode — Hérode
4. Scene Three — Hérode and Polydorus
5. Hérode et les Devins — Hérode; TTBB choir
6. Duet — Marie and Joseph
7. Scene Six — Marie and Joseph; SSAA choir of angels

Part Two: *La Fuite en Egypte*
8. Overture
9. L'Adieu des Bergers à la Sainte Famille — SATB choir
10. Le Repos de la Sainte Famille — Récitant; off-stage SSAA choir

Part Three: *L'Arrivée à Saïs*
11. Introduction
12. Duet — Marie, Joseph; BB choir
13. Scene Two — Père de Famille; SATB choir of Ishmaelites
    Trio for flutes and harp performed by the young Ishmaelites
14. Epilog — Récitant; SATB choir, off-stage SA choir

Movement 9 is the famous Shepherds' Farewell that is often excerpted for independent performance.

Performance Issues: Berlioz indicates in the score that during Part One, the male choristers are on-stage, and the women off-stage around the harmonium. At the beginning of Part Two, the women join the men on-stage. An SSAA octet should remain off-stage for selected effects. There are significant recitatives that are unaccompanied or minimally supported. The off-stage women's choir must be fairly independent. They are harmonically supported by the harmonium, but have some unaccompanied passages. The on-stage choral material is generally well supported by the orchestra. The integration of them and the on-stage orchestra may present some difficulties. The orchestra has some contrapuntally complex material some of which will require attention to balance the layers of musical activity, as there are foreground and background elements at work concurrently. In movement 5, there is a "cabbalistic procession" that maintains a 7/4 meter to great effect. There is a cello solo in movement 6. This appears in duet with the violin I part, which is not labeled solo, but this should be considered. There is some truly challenging rapid passagework for the orchestra intermittently throughout this work. The string parts are particularly challenging in this regard. The bassoons also have critical thematic material throughout the work. There are some unusually conceived contrapuntal passages for both the orchestra and choir. The overture to Part Two is a lovely fugal work, as is the choral portion of movement 13. The trio in movement 14 is completely exposed and quite expressive. The harmonium and harp each appear in only a single movement; likewise, the oboe II part plays English horn in all but one movement. The final movement has an extended a cappella section for the choir. This is a lyrical and sensitively conceived work. It includes some of Berlioz's most accessible and appealing music. The choral material is quite accessible, and this score can be performed by moderate-sized forces. **Soloists:** Marie (mezzo-soprano) - range: c'-f'', tessitura: f'-$e^{b''}$, this is a lyric and simple solo role; Récitant (tenor) - range: $d\#$-a', tessitura: f-f', this is a lyric, "evangelist" role; Centurion (tenor) - range: d-f', tessitura: f-d', this is a simple declamatory role; Joseph (baritone) - range: B^b-e', tessitura: c-c', this is a simple declamatory role; Hérode (bass) - range: F-$e^{b'}$, tessitura: B^b-c', this is a sustained and expressive role that must be clear at the bottom of the range; Père de famille (bass) - range: $F\#$-d', tessitura: d-c', this is a simple declamatory solo; Polydorus (bass) - range: c-$e^{b'}$, tessitura: c-c', this is a simple declamatory solo; **choir:** medium difficult; **orchestra:** difficult.

Selected Discography

Janet Baker, Eric Tappy, Philip Landridge, Thomas Allen, Jules Bastin, Joseph Rouleau, Raimond Herincx; John Alldis Choir, London Symphony Orchestra; conducted by Colin Davis, recorded in London in October 1976. Philips: 416 949-2.

Gilles Cachemaille, Philippe Bernold, Gilles Cottin, José Van Dam, René Schirrer, Michel Fockenoy, Chantal Mathieu, Anne Sofie von Otter, Anthony Rolfe Johnson; Monteverdi Choir; Lyon Opera

Orchestra; conducted by John Eliot Gardiner, recorded in 1988. Erato: 2292-45275-2.

Frederic Caton, Laurent Naouri, Olivier Lallouette, Paul Agnew, Veronique Gens; La Chapelle Royale, Collegium Vocale; Orchestra des Champs Elysées; conducted by Philippe Herreweghe, recorded in 1997. Reissued in 2002. Harmonia Mundi: HMX 290 1632/3.

Christiane Oelze, Christopher Maltman, Mark Padmore, Ralf Lukas, Mikhael Nikiforov, Berhhard Hartmann, Frank Bossert; SWR Vokalensemble; Stuttgart Radio Orchestra; conducted by Roger Norrington, recorded in 2003. Hänssler Classic: CD93.091.

Selected Bibliography

Berlioz, Hector: *The Memoirs of Hector Berlioz*, translated by Rachel and Eleanor Holmes, annotated and revised by Ernest Newman, 475, 479, 482, 483, 488, 489, 506. New York: Knopf, 1932. Reprinted, New York: Dover, 1966.

Barzun, Jacques: *Berlioz and the Romantic Century*, second edition, I: 89-105, 116, 212, 228, 327; II: 91, 93-96, 103, 105 107, 134, 225. New York: Columbia University Press, 1969.

Dickinson, Alan E. F.: *The Music of Berlioz*, 81-90. New York: St. Martin's Press, 1972.

O'Neal, Melinda: *Berlioz's L'Enfance du Christ: trilogie sacrée, Op. 25: A Conductor's Analysis for Performance*. Doctoral dissertation: Indiana University, 1987.

Pahlen, Kurt: *The World of the Oratorio*, translated by Judith Schaefer with additional English-language material by Thurston Dox, 66-68. Portland, OR: Amadeus Press, 1990.

Berger, Melvin: *Guide to Choral Masterpieces: A Listener's Guide*, 59-61. New York: Anchor Books, 1993.

Locke, Ralph P.: "The Religious Works," in *The Cambridge Companion to Berlioz*, edited by Peter A. Bloom, 96-107. Cambridge: Cambridge University Press, 2000.

Smither, Howard E.: *A History of the Oratorio, volume 4: The Oratorio in the Nineteenth and Twentieth Centuries*, 552-565. Chapel Hill, NC: The University of North Carolina Press, 2000.

Rushton, Julian: *The Music of Berlioz*, 60-61, 315-324. Oxford: Oxford University Press, 2001.

La révolution grecque, scène héroïque (1825-1826), H. 21

Duration: ca. 18 minutes

Text: The text is by Humbert Ferrand.

Performing Forces: voices: Greek Priest (bass), Greek Hero (bass) soloists; SATB choir; **orchestra:** 4 flutes, 4 oboes, 4 clarinets (C), 4 bassoons, 4 horns (D, E, G, A), 2 trumpets (A, C), 3 trombones, tuba, timpani (2 drums), percussion (2 players — bass drum, cymbals, tam-tam), and strings.

The score provides the option of using only 2 flutes, 2 oboes, 2 clarinets, and 2 bassoons.

First Performance: 26 May 1828; Salle du Conservatoire, Paris; conducted by Nathan Bloc

Editions: *Scène héroïque* is published in a critical editions in *The New Berlioz Edition*, volume 12a, edited by Julian Rushton, by Bärenreiter (BA 5972). Orchestral parts are also available. It was published by Breitkopf and Härtel in the previous critical edition, *Hector Berlioz: Werke*, volume 10, edited by C. Malherbe and Felix Weingartner, which includes singing translations in German by Emma Klingenfeld and English by John Bernhoff.

Autograph: The composer's manuscript of the full score is lost; however, there is a set of manuscript parts in the library of the Paris Conservatory.

Notes: This work was first published in 1903 as part of the *Hector Berlioz: Werke*.

Performance Issues: There are divisi in all of the choral parts. The choral writing is generally homophonic, and much is set for TTB or SSA choirs, portraying Greek women, priests, soldiers, etc. The choral roles change within movements so that it may be difficult for the audience to clearly identify who is supposed to be singing. The parts are well conceived for the voices and generally well supported by the accompaniment. There are some dissonances placed high in the women's ranges that may prove difficult to tune accurately. In the finale, the women are in unison at a range higher than most altos can produce. It may be best to assign them to the first tenor part, which is in a traditional alto range in the troublesome passages. The instrumental writing is idiomatic and well informed from a player's perspective. Berlioz includes some rapid passagework in the winds that played in unison by the four players he suggests may provide some challenges for precise ensemble playing. This work is suitable to a large symphonic choir, although a medium-sized choral group is sufficient. The composer indicates that the second basses should out-number the firsts. This is a very practical work for less-experienced choirs. It could be a good companion piece with a concert performance of the finale from Mozart's *Don Giovanni*. **Soloists:** Greek Priest (bass) - range: G-e′, tessitura: d-d′, this is a sustained and lyric role; Greek Hero (bass) - range: G-e′, tessitura: d-d′, this is a declamatory solo with some sustained passages; **choir:** medium easy; **orchestra:** medium difficult.

Selected Discography

Lieuwe Visser, Ruud van der Meer; Dutch Radio Choir and Symphony Orchestra; conducted by Jean Fournet, recorded in 1988. Denon: CO-72886.

Selected Bibliography

Berlioz, Hector: *The Memoirs of Hector Berlioz*, translated by Rachel and Eleanor Holmes, annotated and revised by Ernest Newman, 23, 24. New York: Knopf, 1932. Reprinted, New York: Dover, 1966.
Barzun, Jacques: *Berlioz and the Romantic Century*, second edition, I: 65, 68, 83, 88, 92, 240-241. New York: Columbia University Press, 1969.
Dickinson, Alan E. F.: *The Music of Berlioz*, 41-44. New York: St. Martin's Press, 1972.
Rushton, Julian: *The Music of Berlioz*, 13-17, 89-92. Oxford: Oxford University Press, 2001.

A Conductor's Guide to 19th-Century Choral-Orchestra Works 65

Huit scènes du Faust, op. 1 (1828-1829), H. 33

Duration: ca. 36 minutes

Text: The text is from Johann Wolfgang von Goethe's Faust, translated into French by Gérard de Nerval.

Performing Forces: voices: Marguerite (soprano), unnamed (soprano or tenor), Méphistophélès (tenor), and Brander (bass) soloists; SSAATTBB choir; **orchestra:** 2 flutes (both doubling piccolo), 2 oboes (both doubling English horn), 2 clarinets (A, B^b), 2 bassoons, 4 horns (B^b basso, C, D, E^b, F, G), tuba, timpani (2 drums),[25] 2 harps, celeste, guitar, and strings.

First Performance: 1 November 1829; Salle du Conservatoire, Paris; conducted by François-Antoine Habeneck

Editions: *Huit scenes du Faust* is published in a critical editions in *The New Berlioz Edition*, volume 5, edited by Julian Rushton, by Bärenreiter (BA 5445). Orchestral parts are also available. It was published by Breitkopf and Härtel in the previous critical edition, *Hector Berlioz: Werke*, volume 10, edited by C. Malherbe and Felix Weingartner.

Autograph: The composer's manuscript of the full score is lost; however, there is a set of manuscript parts in the library of the Paris Conservatory.

Notes: Much of this composition was reworked to become Berlioz's *La Damnation de Faust* (q.v.). The scenes are arranged as follows:

1.	Chants de la Fête de Pâques	choir
2.	Paysans sous les Tilleuls	S or T soloist and choir
3.	Concert de Sylphes	SSTTBB sextet
4.	Ecot de joyeux Compagnons	Brander and TTB choir
5.	Chanson de Méphistophélès	Méphistophélès and TTB

---

[25] In movement 7, Berlioz calls for four players playing two pairs of timpani. The purpose is to emulate a military retreat. A single player and pair of drums can suffice if necessary.

6. Le Roi de Thulé	Marguerite
7. Romance de Marguerite	Marguerite
Chœurs de Soldats	TTB choir
8. Sérénade de Méphistophélès	Méphistophélès

Performance Issues: There are spoken lines of text at the beginnings and endings of many of the scenes. The choral parts are somewhat contrapuntal, but most of the choral material is homophonic. Sections of the choir are labeled as portraying groups of people within the story. The choral parts are generally well conceived for the singers; however, some of the alto material is quite high. The score divides the women into two SA choirs, which may benefit from spatial separation. If the singers are to be grouped together, some of the divisi may be better redistributed based upon range rather than choir. Movement 4 calls for an SSTTBB solo sextet. This is the most complicated vocal ensemble, and even its recitative-like passages are clearly doubled by the instruments. It does require a sextet of solid singers, but this treatment also considerably reduces the challenge of the work for the full choir. The orchestration varies considerably by movement. The tuba only appears in movement 5, and only two horns are used, except for movements 6 and 7, which calls for four. Likewise the trumpets are only used in movement 7. The harp parts are complex and critical. There is an extended viola solo in movement 6 and an important and exposed English horn solo in movement 7. The final scene is accompanied by solo guitar, which is the only use of this instrument in the work. The choral material is quite accessible, and with the exception of the sextet, this is a men's-choir piece. The solos are all strophic and songlike, and the orchestra parts are fairly easy except as noted. This is a much easier score for singers and players than the composer's later *La Damnation de Faust*. It is also interesting to note that Méphistophélès is converted into a baritone role in the later incarnation. **Soloists:** Marguerite (soprano) - range: c'-a'', tessitura: f'-f'', this is a simple lyric solo appropriate for a soprano or mezzo-soprano; soprano or tenor - range: $c\#'$-a'', tessitura: e'-e'', this is a lyric, folk-like solo that sings a four verse song in movement 2; Méphistophélès (tenor) - range: d-f', tessitura: f-f', this is a lyric solo role; Brander (bass) - range: A-d', tessitura: d-d', this is a straightforward, declamatory solo; **choir:** medium easy; **orchestra:** medium easy.

Selected Discography

Angelika Kirschlager, Frederic Caton, Jean-Paul Fouchecourt, Claude Zibi; Choeur et Orchestre Philharmonique de Radio France; conducted by Yutaka Sado, recorded in 2000. Erato: 8573-80234-2.

Susan Graham, Susanne Mentzer, François Le Roux, John Mark Ainsley; Montréal Symphony Orchestra and Chorus; conducted by Charles Dutoit, recorded in 2003. Decca: 4750972.

Selected Bibliography

Berlioz, Hector: *The Memoirs of Hector Berlioz*, translated by Rachel and Eleanor Holmes, annotated and revised by Ernest Newman, 97-98. New York: Knopf, 1932. Reprinted, New York: Dover, 1966.

Barzun, Jacques: *Berlioz and the Romantic Century*, second edition, I: 96-98, 102, 106-118, 327, 441, 484; II: 66, 220. New York: Columbia University Press, 1969.

Rushton, Julian: "Berlioz's 'Huit scenes de Faust': New Source Material," *Musical Times*, volume 65 (1970), 471-473.

_____: *The Music of Berlioz*, 25-26, 172-176, 181-184, 303-306. Oxford: Oxford University Press, 2001.

Lélio ou le Retour à la vie [Lélio, or The Return to Life], op. 14 bis (1831-1832), H. 55

Duration: ca. 51 minutes

Text: The text is by the composer with the additional poem, "Der Fischer," by Goethe translated into French by A. Dubuys.

Performing Forces: voices: Lélio (tenor), Horatio (tenor), and Captain (baritone) soloists; SATB choir; **orchestra:** 2 flutes (flute II doubling piccolo), 2 oboes (oboe II doubling English horn), 2 clarinets (A, B^b, C), 2 bassoons, 4 horns (C, E, F), 2 cornets (B^b), 2 trumpets (D, E^b, E, F), 3 trombones, tuba, 2 timpanists (4 drums), percussion (2 players — bass drum, cymbals, tam-tam), harp, piano (4-hands), and strings.

First Performance: 9 December 1832; Salle du Conservatoire, Paris; conducted by François-Antoine Habeneck

Editions: *Lélio ou le Retour à la vie* is published in a critical editions in *The New Berlioz Edition*, volume 7, edited by Peter Bloom, by Bärenreiter (BA 5447). Orchestral parts, and a piano-vocal score (BA 5447a) are also available. It was published Breitkopf and Härtel in the previous critical edition, *Hector Berlioz: Werke*, volume 13, edited by C. Malherbe and Felix Weingartner.

Autograph: The composer's manuscript of the full score is in the library of the Paris Conservatory.

Notes: This work was composed as a sequel to Berlioz's *Symphonie fantastique* and is dedicated to the composer's son, Louis. The composer's notes in the score state that this work should be performed as a supplement to the *Symphonie fantastique*. He also indicates that the orchestra is to be invisible and the singers throughout the theater and behind the curtain. Only the actor portraying Lélio is in front of the curtain until the finale, at which point Lélio exits, and the curtain rises to reveal the other musicians. The character of Lélio is a composer. Berlioz indicates that it is more important for this role to be a good actor than a singer, in fact the singing voice should belong an unseen singer who represents Lélio's "imaginary voice." Horatio is his friend, and the choir portrays Musicians, Friends and Pupils of Lélio, Brigands, and Ghosts. The Breitkopf score includes a singing German translation by Peter Cornelius and an English one by John Bernhoff. The work includes substantial spoken text, and is organized as follows:

1. Le Pêcheur (Goethe)	Horatio with piano only
2. Chœur d'ombres	choir and orchestra
3. Chanson de Brigands	Captain, TTBB choir
4. Chant de bonheur	Lélio's imaginary voice
5. La Harpe Eolienne — Souvenirs	orchestra
6. Fantasie sur le Tempête de Shakespeare	SSATT choir

Performance Issues: The choral material is syllabic and clearly doubled by the orchestra. There is significant unison singing by the SATB choir, but the men are presented with the majority of the harmonic material. The finale has the most complex music for the choir and the orchestra. Here the singers must be somewhat independent. The orchestral material is idiomatically conceived. There are significant divisi for all of the strings (4, 4, 2, 4, 2). This may dictate the size of the ensemble in that at minimum there must be four cellos and three doublebasses. The orchestration is quirky, but only heavy-handed in the finale. Here the strings are written as solo parts, so a moderate string and choral component can be used. The string players need to be fairly independent. This is a peculiar melodrama that does require a strong actor in the title role. The staging directions presented in the score may prove impractical, as most of the music is to be performed behind the curtain, which may prove acoustically impossible. The use of a scrim, which is fairly sound-transparent, may be a viable solution. This is a rarely performed work due to its awkward performance demands and challenging text. If presented in the language of the audience as the second half of a concert in sequel to *Symphonie fantastique*, this could be a remarkably powerful examination of the inner workings of the artist. **Soloists:** Lélio (tenor) - range: e-b′, tessitura: g-g′, this is a lyric solo; Horatio (tenor) - range: e-c#″, tessitura: a-a′, this is a lyric role that is exposed at the limits of the range; Captain (baritone) - range: c-f′, tessitura: e-e′, this is an energetic and lyric solo that stresses the top of the range; **choir:** medium, easy; **orchestra:** medium difficult.

Selected Discography

José Carreras, Thomas Allen; John Alldis Choir; London Symphony Orchestra; conducted by Colin Davis, recorded in 1980. Philips: 416 961-2.

Selected Bibliography

Berlioz, Hector: *The Memoirs of Hector Berlioz*, translated by Rachel and Eleanor Holmes, annotated and revised by Ernest Newman, 94-94, 160, 190, 192, 194-195, 508. New York: Knopf, 1932. Reprinted, New York: Dover, 1966.

Newman, Ernest: "*Lélio*," in *Berlioz, Romantic and Classic: Writings by Ernest Newman*, edited by Peter Heyworth, 175-177. London: Victor Gollancz, Ltd., 1972. This particular essay was written in 1949.

Barzun, Jacques: *Berlioz and the Romantic Century*, second edition, I: 133, 137, 150, 158, 220-230, 232-233, 236, 265, 327; II: 88, 109, 146. New York: Columbia University Press, 1969.

Rushton, Julian: *The Music of Berlioz*, 30-33, 86-88. Oxford: Oxford University Press, 2001.

Le Cinq Mai: Chant sur la mort de l'empereur Napoléon, op. 6 (1835), H. 74

Duration: ca. 13 minutes

Text: The text is by Pierre-Jean de Béranger.

Performing Forces: voices: bass soloist; SSTTBB choir; **orchestra:** 2 flutes, 2 clarinets (C), 4 bassoons, 4 horns (C, E^b), 2 trumpets (F), 3 trombones, percussion (1 player — large bass drum), and strings

First Performance: 22 November 1835; Salle du Conservatoire, Paris; conducted by Narcisse Girard

Editions: *Le Cinq mai* is published in a critical edition in *The New Berlioz Edition*, volume 12a, edited by Julian Rushton, by Bärenreiter (BA 5452). Orchestral parts are also available. It was published by Breitkopf and Härtel in the previous critical edition, *Hector Berlioz: Werke*, volume 13, edited by C. Malherbe and Felix Weingartner.

Autograph: The composer's manuscript of the full score is lost; however, there is a set of manuscript parts in the library of the Paris Conservatory.

Notes: The Breitkopf score includes singing translations in German by Felix Weingartner and in English by Percy Pinkerton. The score is dedicated to the French painter, Horace Vernet.

Performance Issues: Much of the choral material is in a unison melody that doubles the soloist at times. The remainder is in block-chord homophonic writing. There are some brief a cappella passages that are clearly prepared and simple. The orchestral parts are very practically written, and the score is within the ability of many amateur ensembles. A small to medium-sized string section will be effective. **Soloist:** bass - range: G-e′, tessitura: c-c′, this is a sustained and lyric solo that is exposed at both extremes of range; **choir:** easy; **orchestra:** medium easy.

Selected Discography

Lieuwe Visser, Ruud van der Meer; Dutch Radio Choir and Symphony Orchestra; conducted by Jean Fournet, recorded in 1988. Denon: CO-72886.

Selected Bibliography

Berlioz, Hector: *The Memoirs of Hector Berlioz*, translated by Rachel and Eleanor Holmes, annotated and revised by Ernest Newman, 291, 304, 331, 333, 336, 340, 343. New York: Knopf, 1932. Reprinted, New York: Dover, 1966.

Barzun, Jacques: *Berlioz and the Romantic Century*, second edition, I: 266-267, 349, 523. New York: Columbia University Press, 1969.

Dickinson, Alan E. F.: *The Music of Berlioz*, 44. New York: St. Martin's Press, 1972.

Tristia, op. 18, (1831-1848), H. 56, 92 b, 103

Duration: *Méditation religieuse* ca. 4 minutes
La Mort d'Ophélie ca. 8 minutes
Marche funébre pour la dernière scène d'"Hamlet" ca. 7 minutes

Text: The text of *Méditation religieuse* is by Louise Belloc, after Thomas Moore. The text of *La Mort d'Ophélie* is by Ernest Legouvé, after William Shakespeare. The third work in this set is for textless choir.

Performing Forces:

Méditation religieuse **voices:** SATTBB choir; **orchestra:** 2 flutes, 2 clarinets (C), 2 bassoons, 2 horns (D), and strings.

La Mort d'Ophélie **voices:** SA choir; **orchestra:** 2 flutes, English horn, 2 clarinets (B^b), 2 bassoons, 2 horns (A^b, E^b), and strings.

Marche funébre pour la dernière scène d'"Hamlet" **voices:** SATB choir; **orchestra:** 2 flutes, 2 oboes, 2 clarinets (C), 4 bassoons (optionally 2), 4 horns (D, F), 2 trumpets (D), 2 cornets (A), 3 trombones, tuba, timpani (2 drums), percussion (9 players — 6 snare drums, bass drum, cymbals, and tam-tam), and strings.

First Performance: It appears that Berlioz compiled this collection of earlier works and had it engraved and published without having heard a note of it performed. It is unclear when the premiere occurred.

Editions: *Tristia* is published in a critical edition in *The New Berlioz Edition*, volume 12b, edited by David Charlton, by Bärenreiter (BA 5790). Orchestral parts are also available. It was published by Breitkopf and Härtel in the previous critical edition, *Hector Berlioz: Werke*, volumes 6 and 14, edited by C. Malherbe and Felix Weingartner.

Autograph: The composer's manuscript of version 2 *Méditation religieuse* is in the library of the Paris Conservatory (ms. 1187), version 1 for chorus and seven wind instruments is lost.

Version 2 of *La Mort d'Ophélie* is in the library of the Paris Conservatory (ms. 1187), version 2 is in the Gesellschaft für Musik in Vienna (A 170).

Marche funébre pour la dernière scène d'"Hamlet" is in the library of the Paris Conservatory (ms. 1187).

Notes: This score is a collection of three works: *Méditation religieuse*, *La Mort d'Ophélie*, and *Marche funébre pour la dernière scène d'Hamlet*. All three works are dedicated to Prince Eugen von Sayn-Wittgenstein.

Méditation religieuse was completed in Rome 4 August 1831. The Breitkopf score includes singing translations in German by F. Graf Spork and in English by Percy Pinkerton.

La Mort d'Ophélie was completed in London on 4 July 1848 and is dedicated to Prince Eugen von Sayn-Wittgenstein. The Breitkopf score includes singing translations in German by Emma Klingenfeld and in English by Percy Pinkerton.

Performance Issues:

Méditation religieuse: The choral writing is homophonic and syllabic. Most of the choral material is a cappella or very lightly accompanied. Passages are exchanged in a call-and-response fashion between the choir and the orchestra. A small choir and chamber orchestra are entirely appropriate for this work. The orchestral material is quite simple. The string parts are simpler than the winds, which may provide good programming opportunities for developing ensembles; **choir:** medium easy; **orchestra:** medium easy.

La Mort d'Ophélie: This is a simple and lyrical score. The choral writing is exclusively two-part. It is homophonic with the majority of the parts moving in parallel thirds or sixths. The instrumental parts are fairly simple and a small orchestra will be quite effective in this work; **choir:** easy; **orchestra:** medium easy.

Marche funébre pour la dernière scène d'"Hamlet": Berlioz indicates in the score that the singers and percussionists should be "behind the scenes at some distance from the orchestra." He also suggests placing 2 violins and a viola near the choir to maintain pitch. The choir actually begins the work unaccompanied on a single "A" natural. This can come from the orchestral tuning. The choir merely lets out an occasional "ah" whole note in octaves. The orchestral writing is rich and expressive and completely idiomatic. Near the end of the piece, there is an indication for "Volley firing at the back of the stage farther away than the side drums." Recorded gunfire or pistols with blanks can be used; **choir:** very easy; **orchestra:** medium difficult.

Selected Discography

John Alldis Choir; London Symphony Orchestra; Colin Davis, recorded in 1980. Philips: 416 431-2.
Orchestre Révolutionnaire et Romantique; conducted by John Eliot Gardiner, recorded in 1996. Philips: 446 676-2.
Montréal Symphony Orchestra and Chorus; conducted by Charles Dutoit, recorded in 2001. Decca: 458 011-2.

Selected Bibliography

Berlioz, Hector: *The Memoirs of Hector Berlioz*, translated by Rachel and Eleanor Holmes, annotated and revised by Ernest Newman, 161. New York: Knopf, 1932. Reprinted, New York: Dover, 1966.
Barzun, Jacques: *Berlioz and the Romantic Century*, second edition, I: 216, 228, 245, 333, 404-405, 518, 543, 547, 562; II: 65, 71, 104, 185. New York: Columbia University Press, 1969.
Dickinson, Alan E. F.: *The Music of Berlioz*, 45-49, 56-61. New York: St. Martin's Press, 1972.
Rushton, Julian: *The Music of Berlioz*, 279-280. Oxford: Oxford University Press, 2001.

Vox populi, op. 20 (1844-1851), H. 120

Duration: *Hymne à la France* ca. 8 minutes
La Menace des Francs ca. 4 minutes

Text: The text of *Hymne à la France* is by Henri-Auguste Barbier. The text of *La Menace des Francs* is by an anonymous author, possibly the composer.

Performing Forces:

Hymne à la France **voices:** SATB choir; **orchestra:** 2 flutes, 2 oboes, 2 clarinets (C), 2 bassoons, 4 horns (D, E), 2 trumpets (D), 2 cornets (A), 3 trombones, tuba, 2 timpanists (2 drums each), percussion (2 players — bass drum, cymbals), and strings.

La Menace des Francs **voices:** TTBB chamber choir and SATTBB choir; **orchestra:** 2 flutes, 2 oboes, 2 clarinets (C), 2 bassoons, 4

A Conductor's Guide to 19th-Century Choral-Orchestra Works 75

horns (B^b basso, C), 2 trumpets (F), 2 cornets (B^b), 3 trombones, tuba, 2 timpanists (2 drums each), and strings.

First Performance: *Hymne à la France*: 1 August 1844; Paris for the closing of an industrial exhibition; conducted by the composer

Editions: *Vox populi* is published in a critical edition in *The New Berlioz Edition*, volume 12a, edited by David Charlton, by Bärenreiter (BA 5452/II). Orchestral parts, a piano-vocal score, and a study score are also available. It appears as op. 20, nos. 1 and 2, in the Breitkopf and Härtel previous critical edition, *Hector Berlioz: Werke*, volume 14, edited by C. Malherbe and Felix Weingartner.

Autograph: As indicated below, this is a compilation of two earlier works.

The autograph full score of *La Menace des Francs* is lost; however, there is a set of manuscript parts in the library of the Paris Conservatory.

A fragment of the autograph of *Hymne à la France* is also in the Paris Conservatory (ms. 1517).

Notes: This work was originally two pieces: *Hymne à la France*, H. 97 and *La Menace des Francs*, H. 117. The Breitkopf score includes singing translations in German by Emma Klingenfeld and in English by Percy Pinkerton. *Hymne à la France* was composed in 1844 and orchestrated in 1859. *Hymne à la France* was composed in 1851. Both scores are dedicated to the French Philharmonic Society.

Performance Issues:

Hymne à la France: The choral writing is generally homophonic and well reinforced by the accompaniment. There are extended passages for the sopranos and basses that could be effectively given to soloists, although balance might prove challenging. The orchestration is varied and the parts are idiomatic. There are many ostinato accompanimental figures throughout the orchestra, some of which are fairly filigreed. The scoring suggests the use of a large choir and sizeable string section. This is a bombastic and impressive short work; **choir:** medium easy; **orchestra:** medium difficult.

La Menace des Francs: This very straightforward composition is truly an overblown hymn. It is generally homophonic with consistent doubling of the singers by the orchestra. Both tenor I parts have fairly high tessituras. Beyond a few imitative gestures among groups of instruments, the orchestra derives nearly all of its material from the choir. The orchestra parts are therefore quite conservative. The size of the ensemble is the greatest complication. Much of the chamber choir's material is actually doubled by the men's section of the full choir. This is a short, powerful work for large choir and orchestra that provides an opportunity for merging a men's choir and a mixed choir; **choir:** easy; **orchestra:** easy.

Selected Discography

No recordings appear to be available.

Selected Bibliography

Barzun, Jacques: *Berlioz and the Romantic Century*, second edition, I: 444, 446, 532, 556; II: 278. New York: Columbia University Press, 1969.
Dickinson, Alan E. F.: *The Music of Berlioz*, 115-116. New York: St. Martin's Press, 1972.

L'Impériale, op. 26 (1854), H. 129

Duration: ca. 10 minutes

Text: The text is by Pierre-Chéri Lafont.

Performing Forces: voices: 2 SATB choirs; **orchestra:** 6 flutes, 6 oboes, 6 clarinets (B^b), 8 bassoons, 8 horns (E^b, F), 6 cornets (B^b), 6 trumpets (E^b), 8 trombones, 5 tubas, 3 timpanists (2 drums each), percussion (5 players — 5 snare drums), and strings.

Berlioz indicates in the score that choir I should have 10 singers on each part and that choir II should be much larger. The score calls

A Conductor's Guide to 19th-Century Choral-Orchestra Works 77

for a string disposition of 36, 34, 28, 25, and 25. The composer also states that in a smaller hall traditional numbers of instruments can be used with choir I becoming a solo quartet. In such an arrangement 2, 2, 2, 2 — 4, 2, 3, 1 (1 perc, timp) — strings will suffice.

First Performance: 15 and 16 November 1855; Palais de l'Industrie at the Exposition Universelle, Paris; conducted by the composer.

Editions: *L'Impériale* is published in a critical edition in *The New Berlioz Edition*, volume 12b, edited by David Charlton, by Bärenreiter (BA 5980). Orchestral parts are also available. It was published by Breitkopf and Härtel in the previous critical edition, *Hector Berlioz: Werke*, volume 13, edited by C. Malherbe and Felix Weingartner.

Autograph: The composer's manuscript of the full score is in the library of the Paris Conservatory (ms. 1191).

Notes: This work was composed in honor of Napoleon III and premiered in a pair of concerts closing the Exposition Universelle that Berlioz presented at the request of Prince Napoleon, the emperor's brother. It was at this enormous concert that Berlioz first used the electric metronome, a device invented by Henri Verbrugghen that allowed the principal conductor to coordinate the beats of "sub-conductors" distributed throughout the ensemble. The Breitkopf score includes singing translations in German by Emma Klingenfeld and English by Percy Pinkerton.

Performance Issues: The choral writing is in unison and homophonic chordal writing. There is one imitative section for the singers, which is clearly doubled and diatonic. This is a bombastic and colorfully orchestrated hymn. The principal challenge is the sheer size of the ensemble. Musically it is a very practical piece. There is some rapid passagework for the winds that provide no significant challenges; **choir:** easy; **orchestra:** medium easy.

Selected Discography

Dutch Radio Choir and Symphony Orchestra; conducted by Jean Fournet, recorded in 1988. Denon: CO-72886.

Selected Bibliography

Berlioz, Hector: *The Memoirs of Hector Berlioz*, translated by Rachel and Eleanor Holmes, annotated and revised by Ernest Newman, 483, 489, 492-493. New York: Knopf, 1932. Reprinted, New York: Dover, 1966.

Barzun, Jacques: *Berlioz and the Romantic Century*, second edition, I: 363; II: 87, 113. New York: Columbia University Press, 1969.

Dickinson, Alan E. F.: *The Music of Berlioz*, 44-45. New York: St. Martin's Press, 1972.

Rushton, Julian: *The Music of Berlioz*, 58-60, 218-220. Oxford: Oxford University Press, 2001.

Brahms, Johannes (b. Hamburg, 7 May 1833; d. Vienna, 3 April 1897)

Life: Brahms's father was a doublebass player in the Hamburg Stadtstheater. He made his debut as a pianist at age 15 and supported himself by teaching lessons and playing the piano in theaters, dance halls, and brothels. In 1853, he accompanied violinist Eduard Reményi on a concert tour. He met another virtuoso violinist on this tour, Joseph Joachim, with whom he maintained a long professional friendship. Joachim provided Brahms with an entrée in the upper echelon of musical Germany. He was famously declared a genius by Robert Schumann. Clara Schumann, who became the object of Brahms's unrequited desire, remained his closest musical confidante for the rest of his life. Soon, Brahms achieved lucrative positions as a piano teacher and conductor. Many of his choral works, especially those for women's choir, were written for his own ensembles. He also enjoyed significant opportunities to conduct orchestras and was highly regarded as a pianist.

Brahms signed a manifesto in 1860 that opposed the musical ideals of the "New German" musical movement espoused by Liszt and Wagner. German musical criticism made Brahms the posterchild for the opposing compositional camp. Much of the rhetoric surrounding the aesthetic differences of these two "schools" was entirely the fabrication of writers on music. Brahms seems to have held no objections to the music of Wagner, and in fact he acquired some of Wagner's manuscripts for his personal music library.

In many ways, Brahms was the most progressive composer of his generation. A dedicated student of music of the past, he developed a compositional technique that seamlessly combined elements of many centuries into logical and impeccably crafted works. His scores demonstrate a mastery of late 19th-century harmonic practices, classical form, and 16th- and 18th-century counterpoint. This conflation of musical devices with an original approach to temporal relationships produced works that were deceptively ahead of their time.

Teachers: Eduard Marxsen, Robert Schumann

Other Principal Works: orchestral: Symphony No. 1 (1855-1876), Symphony No. 2 (1877), Symphony No. 3 (1883), Symphony No. 4 (1884-1885), Violin Concerto (1878), Piano Concerto No. 1 (1854-1858), Piano Concerto No. 2 (1878-1881), Double Concerto (1881), *Variations on a Theme of Haydn* (1873), *Academic Festival Overture* (1880), Tragic Overture (1880); **chamber:** 3 piano trios, 3 string quartets, 2 string quintets, 2 string sextets, 3 piano sonatas, 3 violin sonatas, 2 cello sonatas, numerous works for solo piano including significant sets of variations; **choral:** (without orchestra) *Marienlieder* (1859), 2 Motets, op. 29 (1860), *5 Soldatenlieder* (1861-1862), *Liebeslieder* (1868-1869), *Neue Liebeslieder* (1874), 3 Motets, op. 110 (1889); **songs:** *Magelone Lieder* (1861-1868), *Vier ernste Gesänge* (1896), many folksong arrangements.

Selected Composer Bibliography

Evans, Edwin: *Historical, Descriptive, and Analytical Account of the Entire Works of Johannes Brahms*, volume 1 — The Vocal Works. London: William Reeves, 1912.

Geiringer, Karl: *Brahms: His Life and Work.* London: Oxford University Press, 1948; second edition: New York: Da Capo Press, 1963.

Pascall, Robert, editor: *Brahms: Biographical, Documentary, and Analytical Studies.* Cambridge: Cambridge University Press, 1983.

Hancock, Virginia: *Brahms's Choral Compositions and His Library of Early Music*, UMI Reasearch Press Studies in Musicology Number 76. Ann Arbor: UMI Research Press, 1983.

Musgrave, Michael, editor: *Brahms 2: Biographical, Documentary, and Analytical Studies.* Cambridge: Cambridge University Press, 1985.

Bozarth, Geore S.: *Brahms Studies: Analytical and Historical Perspectives.* Oxford: Oxford University Press, 1990.

MacDonald, Malcolm: *Brahms.* London: Schirmer Books, 1990.

Musgrave, Michael: *The Music of Brahms*, revised edition. Oxford: Oxford University Press, 1994.

Avins, Styra: *Johannes Brahms: Life and Letters.* Oxford: Oxford University Press, 1997.

Swafford, Jan: *Johannes Brahms: A Biography.* New York: Alfred A. Knopf, 1997.

Musgrave, Michael, editor: *The Cambridge Companion to Brahms.* Cambridge: Cambridge University Press, 1999.

Platt, Heather: *Johannes Brahms: A Guide to Research.* New York: Routledge, 2003.

Geiringer, Karl: *On Brahms and His Circle: Essays and Documentary Studies*, revised and enlarged by George S. Bozarth. Sterling Heights, MI: Harmonie Park Press, 2006.

Ave Maria, op. 12 (1858)

Duration: ca. 6 minutes

Text: This text is one of the principal Marian Antiphons from Roman Catholic tradition.

Performing Forces: voices: SSAA choir; **orchestra:** 2 flutes, 2 oboes, 2 clarinets (B^b), 2 bassoons, 2 horns (F), and strings.[26]

First Performance: 2 December 1859; Wörmerscher Saal, Hamburg; Hamburg Frauenchor, conducted by the composer

Editions: *Ave Maria* is published in the critical edition *Johannes Brahms sämtliche Werke*, volume 19, page 113, edited by Eusebius Mandyczewski and published by Breitkopf and Härtel. Complete performing materials are also available from Kalmus.

Autograph: There is a signed, undated score in the Library of Congress.

Performance Issues: The first half of this score makes significant use of paired doubling with the pairs frequently in canon at the octave or in inversion. The vocal parts are doubled by the orchestra intermittently, but the accompaniment provides conspicuous harmonic support throughout. The second half of the score is in four-part homophonic textures that are fully doubled by the orchestra. The vocal parts are conservatively written, and all of the orchestral material is idiomatically conceived. A fairly small choir and string contingent will balance effectively against the winds; **choir:** medium easy; **orchestra:** medium easy.

---

[26] The full score includes a reduction of the orchestral material for organ.

Selected Discography

With organ: Corydon Singer; John Scott, organ; conducted by Matthew Best. Hyperion: CDA66389.
With orchestra: Kammerchor Stuttgart; Deutschen Kammerphilharmonie; conducted by Frieder Bernius. Carus: 83.201.
Danish National Symphony Orchestra and Chorus; conducted by Gerd Albrecht, recorded at the Danish Radio Concert Hall in Copenhagen on 25 to 27 November 2003. Chandos: 10165.

Selected Bibliography

Evans, Edwin: *Historical, Descriptive, and Analytical Account of the Entire Works of Johannes Brahms*, volume 1 — The Vocal Works, 55-57. London: William Reeves, 1912.
Drinker, Sophie: *Brahms and His Women's Chorus*. Merion, PA: A.G. Hess, 1952.

Begräbnisgesang ["Burial Song"], op. 13 (1858) wind band

Duration: ca. 5 minutes

Text: The text is "Nun lasst und den Leib begraben" by Michael Weisse.

Performing Forces: voices: SATBB choir; **orchestra:** 2 oboes, 2 clarinets (B^b), 2 bassoons, 2 horns (E^b), 3 trombones, tuba, and timpani (2 drums).

First Performance: 2 December 1859; Wörmerscher Saal, Hamburg; Hamburg Frauenchor, conducted by the composer

Editions: *Begräbnisgesang* is published in the critical edition *Johannes Brahms sämtliche Werke*, volume 19, page 124, edited by Eusebius Mandyczewski and published by Breitkopf and Härtel. Complete performing materials are also available from Kalmus.

Autograph: There is a signed, undated score in the Library of Congress. The first-draft manuscript has been lost.

Notes: Some scholars have identified the principal tune of this work as one of a number of hymns; however, Brahms stated in a letter that he had not borrowed any folksong or chorale.[27]

Performance Issues: The choral parts are very simple and declamatory. The soprano part has a fairly high tessitura, but it is not a taxing part. The choral material is well supported by the instruments. One passage is labeled "Half Choir." The instrumentation allows the use of a large choral group, but balances should not be an issue even with a small choir. The instrumental parts are idiomatic. The clarinet I and oboe I parts have some exposed filigree-like parts that set triplets against duplets in the rest of the ensemble. A logical pairing would be J. S. Bach's, Cantata No. 118: *O Jesu Christ, mein Lebens Licht*, BWV 118, a seven-minute work for six brass players and choir that was composed for an outdoor burial service. Likewise, Bruckner's Mass No. 2 in E Minor [qv], which is also scored for winds, brass, and choir, would complement both of these pieces very effectively; **choir:** easy; **orchestra:** medium easy.

Selected Discography

Kammerchor Stuttgart; Deutschen Kammerphilharmonie; conducted by Frieder Bernius. Carus: 83.201.
Bavarian Radio Symphony Orchestra and Chorus; conducted by Bernard Haitink. Orfeo: C025821A.
Gächinger Kantorei Stuttgart; Bach-Collegium Stuttgart; conducted by Helmut Rilling. Hänssler: CD98460.

Selected Bibliography

Evans, Edwin: *Historical, Descriptive, and Analytical Account of the Entire Works of Johannes Brahms*, volume 1 — The Vocal Works, 58-59. London: William Reeves, 1912.
Hancock, Virginia: *Brahms's Choral Compositions and His Library of Early Music*, 114, UMI Reasearch Press Studies in Musicology Number 76. Ann Arbor: UMI Research Press, 1983.

---

[27] *Brahms Briefwechsel*, volume 4, page 79. Berlin: Deutsche Brahms-Gesellschaft, 1908-1922.

Avins, Styra: *Johannes Brahms: Life and Letters*, 39, 185. Oxford: Oxford University Press, 1997.

Psalm 13, op. 27 (1859) optional strings

Duration: ca. 4 ½ minutes

Text: The text is from the Book of Psalms in the Bible.

Performing Forces: voices: SSA choir; **orchestra:** organ or piano and strings (ad libitum).

First Performance: 19 September 1864; St. Peter's Church, Hamburg; Hamburg Frauenchor, conducted by the composer

Editions: Psalm 13 is published in the critical edition *Johannes Brahms sämtliche Werke*, volume 20, page 1, edited by Eusebius Mandyczewski and published by Breitkopf and Härtel. Complete performing materials are also available from Kalmus.

Autograph: The composer's manuscript score was in the archives of the Gesellschaft der Musikfreunde in Vienna prior to World War II. It has since been lost.

Notes: The score is labeled for organ or piano "three or four hands." The strings ad libitum, but if they are used the keyboard is not substituted, but rather reinforced. There are portions of the accompaniment that do not appear in the string parts.

Performance Issues: The choral parts are conservatively written and well doubled or supported by the accompaniment. While not musically challenging, the high tessitura of the soprano I part will require singers of at least moderate experience. The string writing is very practical. Solo players may be used effectively, as would solo singers or a small choir; however a full complement of singers will also work well. There is an independent double bass part, although when it does not double the cello, it is doubled by the organ's pedal part. **choir:** medium easy; **orchestra:** medium easy.

Selected Discography

Corydon Singers; conducted by Matthew Best. Released in March 1993. Hyperion: 66389.
St. Bride's Church Choir; conducted by Robert Jones. Recorded in St. Silas Church, June 1996. Naxos: 553877.

Selected Bibliography

Evans, Edwin: *Historical, Descriptive, and Analytical Account of the Entire Works of Johannes Brahms*, volume 1 — The Vocal Works, 90. London: William Reeves, 1912.
Hancock, Virginia: *Brahms's Choral Compositions and His Library of Early Music*, 113, UMI Reasearch Press Studies in Musicology Number 76. Ann Arbor: UMI Research Press, 1983.

Ein deutsches Requiem ["A German Requiem"], op. 45 (1857-1868)

Duration: ca. 72 minutes

Text: Brahms compiled the text using excerpts from Luther's German translation of the Bible as follows:[28]

    I   Gospel of St. Matthew, chapter 5, verse 4
        Psalm 126, verses 5-6

   II   Peter I, chapter 1, verses 24-25
        James, chapter 5, verse 7
        Isaiah, chapter 35, verse 10

  III   Psalm 39, verses 4-8
        Wisdom of Solomon [Apocrypha], chapter 3, verse 1

  IV   Psalm 8, verses 1, 2, and 4

   V   Gospel of St. John, chapter 16, verse 22

---

[28] Luther's Bible differs from modern English editions particularly in emphasis.

Ecclesiasticus [Apocrypha], chapter 51, verse 27
Isaiah, chapter 66, verse 13

VI   Hebrews, chapter 13, verse 14
Corinthians I, chapter 15, verses 51-52 and 54-55
Revelation of St. John, chapter 4, verse 11

VII   Revelation of St. John, chapter 14, verse 13

Performing Forces: voices: soprano and baritone soloists; SATB choir; **orchestra:** piccolo, 2 flutes, 2 oboes, 2 clarinets (B^b, A), 2 bassoons, contrabassoon, 4 horns (B^b basso, C basso, D, E^b, E, F), 2 trumpets (B^b, C, D), 3 trombones, tuba, timpani (3 drums), harp, organ (*ad libitum*), and strings.

First Performance: First three movements: 1 December 1867; Vienna; Gesellschaft der Musikfreunde, Rudolf Panzer, soloist, conducted by Johann Herbeck

First four and last two movements: 10 April 1868 (Good Friday concert); Bremen Cathedral; Bremen Cathedral Choir, Julius Stockhausen, soloist, conducted by the composer

Complete work: 18 February 1869; Gewandhaus, Leipzig; Emilie Bllingrath-Wagner and Franz Krückl, soloists, conducted by Karl Reinecke

Editions: *Ein deutsches Requiem* is published in the critical edition *Johannes Brahms sämtliche Werke*, volume 17, page 3, edited by Eusebius Mandyczewski and published by Breitkopf and Härtel. Complete performing materials are also available from Breitkopf and Härtel, C. F. Peters, Hinshaw, and Kalmus.

Autograph: The autograph score, the composer's copy of the first published edition, and the original set of parts used in the Vienna performances led by the composer are in the Gesellschaft der Musikfreunde in Vienna. The composer's manuscript of the piano reduction is in the Brahms Archive of the Universitätsbibliothek in Hamburg, Germany.

Notes: The Hinshaw full score includes a singing English translation and a comparative table of tempi extracted from selected recordings of the work.

Performance Issues: Most of the choral material is clearly supported by the accompaniment. There is significant use of paired doubling in the choir, as well as some complex close imitation and some exceedingly complex extended fugues. There are exposed and intricate solo passages for each of the principal winds. A full symphonic complement of strings is appropriate, and there are some significant divisi within the strings, including three viola parts in one section. Likewise, a large choral component is desirable, although credible performances are given regularly by smaller ensembles. The score makes productive use of pedal point and rhythmic ostinati as a unifying element and to establish forward momentum. This contributes some efficiency to rehearsal time. The piccolo part requires a discrete player. Although many performances are given without organ, the timbral depth this instrument adds to the score is significant. Care should be given to general registration of the organ part, but particular attention should be given to the selection of pedal stops. The "Vivace" section of movement #6 will require attention in rehearsal to establish accuracy and tempo stability. This score uses a number of less-common meters, including 4/2, which is some instances produces measures that contain many notes and may produce some challenges to visual clarity. Adding a few dotted barlines in the parts may save rehearsal time. Brahms's alternations of meter within movements have implicit tempo relationships within them. These metric modulations should be carefully calculated ahead of time. This is one of the great canonic works of the choral-orchestral literature. Because of its familiarity, it is easy to gloss over the many sophisticated technical achievements of metrical organization and extended contrapuntal virtuosity within the score that add vibrancy to a good performance. Careful attention to nuances, especially related to displaced stresses will do much to enhance to final product. **Soloists:** soprano - range: f'-b♭'', tessitura: a'-f#'', this is a lyric and declamatory solo best suited to a clear and focused voice; bass - range: A-f#', tessitura: d-d', this is a lyric solo role that is fairly syllabic with some sustained passages, Brahms labels to part as "bass" in movement #3 and "baritone" in movement #6; however, a single vocalist is the norm; **choir:** difficult; **orchestra:** difficult.

Selected Discography

Elisabeth Schwarzkopf, Hans Hotter; Singverein der Gesellschaft der Musikfreunde; Wiener Philharmonic; conducted by Herbert von Karajan. EMI: 0724356281127.

Elisabeth Schwarzkopf, Dietrich Fischer-Dieskau; Philharmonia Chorus and Orchestra; conducted by Otto Klemperer. EMI: 0724356690325.

Anna Tomowa-Sintow, José van Dam; Wiener Singverein; Berlin Philharmonic; conducted by Herbert von Karajan. EMI: 0724358505320.

Kathleen Battle, Håkan Hagegård; Chicago Symphony Chorus (Margaret Hillis, director), Chicago Symphony Orchestra; conducted by James Levine. RCA: RCD1-5003.

Arleen Auger, Franz Gerihsen; Munich Philarmic Choir and Orchestra; conducted by Sergiu Celibidache. EMI: 0724355684325.

Margaret Price, Samuel Ramey; Ambrosian Singers; Royal Philharmonic Orchestra; conducted by André Previn. Apex: 8573-89081-2.

Barbara Bonney, Andreas Schmidt; Vienna State Opera Chorus; Vienna Philharmonic; conducted by Carlo Maria Giulini. Deutsche Grammophon: 44546-2.

Sylvia McNair, Håkan Hagegård; Westminster Symphonic Choir; New York Philharmonic; conducted by Kurt Masur. Teldec: 4509-98413-2.

Charlotte Margiono, Rodhey Gilfry; Monteverdi Choir; Orchestra Révolutionnaire et Romantique; conducted by John Eliiot Gardiner, recorded in 1990. Philips: 432140-2.

Cheryl Studer, Andreas Schmidt; Eric-Ericson Chamber Choir; Berlin Philharmonic; conducted by Claudio Abbado. Deutsche Grammophon: 437517-2.

Donna Brown, Gilles Cahemaille; Gächinger Kantorei; Bach-Collegium Stuttgart; conducted by Helmut Rilling. Hänssler: CD 91102.

Jessye Norman, Jorma Hynninen; London Philharmonic Chorus and Orchestra; conducted by Klaus Tennstedt. EMI: 0724357572224.

Selected Bibliography

Upton, George: *The Standard Oratorios*, 80-81. Chicago: A. C. McClurg and Company, 1893.

Evans, Edwin: *Historical, Descriptive, and Analytical Account of the Entire Works of Johannes Brahms*, volume 1 — The Vocal Works, 163-181. London: William Reeves, 1912.

Tovey, Francis: "Brahms: Requiem, Op. 45," in *Essays in Musical Analysis*, volume 5, 211-224. London: Oxford University Press, 1937.

Newman, William S.: "A 'Basic Motive' in Brahms's 'German Requiem.'" *Music Review*, volume 24 (1963), 190.

Robertson, Alec: *Requiem: Music of Mourning and Consolation*, 175-182. New York: Frederick A. Praeger, 1967.

Boyd, Malcolm: "Brahms's Requiem: A Note on Thematic Integration," *The Musical Times*, volume 113 (1972), 140-141.

Musgrave, Michael: "Historical Influences on Brahms's 'Requiem,' *Music and Letters*, volume 53, number 1 (January 1972), 3-17.

Zeileis, Friedrich G.: "Two Manuscript Sources of Brahms's German Requiem," *Music and Letters*, volume 60 (1979), 149-155.

Reynolds, Christopher: "A Choral Symphony by Brahms?," *19th-Century Music*, volume 9, number 1 (1985), 3-25.

Pahlen, Kurt: *The World of the Oratorio*, translated by Judith Schaefer with additional English-language material by Thurston Dox, 73-78. Portland, OR: Amadeus Press, 1990.

Berger, Melvin: *Guide to Choral Masterpieces: A Listener's Guide*, 81-88. New York: Anchor Books, 1993.

Struck, Michael: "Ein deutsches Requiem—handlich gemacht. Der Klavierauszug und seine Stichvorlage," *Patrimonia*, volume 80 (1994), 5-18.

Musgrave, Michael: *Brahms: A German Requiem* [from the series, *Cambridge Music Handbooks*]. Cambridge: Cambridge University Press, 1996.

Avins, Styra: *Johannes Brahms: Life and Letters*, 320-322, 355, 356, 357, 375-376, 378, 384-385, 390, 413, 416, 480. Oxford: Oxford University Press, 1997.

Rudolf, Max: "Brahms's *German Requiem*: A Report on a Composer-Annotated Score," in *Max Rudolf: A Musical Life Writings and Letters*, 135-150. Hillsdale, NY: Pendragon Press, 2001. Originally published as "A Recently Discovered Composer-Annotated Score of the Brahms Requiem" in the *Quarterly Journal of the Riemenschneider Bach Institute*, volume 7, number 4 (1976).

Rinaldo, op. 50 (1863-1868)

Duration: ca. 45 minutes

Text: The text is by Johann Wolfgang von Goethe.

Performing Forces: voices: tenor soloist; TTBB choir; **orchestra:** piccolo, 2 flutes, 2 oboes, 2 clarinets (B^b, A), 2 bassoons, 2 horns (E^b), 2 trumpets (E^b), 3 trombones, timpani (3 drums), and strings.

First Performance: 28 February 1869; Great Redoutensaal, Vienna; Gustav Walter, soloist, Akademischer Gesangverein of Vienna, Vienna Hofopernorchester, conducted by the composer

Editions: *Rinaldo* is published in the critical edition *Johannes Brahms sämtliche Werke*, volume 18, page 192, edited by Eusebius Mandyczewski and published by Breitkopf and Härtel. Other editions which are available for purchase include: Simrock, Lucks, and Kalmus.

Autograph: A signed, undated score is in the Moldenhauer Archives in Spokane, Washington.

Notes: This is the closest Brahms comes to writing dramatic music. This is an operatic work in spirit. It was composed amid the heat of critical arguments within Germany of the "new" music of the Wagner camp, and the "conservative" music embodied by Brahms. While in hindsight, we know Brahms's music to have been as progressive, albeit in very different ways, as Wagner's, the public debates of style and Brahms's awareness of the paucity of staged music on the "conservative" front must have done much to shape his musical decisions.

Performance Issues: The choral writing is primarily homophonic in three- and four-part block harmonies. The choral material is supported by the orchestra, but not consistently doubled. The parts are vocally demanding, but well written for the voices. A mature vocal ensemble is necessary to balance the ranges across the choir. There are some significant high passages for the tenor I and bass I parts. The orchestration requires a moderate to large-sized choir. There are some brief solo quartets of choristers throughout the work. Some of these indicate a second singer to rotate in intermittently. There is also a brief section at the end in which the choir is broken into eight parts. The score demands a broad palette of colors and dynamics from the singers as well as some important rhythmic clarity. The orchestral parts are idiomatic and present few technical challenges for experienced players. There are some rapid alternations of extreme dynamics and a recurring 32nd-note figure that needs a lightness and precision of articulation. Some of the writing may require attention to guarantee good balances between the choir and orchestra. Thoughtful attention should be given to the tempo relationships between sections of this piece. This is a dramatic and effective work that is rarely performed. It is an excellent showpiece for a gifted tenor soloist, and it would make an interesting pairing with Brahms's *Alto Rhapsodie* (*qv*), which features an alto soloist with men's choir and orchestra. **Soloist:** tenor - range: (c# optional) e^b-a', tessitura: f#-f#', this is a lyric solo with long sustained phrases and some declamatory writing that requires a strong singer; **choir:** medium difficult; **orchestra:** medium difficult.

Selected Discography

Steve Davislim; Dresden Philharmonc Orchestra and Chorus; conducted by Michel Plasson. EMI: 0724357572224.
Carsten Süss; Gächinger Kantorei Stuttgart; Radio-Sinfonieorchester Stuttgart; conducted by Helmut Rilling. Hänssler: CD98228.

Selected Bibliography

Evans, Edwin: *Historical, Descriptive, and Analytical Account of the Entire Works of Johannes Brahms*, volume 1 — The Vocal Works, 206-222. London: William Reeves, 1912.
Hancock, Virginia: *Brahms's Choral Compositions and His Library of Early Music*, 128, UMI Reasearch Press Studies in Musicology Number 76. Ann Arbor: UMI Research Press, 1983.
Avins, Styra: *Johannes Brahms: Life and Letters*, 188 n. 8, 287, 385, 751-752. Oxford: Oxford University Press, 1997.

Alto Rhapsodie, op. 53 (1869)

Duration: ca. 14 minutes

Text: The text is taken from Goethe's poem, *Harzreise im Winter*.

Performing Forces: voices: alto soloist; TTBB choir; **orchestra:** 2 flutes, 2 oboes, 2 clarinets (B^b), 2 bassoons, 2 horns (C basso), and strings

First Performance: 3 March 1870; Jena; Pauline Viardot-Garcia, soloist, Choral Society of the Academy of Jena, conducted by the composer[29]

Editions: *Alto Rhapsodie* is published in the critical edition *Johannes Brahms sämtliche Werke*, volume 19, page 1, edited by Eusebius Mandyczewski and published by Breitkopf and Härtel. Other editions that are available for purchase include: Breitkopf and Härtel, C. F. Peters, Carl Fischer, and Kalmus.

Autograph: The signed, undated score is in the Music Division of the New York Public Library. A facsimile has been published by Walter Frisch, 1983.

Notes: This work was composed in heartsunk response to the engagement of Julie Schumann, daughter of Robert and Clara, for whom Brahms had been carrying an undeclared torch.

Performance Issues: The choral writing is primarily homophonic. The vocal material is harmonically, but not melodically, supported by the orchestra. The choral style of the ensemble is that of a mid-19th-century partsong. With the exception of the soloist, the vocal writing is conservative and well within the abilities of a moderately experienced amateur ensemble. The orchestral parts are idiomatic and not technically challenging. Some of the tutti passages are harmonically dense due to the voicing of the orchestral parts. **Soloist:** alto - range: a^b-g$^{b''}$, tessitura: d'-d'', this solo is the heart of

---

[29] There was an unofficial performance given in Karlsruhe in late 1869 to test the work before its offical premiere.

this work, it requires a lyric and clear voice capable of very wide melodic leaps; **choir:** medium easy; **orchestra:** medium difficult.

Selected Discography

Christa Ludwig; Philharmonia Orchestra and Chorus; conducted by Otto Klemperer. EMI: 0724356702929.

Janet Baker; London Philharmonic Orchestra and Chorus; conducted by Adrian Boult. EMI: 072435679124.

Christa Ludwig; Vienna Philharmonic; conducted by Karl Böhm. Deutsche Grammophon: 471443-2.

Janet Baker; City of London Sinfonia; conducted by Richard Hickox. EMI: 0724357572224.

Marilyn Horne; Atlanta Symphony Orchestra and Chorus, conducted by Robert Shaw, recorded 14-16 March 1988 in Symphony Hall, Atlanta. Telarc: CD-80176.

Marianna Lipovsek; Ernst Senff Chorus; Berlin Philharmonic Orchestra; conducted by Claudio Abbado. Deutsche Grammophon: 435791-2.

Brigitte Fassbaender; Prague Philharmonic Choir; Czech Philhamonic; conducted by Giuseppe Sinopoli. Deutsche Grammophon: 435066-2.

Alfreda Hopson; Bavarian Radio Symphony Orchestra and Chorus; conducted by Bernard Haitink. Orfeo: C025821A.

Lioba Braun; Gächinger Kantorei Stuttgart; Radio-Sinfonieorchester Stuttgart; conducted by Helmut Rilling. Hänssler: CD98228.

Selected Bibliography

Tovey, Francis: "Brahms: Rhapsodie for Alto Voice, Male Chorus, and Orchestra, Op. 53," in *Essays in Musical Analysis*, volume 5, 225-226. London: Oxford University Press, 1937.

Evans, Edwin: *Historical, Descriptive, and Analytical Account of the Entire Works of Johannes Brahms*, volume 1 — The Vocal Works, 233-237. London: William Reeves, 1912.

Hancock, Virginia: *Brahms's Choral Compositions and His Library of Early Music*, 128, UMI Reasearch Press Studies in Musicology Number 76. Ann Arbor: UMI Research Press, 1983.

Pahlen, Kurt: *The World of the Oratorio*, translated by Judith Schaefer with additional English-language material by Thurston Dox, 81-82. Portland, OR: Amadeus Press, 1990.

Berger, Melvin: *Guide to Choral Masterpieces: A Listener's Guide*, 88-89. New York: Anchor Books, 1993.

Avins, Styra: *Johannes Brahms: Life and Letters*, 394. Oxford: Oxford University Press, 1997.

Webster, James: "The *Alto Rhapsody*: Psychology, Intertextuality, and Brahms's Artistic Development," in *Brahms Studies 3*, edited by David Brodbeck, 19-45. Lincoln, NE: University of Nebraska Press, 2001.

Schicksalslied ["Song of Destiny"], op. 54 (1868-1871)

Duration: ca. 17 minutes

Text: The text is derived from the German poem, "Hyperion's Schicksalslied," which appears in the novel, *Hyperion*, by Friedrich Hölderlin.

Performing Forces: voices: SATB choir; **orchestra:** 2 flutes, 2 oboes, 2 clarinets (B^b), 2 bassoons, 2 horns (E^b), 2 trumpets (C), 3 trombones, timpani (3 drums), and strings.

First Performance: 18 October 1871; Karlsruhe; conducted by the composer

Editions: *Schicksalslied* is published in the critical edition *Johannes Brahms sämtliche Werke*, volume 19, page 22, edited by Eusebius Mandyczewski and published by Breitkopf and Härtel. Other editions that are available for purchase include: Breitkopf and Härtel, Simrock, and Kalmus.

Autograph: The signed, undated manuscript is in the Library of Congress in Washington, D.C.

Notes: There has been much written about the closing orchestral section of this work. It is often suggested by earlier writers that the composer was trying to dispel the gloom of the previous section or that he was presenting a musical subtext as a way of commenting on the poem. A much more reasonable conclusion is to provide a balanced classical structure. The return of material from the E^b introduction in the new key of C provides a brilliant denouement to this minor masterpiece.

Performance Issues: The choral writing is primarily homophonic with a few passages in pervasive imitation. In the latter, the choral entrances are often in unorthodox pitch sequences. The choral parts are generally well supported by the accompaniment, although there are a few brief a cappella passages, which are well prepared and present no challenges. The choral writing is all vocally practical. There is an extended middle section of the composition that utilizes significant choral unisons with octave doublings. This same section uses frenetic unison string writing all of which is idiomatic and plays well. The nature of the orchestration allows this work to be performed by medium-sized choirs; however, a large symphonic choir and string section are also appropriate. The orchestral writing is conservative, but expressive. The score exploits sharp dynamic contrasts and significant use of hemiolas. This is a particularly good work to introduce Brahms's symphonic choral music to developing choirs; **choir:** medium easy; **orchestra:** medium difficult.

Selected Discography

Atlanta Symphony Orchestra and Chorus; conducted by Robert Shaw, recorded 14-16 March 1988 in Symphony Hall, Atlanta. Telarc: CD-80176.
Ernst Senff Chorus; Berlin Philharmonic Orchestra; conducted by Claudio Abbado. Deutsche Grammophon: 435791-2.
Prague Philharmonic Choir; Czech Philhamonic; conducted by Giuseppe Sinopoli. Deutsche Grammophon: 435066-2.
Dresden Philharmonc Orchestra and Chorus; conducted by Michel Plasson. EMI: 0724357572224.
Danish National Symphony Orchestra and Chorus; conducted by Gerd Albrecht, recorded at the Danish Radio Concert Hall in Copenhagen on 8 and 9 November 2001. Chandos: 10165.
Gächinger Kantorei Stuttgart; Bach-Collegium Stuttgart; conducted by Helmut Rilling. Hänssler: CD98460.

Selected Bibliography

Tovey, Francis: "Brahms: 'Song of Destiny' (Schicksalslied), for Chorus and Orchestra Op. 54," in *Essays in Musical Analysis*, volume 5, 226-229. London: Oxford University Press, 1937.

Evans, Edwin: *Historical, Descriptive, and Analytical Account of the Entire Works of Johannes Brahms*, volume 1 — The Vocal Works, 238-247. London: William Reeves, 1912.

Hancock, Virginia: *Brahms's Choral Compositions and His Library of Early Music*, 129-130, UMI Reasearch Press Studies in Musicology Number 76. Ann Arbor: UMI Research Press, 1983.

Berger, Melvin: *Guide to Choral Masterpieces: A Listener's Guide*, 90-91. New York: Anchor Books, 1993.

Avins, Styra: *Johannes Brahms: Life and Letters*, 427, 429. Oxford: Oxford University Press, 1997.

Triumphlied ["Song of Triumph"], op. 55 (1870-1871)

Duration: ca. 24 minutes

Text: The text is from the *Book of Revelation*, chapter 19.

Performing Forces: voices: baritone soloist; two SATB choirs; **orchestra:** 2 flutes, 2 oboes, 2 clarinets (A), 2 bassoons, contrabassoon, 4 horns (D), 3 trumpets (D), 3 trombones, tuba, timpani (2 drums), organ (*ad libitum*), and strings.

First Performance: 5 June 1872; Hoftheater, Karlsruhe; Julis Stockhausen, soloists, Hoftheater Choir and Orchestra, conducted by Hermann Levi

The first movement was performed 7 April 1871; Bremen Cathedral; Singakademie, conducted by the composer

Editions: *Triumphlied* is published in the critical edition *Johannes Brahms sämtliche Werke*, volume 18, page 1, edited by Eusebius Mandyczewski and published by Breitkopf and Härtel. Complete performing materials are also available from Kalmus.

A Conductor's Guide to 19th-Century Choral-Orchestra Works 97

Autograph: The composer's manuscript is in the Biblioteka Jagiellonska in Krakow.

Notes: This work was written to celebrate Germany's victory over France in the war of 1870-1871. It is dedicated to Wilhelm I who had recently been crowned Emperor of the new German Empire. It is organized in three movements with the soloist appearing only in the third.

Performance Issues: The choral writing juxtaposes block homophonic singing with free counterpoint. There are some rapid melismatic passages for the singers. The contrapuntal organization of this work would benefit from a physical separation of the two choirs. There is rapid unison passagework for the winds and strings that demands secure players. All of the principal wind parts have significantly challenging passagework. Some of the string writing is fairly high, and may require attention for accurate intonation. The voicing of the winds and brass require the use of a large choral ensemble and a full complement of strings. Although the organ is optional it provides coloristic punctuation to the orchestration that greatly enhances the effect of the score. Also, the organ is sometimes the only instrument doubling the choir. This score includes some of Brahms's most virtuosic orchestral writing. It is an atypical work, but one that has the potential of great dramatic effect. It is a fairly bombastic and difficult work. **Soloist:** baritone - range: A-f#', tessitura: e-e', this is a brief declamatory solo role; **choir:** difficult; **orchestra:** very difficult.

Selected Discography

Wolfgang Brendel; Prague Philharmonic Choir; Czech Philhamonic; conducted by Giuseppe Sinopoli. Deutsche Grammophon: 435066-2.

Dietrich Henschel; Dresden Philharmonc Orchestra and Chorus; conducted by Michel Plasson. EMI: 0724357572224.

Bo Skovhus; Danish National Symphony Orchestra and Chorus; conducted by Gerd Albrecht, recorded at the Danish Radio Concert Hall in Copenhagen on 25 to 27 November 2003. Chandos: 10165.

Selected Bibliography

Upton, George P.: *The Standard Cantatas*, seventh edition, 83-85. Chicago: A. C. McClurg and Company, 1899.

Evans, Edwin: *Historical, Descriptive, and Analytical Account of the Entire Works of Johannes Brahms*, volume 1 — The Vocal Works, 248-252. London: William Reeves, 1912.

Hancock, Virginia: *Brahms's Choral Compositions and His Library of Early Music*, 128-129, UMI Reasearch Press Studies in Musicology Number 76. Ann Arbor: UMI Research Press, 1983.

Avins, Styra: *Johannes Brahms: Life and Letters*, 559. Oxford: Oxford University Press, 1997.

Nänie, op. 82 (1880-1881)

Duration: ca. 13 minutes

Text: The text is a German poem by Friedrich Schiller.

Performing Forces: voices: SATB choir; **orchestra:** 2 flutes, 2 oboes, 2 clarinets (A), 2 bassoons, 2 horns (D), 3 trombones, timpani (2 drums), harp, and strings.

First Performance: 6 December 1881; Zurich Concert Society; conducted by the composer[30]

Editions: *Nänie* is published in the critical edition *Johannes Brahms sämtliche Werke*, volume 19, page 60, edited by Eusebius Mandyczewski and published by Breitkopf and Härtel. Other editions that are available for purchase include: Breitkopf and Härtel, C. F. Peters, and Kalmus.

Autograph: An unsigned and undated manuscript is in the Musikbibliothek der Stadt Leipzig.

---

[30] This concert included the second performance of Brahms's Piano Concerto No. 2 with the composer as soloist, the *Academic Festival Overture*, and the Second Symphony.

Notes: Brahms composed this lament in response to the death of his friend, the painter Anselm Feuerbach. The score is dedicated to the artist's mother.

Performance Issues: The choral writing juxtaposes passages of pervasive imitation with purely homophonic writing. Much of the choral material is clearly supported by the orchestra; however, there are a number of exposed a cappella passages. Each section of the choir has exposed melodic moments, and the composer introduces some very effective paired doubling in selected passages. The harp part adds tremendous color to the orchestration, but there are occasional cued passages in the strings should a harpist not be available. Some significant melodic material is given to the oboe I player. This score is filled with intricate hemiola constructions, many of which require careful analysis as they begin on unusual beats within measures. Attention to these details in rehearsal will reveal an exceptional metric vitality. This is a particularly expressive composition that is conceived with great insight into the role of each part. It is exceedingly playable and singable in spite of significant structural complexity. It is truly a minor masterpiece; **choir:** medium difficult; **orchestra:** medium difficult.

Selected Discography

Atlanta Symphony Orchestra and Chorus; conducted by Robert Shaw, recorded 14-16 March 1988 in Symphony Hall, Atlanta. Telarc: CD-80176.
Berlin Radio Chorus; Berlin Philharmonic Orchestra; conducted by Claudio Abbado. Deutsche Grammophon: 435791-2.
New Philharmonia Orchestra and Chorus; conducted by Wilhelm Pitz. EMI: 0724357572224.
Prague Philharmonic Choir; Czech Philharmonic; conducted by Giuseppe Sinopoli. Deutsche Grammophon: 435066-2.
Danish National Symphony Orchestra and Chorus; conducted by Gerd Albrecht, recorded at the Danish Radio Concert Hall in Copenhagen on 8 and 9 November 2001. Chandos: 10165.
Bavarian Radio Symphony Orchestra and Chorus; conducted by Bernard Haitink. Orfeo: C025821A.
Gächinger Kantorei Stuttgart; Bach-Collegium Stuttgart; conducted by Helmut Rilling. Hänssler: CD98460.

Selected Bibliography

Evans, Edwin: *Historical, Descriptive, and Analytical Account of the Entire Works of Johannes Brahms*, volume 1 — The Vocal Works, 372-376. London: William Reeves, 1912.

Hancock, Virginia: *Brahms's Choral Compositions and His Library of Early Music*, 129, UMI Reasearch Press Studies in Musicology Number 76. Ann Arbor: UMI Research Press, 1983.

Avins, Styra: *Johannes Brahms: Life and Letters*, 579. Oxford: Oxford University Press, 1997.

Gesang der Parzen ["Song of the Fates"], op. 89 (1882)

Duration: ca. 12 minutes

Text: The text is from Johann Wolfgang von Goethe's *Iphigenie auf Tauris*.

Performing Forces: voices: SAATBB choir; **orchestra:** 2 flutes (flute I doubling piccolo), 2 oboes, 2 clarinets in (B^b), 2 bassoons, contrabassoon, 4 horns (D, F), 2 trumpets (D), 3 trombones (alto, tenor, and bass), tuba, timpani, and strings.

First Performance: 10 December 1882; Basel; Allgemeinen Musik-Gesellschaft, conducted by the composer

Editions: *Gesang der Parzen* is published in the critical edition *Johannes Brahms sämtliche Werke*, volume 19, page 86, edited by Eusebius Mandyczewski and published by Breitkopf and Härtel. Complete performing materials are also available from Kalmus.

Autograph: The signed and dated manuscript is in the Stadtarchiv in Krefeld, Germany.

Notes: Virginia Hancock (see bibliography below) suggests that the harmonic and contrapuntal language of this work was significantly shaped by Brahms's study of the music of J. S. Bach.

Performance Issues: The choral writing is primarily homophonic with occasional paired imitation and some passages in close imitation.

A Conductor's Guide to 19th-Century Choral-Orchestra Works   101

The pitch material for the choir is well supported in the accompaniment, although at times in the form of pedal point. The orchestral material is much more varied than the choral. There are some challenging passages for each section of the orchestra. Some of the instrumental counterpoint may provide intonation difficulties. There are some dramatic contrasts in this work, which can be effectively performed by medium and large choral ensembles. There is a dark timbral quality to the orchestration that is heightened by the voicing of the choir to exploit the lower choral sections of both genders. This dark quality is best maintained through the use of mature-sounding ensembles, both choral and orchestral; **choir:** medium difficult; **orchestra:** medium difficult.

Selected Discography

Atlanta Symphony Orchestra and Chorus; conducted by Robert Shaw, recorded 14-16 March 1988 in Symphony Hall, Atlanta. Telarc: CD-80176.
Ernst Senff Chorus; Berlin Philharmonic Orchestra; conducted by Claudio Abbado. Deutsche Grammophon: 435791-2.
Dresden Philharmonic Orchestra and Chorus; conducted by Michel Plasson. EMI: 0724357572224.
Bavarian Radio Symphony Orchestra and Chorus; conducted by Bernard Haitink. Orfeo: C025821A.
Gächinger Kantorei Stuttgart; Bach-Collegium Stuttgart; conducted by Helmut Rilling. Hänssler: CD98460.

Selected Bibliography

Evans, Edwin: *Historical, Descriptive, and Analytical Account of the Entire Works of Johannes Brahms*, volume 1 — The Vocal Works, 396-401. London: William Reeves, 1912.
Hancock, Virginia: *Brahms's Choral Compositions and His Library of Early Music*, 130-131, UMI Reasearch Press Studies in Musicology Number 76. Ann Arbor: UMI Research Press, 1983.
Pahlen, Kurt: *The World of the Oratorio*, translated by Judith Schaefer with additional English-language material by Thurston Dox, 82. Portland, OR: Amadeus Press, 1990.

Bruch, Max (b. Cologne, 6 January 1838; d. Friedenau, Germany, 2 October 1920)

Life: Bruch's father was a government official, and his mother an accomplished amateur singer. His initial training came from Breidenstein in Bonn. In 1852, he won a scholarship from the Mozart Foundation that allowed him to move to Cologne where he studied with Hiller, Reinecke, and Breuning.

Bruch taught in Cologne from 1858 to 1861. He was music director in Koblenz from 1865 to 1867, and was subsequently Kapellmeister in Sonderhausen. From 1880 to 1883, he was conductor of the Liverpool Philharmonic and director of the Orchesterverein of Breslau from 1883 to 1890. In 1891 he became professor of composition at the Hochschule für Musik in Berlin, remaining there until his retirement in 1910.

Bruch's entire musical output has been eclipsed by the success of his first Violin Concerto, *Scottish Fantasy*, and *Kol Nidrei*. He was a successful opera composer during the first half of his career and one of the most significant composers of oratorios during the second half of the 19th century. Most of these works have fully fallen from the repertoire, and complete materials for their performance have, in some cases, become unavailable. Based upon the works for which full scores or vocal scores were reviewed, this is an important body of works for large choral ensembles and orchestra. A number of them also reflect his Jewish faith and heritage. Like the entry for Amy Beach, I have included incomplete information for those works for which a full score, or even piano-vocal scores, was not readily available with the expectation that some conductors may take the effort to revive these remarkable compositions.

Teachers: Breidenstein, Breuning, Ferdinand Hiller, Carl Reinecke

Students: Gian Francesco Malipiero, Wallingford Riegger, Oscar Straus, Arthur Thomas, Ralph Vaughan Williams

Other Principal Works: opera: Loreley (1863), *Hermione* (1872); **orchestral:** Symphony No. 1 (1870), Symphony No. 2 (1870), Symphony No. 3 (1887), Violin Concerto No. 1 (1868), Violin Concerto No. 2 (1878), Violin Concerto No. 3 (1891), *Scottish*

Fantasy (1880), *Kol Nidrei* (1881); **chamber music**: 2 string quartets.

Selected Composer Bibliography

Pfitzner, Hans: *Meine Beziehungen zu Max Bruch*, Munich: Langen-Müller, 1938.

Max Bruch Studien, zum 50 Todestag des Komponisten, Dietrich Kämper, editor, in the series *Beiträge zur rheinischen Musikgeschichte*, lxxxvii. Colgne: Arno, 1970.

Fellerer, Karl Gustav: *Max Bruch*, in the series *Beiträge zur rheinischen Musikgeschichte*, ciii. Cologne: Arno, 1974.

Vick, Bingham Lafayette: *The Five Oratorios of Max Bruch*. Doctoral dissertation: Northwestern University, 1977.

Luyken, Sonja: *Max Bruch*, in the series, *Kölner Biografen*, xvii. Cologne: Stadt Köln, Der Oberstadtdirektor, 1984.

Fifield, Christopher: *Max Bruch: His Life and Works*. New York: George Braziller, 1988.

Schwarzer, Matthias: *Die Oratorien von Max Bruch: Eine Quellenstudie*. Berlin: Merseburger, 1988.

Arminius, op. 43 (1875)

Duration: ca. 90 minutes

Text: The text was written by Friedrich Hellmuth for this work using the pseudonym J. Küppers.

Performing Forces: voices: Priestess (alto), Siegmund (tenor), and Arminius (baritone) soloists, SATB choir; **orchestra:** 2 flutes, 2 oboes, 2 clarinets (B^b), 2 bassoons, 4 horns, 2 trumpets, 3 trombones, tuba, timpani (2 drums), organ, and strings.

First Performance: 4 December 1875;[31] Barmen Germany; George Henschel, baritone; Barmen Konzertgesellschaft, prepared by Anton Krause; conducted by the composer

---

[31] Christopher Fifield indicates 4 December as the premiere date, but Bingham Vick cites 10 December. See "Work Bibliography" below.

Revised version: 21 January 1877, Zürich; George Henschel, baritone [also singing the tenor solos for an ailing colleague]; conducted by the composer

American premiere: 5 May 1883, Boston; conducted by the composer

Editions: *Arminius* was first published in 1878 by Simrock. Full scores and parts are available from Edwin F. Kalmus. Piano-vocal scores are available from G. Schirmer.

Notes: The oratorio is based on the historical story of the battle between the Germanic tribe, Cherusci, led by Arminius (Latin for Hermann), who defeated the Romans, led by Varus, in a battle in the Teutonburger Forest. The work, which was composed on the heels of the Franco-Prussian War, was conceived in conjunction with the dedication of a memorial to the ancient tribal leader constructed by Ernst von Bandel in Grotenburg.

After three performances, Bruch chose to revise the score. It is dedicated to George Henschel who served as the lead in the premieres of both versions. The work in its final format is organized as follows:

Part I: Einleitung — Introduction
1. Chorus
2. Recitative (Siegmund and Arminius) and chorus
3. Roman chorus[32]
4. Recitative (Arminius)
5. Duet (Siegmund and Arminius) and chorus

Part II: Im heiligen Hain — In the Sacred Forest
6. Scene (Priestess and choir)
7. Chorus

Part III: Der Aufstand — The Insurrection
8. Recitative (Arminius) and chorus

---

[32] Given the forces needed for this movement, the full choral component should be used to portray the Romans instead of a separate semi-choir.

9. Recitative and aria (Siegmund)
10. Chorus
11. Scene
12. Battle Song (Arminius and choir[33])

Part IV: Die Schlacht — The Battle
13. Recitative and aria (Priestess)
14. Chorus
15. Recitative (Priestess) and chorus
16. Scene (Siegmund and choir)
17. Chorus
18. Recitative (Arminius)
19. Final Hymn (Priestess, Arminius, and choir)

Performance Issues: The choral parts are primarily homophonic and declamatory. The choral material is thoroughly doubled by the orchestra, usually the winds and brass. There are numerous divisi for the sopranos and basses and a few for the altos and tenors. The choral writing is melodic and well conceived for the voices. The tessituri of the choral parts (particularly the tenors) require choristers with reasonable vocal prowess. The orchestration and use of the choir suggests the need for a large vocal ensemble. Nearly all of the choral writing is homophonic and syllabic. The few contrapuntal passages are skillfully executed and very accessible. Despite the date of composition, Siegmund and the choral tenors are notated in tenor clef in the full score. The organ part is minimal and serves as orchestral color while not being musically necessary. The orchestral writing is all very practical. The winds and brass mostly double the melodic material of the singers or play fanfare-like material. All of these parts are musically easy, but in the case of the brass, strong players are needed for endurance and dynamic control. Some of the orchestration may prove difficult for achieving good balance unless the choir and soloists are particularly athletic singers. The string parts are much more involved, but are very idiomatic. There is more than a little resemblance between this work and Wagner's Teutonic operas, both in subject and treatment. Bruch's work with folksong and his less progressive harmonic language and orchestration temper this effect. This oratorio is a good

---

[33] Siegmund doubles the choral tenors in this movement.

choral complement to Wagner's traditional orchestral concert extracts. The musical language is very accessible for larger choirs of moderate experience, while the soloists must be vocally strong. **Soloists:** Priestess (alto) - range: a^b-g'', tessitura: d'-d'', this is a dramatic and declamatory solo best suited to a powerful and darker voice; Siegmund (tenor) - range: e^b-$b^{b'}$, tessitura: f-f', this is a declamatory and sustained solo requiring flexibility in the upper range; Arminius (baritone) - range: A^b-f#', tessitura: e^b-$e^{b'}$, this is a helden baritone role with extended lyric passages and dramatic declamations; **choir:** medium difficult; **orchestra:** medium difficult.

Selected Discography

At the time of this writing, no recordings were available.

Selected Bibliography

Chrysander, Friedrich: "Arminius, Oratorium von Max Bruch [review]," *Allgemeine Musikalische Zeitung* (29 December 1875), 817.

Vick, Bingham Lafayette: *The Five Oratorios of Max Bruch*, 76-114. Doctoral dissertation: Northwestern University, 1977.

Fifield, Christopher: *Max Bruch: His Life and Works*, 145-149. New York: George Braziller, 1988.

Schwarzer, Matthias: *Die Oratorien von Max Bruch: Eine Quellenstudie*, 86-149. Berlin: Merseburger, 1988.

Additional works by Max Bruch

Frithjof, op. 23 (1857-1864)

Text: The text is the composer's adaptation of the German translation by Gottlieb Mohnike of a Swedish poem by Esaias Tegner.

Performing Forces: voices: soprano (Ingeborg) and baritone (Frithjof) soloists, TTBB choir; **orchestra**.

First Performance: 20 November 1864, Aachen, Germany; Concordia Male Choir and orchestra; conducted by the composer

Editions: Full scores and parts for *Frithjof* were published by C. F. W. Siegel Musikalienhandlung.

Notes: Tegner's poem is based upon a 13th-century Icelandic legend.

Performance Issues: There is a solo TTBB quartet accessible to a group of strong choristers. **Soloists:** soprano - range: d'-g'', tessitura: f'-'', this is a declamatory role for a powerful voice; baritone - range: c-f', tessitura: e-e', this is a very lyric role with sustained singing in the top of the range; **choir:** difficult.

Selected Discography

At the time of this writing, no recordings were available.

Selected Bibliography

Upton, George P.: *The Standard Cantatas*, seventh edition, 87-92. Chicago: A. C. McClurg and Company, 1899.

Fifield, Christopher: *Max Bruch: His Life and Works*, 52-58. New York: George Brazillier, 1988.

Schön Ellen, op. 24 (1866)

Duration: ca. 12 minutes

Text: The text is by Emanuel Geibel.

Performing Forces: voices: soprano (Fair Ellen) and baritone (Lord Edward) soloists; SATB choir; **orchestra**.

First Performance: 22 February 1867, Coblenz, Germany

Editions: Piano-vocal scores are available for purchase from G. Schirmer, which also provides orchestral materials for rent.

Notes: The score incorporates the Scottish folksong, "The Campbells Are Coming." The story is loosely based upon an uprising in India between 1857 and 1858 during which a British fort in Lucknow was under siege for two months. In this ballad, the character of Ellen hears the drums of the Scottish Highland Regiment coming to the relief of the besieged British. Twice no one else hears them, and she is thought to be crazy, but on her third expostulation, she is believed, and they are, in fact, saved.

Selected Discography

Claudia Braun, Thomas Laske; Kantorei Barmen-Gemarke; Wuppertal Symphony Orchestra; conducted by George Hanson. MD&G: 3351096.

Selected Bibliography

Upton, George P.: *The Standard Cantatas*, seventh edition, 93-95. Chicago: A. C. McClurg and Company, 1899.
Fifield, Christopher: *Max Bruch: His Life and Works*, 61, 62, etc. New York: George Braziller, 1988.

Salamis, op. 25 (1866)

Text: The text is by Hermann Lingg.

Performing Forces: voices: 4 male soloists, TTBB choir; **orchestra.**

Notes: The drama set in this work centers around Greek troops returning from their victory over Xerxes and the Persians.

Selected Discography

At the time of this writing, no recordings were available.

Selected Bibliography

Upton, George P.: *The Standard Cantatas*, seventh edition, 92-93. Chicago: A. C. McClurg and Company, 1899.
Fifield, Christopher: *Max Bruch: His Life and Works*, 61, 62, etc. New York: George Braziller, 1988.

Odysseus, op. 41 (1872)

Duration: ca. 107 minutes

Text: The text was written for this work by the poet, Wilhelm Paul Graff based upon scenes from Homer's *Odyssey* on an outline from the composer.

Performing Forces: voices: Nausicaa (soprano), Pallas Athene (soprano), Leucothea (soprano), Penelope (alto), Arete (alto), Spirit of Anticlea (alto), Hermes (tenor), Odysseus (bass-baritone), Alcinoos (bass), Helmsman (bass), Spirit of Tiresias (bass); SATB choir;[34] **orchestra:** 2 flutes, 2 oboes, 2 clarinets, 2 bassoons, 4 horns, 2 trumpets, 3 trombones, tuba, timpani, harp, and strings.

First Performance: 8 February 1873, Barmen Germany; Barmen Konzertgesellschaft, prepared by Anton Krause; conducted by the

---

[34] The score reconfigures the choral forces into male, female, and mixed ensembles to represent various groups of people.

composer. Amalie Joachim and Julius Stockhausen were scheduled as soloists, but both were forced to cancel late that day. They were replaced by Adele Graf and Josef Bletzacher.

Six completed scenes (1, 2, 3, 4, 7, and 10) were performed in Bremen by the Choral Society of Bremen, under the direction of Carl Rheinthaler, 6 May 1872.

Editions: N. Simrock published full scores and parts for *Odysseus* in 1872. This first edition included an English singing translation prepared by Natlie Macfarren. The score is organized into eight scenes in two acts as follows:

Act I
1. Overture
2. Odysseus to Calypso
3. Odysseus in the Underworld
4. Odysseus to the Sirens
5. Sea Storm

Act II
6. Odysseus to the Phäaken
   a. Nausicaa
   b. Festival in Ithaca
   c. Entsendung — Homeward
7. Penelope
8. Final Scene

Notes: The score is dedicated to the Choral Society of Bremen. It was conceived in September of 1871 and completed in November 1872. Between 1872 and 1875, over 40 performances were given throughout Germany, England, and the United States. Bruch married the soprano, Clara Tuczek, in 1882, after which she often sang the role of Penelope when her husband conducted performances of this work.

Performance Issues: In performances during Bruch's lifetime, the roles of Nausicaa, Pallas Athene, Arete, and the Spirit of Anticlea were often doubled by Penelope and Leucothea. The clarity of the drama is better served with individual soloists for each role. These smaller roles may be best assigned to choristers.

Selected Discography

Camilla Nylund, Nancy Maultsby, Jeffrey Kneebone; Budapest Radio Chorus; North German Radio Orchestra; conducted by Leon Botstein, recorded in 1997. Koch Schwann: 3-6557-2.

Selected Bibliography

Upton, George P.: *The Standard Cantatas*, seventh edition, 95-100. Chicago: A. C. McClurg and Company, 1899.

Kahl, Willi: "Zur Barmer Erstauffuhrung des 'Odysseus' von Max Bruch (1873): Nach unveroffentlichten Briefen," Beiträge zur rheinische Musikgeschichte, v (1954), 32-50.

Geck, Martin: "Max Bruchs weltliche Oratorien," *Beiträge zur rheinische Musikgeschichte*, lxxxvii (1970), 80-88.

Vick, Bingham Lafayette: *The Five Oratorios of Max Bruch*, 32-75. Doctoral dissertation: Northwestern University, 1977.

Fifield, Christopher: *Max Bruch: His Life and Works*, 129-135. New York: George Braziller, 1988.

Schwarzer, Matthias: *Die Oratorien von Max Bruch: Eine Quellenstudie*, 1-85. Berlin: Merseburger, 1988.

Das Lied von der Glocke, op. 45 (1877-1878)

Duration: ca. 110 minutes

Text: The text is a poem by Friedrich Schiller to whose memory the score is dedicated.

Performing Forces: voices: soprano, alto, tenor and bass soloists; SATB choir; **orchestra**.

First Performance: 12 May 1878, Gürzenich Hall, Colgne, conducted by the composer

Final version: January and February 1879, Barmen, Germany; conducted by the composer

English premiere: 26 August 1879, Birmingham; Birmingham Triennial Festival, conducted by the composer

Editions: *Das Lied von der Glocke* was first published by Simrock in 1879 (number 8088); however, the composer paid for the initial engraving. This edition includes an English singing translation by Nathalia Macfarren.

Notes: The fair copy of the score was completed 8 January 1878.

Selected Discography

Ute Selbig, Elisabeth Graf, Matthias Blidorn, André Eckert; Dresden State Opera Chorus; Dresden Philharmonic; conducted by Hans-Christoph Rademann, recorded in 1995. Thorofon: DCTH-2291/92.

Eleonore Marguerre, Annette Markert, Klaus Florian Vogt, Mario Hoff; Kuehn's Mixed Chorus, Prague Philharmonic Chorus; Staatskapelle Weimar; conducted by Jac van Steen. CPO: 777130-2.

Selected Bibliography

Fifield, Christopher: *Max Bruch: His Life and Works*, 158-165. New York: George Braziller, 1988.

Steinert, Daniel A.: *Max Bruch's Dramatic Cantata on Friedrich Schiller's Poem, "Das Lied von der Glocke": A Conductor's Analysis for Performance*. Doctoral dissertation: University of North Carolina at Greensboro, 1995.

Achilleus, op. 50 (1882-1885)

Duration: ca. 180 minutes

Text: The text, which is based upon Homer's *Iliad*, was commissioned for this work from Heinrich Bulthaupt.

Performing Forces: voices: Andromache (alto), Achilles (tenor), Hector (baritone), Priam (bass) soloists; SSAATTBB choir; **orchestra:**

A Conductor's Guide to 19th-Century Choral-Orchestra Works   113

2 flutes, 2 oboes, 2 clarinets, 2 bassoons, 4 horns, 2 trumpets, 3 trombones, tuba, timpani, cymbals, harp, and strings.

First Performance: 28 June 1885, Bonn, Germany; Amalie Joachim, Emil Götze, George Henschel, Bonn Music Festival, conducted by the composer

Notes: The score is organized as follows:

Act One
1. Scene — "Volkversammlung"
2. Scene — Am Gestade des Meeres / Achilleus
3. Chorus
4. Recitative
5. Soprano and women's choir — Thetis und die Meergöttinen
6. Recitative and duet
7. Chorus

Act Two
8. Scene
9. Morgengesang der Trojaner
10. Duet — Andromache and Hector
11. Quartet and choir
12. Scene — choir

Act Three
13. Die Leichenfeier des Patroklas
14. Chorus
15. Recitative and Duet — Achilleus and Priam / Scene im Zelt des Achilleus / Nacht
16. Scene — Andromache
17. Choral Epilogue

Performance Issues: "The orchestration has none of the subtle colors and tender beauties of *Odysseus*. It is overburdened with instrumental doublings and overwhelmed by a thickened texture...Clarity is lost in the frenetic string passages at melodramatic moments."[35]

---

[35] Christopher Fifield: *Max Bruch: His Life and Works*, 222. New York: George Braziller, 1988.

Selected Discography

At the time of this writing, no recordings were available.

Selected Bibliography

Kahl, Willi: "Zur Entstehung und Bonner Uraufführung von Max Bruchs 'Achilleus' 1885," *Beiträge zur rheinische Musikgeschichte*, xxxv (1959), 26-54

Vick, Bingham Lafayette: *The Five Oratorios of Max Bruch*, 115-167. Doctoral dissertation: Northwestern University, 1977.

Fifield, Christopher: *Max Bruch: His Life and Works*, 220-224. New York: George Braziller, 1988.

Schwarzer, Matthias: *Die Oratorien von Max Bruch: Eine Quellenstudie*, 150-269. Berlin: Merseburger, 1988.

Das Feuerkreuz [The Cross of Fire], op. 52 (1888)

Text: The text was written for this work by Heinrich Alfred Bulthaupt based upon an incident in Sir Walter Scott's *The Lady of the Lake*.

Performing Forces: voices: Mary (soprano), Norman (baritone), Angus (bass); SATB choir; **orchestra**.

First Performance: 26 February 1889; Breslau, Germany; Breslau Sing-Akademie, conducted by the composer

Notes: The work was initially conceived in 1874 with Wilhelm Graff as librettist. Bruch's dissatisfaction with Graff's work and their eventual estrangement led him to commission the text from Bulthaupt. Bruch initially intended to dedicate the score to the Kaiser, but chose instead to dedicate it to the Breslau Sing-Akademie. The "Ave Maria" movement was extracted for independent performance as op. 52, no. 6. Bruch later also adapted it for solo cello and orchestra as op. 61.

Selected Discography

At the time of this writing, no recordings were available.

A Conductor's Guide to 19th-Century Choral-Orchestra Works 115

Selected Bibliography

Fifield, Christopher: *Max Bruch: His Life and Works*, 224-228. New York: George Braziller, 1988.

Moses, op. 67 (1895)

Duration: ca. 120 minutes

Text: The text, based upon the Bible, is by Ludwig Spitta.

Performing Forces: voices: soprano (The Angel of the Lord), tenor (Aaron), and bass (Moses) soloists; SATB choir; **orchestra:** 2 flutes, 2 oboes (oboe II doubling English horn), 2 clarinets, 2 bassoons, 4 horns, 3 trumpets, 3 trombones, tuba, timpani, percussion (1 player — triangle and cymbals), organ, harp, and strings.

First Performance: 19 January 1895; Barmen, Germany; Konzertgesellschaft, conducted by the composer

American premiere: 6 February 1896; Baltimore; in an English translation by Paul England

Editions: Full scores and parts for *Moses* were published by Simrock in 1895. Simrock also published a piano-vocal score with a singing English translation by Paul England.

Autograph: The autograph full score is in the Moldenhauer Archive of Northwestern University in Enavston, Illinois.

Notes: The score is organized as follows:

Act One: Am Sinai
1. The People (Choir)
2. The Angel of the Lord
3. Moses
4. Song of Praise
5. The Angel of the Lord, Moses, Aaron
6. The People

Act Two: Das goldene Kalb
   7. Scene
   8. Aaron, The People
   9. Moses, Aaron, The People

Act Three: Die Rückkehr der Kundschafter aus Kanaan
  10. Choir of Kundschafter
  11. Moses
  12. Scene — Aaron, The People
  13. Moses, The Angel of the Lord, The People

Act Four: Das Land der Verheißung
  14. The Angel of the Lord
  15. Moses
  16. Choir
  17. Der letzte Segen Moses
  18. Choir, recitative
  19. Die Klage des Volks über Moses

Selected Discography

Elizabeth Whitehouse, Robert Gambill, Michael Volle; Bamberg Symphony Orchestra and Chorus; conducted by Claus Peter Flor. Orfeo: C 438 982 H.

Brigitte Christensen, Peter Lika, Stefan Vinke; Maulbronn Choir; Russian Chamber Philharmonic, St. Petersburg; conducted by Jurgen Budday, recorded live in the Maulbronn Monastery. K&K: KUK96.

A Conductor's Guide to 19th-Century Choral-Orchestra Works 117

Selected Bibliography

Fellinger, Imogen: "Zur Entstehung von Bruchs 'Moses,'" *Max Bruch-Studien*, lxxxvii, edited by Dietrich Kämper, 89-103. Cologne: Arno Volk-Verlag, 1970.

Vick, Bingham Lafayette: *The Five Oratorios of Max Bruch*, 168-204. Doctoral dissertation: Northwestern University, 1977.

Fifield, Christopher: *Max Bruch: His Life and Works*, 256-260. New York: George Braziller, 1988.

Schwarzer, Matthias: *Die Oratorien von Max Bruch: Eine Quellenstudie*, 270-332. Berlin: Merseburger, 1988.

Gustav Adolf, op. 73 (1898)

Text: Albert Hackenburg wrote the text.

Performing Forces: voices: Gustav Adolf, Duke Bernard, Leubelfing; SATB and TTBB choirs; **orchestra:** 2 flutes (flute II doubling piccolo), 2 oboes (oboe II doubling English horn), 2 clarinets, 2 bassoons, 4 horns, 3 trumpets, 3 trombones, tuba, timpani, percussion (3 players — snare drum, bass drum, triangle, and cymbals), organ, and strings.

First Performance: 22 May 1898; Barmen, Germany; Konzertgesellschaft, conducted by the composer

Editions: Full scores and parts for *Gustav Adolf* were published by Simrock in 1898. This set is reprinted by Edwin Kalmus (A3291-STP).

Notes: *Gustav Adolf* was performed in Berlin in 1917 for the celebration of 400 years of Protestantism in Germany. The score is organized as follows:

Act One: Erwartung und Ankunft Gustav Adolfs
1. Am Meergestade
2. People, Priest, Swedish Soldiers

Act Two: Magdeburgszene
3. Im Lager an der Havel

4. Duke Leubelfing, the King
5. Kriegslied — War Song
6. Folksong — maiden, women, the King
7. The King, Bernhard, Choir

Act Three: Münchenszene
8. Vor München
9. Leubelfings Lied
10. Herzog, Bernhard, Gustav, Choir
11. Scene

Act Four: Tod und Verklärung Gustav Adolfs
12. Bei Lützen
13. Im Naumburg
14. Schlosskirche zu Wittenburg

Selected Discography

At the time of this writing, no recordings were available.

Selected Bibliography

Geck, Martin: "Max Bruchs Oratorium 'Gustav Adolf' — ein Denkmal des Kultur-Protestantismus," *Archiv für Musikwissenshaft*, xxvii (1970), 138-149.
Vick, Bingham Lafayette: *The Five Oratorios of Max Bruch*, 205-240. Doctoral dissertation: Northwestern University, 1977.
Fifield, Christopher: *Max Bruch: His Life and Works*, 256-260. New York: George Braziller, 1988.
Schwarzer, Matthias: *Die Oratorien von Max Bruch: Eine Quellenstudie*, 333-400. Berlin: Merseburger, 1988.

Bruckner, Anton (b. Ansfelden, Austria, 4 September 1824; d. 11 October 1896)

Life: Bruckner's father was a schoolmaster. He was a choirboy at St. Florian's monastery. He moved to Linz to prepare to become a schoolmaster and continued his music training there. He became a vituoso organist, he would later tour throughout Europe giving concerts of improvisations, and returned to St. Florian to teach. There he produced his first significant works. In 1868, he moved to Vienna to succeed his teacher, Sechter, as professor of harmony and counterpoint.

Bruckner became an ardent admirer of Wagner's music, and he dedicated his third symphony to his senior composer, which labeled him as part of the "New German" movement bringing him the undeserved indignation of the critic, Eduard Hanslick and his contemporaries in the Viennese press.

Bruckner's music displays consummate technical brilliance. He integrated the harmonic language of his time with imitative procedures from the 16th century producing exquisite and highly individual compositions; however, he was plagued by self-doubt, which has led to one of the great challenges for performers and scholars of his music. He revised compositions, especially the symphonies, many times, leaving two and three finished versions. These were sometimes in response to criticism from feable sources. The critical edition under the direction of Robert Haas and Alfred Orel produced a number of multi-versioned works. Haas's successor, Leopold Nowak, continued to produce discrete editions for each version of a work, but also made subsequent revisions of many of the editions of the works published under the Haas regime. Those conductors wishing to select materials for performances of the symphonies should consult David Daniels's *Orchestral Music*[36] for recommendations of editions, scores, and parts. Fortunately, the choral works, including those with orchestra seem to have been spared such capriciousness, and therefore the Bruck-

---

[36] David Daniels: *Orchestral Music*, fifth edition. Lanham, MD: Scarecrow Press, 2006.

ner Gesellschaft editions appear in single versions, and they are ideal for concert use.

Teachers: Otto Kitzler, Simon Sechter, Johann Baptist Weiss, Leopold Edler von Zenetti

Students: Guido Adler, Emile Jaques-Dalcroze, Hans Rott, Heinrich Schenker, Franz Schmidt

Other Principal Works: orchestra: Symphony No. 0 (1863-1864), Symphony No. 1 (1865-1866), Symphony No. 2 (1871-1872), Symphony No. 3 (1873), Symphony No. 4 (1874), Symphony No. 5 (1875-1876), Symphony No. 6 (1879-1881), Symphony No. 7 (1881-1883), Symphony No. 8 (1884-1887), Symphony No. 9 (1887-1894); **choir:** (without orchestra) numerous motets.

Selected Composer Bibliography

Orel, Alfred: *Bruckner-Brevier: Briefe, Dokumente, Berichte.* Vienna: Musikwissenschaftlicher Verlag, 1959.
Cook, Deryck: "The Bruckner Problem Simplified," *in The Musical Times* (1969), compiled as a monograph, New York: The Musical Newsletter, 1975.
Grasberger, Renate: *Werzeichnis Anton Bruckner.* Tutzing: Hans Schneider, 1977.
Howie, A. C.: "Traditional and Novel Elements in Bruckner's Sacred Music," *Musical Quarterly* (October 1981), volume 67, 544-567.

Requiem in D minor, WAB 39 (1848-1849)

Duration: ca. 37 minutes

Text: The text is from the Roman Catholic Mass for the Dead.

Performing Forces: voices: soprano, alto, tenor, and bass soloists; SATB choir; **orchestra:** 3 trombones (alto, tenor, and bass), organ, and strings.

First Performance: 15 September 1849; St. Florian

A Conductor's Guide to 19th-Century Choral-Orchestra Works   121

Editions: *Requiem in D minor* is published in the critical editions *Anton Bruckner: Sämtliche Werke*, volume 15, edited by Robert Haas, and *Anton Bruckner Gesamtausgabe*, volume 14, edited by Leopold Nowak. It also appears in a study-score published by the Bruckner-Gesellschaft, which is published by Musikwissenschaftlicher Verlag and distributed in the United States by C. F. Peters. Editions, which are available for purchase include: Musikwissenschaftlicher Verlag.

Autograph: The composer's manuscript is in the Music Collection of the Österreichischen Nationalbibliothek in Vienna (S. m. 2125).

Notes: This work was composed for a memorial service for Bruckner's friend, Franz Sailer. The score is organized as follows:

1.	Requiem	SATB choir
2.	Dies irae	all soloists and choir
3.	Domine Deus	soprano and bass soloists and choir
4.	Hostias	TTBB choir
5.	Quam olim	SSATB choir
6.	Sanctus	all soloists and choir
7.	Benedictus	all soloists and choir
8.	Agnus Dei	A, T, B soloists and choir
9.	Requiem	SATB choir
10.	Cum Sanctis	SATB choir

Performance Issues: The choral writing freely intersperses homophonic and polyphonic textures. Much of the choral material is harmonically supported by the instruments, but the choral singers must exercise a fair degree of musical independence. The scoring allows for the use of a small choir and reduced, or even single strings. Movement 3 begins with a dramatic soli section for the basses that seems to be intended for the soloist, which is reinforced by a similar solo passage for the soprano in the middle of the movement. Movement 4 is nearly a cappella and movement 9 is an a cappella chorale. The trombones are used to reinforce choral harmonies and to "set" beginning pitches of other choral passages. This practice appears to be informed by the practice of Bach. The organ is written as a figured-bass part. All of the solos are appropriate for strong choristers. **Soloists:** soprano - range: $e'-g''$, tessitura: $g'-e''$, this is a lyric role; alto - range: $b-e^{b''}$, tessitura: $d'-c''$, this is a sustained lyric role; tenor - range: e-a', tessitura: g-f', this is a lyric solo part; bass - range: F-e$^{b'}$, tessitura: B^b-b^b, this is a declamatory role; **choir:** medium difficult; **orchestra:** medium easy.

Selected Discography

Joan Rodgers, Catherine Denley, Maldwyn Davies, Michael George; Corydon Singers; English Chamber Orchestra; conducted by Matthew Best. Hyperion: CDA66245.

Selected Bibliography

Müller, Franz Xaver: "Bruckners Requiem," *Bruckner-Blätter*, volume 2 (1930), 80-82.
Bayer, Julia: "Anton Bruckners d-Moll-Requiem," *Chorblätter*, volume 6 (1951), 19.
Diether, Jack: "Flashes of Greatness from the 25-Year-Old Bruckner: A Moving Masterly Requiem (Recording)," *American Record Guide*, volume 37 (1971), 428-429.

Missa Solemnis in B^b minor, WAB 29 (1854)

Duration: ca. 31 minutes

Text: The text is from the Roman Catholic communion liturgy.

Performing Forces: voices: soprano, alto, tenor, and bass soloists; SATB choir; **orchestra:** 2 oboes, 2 bassoons, 2 trumpets (B^b), 3 trombones (alto, tenor, and bass), timpani (2 drums), organ, and strings.

First Performance: 14 September 1854; St. Florian

Editions: *Missa Solemnis in B^b minor* is published in the critical editions *Anton Bruckner: Sämtliche Werke*, volume 15, edited by Robert Haas, and *Anton Bruckner Gesamtausgabe*, volume 15, edited by Leopold Nowak. It also appears in a study-score published by the Bruckner-Gesellschaft, which is published by Musikwissenschaftlicher Verlag and distributed in the United States by C. F.

A Conductor's Guide to 19th-Century Choral-Orchestra Works 123

Peters. Editions, which are available for purchase include: Musikwissenschaftlicher Verlag.

Autograph: The composer's manuscript is in the archives of the St. Florian Monastery.

Notes: Bruckner composed this mass for the induction ceremony of Friedrich Mayr at St. Florian.

Performance Issues: The choir is well supported harmonically by the instruments, but it is not often clearly doubled by the accompaniment. There are alternate text underlays in the "Kyrie" that provide differing sequences of repetition of the Kyrie and Christe iterations. The organ is a continuo part. There is an extended oboe solo in the "Qui tollis" movement. The orchestral parts are conservatively written and the choral parts are more musically than vocally demanding, which makes this an excellent work for good church choirs with a pick-up orchestra. A small string section is appropriate, and single players can be used effectively. **Soloists:** soprano - range: f'-$b^{b''}$, tessitura: g'-f'', this is a lyric solo with some wide melodic leaps; alto - range: a-$e^{b''}$, tessitura: d'-a', this is a sustained solo role; tenor - range: f-$a^{b'}$, tessitura: a-f', this is a lyric solo; bass - range: (D) F-$e^{b'}$, tessitura: F-a, this is a powerful declamatory role for which the parenthetical low note is offered optionally an octave higher; **choir:** medium difficult; **orchestra:** medium difficult.

Selected Discography

Christiane Oelze, Claudia Schubert, Jürg Dürmüller, Reinhard Hagen; Bamberg Symphony Orchestra and chorus; conducted by Karl Anton Rickenbacher. Virgin Classics: 5615012.

Selected Bibliography

Schnerich, Alfred: "Bruckners B-Messe," *Musica sacra*, volume 55 (1925), 228.
Habel, Ferdinand: "'Missa solemnis' B-moll" *Bruckner-Blätter*, volume 6, number 3 (1934), 31-34.
Strehlen, Oswald: "Anton Bruckner's erste Messe," Der neue Wille, volume 2, number 43 (1940), 8.

Psalm 146, WAB 37 (1854?)

Duration: ca. 35 minutes

Text: The text is from the Bible. It is in German.

Performing Forces: voices: soprano, alto, tenor, and bass soloists; SSAATTBB choir; **orchestra:** 1 flute, 2 oboes, 2 clarinets (A), 2 bassoons, 4 horns, (B^b basso, D, F), trumpets (D), 4 trombones (alto, tenor, and 2 bass), timpani (2 drums), and strings.

First Performance: unknown

Editions: *Psalm 146* is published in a critical edition by the Bruckner-Gesellschaft volume 20, number 4, as prepared by Paul Hawkshaw, which was published in 1996 by Musikwissenschaftlicher Verlag and distributed in the United States by C. F. Peters.

Autograph: There is an incomplete score in the composer's hand (Mus.-Hs. 40.500) and a complete score by an unknown copyist with annotations in Bruckner's hand (Mus.-Hs. 6011). Both are in the Music Collection of the Österreichischen Nationalbibliothek in Vienna.

Notes: The dating of this work is problematic, but the mid-1850s are a reasonable assumption. There is no reference to this composition in Bruckner's correspondence, and there is no evidence that it was performed during the composer's lifetime. The score is organized as follows:

1.	Alleluia, Lobet den Herrn	choir
2.	Der Herr bauet Jerusalem	S, T, B recitatives
3.	Groß ist unser Gott	double choir
4.	Der Herr nimmt auf die Sanften	S, A, T, B and choir
5.	Der Herr hat Wohlgefallen an denen	soprano
6.	Alleluia, lobet den Herrn	choir with fugue

Performance Issues: The choral writing freely alternates between four-part textures and assorted divisi. The choral material is often clearly supported by the orchestra, but there are also extended a cappella passages. The choral parts are vocally demanding. There is rapid coloratura passagework for all of the voices, and the tessituras of the soprano and tenor parts are fairly high. The double-choir writing in movement 3 would benefit from a physical separation of these groups as much of the material is in block imitation between the choirs. There is an important oboe solo in movement 4 that is florid, but accessible. In movement 1, there is a horn part labeled solo and two additional parts labeled 1 and 2. There are 4 horn parts in movement 4, but only two in the remaining movements. The wind and brass parts are generally idiomatic and not overly demanding. There is some rapid passagework for the strings that requires solid players. The scoring for the bass suggests the use of a large symphonic choir and a full complement of strings. This is a rarely-performed, but impressive symphonic choral work reflecting an awareness of the music of Mendelssohn. **Soloists:** soprano - range: c'-a'', tessitura: f'-f'', this is a lyrica role that has the most singing of the soloists and must be able to penetrate the full ensemble; alto - range: b♭-c'', tessitura: d'-a', this is a simple solo that appears only in an ensemble context; tenor - range: c-a', tessitura: f-f', this is a lyric role; bass - range: A-e', tessitura: c-c', this is a declamatory role; **choir:** medium difficult; **orchestra:** medium difficult.

Selected Discography

Wendt, Russ, Stricker, Nimsgern; Sachs Choir, Lehrergesangverein Nürnberg, Nürnberg Symphony Orchestra; conducted by Riedelbach. Colosseum: 548 [LP].

Selected Bibliography

Hawkshaw, Paul: "Foreword" to the critical edition. Vienna: Musikwissenschaftlicher Verlag, 1996.

Psalm 112, WAB 35 (1863)

Duration: ca. 14 minutes

Text: The text is from the Bible. It is in German.

Performing Forces: voices: double SATB choir; **orchestra:** 2 flutes, 2 oboes, 2 clarinets (B^b), 2 bassoons, 2 horns, (F), 2 trumpets (E^b), 3 trombones (alto, tenor, and bass), timpani (2 drums), and strings.

First Performance: 14 March 1926; Vöcklabruck, Austria

Editions: *Psalm 112* is published in a critical edition by the Bruckner-Gesellschaft, volume 20, number 5, as prepared by Paul Hawkshaw, which was published in 1996 by Musikwissenschaftlicher Verlag and distributed in the United States by C. F. Peters. Additional materials are published by Universal Edition.

Autograph: The composer's manuscript is in the Music Collection of the Österreichischen Nationalbibliothek in Vienna (Mus.-Hs. 3156).

Notes: This is the final work Bruckner composed as part of his studies with Otto Kitzler.

Performance Issues: The choral writing is primarily homophonic with the two choirs in close imitation of each other. The choral material is generally well supported harmonically, but the choral parts are rarely directly doubled by the instruments. Bruckner's work with Kitzler was focused on orchestration and the study of form. There are a number of coloristic orchestrational effects including tremolos and trills that one rarely sees in Bruckner's concerted choral music that are surely the result of those endeavors. The choral writing is practical and the grand fugue at the end of the score reduces the choral component to four parts. The instrumental parts are practically written and the density of orchestration is more varied than in much of Bruckner's music. A da capo of the opening section is suggested at the end of the score. This was introduced in the first published edition of 1926 by Josef V. Wöss. It has been retained in the critical edition and is advisable in performance; **choir:** medium difficult; **orchestra:** medium difficult.

Selected Discography

Corydon Singers; English Chamber Orchestra; conducted by Matthew Best. Hyperion: CDA66245.

Bamberg Symphony Orchestra and chorus; conducted by Karl Anton Rickenbacher. Virgin Classics: VC 7 91481 and CDC 59060.

Selected Bibliography

Hawkshaw, Paul: "Foreword" to the critical edition. Vienna: Musikwissenschaftlicher Verlag, 1996.

Mass No. 1 in D minor, WAB 26 (1864)

Duration: ca. 43 minutes

Text: The text is from the Roman Catholic communion liturgy.

Performing Forces: voices: soprano, alto, tenor, and bass soloists; SATB choir; **orchestra:** 2 flutes, 2 oboes, 2 clarinets (B^b), 2 bassoons, 2 horns (F), 2 trumpets (F), 3 trombones (alto, tenor, and bass), timpani (2 drums), organ, and strings.

First Performance: 20 November 1864; Linz cathedral; conducted by the composer

Editions: *Mass No. 1 in D minor* is published in the critical edition *Anton Bruckner Gesamtausgabe*, volume 15, edited by Leopold Nowak. It also appears in a study-score published by the Bruckner-Gesellschaft, which is published by Musikwissenschaftlicher Verlag and distributed in the United States by C. F. Peters.

Autograph: The composer's manuscript is in the music collection of the Österreichishen Nationalbibliothek (Cod. 19.483).

Notes: Leopold Nowak indicates in "Foreword" to his edition of the score that, "Bruckner did not include the organ in his original score, except for the small solo in the Credo, and a figured thorough-bass is also missing. Its use, however, is indispensable in this kind of sacred music."[37] This score established Bruckner's reputation as an important composer.

Performance Issues: The choral material combines homophonic and imitative writing. There are limited divisi in all choral parts. The accompaniment does not always clearly support the singers, which necessitates a strong and independent vocal ensemble. The wind scoring allows the use of a moderate-sized choir, although a symphonic group could be effective. The wind parts do not pose any technical challenges, although there are some significant sustained passages. The string writing is quite challenging and will demand skilled players and may warrant a separate instrumental rehearsal. The vocal solos are interspersed occasionally throughout the choral material. With the exception of the bass, the soloists appear only in ensemble textures. The organ part is not difficult and is appropriate for a small instrument. It actually appears as an independent part for only a few measures in the "Credo." There are optional wind parts should an organ not be available. **Soloists:** soprano - range: c′-g″, tessitura: e′-e″, this is a simple solo role suitable for a chorister; alto - range: b-d″, tessitura: e′-b′, this is a simple solo role suitable for a chorister; tenor - range: d-a′, tessitura: a-f#′, this is a simple solo role suitable for a chorister; bass - range: F-e′, tessitura: d-c′, this role has more exposed material than the others and requires clarity at the bottom of the range, but it is also appropriate for a strong chorister; **choir:** difficult; **orchestra:** difficult.

Selected Discography

Edith Mathis, Marga Schiml, Wieslaw Ochman, Karl Ridderbusch; Elmar Schloter, organ; Bavarian Radio Chorus and Orchestra; conducted by Eugen Jochum, recorded in January 1971 in the Herkules Saal, Residenz, Munich. Re-released on CD as Deutsche Grammophon: 423 127 2.

Joan Rodgers, Catherine Wyn-Rogers, Keith Lewis, Alastair Miles; James O'Donnell, organ; Corydon Singers and Orchestra; conducted by Matthew Best; recorded 5-7 February 1993. Hyperion: CDA66650.

---

[37] Leopold Nowak: preface to *Mass No. 1 in D minor*, translated by Christl Schönfeldt. Vienna: Musikwissenschaftlicher Verlag, 1957.

Luba Orgonasova, Bernarda Fink, Christoph Prégardien, Eike Wilm Schulte; Ian Watson, organ; Monteverdi Choir; Vienna Philharmonic; conducted by John Eliot Gardiner, recorded 1 June 1996. Deutsche Grammophon: 028945967424.

Isabelle Müller-Kant, Eibe Möhlmann, Christoph Fischesser, Daniel Sans; Chamber Choir of Europe; Württembergische Philharmonic Reutligen; conducted by Nicol Matt, recorded 20-25 January 2003. Brilliant Classics: 92002.

Selected Bibliography

Auer, Max: "Anton Bruckners ertes Meisterwerk für Ischl geplant (d-Moll-Messe)," *Festchrift zum 400jährigen Jubiläum der römankatholische*, 36-39. Bad Ischl: Pfarre Bad Ischl, 1954.

Nowak, Leopold: "Foreword" to *Messe D-Moll, Anton Bruckner Gesamtausgabe*, volume 16. Vienna: Musikwissenschaftlicher Verlag, 1957.

Newlin, Dika: "Bruckner's Three Great Masses," *Chord and Discord*, volume 2, number 8 (1958), 3-16.

Sullivan, Cornelius Fancis: *The D minor and F minor Masses of Anton Bruckner as the Culmination of the Viennese Classical Mass Tradition*. Columbia University: dissertation, 1972.

Mass No. 2 in E minor, WAB 27 (1866)

Duration: ca. 37 minutes

Text: The text is from the Roman Catholic communion liturgy.

Performing Forces: voices: SSAATTBB choir; **orchestra:** 2 oboes, 2 clarinets (A, C), 2 bassoons, 4 horns (D, F), 2 trumpets (C), 3 trombones (alto, tenor, and bass).

First Performance: 29 September 1869; the cathedral square in Linz; conducted by the composer for the dedication of a new votive chapel in the cathedral

Editions: The 1866 version is published in the critical edition *Anton Bruckner Gesamtausgabe*, volume 17, part 1, edited by Leopold Nowak.

The revised 1882 version of *Mass No. 2 in E minor* is published in the critical editions *Anton Bruckner: Sämtliche Werke*, volume 13, edited by Robert Haas, and *Anton Bruckner Gesamtausgabe*, volume 17, part 2, edited by Leopold Nowak.

Both versions appear in study-scores by the Bruckner-Gesellschaft, which are published by Musikwissenschaftlicher Verlag and distributed in the United States by C. F. Peters. Editions that are available for purchase include: Musikwissenschaftlicher Verlag.

Autograph: The composer's manuscript is in the archives of the New Cathedral in Linz. The original presentation score is in the Bishop's Palace in Linz. A set of parts copied in 1885 is in the St. Florian Monastery.

Notes: In the "Sanctus," Bruckner quoted a phrase from the Missa brevis of Palestrina.[38] The score is dedicated to Bishop Rudigier who had commissioned it for the cornerstone dedication of the votive chapel of the Virgini Mary.

Performance Issues: This score combines Palestrinan contrapuntal techniques with 19th-century harmonic practices and romantic wind and brass scoring. The 8-part polyphonic textures of the choral writing are frequently a cappella and at other time placed against accompanimental figures sharply contrasted with the vocal material. The soprano I part has an unusually high tessitura, and there are some awkward and broad melodic leaps for the singers, particularly the basses. One notable challenge for the singers is Bruckner's use of chromatic variation as a method of melodic development. Motives are repeated with selected notes altered by semitone often leaving the rest of the harmonic context unaltered. The wind parts are generally interspersed with frequent rests so that fatigue for the players should not be a concern. The individual parts do require secure and experienced players. The bassoons have the most technically demanding of the wind parts. This remarkable composition demonstrates Bruckner's supreme mastery of counterpoint and his avant-garde harmonic practices. It is an ex-

---

[38] Cooke, Deryck: "Anton Bruckner," *The New Grove Late Romantic Masters*, 41. New York: W.W. Norton, 1985.

ceedingly effective work filled with moments of drama and beauty. An interesting pairing would be J. S. Bach's, Cantata No. 118: *O Jesu Christ, mein Lebens Licht*, BWV 118, a seven-minute work for six brass players and choir and Brahms's *Begräbnisgesang* [*qv*]; **choir:** difficult; **orchestra:** medium difficult.

Selected Discography

Bavarian Radio Chorus and Orchestra; conducted by Eugen Jochum, recorded in February 1971 in the Herkules Saal, Residenz, Munich. Re-released on CD as Deutsche Grammophon: 423 127 2.

John Alldis Choir; New English Chamber Orchestra; conducted by Daniel Barenboim. EMI: 0724358550825.

Corydon Singers; English Chamber Orchestra Winds; conducted by Matthew Best; recorded 1985. Hyperion: CDA66650.

Gächinger Kantorei; Stuttgart Bach Collegium; conducted by Helmut Rilling. Hänssler: CD 98.119.

Selected Bibliography

Diether, Jack: "An Introduction to Bruckner's Mass in E minor," *Chord and Discord*, volume 2, number 6 (1950), 60-65.

Newlin, Dika: "Bruckner's Three Great Masses," *Chord and Discord*, volume 2, number 8 (1958), 3-16.

Brauckmann, Rudolf: "Einige Gedanken über Anton Bruckner sowie praktische Hinweise zur Einstudierung seiner Messe in e-moll," *Musica sacra*, volume 94 (1974), 204-206.

Nowak, Leopold: "Foreword" to *Messe e-Moll, Anton Bruckner Gesamtausgabe*, volume 17, part 1. Vienna: Musikwissenschaftlicher Verlag, 1977.

Berger, Melvin: *Guide to Choral Masterpieces: A Listener's Guide*, 98-100. New York: Anchor Books, 1993.

Mass No. 3 in F minor "The Great," WAB 28 (1867-1868)

Duration: ca. 60 minutes

Text: The text is from the Roman Catholic communion liturgy.

Performing Forces: voices: soprano, alto, tenor, and bass soloists; SATB choir; **orchestra:** 2 flutes, 2 oboes, 2 clarinets (B^b), 2 bassoons, 2 horns (F), 3 trombones (alto, tenor, and bass), organ,[39] and strings.

First Performance: 16 June 1872; St. Augustine's Church, Vienna; conducted by the composer

Editions: *Mass No. 3 in F minor* is published in the critical editions *Anton Bruckner: Sämtliche Werke*, volume 13, edited by Robert Haas, and *Anton Bruckner Gesamtausgabe*, volume 18, edited by Leopold Nowak. It also appears in a study-score published by the Bruckner Gesellschaft, which is published by Musikwissenschaftlicher Verlag and distributed in the United States by C. F. Peters. Editions that are available for purchase include a study score of the critical edition from Musikwissenschaftlicher Verlag.

Autograph: The composer's manuscript is in the Music Collection of the Österreichische Nationalbibliothek in Vienna (S.m. 2105). This collection has additional manuscript materials (S.m. 6015) and a score annotated with expanded scoring by Joseph Schalk (S.m. 19.302).

Notes: Bruckner had the opportunity to hear a performance of this work elaborated by Joseph Schalk. He rejected these changes; however, he made some changes of his own in preparation for various performances over two decades that were not used in the preparation of the Haas edition. The Nowak edition has carefully

---

[39] There are indications for the organ to play in a handful of passages in the Kyrie, but nowhere else. Given the performance tradition of the time and place, a thoroughbass organ part is entirely appropriate if an instrument is available in the performance venue.

rectified any discrepancies and should be the one used for performance.

Performance Issues: The choral material combines homophonic and imitative textures. There are divisi in all parts. A number of choral passages are unaccompanied. These are all clearly and logically prepared by previous choral material or the preceding accompaniment. Much of the accompaniment provides a harmonic framework for the vocal parts, but there is little direct doubling. The choir must be strong and musically independent. Some sections of this composition are fairly demanding vocally requiring sustained and powerful singing and broad vocal ranges for the choristers. The string parts are quite challenging throughout the mass with some intricate passagework. This includes a violin solo in the Kyrie that is exposed and technically demanding. The wind parts have some rapid chromatic passagework as well. The brass scoring is rich in color and should provide no balance problems, although experienced and sensitive players are advisable. The size of the orchestration allows the use of a medium-sized choral ensemble, which given the contrapuntal complexities would be preferable to a symphonic group. The solos are not overly challenging, but the score suggests the use of an independent solo quartet. **Soloists:** soprano - range: b-b$^{b''}$, tessitura: f'-f'', this is a lyric solo with some sustained passages; alto - range: b-f'', tessitura: d'-d'', this is a sustained solo best suited to a mezzo-soprano voice; tenor - range: d#-a'', tessitura: f-f', this is a lyric solo; bass - range: G-f', tessitura: c-d', this is a declamatory solo with some sustained singing; **choir:** difficult; **orchestra:** difficult.

Selected Discography

Maria Stadter, Claudia Hellman Ernst Haefliger, Kim Borg; Anton Nowakowski, organ; Bavarian Radio Chorus and Orchestra; conducted by Eugen Jochum, recoded in July 1967 in the Herkules Saal, Residenz, Munich. Re-released on CD as Deutsche Grammophon: 423 127 2.

Heather Harper, Anna Reynolds, Robert Tear, Marius Rintzler; New Philharmonia Chorus and Orchestra; conducted by Daniel Barenboim. EMI: 0724358550825.

Juliet Booth, Jean Rigby, John Mark Ainsley, Gwynne Howell; Corydon Singers and Orchestra; conducted by Matthew Best; recorded February 1992. Hyperion: CDA66650.

Selected Bibliography

Zentner, Wilhelm: *Anton Bruckner: Messe in f-moll.* Munich: Schnell and Steiner, 1948.

Newlin, Dika: "Bruckner's Three Great Masses," *Chord and Discord,* volume 2, number 8 (1958), 3-16.

Nowak, Leopold: "Foreword" to *Messe F-Moll, Anton Bruckner Gesamtausgabe,* volume 18. Vienna: Musikwissenschaftlicher Verlag, 1960.

Sullivan, Cornelius Fancis: *The D minor and F minor Masses of Anton Bruckner as the Culmination of the Viennese Classical Mass Tradition.* Columbia University: dissertation, 1972.

Te Deum, WAB 45 (1881)

Duration: ca. 22 minutes

Text: This is an anonymous hymn of thanksgiving in church use since the sixth century. It is usually sung during the Matins service. The apocryphal source of its genesis is that it was spontaneously sung by Ss. Ambrose and Augustine on the evening when Augustine was baptized.[40]

Performing Forces: voices: soprano, alto, tenor, and bass soloists; SATB choir; **orchestra:** 2 flutes, 2 oboes, 2 clarinets (A), 2 bassoons, 4 horns (F), 3 trumpets (F), 3 trombones (alto, tenor, and bass), tuba, timpani, organ,[41] and strings.

---

[40] Jeffers, Ron: *Translations and Annotations of Choral Repertoire, Volume I: Sacred Latin Texts,* 218. Corvallis, OR: Earthsongs, 1988.

[41] Some resources list the organ as optional, but that is not indicated in the critical score. It is the supposition of the editorial committee that this indication in earlier editions was to increase the number of likely performances. It should be noted that the organ part is well doubled by the winds.

First Performance: With two pianos: 2 May 1885; Vienna; Mrs. Ulrich-Linde, Emilie Zips, Richard Exleben, Heinrich Gassner; Wiener Akademischer Richard Wager Verein Choir; Robert Erben and Josef Schalk, pianists; conducted by the composer

With orchestra: 10 January 1886; Vienna; Gesellschaft der Musikfreunde; conducted by Hans Richter

Editions: *Te Deum* is published in the critical edition *Anton Bruckner Gesamtausgabe*, volume 19, edited by Leopold Nowak. A full score and parts are also available from C. F. Peters.

Autograph: The composer's manuscript is in the Music Collection of the Österreichische Nationalbibliothek in Vienna (Cod. 19.486). Additional sketches are in the archive of the Monastery in Kremsmünster.

Notes: This score was one of Bruckner's most successful; during his own lifetime it was performed around the world. The score is organized as follows:

1. Te Deum — soloists and choir
2. Te ergo — solo quartet
3. Aeterna fac — soloists and choir
4. Salvum fac — soloists and choir
5. In te Domine speravi — soloists and choir

Performance Issues: There are divisi in each choral part, and all of the parts require vocally strong singers. The choral writing is homophonic and in close imitation. Some of the harmonic language is more progressive than the contrapuntal procedures would suggest, which may require extra attention in the preparation of the choir. The orchestration is full and powerful, which demands a large symphonic choir and full string complement. While much of the choral material is clearly doubled by the orchestra, there are passages that are a cappella or sparsely accompanied. The orchestra writing is straightforward and practical. There is a significant amount of ostinato usage in the strings. The brass and winds must be capable of full sustained playing for extended passages. Some of these may prove troublesome for intonation. There is a florid violin solo in movement 2. **Soloists:** soprano - range: c'-a'', tessitura: f′-f″, this is a sustained lyric role; alto - range: a-c″, tessitura: c′-g′, this is a sustained solo; tenor - range: d^b-b$^{b\prime}$, tessitura: g-g′, this is a dramatic solo role; bass - range: F-c′, tessitura: B^b-b^b, this is a declamatory solo; **choir:** difficult; **orchestra:** medium difficult.

Selected Discography

Anneliese Kupper, Ruth Siewert, Lorenz Fehenberger, Kim Borg; Bavarian Radio Orchestra and Chorus; conducted by Eugen Jochum, recorded in 1954, re-released on CD as Orfeo d'Or: 195892.

Leontyne Price, Fritz Wunderlich, Walter Berry; Singverein der Gesellschaft der Musikfreunde; Vienna Philharmonic Orchestra; conducted by Herbert von Karajan. EMI: 0724356688025.

Maria Stadter, Sieglinde Wagner, Ernst Haefliger, Peter Lagger; Bavarian Radio Chorus, Berlin German Opera Chorus; Berlin Philharmonic; conducted by Eugen Jochum. Deutsche Grammophon: 457743-2.

Joan Rodgers, Catherine Wyn-Rogers, Alastair Miles; James O'Donnell, organ; Corydon Singers and Orchestra; conducted by Matthew Best, recorded 5-7 February 1993. Hyperion: CDA66650.

Anne Pashley, Birgit Finnila, Robert Tear, Don Garrard; New Philharmonia Chorus and Orchestra; conducted by Daniel Barenboim. EMI: 0724358550825.

Margaret Price, Christel Borchers, Karl Helm, Elmar Schloter; Munich Bach Choir, Munich Philharmonic Orchestra and Chorus; conducted by Sergiu Celibidache. EMI: 0724355669520.

Pamela Coburn, Ingeborg Danz, Christian Elsner, Franz-Joseph Selig; Gächinger Kantorei; Stuttgart Bach Collegium; conducted by Helmut Rilling. Hänssler: CD 98.119.

Selected Bibliography

Engel, Gabriel: "The Grand Te Deum," *Chord and Discord*, volume 1, number 7 (1935), 9-10.

Newlin, Dika: "Bruckner's Te Deum," *Chord and Discord*, volume 2, number 8 (1958), 71-75.

Nowak, Leopold: "Foreword" to the critical edition. Vienna: Musikwissenschaftlicher Verlag, 1962.

Pahlen, Kurt: *The World of the Oratorio*, translated by Judith Schaefer with additional English-language material by Thurston Dox, 95-97. Portland, OR: Amadeus Press, 1990.

Berger, Melvin: *Guide to Choral Masterpieces: A Listener's Guide*, 100-101. New York: Anchor Books, 1993.

Psalm 150, WAB 38 (1892)

Duration: ca. 9 minutes

Text: The text is from the Book of Psalms in the Bible.

Performing Forces: voices: soprano soloist; SATB choir; **orchestra:** 2 flutes, 2 oboes, 2 clarinets (B^b), 2 bassoons, 4 horns (F), 3 trumpets (F), 3 trombones, tuba, timpani (2 drums), and strings.

First Performance: 15 November 1892; Geselleschaft der Musikfreunde, Vienna; conducted by Wilhelm Gericke

Editions: *Psalm 150* is published in the critical edition *Anton Bruckner Gesamtausgabe*, volume 20/6, edited by F. Grasberger. It also appears in a study-score published by the Bruckner-Gesellschaft, which is published by Musikwissenschaftlicher Verlag and distributed in the United States by C. F. Peters. Editions that are available for purchase include: Musikwissenschaftlicher Verlag.

Autograph: The composer's manuscript is in the Music Collection of the Österreichische Nationalbibliothek in Vienna (Mus. H 19.484).

Notes: This work was originally composed for a music festival planned for 1892 in Vienna that did not come to fruition. It was fortunately performed later in the year as listed above.

Performance Issues: There are significant unison passages for the choir and orchestra. There are also frequent iterations of a double-dotted rhythmic figure that will require attention. This is a bombastic score that requires a large choir and full complement of strings. There are a number of a cappella passages throughout the work to give balance to the powerful wind and brass sections. The part writing is exquisite. The choral parts are vocally challenging with broad ranges in all parts and wide melodic leaps throughout. There are two-part divisi for the alto and sopranos and three-part divisi in each of the men's parts. The tessitura of the soprano part is fairly high. The orchestration is brilliant and full, but there may be challenges to balance within the orchestra and between the instruments and the singers. There are some intricate and exposed passages for the flutes. The brass and string parts will likewise require seasoned players. This would be a fine complement to Holst's *Hymn to Jesus*. **Soloists:** soprano - range: e'-b'', tessitura: g'-g'', this is a brief lyric role with some chromaticisms, the orchestration is very light when accompanying this soloist; **choir:** difficult **orchestra:** difficult.

Selected Discography

Maria Stadter, Sieglinde Wagner, Ernst Haefliger, Peter Lagger; Bavarian Radio Chorus, Berlin German Opera Chorus; Berlin Philharmonic; conducted by Eugen Jochum. Deutsche Grammophon: 457743-2.
Bamberg Symphony Orchestra and chorus; conducted by Karl Anton Rickenbacher. Virgin Classics: 5615012.
Pamela Coburn, Ingeborg Danz, Christian Elsner, Franz-Joseph Selig; Gächinger Kantorei; Stuttgart Bach Collegium; conducted by Helmut Rilling. Hänssler: CD 98.119.

Selected Bibliography

Graf, Max: "Bruckners 150. Psalm," *Neues Wiener Journal* (21 January 1901).
Botstiber, Hugo: *Anton Bruckner, der 150. Psalm: Erläuert*. Berlin: Schlesinger, 1907.
Berger, Melvin: *Guide to Choral Masterpieces: A Listener's Guide*, 102-103. New York: Anchor Books, 1993.

Helgoland, WAB 71 (1893)

Duration: ca. 14 minutes

Text: The text is by August Silberstein.

A Conductor's Guide to 19th-Century Choral-Orchestra Works 139

Performing Forces: voices: TTBB choir; **orchestra:** 2 flutes, 2 oboes, 2 clarinets (B^b), 2 bassoons, 4 horns (B^b basso, F), 3 trumpets (F), 3 trombones (alto, tenor, and bass), tuba, timpani (2 drums), percussion (1 player — cymbals), and strings.

First Performance: 8 October 1893; Vienna; Wiener Männergesang-Verein and Vienna Philharmonic, conducted by Eduard Kremser on the event of the choir's 50th anniversary

Editions: *Helgoland* is published in a critical edition by the Bruckner-Gesellschaft, volume 22, part 2, which is published by Musikwissenschaftlicher Verlag and distributed in the United States by C. F. Peters. Editions that are available for purchase include: Musikwissenschaftlicher Verlag, Bärenreiter, and Universal Edition.

Autograph: The composer's manuscript is in the Music Collection of the Österreichische Nationalbibliothek in Vienna (Mus. H 19.485).

Notes: This is Bruckner's last completed composition.

Performance Issues: The choral writing is almost entirely homophonic. Because of this, the tessitura of the tenor I part remains narrow and high, which may prove problematic for endurance. There are some extended soli passages for tenor I that could be effectively assigned to a soloist and provide some rest to the section. The work is musically accessible for the singers, but may prove too vocally demanding for most ensembles. Mature voices are needed. The score of this work requires a large men's choir and a full string section. The instrumental writing is fairly conservative and should be within the abilities of most players. This work would make an excellent complement to Brahms's *Alto Rhapsody*; **choir:** difficult; **orchestra:** medium difficult.

Selected Discography

Berlin Radio Chorus; Berlin Philharmonic; conducted by Daniel Barenboim. Warner Classics: 2564-61891-2.

Selected Bibliography

Nowak, Leopold: "Foreword" to the critical edition. Vienna: Musikwissenschaftlicher Verlag, 1987.

Cherubini, Luigi (b. Florence, 14 September 1760; d. Paris, 15 March 1842)

Life: Cherubini was a prolific composer. He produced 30 operas, 14 masses, 14 cantatas, and a number of orchestral works. He spent time in London as a young man and was greatly affected by the Gluck operas he saw there. Moving to Paris in 1788, he began producing works in that style. When Napoleonic France became too heated for him, he visited Vienna, where he is said to have exerted significant influence upon Beethoven, especially in the composition of *Fidelio*.

Cherubini returned to France at the request of the French throne. He joined the faculty of the Paris Conservatory in 1816 and served as its director from 1821 to 1841. In 1841, he was the first musician to be made a Commander of the Légion d'honneur.

Teachers: Bizarri, Castrucci, Alessandro Felici, Bartolomeo Felici, Giuseppe Sarti

Students: Pierre Baillot, César Franck, Fromental Halévy, Aimé-Ambroise-Simon Leborne, Pierre-Joseph-Guillaume Zimmerman

Writings: *A Treatise on Counterpoint and Fugue* (originally published in Paris in 1833, translated into English by Mary Cowden Clarke, revised by Joseph Bennett). London: Novello and Ewer, 1884.

Other Principal Works: opera: *Armida* (1782), *Médée* (1797), *Deux Journées* (1800), *Anacréon* (1803), *Les Abencérages* (1813); **orchestral:** Symphony in D major (1815); **choral:** Requiem in D minor (1811), Requiem in C minor (1816), Coronation Mass in A major (1825).

Selected Composer Bibliography

Bellasis, Edward: *Cherubini: Memorials Illustrative of His Life and Work*. Birmingham: Cornish Brothers Limited, 1912; reprinted, New York: Da Capo Press, 1971.

Requiem Mass in D minor (1836)

Duration: ca. 35 minutes[42]

Text: The text is from the Roman Catholic liturgy of the Mass for the Dead.

Performing Forces: voices: TTB choir; **orchestra:** piccolo, flute, 2 oboes, 2 clarinets, 2 bassoons, 4 horns (F, D), 2 trumpets (D), 3 trombones, timpani and strings.

First Performance: 25 March 1838; Société des Concerts, Paris

Editions: Full scores for Requiem Mass in D minor are available for purchase from C. F. Peters (EP 2005) and Kalmus. Eulenberg publishes a study score of the Peters edition. Parts are available for rental from Peters and for sale or rent from Kalmus.

Autograph: The location of the composer's manuscript is unknown.

Notes: A lesser-known Requiem in D minor was composed in 1811. It is for mixed voices. This led to the originial title of "Deuxième Requiem." Cherubini was inspired to compose this work, which he intended to be for his own funeral, upon the death of the composer Boieldieu in 1834 for whose funeral Cherubini's C Minor Requiem was performed. That event provoked complaints from the Archbishop over the participation of women in the service. The work was performed for the composer's funeral four years after its premiere.[43]

Performance Issues: There are divisi in all of the choral parts. Most of the choral writing is homophonic. Polyphonic writing is in close imitation, and although these passages are not always conspicuously doubled, there is significant harmonic and melodic support of all choral parts by the orchestra. The exception to this is in the

---

[42] This duration is indicated in the score and appears accurate; however, a variety of sources give durations ranging from 45 to 52 minutes.

[43] Rudolf Lück: "Foreword" to *Requiem für Männerchor und Orchester*, edited by Rudolf Lück. London: Ernst Eulenberg, n.d.

"Pie Jesu" in which virtually all the choral passages are unaccompanied. The tessitura of the tenor I part is quite high, remaining within a compass of a perfect fifth for (c'-g') for extended periods of time. An odd feature of this score is the placement of the bassoons between the trumpets and trombones. The orchestral writing is idiomatic and colorful. There are exposed passages for all principal players, but the score as a whole would work well for a good college or amateur ensemble. The significant brass writing will require player with some stamina and control. The scoring of the tutti passages suggests the use of a large string section and a sizeable choir; **choir:** medium difficult, **orchestra:** medium difficult.

Selected Discography

Czech Philharmonic Orchestra, Prague Philharmonic Chorus; conducted by Igor Markevitch; Supraphon: SU3429-2.

Selected Bibliography

Lück, Rudolf: "Foreword" to *Requiem für Männerchor und Orchester*, edited by Rudolf Lück. London: Ernst Eulenberg, n.d.

Pahlen, Kurt: *The World of the Oratorio*, translated by Judith Schaefer with additional English-language material by Thurston Dox, 108. Portland, OR: Amadeus Press, 1990.

Coleridge-Taylor, Samuel (b. London, 15 August 1875; d. Croydon, England, 1 September 1912)

Life: Coleridge-Taylor was a prominent and very successful black English composer whose father had been born in Sierra Leone. He studied at the Royal College of Music in London and later taught violin at the Royal Academy of Music and composition at Trinity College in London and the Guildhall School.

Coleridge-Taylor's music is tuneful and highly refined in a distinctively Edwardian style. He is best remembered today for his *Song of Hiawatha* trilogy.

Teacher: Charles Villiers Stanford

Other Principal Works: opera: *Thelma* (1909); **orchestral:** Symphony in A minor (1896), *Idyll* (1901), *Symphonic Variations on an African Air* (1906), *Bamboula* (1910), Violin Concerto (1911).

Selected Composer Bibliography

Coleridge-Taylor, Jessie Fleetwood: *A Memory Sketch or Personal Reminiscences of My Husband: Genius and Musician S. Coleridge-Taylor.* London: Bobby and Co., 1912.
Thompson, Jewel Taylor: *Samuels Coleridge-Taylor: The Development of His Compositional Style.* Metuchen, NJ: Scarecrow Press, 1994.
Self, Geoffrey: *The "Hiawatha Man."* Aldershot: Scolar Press, 1995.
Tortolano, William: *Samuel Coleridge-Taylor: Anglo-Black Composer, 1875-1912*, second edition. Lanham, MD: Scarecrow Press, 2002.

The Song of Hiawatha (1898-1900)

Text: Henry Wadsworth Longfellow.

Notes: This oratorio comprises three works, which were composed independently, and can each be performed as a freestanding composition. The proper nouns used by Longfellow have traditional pronunciations that may not be evident to a newcomer to the text. Care should be taken to become familiar with these names prior to the first rehearsal. Each is described independently below.

I. Hiawatha's Wedding Feast (1898)
1. Chorus: You shall hear how Pau-Puk-Keewis
2. Chorus: Then shall the handsome Pau-Puk-Keewis
3. Chorus: He was dress'd in shirt of doe-skin
4. Chorus: First he danc'd a solemn measure
5. Chorus: Then said they to Chibiabos
6. Tenor Solo: Onaway! Awake, beloved!
7. Chorus: Thus the gentle Chibiabos
8. Chorus: Very boastful was Iagoo
9. Chorus: Such was Hiawatha's Wedding

Duration: ca. 34 minutes

Performing Forces: voices: soprano, tenor, and baritone soloists, SATB choir; **orchestra:** piccolo, 2 flutes, 2 oboes, 2 clarinets (A), 2 bassoons, 4 horns (F), 2 trumpets (F), 3 trombones, tuba, percussion (2 players: triangle, cymbals, and bass drum), timpani, harp, and strings.

II. The Death of Minnehaha (1899)

10. Chorus: Oh, the long and dreary winter
11. Chorus: Into Hiawatha's wigwam
12. Baritone Solo: And the foremost said, 'Behold me!'
13. Soprano Solo: And the other said, 'Behold me!'
14. Chorus: And the lovely Minnehaha
15. Chorus: Forth into the empty forest
16. Baritone Solo: Gitchie Manito, the Mighty!
17. Chorus: Into the wigwam with Nokomis
18. Soprano Solo: Hark! She said, I hear a rushing
19. Soprano Solo: Wahonomin! Wahonomin!
20. Baritone Solo: Wahonomin! Wahonomin!
21. Chorus: And he rush'd into the wigwam
22. Soprano Solo: Then he sat down, still and speechless
23. Chorus: Then they buried Minnehaha
24. Baritone Solo and Chorus: Farewell! said he, Minnehaha

Duration: ca. 37 minutes

Performing Forces: voices: soprano, tenor, and baritone soloists, SATB choir; **orchestra:** piccolo, 2 flutes, 2 oboes, 2 clarinets (A),

2 bassoons, 4 horns (F), 2 trumpets (F), 3 trombones, tuba, percussion (2 players — triangle, cymbals, and bass drum), timpani, harp, and strings.

III. The Departure of Hiawatha (1900)

25. Soprano Solo: Spring had come with all its splendour
26. Chorus: From his wand'rings far to Eastward
27. Tenor Solo: He had seen, he said, a water
28. Chorus: Only Hiawatha laughed not
29. Baritone Solo: True is all Iagoo tells us
30. Chorus: By the shore of Gitche Gumee
31. Soprano Solo: From the brow of Hiawatha
32. Chorus: It was neither goose nor diver
33. Baritone Solo: Beautiful is the sun, O strangers
34. Tenor Solo and Chorus: And the Black-Robe chief made answer
35. Chorus: Then the generous Hiawatha
36. Tenor Solo: Then the Black-Robe chief, the prophet
37. Male Chorus: And the chiefs made answer, saying
38. Chorus: Then they rose up and departed
39. Baritone Solo: I am going, O Nokomis
40. Chorus: Forth into the village went he
41. Baritone Solo: I am going, O my people
42. Chorus: On the shore stood Hiawatha

Duration: ca. 48 minutes

Performing Forces: voices: soprano, tenor, and baritone soloists, SATB choir; **orchestra:** piccolo, 2 flutes, 2 oboes, 2 clarinets (A), 2 bassoons, 4 horns in F, 2 trumpets in F, 3 trombones, tuba, percussion (2 players: triangle, cymbals, and bass drum), timpani, harp, organ (optional), and strings.

Editions: Full scores and parts these three works are published by Edwin F. Kalmus.

Performance Issues: The choral writing is conservative and lyrical allowing for the use of a large, but marginally experienced ensemble. The choral parts are well supported by the orchestra. The orchestral writing is rich, but none of the individual parts is particularly challenging. If an amateur ensemble is used, some issues of balance between the choir and orchestra may require additional attention, as the delicacy of the writing may not be patently obvious to inexperienced players. The organ part is entirely optional and its absence does not require the playing of any cues in the winds. **Soloists:** soprano - range: f#'-a'', tessitura: b'-g'', this is a lyric solo reuiring a fairly strong voice; tenor - range: g#-g#' (b'), tessitura: b-g#', this is a declamatory solo with the bracketed pitch offered as an optional high note; baritone - range: B-f', tessitura: e-e', this is a lyric solo reuiring a flexible a strong singer; **choir:** medium easy, **orchestra:** medium difficult.

Selected Discography

Helen Field, Arthur Davies, Bryn Terfel; Chorus of the Welsh National Opera (Andrew Greenwood, chorusmaster), Orchestra of the Welsh National Opera; conducted by Kenneth Alwyn, recorded in Brabgwyn Hall, Swansea, Wales, January 1990. Argo: CD 430 356-2.

Bibliography

Self, Geoffrey: *The "Hiawatha Man,"* 69-108. Aldershot: Scolar Press, 1995.
Tortolano, William: *Samuel Coleridge-Taylor: Anglo-Black Composer, 1875-1912*, second edition, 17-39. Lanham, MD: Scarecrow Press, 2002

Delibes, Léo (b. St.-Germain-du-Val, 21 February 1836; d. Paris, 16 January 1891)

Life: Delibes received early musical training from his mother and uncle. He then studied organ and composition at the Paris Conservatory. In 1853 was appointed organist at St. Pierre de Chaillot and became an accompanist at the Théâtre-Lyriques. Three years later his first operetta was produced at the Folies-Nouvelle. He became a prolific composer of operettas, ballets, and opera.

Delibes possessed a great lyric gift and an innate elegance, which has led a number of his melodies to gain virtual universal recognition.

Teachers: Adolphe Adam

Students: Emile Jaques-Dalcroze

Other Principal Works: opera: *Lakmé* (1883); **ballet:** *Coppélia* (1870), *Sylvia* (1876); **songs:** *Les filles de Cadiz.*

Selected Composer Bibliography

Curzon, Henri de: *Léo Delibe: Sa vie et ses œuvres.* Paris: Legouix, 1926.
Studwell, W., editor: *Adolphe Adam and Léo Delibes: A Guide to Research.* New York: Garland, 1987.

Messe Brève (n.d.)

Duration: ca. 20 minutes

Text: The text is from the Roman Catholic communion liturgy.

Performing Forces: voices: SA choir; **orchestra:** strings and organ.

Editions: Full scores (30/1196R), piano-vocal scores (30/1150R), and parts (30/1197R) for *Messe Brève* are available from Roger Dean Music as edited by Dan Krunnfuss.

Performance Issues: The organ part is optional. It merely reinforces pitch material in the choir and strings. All of the choral material is clearly double by the orchestra. This is a homophonic and declamatory work for the singers. The voicing is appropriate for women's choir or children's choir. The score is simple enough for the use of solo strings; **choir:** easy; **orchestra:** easy.

Selected Discography

At the time of this writing, no recordings were available.

Selected Bibliography

Curzon, Henri de: *Léo Delibe: Sa vie et ses œuvres*, 213. Paris: Legouix, 1926.

Dvorák, Antonin (b. Mühlhausen, Czechslovakia, 8 September 1841; d. Prague, 1 May 1904)

Life: Dvorak was the son of a butcher. He developed as a young violinist and was sent to the Organ School in Prague where he studied with the school's director and began to compose prolifically. He eventually left the school to play viola, eventually becoming a member of the orchestra of the Prague National Theater. In 1874, he won the Austrian State Prize for his Symphony No. 3. He would win the prize two more times in 1877. One of the judges was Brahms who introduced him to his publisher, Simrock.

Dvorak's works were championed by the leading conductors and soloists of the time, including Joachim, Richter, and von Bülow. He made nine trips to England to conduct performances of his works. In 1892, Dvorak was invited to serve as the director of the National Conservatory of Music in New York, which would later become the Juilliard School, a post he held for three years. During his American sojourn, Dvorak summered in a part of Iowa with a large Bohemian population. It is believed that it was here that he encountered the African-American folktune that became the celebrated melody of the slow movement of hie New World Symphony. He published an article, "Music in America," in *Harper's New Monthly Magazine* (February 1895) that encourages composers to utilize the rich folk and popular musical resources that he found so fertile.

Dvorak's music is an intriguing amalgamation of style including formal and rhythmic elements of Brahms, harmonic principles of Wagner, with a significant tincture of Czech folkmusic.

Teachers: Joseh Krejci, Karel Pitsch

Students: Rubin Goldmark, Rudolf Karel, Vitezslav Novák, Alois Reiser, Josef Suk

Other Principal Works: opera: *Rusalka* (1900); **orchestral:** Symphony No. 1 (1865), Symphony No. 2 (1865), Symphony No. 3 (1873), Symphony No. 4 (1874), Symphony No. 5 (1875), Symphony No. 6 (1880), Symphony No. 7 (1884-1885), Symphony No. 8 (1889), Symphony No. 9 (1893), Piano Concerto (1876),

A Conductor's Guide to 19th-Century Choral-Orchestra Works   151

Violin Concerto (1879-1880), Cello Concerto (1894-1895), *Slavonic Dances*, op. 46 (1878), *Slavonic Dances*, op. 72 (1886-1887), *Carnival Overture* (1891-1892); **chamber music:** "Dumky" Trio (1890-1891), Piano Quintet, op. 81 (1882).

Selected Composer Bibliography

Stefan, Paul: *Anton Dvorak*, translated by Y. W. Vance. New York: Greystone Press, 1941.
Robertson, Alec: *Dvorak*. New York: Pellegrini and Cudahy, 1949.
Burghauser, Jarmil: *Antonin Dvorak: Thematic Catalogue*. Prague: Artia, 1960.
Clapham, John: *Dvorak*. New York: W. W. Norton, 1979.
Schönzeler, Hans-Hubert: *Dvorak*. London: Marion Boyars, 1984.

Stabat Mater, op. 58, B. 71 (1876-1877)

Duration: ca. 90 minutes

Text: The authorship of this text is highly disputed. It has been attributed to Jacopone da Todi who died in 1306. It was removed from sanctioned use at the Council of Trent, and restored to the liturgical canon in 1727. The text addresses the "Seven Sorrows of the Virgin Mary." It is used as the Sequence Hymn on the first Friday after Passion Sunday and on 15 September.[44]

Performing Forces: voices: soprano, alto, tenor, and bass soloists; SATB choir; **orchestra:** 2 flutes, 2 oboes, English horn, 2 clarinets, 2 bassoons, 4 horns (F, D), 2 trumpets (D), 3 trombones, tuba, timpani, organ (or harmonium), and strings.

First Performance: 23 Devember 1880; Society of Musicians in Prague; Eleonora Ehrenberg, Betty Fibich, Antonín Vávra, and Karel Cech, soloists; choir and orchestra of the Czech Provisional Theatre; conducted by Adolf Cech. A second performance was given on 2 April 1882, conducted by Leos Janácek.

---

[44] Jeffers, Ron: *Translations and Annotations of Choral Repertoire, Volume I: Sacred Latin Texts*, 200-207. Corvallis, OR: Earthsongs, 1988.

Editions: *Stabat Mater* is published in a critical edition as part of *Antonin Dvorak: Complete Edition*, series 2, volume 1. Prague: Artia, 1961. A new critical edition, edited by Otakar Sourek was published by Editio Bärenreiter Praha in 2004, for which a study score (H 2268) is available. It was first published in1881 by Simrock and soon appeared in English translation as a Novello publication.

Autograph: The composer's manuscript is in the Music Department of the National Museum in Prague (sign. 834/52).

Notes: Like a number of Dvorak's compositions, this work has been assigned two different numbers. It was first composed as op. 28, but later published as op. 58. The work was begun in response to the death of the composer's daughter, Josefa (21 September 1875); before it was completed two others passed away, Ruzena (13 August 1877) and Otakar (13 November 1877).

Performance Issues: This is a very dramatic work that demands a seasoned and vocally athletic choir and a skilled and cohesive orchestra. The choral writing is generally syllabic, and although there is a fair amount of imitative counterpoint, the parts are conceived in a chorale-like fashion. The vocal writing is primarily diatonic. Many of the chromatic elements provide a "Czech" quality to the music. The orchestra doubles most of the choral parts, and the remaining passages are well supported harmonically by the accompaniment. There are occasional divisi in the choral parts, and the voices are asked to produce a broad and quickly changing dynamic palette. The sixth movement is written for tenor soloist and four-part men's choir, which includes some closely voiced melismatic writing for the choristers that will need attention to guarantee harmonic clarity. The final movement has very dramatic and sustained eight-part choral writing. This movement will test the endurance of less experienced ensembles. The orchestral writing is expressive, and the orchestration is colorful. Some balances in the piano passage in the winds may present challenges for less sophisticated ensembles. The wind writing suggests a full string section and large choir. Operatic soloists will be needed to properly balance with the orchestra. **Soloists:** soprano - range: f#'-b'', tessitura: a'-f#'', this is a declamatory role that must be capable of a full diversity of dynamics at the top of the range; alto - range: a-f'', tessitura: f'-d'', this is a sustained mezzo-soprano role with significant melismatic writing that is sometimes in unison with the soprano and should therefore have a contrasting, but compatible timbre; tenor - range: e^b-a′, tessitura: a-f#′, this is a sustained role requiring a strong voice; bass - range: E-f#′, tessitura: c-c′, this singer must have clear projection at the bottom of the indicated range; **choir:** difficult; **orchestra:** difficult.

Selected Discography

Marina Shaguch, Ingeborg Danz, James Taylor, Thomas Quasthoff; Oregon Bach Festival Chorus and Orchestra; conducted by Helmut Rilling, recorded in July 1995. Hänssler Classic: 98935.

Stefania Woytowicz, Vera Soukupová, Ivo Žídek, Kim Berg; Prague Philharmonic Choir, Czech Philharmonic Orchestra; conducted by Václav Smetácek. Supraphon: SU3775-2.

Selected Bibliography

Upton, George: *The Standard Oratorios*, 92-95. Chicago: A. C. McClurg and Company, 1893.

Pahlen, Kurt: *The World of the Oratorio*, translated by Judith Schaefer with additional English-language material by Thurston Dox, 118-119. Portland, OR: Amadeus Press, 1990.

Berger, Melvin: *Guide to Choral Masterpieces: A Listener's Guide*, 112-113. New York: Anchor Books, 1993.

Sourek, Otakar: "Preface" and "Editor's Notes" for *Dvorak: Stabat Mater* (H 2268). Prague: Editio Bärenreiter Praha, 2004.

Psalm 149, op. 79, B. 91 (1879); revised as B. 154 (1887)

Duration: ca. 10 minutes

Text: The text is from the Book of Psalms in the Bible. It was premiered in Czech, but is available with singing translations in many languages.

Performing Forces: voices: SATB choir; **orchestra:** 2 flutes, 2 oboes, 2 clarinets (C), 2 bassoons, 4 horns (C, F), 2 trumpets (C), 3 trombones, tuba, timpani (2 drums), and strings.

First Performance:

Version 1: 16 March 1879; Sophia Island; Prague Hlahol Vocal Society, conducted by Karel Knittl.

Version 2: 16 November 1890; Olomouc; conducted by the composer at the Jubilee Concert of the Zerotin Vocal Society

Editions: *Psalm 149* is published in a critical edition as part of *Antonin Dvorak: Complete Edition*, series 2, volume 6. Prague: Artia, 1968. This edition includes a complete score of both versions.

Autograph: The composer's manuscript is in the Music Department of the National Museum in Prague (846/52).

Notes: This work was composed for Hlahol, a Czech chorus that served as an early proponent of Czech culture. It was initially written for men's choir, but was later rewritten for mixed choir. It is this latter version that was originally published by Simrock.

Performance Issues: In addition to voicing changes, the SATB version has a number of textual and rhythmic deviations from the TTBB, but the general performance issues remain the same. Either version would make an effective concert work. The score includes singing texts in Czech, German, and English. The choral writing is generally homophonic and syllabic. There is one brief fugal section. All of the vocal material is clearly doubled by the orchestra, and none of the parts is vocally demanding. The scoring requires a large choir and full string section. The trombone I and II parts are written in alto clef, but appear to be intended for tenor trombones. There are sudden dramatic shifts in dynamics, and there are passages wherein the ensemble must be powerful to be effective. The string writing has some challenging figures, but they are idiomatically conceived, and should play well; **choir:** medium easy; **orchestra:** medium difficult.

A Conductor's Guide to 19th-Century Choral-Orchestra Works   155

Selected Discography

Christine Brewer, Marietta Simpson, John Aler, Ding Gao; Washington Orchestra and Chorus; conducted by Robert Shafer. Naxos: 8.555301-02.

Selected Bibliography

Burghauser, Jarmil: "Editors' Notes" for *Dvorak: Psalm 149* in *Antonin Dvorak: Complete Edition*, series 2, volume 6, vi-vii and unnumbered pages at the end, translated into English by R. F. Samsour. Prague: Artia, 1968.

Pahlen, Kurt: *The World of the Oratorio*, translated by Judith Schaefer with additional English-language material by Thurston Dox, 119. Portland, OR: Amadeus Press, 1990.

Svatební kosile ["The Spectre's Bride"], op. 69, B. 135 (1884)

Duration: ca. 85 minutes

Text: The text is from *Garland of Folk Poesy* [Kytice z povestí národích] by Karel Jaromír Erben

Performing Forces: voices: soprano (Maiden), tenor (Spectre), and bass (Narrator) soloists; SATB choir; **orchestra:** 2 flutes (flute II doubling piccolo), 2 oboes, English horn, 2 clarinets (A, B♭), bass clarinet (B♭), 2 bassoons, 4 horns (B♭ basso, D, E♭, E, F), 2 trumpets (C, D, E, F), 3 trombones, tuba, timpani (2 drums), percussion (3 players — triangle, tam, tam, chimes [e′, a′, e″, g#″]),[45] harp, and strings.

First Performance: 28 March 1885; Plzen; Royal and Imperial 35th Regimental Band, local singers and instrumentalists and students from the Realgymnasium; conducted by the composer [46]

---

[45] The instrument list calls for all four pitches, but only e′, a′, and e″ appear in the score.

[46] The score's premiere was originally intended for a music festival in Birmingham, England, where it was performed in August 1885 in English.

Editions: *Svatební košile* is published in a critical edition as part of *Antonin Dvorak: Complete Edition*, series 2, volume 6. Prague: Artia, 1969. A piano-vocal score arranged by Heinrich von Káan with and English singing translation by Troutbeck was published by Novello, Ewer, and Co.

Autograph: The sketches and manuscript of the full score were in the collection of the Dvorak family at the time of the creation of the critical edition and thematic catalogue.

Notes: The score is organized as follows:

1. Chorus: The stroke of midnight soon will sound
2. Soprano solo: Where Art Thou, Father?
3. Bass and Tenor soli and Chorus: The picture on a sudden moves
4. Soprano and Tenor duet: Ah, dearest child, how is't with thee?
5. Bass solo and Chorus: Nature was clad in gloom
6. Bass solo and Chorus: And on he went, with rapid gait
7. Soprano and Tenor duet: Fair is the night
8. Bass solo and Chorus: He grips the book
9. Bass solo and Chorus: Out of caverns under ground
10. Soprano and Tenor duet: Fair is the night
11. Baritone solo and Chorus: The pathway now less rugged grows
12. Soprano and Tenor duet: Now, when the night so fair doth show
13. Bass solo and Chorus: There stood a pile
14. Recitative: Soprano and Tenor and Chorus: See now, my sweet-heart
15. Baritone solo and Chorus: He leapt the wall
16. Bass solo and Chorus: And at the door there came a knock
17. Soprano solo: O Virgin-Mother, gracious be
18. Bass solo and Chorus: There crew a cock

Performance Issues: The score includes singing texts in Czech, German, and English. The choral writing is generally homophonic and syllabic. It is not vocally difficult. The choral material is clearly doubled by the orchestra. There are divisi throughout the choir, except for the altos. Movement 15 asks for a small group of basses singing in the distance. There are challenging passages throughout

A Conductor's Guide to 19th-Century Choral-Orchestra Works   157

the orchestra, including exposed solo figures for the principal winds. There is also an extended solo for the flute II in movement 12. There are some very difficult passages for the horns. The trombone I and II parts are written in alto clef, but appear to be intended for tenor trombones. The text must be very clearly delivered to guarantee the appropriate effect. Presenting this work in the language of the audience is advised. The score includes a wide variety of scoring and articulations. It is a very melodramatic presentation of the text that needs to me performed stylishly. This is an excellent work for a large community choir and professional orchestra. This gothic folktale in verse provides an intriguing secular drama for the concert hall. It would actually be a great adult Halloween program. **Soloists:** soprano - range: c'-$a^{b''}$ ($b^{b''}$), tessitura: f'-f'', this is a dramatic solo with some rapid coloratura figures; tenor - range: $c\#$-a', tessitura: f-f', this is a sustained lyric role; bass - range: A-$g^{b'}$, tessitura: e^b-$e^{b'}$, this is a declamatory solo for a baritone or lyric bass; **choir:** medium easy; **orchestra:** difficult.

Selected Discography

Drahomíra Tikalová, Beno Blachut, Ladislav Mráz; Czech Philharmonic Orchestra and Chorus; conducted by Jaroslav Krombholc. Supraphon: DV 5792-93 [LP].

Selected Bibliography

Upton, George P.: *The Standard Cantatas*, seventh edition, 136-139. Chicago: A. C. McClurg and Company, 1899.
Berkovec, Jírí: "Editors' Notes" for *Dvorak Svatební kosile* in *Antonin Dvorak: Complete Edition*, series 2, volume 2, vii-viii, translated into English by R. F. Samsour. Prague: Artia, 1969.
Philippi, Daniela: *Antonín Dvorak: Die Geisterbraut/Svatební kosile op. 69 – Die heilige Ludmilla/Svatá Ludmila op. 71, Studien zur "großen Vokalform" im 19 Jahrhundert*. Tutzing: Hans Schneider, 1993.

Svata Ludmila [St. Ludmila], op. 71, B. 144 (1885-1886)

Duration: ca. 120 minutes

Text: The text is by the Czech poet, Jaroslav Vrchlicky. The premiere was given in English, and singing translations have since been made in many languages. The critical edition includes text underlay in Czech, English, and German.

Performing Forces: voices: soprano (Ludmila), alto (Svatava and young countryman), tenor (Borivoj), and bass (Ivan) soloists; SATB choir; **orchestra:** 2 flutes, 2 oboes, English horn, 2 clarinets (A, B^b), bass clarinet (A, B^b), 2 bassoons, contrabassoon, 4 horns (B^b basso, C, D, E^b, E, F, B^b), 3 trumpets (B^b, C, E^b, E, F), 3 trombones,[47] tuba, timpani (2 drums), percussion (1 player — triangle), harp, organ, and strings.

First Performance: 15 October 1886; Leeds, England; conducted by the composer

Editions: *Svata Ludmila* is published in a critical edition as part of *Antonin Dvorak: Complete Edition*, series 2, volume 3. Prague: Artia, 1964.

Autograph: The composer's manuscript of the full score was in the collection of the Dvorak family at the time of the creation of the critical edition and thematic catalogue.

Notes: The score is dedicated to the Zerotin Musical Society of Olomouc. The text presents the medieval Bohemian legend of St. Ludmila (the grandmother of St. Wenceslas). The three sections of the work address Ludmila's conversion, the conversion of her husband, Prince Boriwoj I, and the baptism of the couple and their followers.

---

[47] The composer indicates that the trombone III part is for bass trombone. It seems clear that parts I and II are intended for tenor trombone, but the parts in the critical edition are in alto clef.

A Conductor's Guide to 19th-Century Choral-Orchestra Works   159

Performance Issues: The choral writing is primarily homophonic and the choral material is clearly supported by the orchestra. There are divisi in all choral parts. There are some important passages for the choral basses that are below the staff. Most of the vocal material is syllabic and quite declamatory. The choral ranges are varied enough to avoid fatigue. There are some sections that use two choirs for which physical division is not necessary, but could be effective. The instrumental writing is informed and practical. There are a number of exposed solo passages for the winds, and some of the string writing provides some technical challenges, but should not present any obstacle for a successful performance. The organ and harp parts are minimal and easy. The bass clarinet appears in only two movements, but it appears simultaneously with the two clarinets, necessitating an independent player. Other wind players are unoccupied at those times, so a doubler could be navigated. There are some powerfully orchestrated passages that will require a large, mature choir. The recording made in conjunction with the critical edition had the part of the young man sung by a boy. In the score, it is assigned to the alto soloist. This is a well-crafted work with attractive tunes that is rarely performed outside the Czech Republic. The relevance of St. Ludmila beyond Eastern Europe may contribute to this neglect. The length of the work may also be a prohibition; however, it is an excellent choice for a single-work concert. **Soloists:** soprano - range: d'-b", tessitura: f'-f", this is a lyric solo with some coloratura and long phrases; alto - range: b-g", tessitura: f'-f", this role combines declamatory and lyric material, there are many ossia pitches that allow singers to shift the tessitura down; tenor - range: d-a', tessitura: g-g', this is a sustained lyric role; bass - range: G-e', tessitura: B-d', this is a powerful declamatory role; **choir:** medium difficult; **orchestra:** medium difficult.

Selected Discography

Eva Zikmundová, Vera Soukupová, Beno Blachut, Richard Novák, Vladimir Krejcik; Bohemian Choir (Josef Veselka, choirmaster), Prague Symphony Orchestra; conducted by Vaclav Smetácek. Supraphon: DV 6064-66 [LP], re-released on CD.
Livia Àghová, Michelle Breedt, Piotr Beczala, Ludek Vele; Prague Chamber Choir. Cologne WDR Radio Choir and Symphony Orchestra; conducted by Gerd Albrecht. WDR: 513992.

Selected Bibliography

Sychra, Antonin: "Editors' Notes" for *Dvorak: Svata Ludmila* in *Antonin Dvorak: Complete Edition*, series 2, volume 3, part 2, 722-727, translated into English by John Clapham. Prague: Artia, 1964.
Philippi, Daniela: *Antonín Dvorak: Die Geisterbraut/Svatební kosile op. 69 — Die heilige Ludmilla/Svatá Ludmila op. 71, Studien zur "großen Vokalform" im 19 Jahrhundert*. Tutzing: Hans Schneider, 1993.

Requiem Mass, op. 89, B. 165 (1890)

Duration: ca. 95 minutes

Text: The text is from the Roman Catholic liturgy of the Mass for the Dead.

Performing Forces: voices: soprano, alto, tenor, and bass soloists, SATB choir; **orchestra:** piccolo, 2 flutes, 2 oboes, English horn, 2 clarinets (A, B^b), bass clarinet (A, B^b), 2 bassoons, contrabassoon, 4 horns[48] (D, F), 4 trumpets (B^b, D, E^b, F), 3 trombones, tuba, timpani (3 drums), percussion (1 player — tam-tam), organ, and strings.

First Performance: 9 October 1891; Birmingham, England; conducted by the composer

Editions: *Requiem* is published in a critical edition as part of *Antonin Dvorak: Complete Edition*, series 2, volume 4. Prague: Artia, 1961. Full scores and parts are available for purchase from: Bärenreiter, Kalmus, and Supraphon.

Autograph: The composer's manuscript of the full score was in the collection of the Dvorak family at the time of the creation of the critical edition and thematic catalogue.

---

[48] Some sources list a fifth horn part, but it is not in the score.

Notes: The score was begun on New Year's Day in 1890, the sketches were completed in July, and the full score was finished 31 October. The work is in two large sections organized as follows:

Part I

Requiem aeternam	SATB soli and choir
Graduale	S solo and choir
Dies Irae	choir
Tuba mirum	ATB soli and choir
Quid sum miser	SATB soli and choir
Recordare, Pie Jesu	SATB soli
Confutatis maledictus	choir
Lacrimosa	SATB soli and choir

Part II

Offertorium	SATB soli and choir
Hostias	SATB soli and choir
Sanctus	SATB soli and choir
Pie Jesu	SATB soli and men's choir
Agnus Dei	SATB soli and choir

Performance Issues: The choral writing is generally syllabic and homophonic. There are some extended passages of unison singing for the choir. The choral material is well supported by the accompaniment with some interspersed a cappella passages. There are divisi in all choral sections, and some passages are labeled "coro piccolo." Dvorak creates some very effective textural contrasts between the solo quartet and the choir. Placement of the soloists will be important to keep these layers clear. There are some challenging figures for all of the winds often in unison combinations, and some of the string material is quite challenging, but written from a string-player's perspective. The organ part is brief and primarily sustained pedals. There are some horn figures in the "Offertorium" that are wholly impractical and will be deemed unplayable by some hornists. Dvorak indicates that the tam-tam can be replaced with a bell, which may have a better effect. This is a complicated score that explores a wide array of textures and voicings. It is a distinctive setting of this text that will be very dramatic when presented by the best ensembles. **Soloists:** soprano - range: c'-b'', tessitura: f'-f'', this is a lyric solo; alto - range: a-e'', tessitura: e'-c'', this is a sustained and declamatory mezzo-soprano solo; tenor -

range: d-a', tessitura: g-g', this is a lyric solo with very long phrases; bass - range: G-e', tessitura: c-c', this is a lyric role; **choir:** difficult; **orchestra:** very difficult.

Selected Discography

Pilar Lorengar, Erzebet Komlossy, Robert Ilosfalvy, Tom Krause; Ambrosian Singers (John McCarthy, choirmaster), London Symphony Orchestra; conducted by István Kertész. Decca: 028946868722.

Selected Bibliography

Burghauser, Jarmil: "Editors' Notes" for *Dvorak: Requiem* in *Antonin Dvorak: Complete Edition*, series 2, volume 4, ix-xii and unnumbered pages at the end, translated into English by R. F. Samsour. Prague: Artia, 1961.

Robertson, Alec: *Requiem: Music of Mourning and Consolation*, 110-116. New York: Frederick A. Praeger, 1967.

Pahlen, Kurt: *The World of the Oratorio*, translated by Judith Schaefer with additional English-language material by Thurston Dox, 117-118. Portland, OR: Amadeus Press, 1990.

Berger, Melvin: *Guide to Choral Masterpieces: A Listener's Guide*, 114-115. New York: Anchor Books, 1993.

Te Deum, op. 103, B. 176 (1892)

Duration: ca. 22 minutes

Text: This is an anonymous hymn of thanksgiving in church use since the sixth century. It is usually sung during the Matins service. The apocryphal source of its genesis is that it was spontaneously sung by Ss. Ambrose and Augustine on the evening when Augustine was baptized.[49]

Performing Forces: voices: soprano and bass soloists; SATB choir; **orchestra:** 2 flutes, 2 oboes, English horn, 2 clarinets (A, B^b), 2 bassoons, 4 horns (F), 2 trumpets (F), 3 trombones, tuba, timpani

---

[49] Jeffers, Ron: *Translations and Annotations of Choral Repertoire, Volume I: Sacred Latin Texts*, 218. Corvallis, OR: Earthsongs, 1988.

(2 drums), percussion (3 players — bass drum, triangle, cymbals), and strings

First Performance: 21 October 1892; New York Music Hall; conducted by the composer. This was Dvorak's first independent concert upon arriving in New York to head the National Conservatory.

Editions: *Te Deum* is published in a critical edition as part of *Antonin Dvorak: Complete Edition*, series 2, volume 6. Prague: Artia, 1969. Full scores and parts for *Te Deum* are available for purchase from Bärenreiter, Kalmus, Simrock, and Supraphon.

Autograph: The sketches and manuscript of the full score were in the collection of the Dvorak family at the time of the creation of the critical edition and thematic catalogue.

Notes: Jeanette Thurber, the founder of the National Conservatory, had contacted Dvorak about writing a choral work in celebration of the 400th anniversary of Columbus's voyages, which he could conduct upon his arrival in New York as director of the new school. Dvorak set the *Te Deum* in anticipation of this concert; however, Mrs. Thurber sent him the text for *The American Flag* shortly before he sailed for the United States, giving him inadequate time to compose and displacing the *Te Deum* to another concert.

Performance Issues: The choral writing of the first movement maintains significant rhythmic independence between the parts giving a sense of imitative counterpoint without actual imitation. There are significant passages with differing text declamation or the presentation of multiple passages of the text occurring simultaneously, which will require special attention to guarantee clarity in performance. The remaining movements are homophonic or unison passages. The choral writing is not vocally demanding, but requires a fairly musically savvy ensemble. There are intricate sections for all of the winds, including exposed passages for the pricipal players. The horn parts are quite difficult. The brass writing overall is fairly heavy. The trombone I and II parts are written in alto clef, but appear to be intended for tenor trombones. This is combined with some pervasive percussion parts necessitating a large choral group. The premiere featured 250 singers. This is a flashy and effective setting that has a real Czech flavor. **Soloists:**

soprano - range: f'-b'', tessitura: a'-g'', this is a sustained lyric solo; bass - range: c-g$^{b\prime}$, tessitura: e^b-e$^{b\prime}$, this is a sustained and declamatory solo; **choir:** medium difficult; **orchestra:** medium difficult.

Selected Discography

Czech Philharmonic Chorus and Orchestra; conducted by Vaclav Neumann. Supraphon: 111961-2.

Pamela Coburn; Gächinger Kantorei Stuttgart, Bach-Collegium Stuttgart; conducted by Helmuth Rilling. Hänssler: CD98421.

Selected Bibliography

Bartos, Frantisek: "Editors' Notes" for *Dvorak: Te Deum* in *Antonin Dvorak: Complete Edition*, series 2, volume 6, vi-vii and unnumbered pages at the end, translated into English by R. F. Samsour. Prague: Artia, 1969.

Pahlen, Kurt: *The World of the Oratorio*, translated by Judith Schaefer with additional English-language material by Thurston Dox, 120-121. Portland, OR: Amadeus Press, 1990.

Elgar, Edward (b. Lower Broadheath, Worcester, 2 June 1857; d. Worcester, 23 February 1934).

Life: As a youth, Elgar worked in his father's music store and served as assistant organist to his father at St. George's, Worcester. He played violin in a number of regional orchestras some of which he also conducted. He began to establish a national reputation as a composer with a number of works for the Three Choirs Festival in Worcester. His first triumph in London was the debut of the *Enigma Variations* (1899). This was followed by the oratorio *The Dream of Gerontius* (1900), which secured his fame. He is best known for his five *Pomp and Circumstance* Marches (1901-1930), the first of which has virtually become Britain's second national anthem with the addition of the text, "Land of Hope and Glory."[50]

Elgar was knighted in 1904, was made a member of the Order of Merit in 1911. This was followed by the title, Master of the King's Music in 1924 and a baronet in 1931. He also received several honorary doctorates, notably from Cambridge (1900) and Yale (1905). He served as conductor of the London Symphony for the 1911-12 season. After his wife's death he completed few scores.

Elgar's music was surely the finest of Britain's romantic composers. His fame was instantly established by the success of the *Enigma Variations* and the oratorios. His style is one of elegance and regal grandeur. The harmonic language is that of the late 19th century, and Elgar's method of composition is purposefully nonprovincial. Outspoken with regard to the lack of quality English music at the beginning of the 20th century, Elgar strove to adopt the fluid musical style of the continent. One can hear an English quality in his music, but in fact one probably hears a bit of Elgar in all of the English music to follow him. He became the paradigm of the English musical sound.[51] The orchestration is lush and very knowledgeable of instrumental potentials, especially in his string writing, which is frequently challenging but always effective.

---

[50] Michael Kennedy: *Portrait of Elgar*, revised. London: Oxford University Press, 1983.

[51] Jerrold Northrop Moore: *Spirit of England: Edward Elgar in his World*. London: Oxford University Press, 1984.

Other Principal Works: choral-orchestral: *The Black Knight* (1889-1892), *Scenes from the Saga of King Olaf* (1897), *The Banner of St. George* (1897), *The Dream of Gerontius* (1900), *The Apostles* (1903), *The Kingdom* (1901-1906), *The Music Makers* (1902-1912), *The Spirit of England* (1915-1917); **orchestral:** *Variations on an Original Theme* ("Enigma," 1898-1899), *Froissart* (1890), *Cockaigne* (1901), *The Wand of Youth* Suites 1 and 2 (1907), Symphony No. 1 (1907-1908), Symphony No. 2 (1903-1911), *Coronation March* (1911), *Crown of India* (1912), *Pomp and Circumstances Marches* (1901, 1901, 1904, 1907, 1930), Violin Concerto (1909-10), Cello Concerto (1918-1919); many songs and chamber music.

Selected Composer Bibliography

Maine, Basil: *Elgar: His Life and Works*, 2 volumes. Reprint of 1933 edition, New York: AMS Press, (no date given, but still listed in print as of January 1993).
Young, Percy, editor: *Letters of Edward Elgar and Other Writings.* London: Collins, 1956.
Moore, Eleanor Marie: *A Study of the Vocal Works of Sir Edward Elgar.* University of Rochester: Dissertation, 1961.
Redwood, Christopher, editor: *An Elgar Companion.* Ashbourne: Sequoia Publishing, 1982.
Kennedy, Michael: *Portrait of Elgar*, revised. London: Oxford University Press, 1983.
Moore, Jerrold Northrop: *Spirit of England: Edward Elgar in his World.* London: Oxford University Press, 1984.
Philip, Robert: "The recordings of Edward Elgar (1857-1934), authenticity and performance practice," *Early Music*, xii/4 (1984), 481-489.
Willets, Pamela: "The Elgar Sketch-books," *British Library Journal*, xi/1 (1985), 25.
McVeagh, Diana: "Edward Elgar," *The New Grove Twentieth-Century English Masters*, 1-68. New York: W. W. Norton, 1986.
Moore, Jerrold Northrop: *Elgar and His Publishers: Letters of a Creative Life*, 2 volumes. Oxford: Clarendon Press, 1987.
_____: *Edward Elgar: The Windflower Letters, Correspondence with Alice Caroline Stuart Wortley and Her Family.* Oxford: Clarendon Press, 1989.

_____: *Edward Elgar: Letters of a Lifetime.* Oxford: Clarendon Press, 1990.

Reed, William H.: *Elgar as I Knew Him.* Oxford: Oxford University Press, 1989.

Anderson, Robert: *Elgar in Manuscript.* Portland, OR: Timber Press, 1990.

Monk, Raymond, editor: *Elgar Studies.* Aldershot, England: Scolar Press, 1990.

The Light of Life (Lux Christi), op. 29 (1896)

Duration: ca. 65 minutes

Text: The libretto was written by Edward Capel-Cure (1860-1949), based upon the Gospel of John.

Performing Forces: voices: Mother of the Blind Man (soprano), narrator (alto), Blind Man (tenor), Jesus (baritone); SSAATTBBBB choir; **orchestra:** 2 flutes (II doubling piccolo), 2 oboes, 2 clarinets, 2 bassoons, contrabassoon, 4 horns, 2 trumpets, 3 trombones, tuba, timpani (2 drums), percussion (cymbals),[52] harp, organ, and strings.

First Performance: 8 September 1896; Worcester, England; Anna Williams, Jessie King, Edward Lloyd, Watkin Mills, Worcester Three Choirs Festival

Editions: A critical edition and performing materials for *The Light of Life* are published by Novello.

Autograph: The composer's manuscript of the full score and proofs of the vocal score are in the Elgar Birthplace Museum (ms. 103). Additional sketches are in the British Library (add. ms. 47900A).

Notes: The score was commissioned by the Worcester Three Choirs Festival. The score is organized as follows (All of the text is de-

---

[52] The cymbal part is cued in the timpani part and does not require an independent player.

rived from scripture, direct quotes from scripture are indicated parenthetically):

1. Meditaion: orchestra
2. Chorus (Levites) and tenor: Seek Him that maketh the seven stars (*Amos* v.8, *Psalm* cxxxvi. 1, 7-9)
3. Alto recitative and chorus (Disciples): As Jesus passed by
4. Soprano: Be not extreme, O Lord (*St. John* ix. 1-2, Job viii.20)
5. Baritone: Neither hath this man sinned
6. Chorus: Light out of darkness (*St. John* ix.3-5, viii.12)
7. Alto and baritone recitative: And when He had thus spoken
8. Chorus and soprano/alto duet: Doubt not thy Father's care (*St. John* ix.6-7)
9. Contralto and tenor solos and chorus: He went his way therefore
10. Tenor solo: As a spirit didst Thou pass before mine eyes (*St. John* ix.7-10, 32, 11-12; *Isaiah* xxix. 14, 18)
11. Alto recitative and chorus: They brought him to the Pharisees
12. Alto solo: Thou only hast the words of life (*St. John* ix.13-14, 16; *Exodus* xxxi.12-14; *St. John* x.21; ix.17)
13. Soprano, alto, and tenor recitatives and chorus: But the Jews did not believe
14. Soprano solo and chorus of women: Woe to the shepherds of the flock (*St. John* ix.18, 20-21, 24-25, 29-31, 33-34)
15. Alto, tenor and baritone recitatives: Jesus heard that they had cast him out; baritone solo: I am the Good Shepherd (*Ezekiel* xxxiv.35-38; x.14, 10; xvii.11, 17, 24)
16. Chorus: Light of the World, we know Thy praise (*St. John* ix.35-38; x.14, 10; xvii.11, 17, 24)

Performance Issues: The choral writing is vocally conservative, although the bass part has important passages below the staff. All of the choral material is well supported by the accompaniment. A large vocal ensemble is required. The only choral complications are a few brief sections with significant divisi. The composer has indicated that horns III and IV and the contrabassoon parts may be left out. The string parts are the most demanding within the orchestra, but they are well informed by a violinist composer. This is a colorful score that presages the timbral palette of Elgar's later oratorios. The horn I and II parts require control and endurance. Some attention will be required to establish appropriate balances within the orchestra. **Soloists:** soprano - range: c'-$a^{b''}$, tessitura: f'-f'', this is a gentle lyric role; alto - range: a-e'', tessitura: d'-c'', this is a straightforward declamatory role; tenor - range: e-a', tessitura: f-f', this is a lyic solo with sustained passages; bass - range: c-$e^{b'}$ (g'), tessitura: g-d', this is a declamatory role; **choir:** medium easy; **orchestra:** medium difficult.

Selected Discography

Judith Howarth, Linda Finnie, Arthur Davies, John Shirley-Quirk; London Symphony Orchestra and Chorus; conducted by Richard Hickox. Chandos: 9208.

Selected Bibliography

Moore, Jerrold Northrop: *Elgar and His Publishers: Letters of a Creative Life*, 30-39, 69-70, 93-94, 96, 125, 128-130, 136, 138-139, 351, 410, 412-413, 463, 582, 606, 795. Oxford: Clarendon Press, 1987.

Stam, John Campbell: *Four English Music Festivals and Their Influence on the Careers and Selected Major Choral Works of Parry, Stanford, and Elgar*, 115-121. Doctoral dissertation: University of Iowa, 1991.

Caractacus, op. 35 (1898)

Duration: ca. 105 minutes

Text: Harry Acworth wrote the libretto at Elgar's request. It is based upon the legend of the ancient British hero of its title.

Performing Forces: voices: Eigen (soprano), Orbin (tenor), Caractacus (baritone), Arch-Druid (bass), a Bard (bass), and Claudius (bass); SSAATTBB choir; **orchestra:** 2 flues (flute II doubling piccolo), 2 oboes, 2 clarinets, bass clarinet, 2 bassoons, contrabassoon, 4 horns, 4 trumpets, 3 trombones, tuba, timpani (3 drums), percussion (4 players[53] — snare drum, bass drum, triangle, cym-

---

[53] The parts can be navigated with three players, but four are called for.

bals, gong, small gong in E^b, and glockenspiel), harp, organ, and strings.

The score indicates that the bass clarinet, contrabassoon, and trumpet IV are optional. It also states that in Scene VI, additional snare drums may be employed.

First Performance: 1898; Leeds, England; Medora Henson, Edward Lloyd, Andrew Black, Leeds Festival, conducted by the composer

Editions: *Caractacus* is published in a critical edition by Novello, which was prepared by Robert Anderson and Jerrold Northrop Moore in 1985. Earlier editions are also available for purchase or rental from Novello; this includes a set of orchestral parts matching the critical edition, which is available for rental.

Autograph: The manuscript vocal score (Add. MSS. 58000 and 58001), sketches (Add. MS. 47901), and manuscript full score (Add. MS. 58002) are in the British Library. Additional proof score are in the Elgar Birthplace Museum.

Notes: *Caractacus* was commissioned by the Leeds Festival. It is based upon mystical legends of early Britain. is dedicated to Queen Victoria. The score is organized into six scenes. The composer indicates that if an intermission is desired, it should occur after the second scene.

Performance Issues: The choral material is loosely homophonic most of the time. The orchestra provides significant harmonic support for the singers, but they must be somewhat musically independent. There are some divisi for each choral section. All of the choral parts are vocally demanding. The orchestration is brilliant requiring execution of complex figurations from all sections. This work was written for very large choral forces and a sizable string section. The string writing is particularly involved, but the composer's experience as a violinist leads them to be remarkably playable. Great care has been taken to balance the soloists. The instrumental colors are varied and quite effective. Elgar indicates that all of the bass roles may be sung by a single soloist, which is how they are evaluated here; however, he indicates that separate singers are preferred. The stage must be set to allow the choristers to be seated at times. The peculiar subject matter of the text has probably contributed to its current neglect. The lament in scene IV is in 7/4. This is an exceptionally refined composition that may in fact be compelling to contemporary audiences who seem to embrace fantasies of this ilk. Costuming of the soloists may be desirable. **Soloists:** Eigen (soprano) - range: c'-b'', tessitura: f'-f'', this is a dramatic solo role; Orbin (tenor) - range: f#-b$^{b\prime}$, tessitura: g-g', this is a sustained and lyric role; Caractacus (baritone) - range: B^b-g', tessitura: c-e$^{b\prime}$, this is a dramatic role with some very sustained passages; Arch-Druid, Bard, and Claudius (bass) - range: (F) G-e$^{b\prime}$ (f'), tessitura: c-c', this is a declamatory role that would dramatically benefit from three distinct singers; **choir:** difficult; **orchestra:** difficult.

Selected Discography

Judith Howarth, Arthur Davies, David Wilson-Johnson, Alastair Miles, Stephen Roberts; London Symphony Orchestra and Chorus; conducted by Richard Hickox. Chandos: 9156/7.

Selected Bibliography

Moore, Jerrold Northrop: *Elgar and His Publishers: Letters of a Creative Life*, 59-61, 63-67, 70-93, 102-105, 110, 115-116, 119-120, 142, 144-145, 154-155, 160, 171, 187, 318, 399, 450, 513, 531-532, 539, 582, 585, 586, 588, 596, 629-630, 799. Oxford: Clarendon Press, 1987.

Stam, John Campbell: *Four English Music Festivals and Their Influence on the Careers and Selected Major Choral Works of Parry, Stanford, and Elgar*, 121-127. Doctoral dissertation: University of Iowa, 1991.

Fauré, Gabriel (b. Palmiers, Ariège, France, 12 May 1845; d. Paris, 4 November 1924)

Life: Fauré's father, a school inspector, recognized his son's musical talent and took him to Paris where he studied at the École Niedermeyer and then with Saint-Saëns. He held a number of organ positions, and in 1874 he was appointed deputy organist to Saint-Saëns at the church of the Madeleine, succeeding his teacher as principal organist in 1896. That same year, he became professor of composition at the Paris Conservatory. In 1905, he was named director, a post he held with distinction until his retirement in 1920.

Fauré is widely regarded as one of the great teachers of composition. He is a cusp composer, serving as a bridge from the generation of Franck and Saint-Saëns to that of Debussy and Ravel. His music is a unique blending of church modes with the spirit and harmonies of the impressionists. The *Requiem*, *Pelléas et Mélisande Suite*, *Pavane*, and many of the songs have become staples of the repertoire. His chamber music is of equally high quality.

Teachers: Louis Niedermeyer, Camille Saint-Saëns

Students: Nadia Boulanger, Alfredo Casella, Eugene Cools, Georges Enescu, Jacques Ibert, Emile Jaques-Dalcroze, Charles Koechlin, André Messager, Maurice Ravel, Jean Roger-Ducasse, Florent Schmitt

Writings: *Opinions musicales* [a posthumous compilation of his reviews in *Le Figaro*], edited by P.B. Gheusi. Paris: Rieder, 1930.

Other Principal Works: opera: *Prométhée* (1900), *Pénélope* (1913), *Masques et Bergamasques* (divertissement, 1919); **orchestral:** *Pelléas et Mélisande* (incidental music, 1898); **choral:** *Cantique de Jean Racine* (1876), *Messe basse* (1881), *Tantum ergo* (1890), *Salve Regina* (1895), *Ave Maria* (1895); **songs:** *Nell* (1880), *Mandoline* (1891), *Green* (1891), *Clair de Lune* (1892), *La Bonne Chanson* (1892-1893), many others.

Selected Composer Bibliography

Fauré-Fremiet, Philippe: *Gabriel Fauré*. Paris, Les Éditions Rieder, 1929.
Koechlin, Charles: *Gabriel Fauré*, second edition, translated by Leslie Orrey. London: Dennis Dobson Limited, 1946.
Suckling, Norman: *Fauré*. London: J. M. Dent, 1946; reprinted, Greenwood Press, 1979.
Fauré, Gabriel: *Correspondance*, edited by Jean-Michel Nectoux. Paris: Flammarion, 1980.
_____: *A Life in Letters*, translated and edited by J. Barrie Jones. London: B. T. Batsford, 1988.
Nectoux, Jean-Michel: *Gabriel Fauré: A Musical Life*, translated by Roger Nichols. Cambridge: Cambridge University Press, 1991.

Pavane, op. 50 (1887) optional choir

Duration: ca. 7 minutes

Text: The text is by Count R. de Montesquiou.

Performing Forces: voices: SATB choir; **orchestra:** 2 flutes, 2 oboes, 2 clarinets (A), 2 bassoons, 2 horns (F), and strings.

First Performance: 28 April 1888; Paris; Société nationale de musique

Editions: Full scores and parts for *Pavane* are available for purchase from Hamelle et Cie, Broude Brothers, and Kalmus.

Autograph: The composer's manuscript is in the Bibliotheque Nationale in Paris.

Notes: This brief work is probably Fauré's most recognized composition. It is often performed without the choir. The Broude score contains only an English text, which is "freely adapted" by Harold Heilberg.

Performance Issues: The choral material is quite simple and completely supported by the orchestra. There are exposed but simple solos for all of the principal winds. This work is quite effective with a small choir and reduced strings. This is a beautiful and easily prepared secular work that is commonly paired with Fauré's Requiem. It would also be a very effective complement to Brahms's *Nänie*; **choir:** easy; **orchestra:** easy.

Selected Discography

Academy of St. Martin in the Fields; conducted by Neville Marriner. Classics for Pleasure: 85624.
St. Louis Symphony Orchestra; conducted by Leonard Slatkin. Telarc: 60641.
King's College Choir, New Philharmonia Orchestra; conducted by David Willcocks. Recorded in 1967. EMI Classics: 64715.
Montréal Symphony Orchestra and Chorus; conducted by Charles Dutoit. Recorded in 1987. London: 421440.

Selected Bibliography

Fauré, Gabriel: *A Life in Letters*, translated and edited by J. Barrie Jones, 98, 100-101, 110, 131, 174, 178-181. London: B. T. Batsford, 1988.
Nectoux, Jean-Michel: *Gabriel Fauré: A Musical Life*, translated by Roger Nichols, 34, 108-109, 172, 256, 258, 260, 275, 339, 394-395, 485, 509-512, 515, 520, 540, 556. Cambridge: Cambridge University Press, 1991.

Messe de Requiem, op. 48 (1886-1887, 1889, 1900)

Duration: ca. 39 minutes

Text: The text is from the Roman Catholic liturgy of the Mass for the Dead.

Performing Forces: voices: soprano and baritone soloists; SATB choir; **orchestra:** *Version 1 (1887):* solo violin, 2 horns, 2 trumpets, harp, organ, timpani, and strings (without violins)

Version 2 (1900): 2 flutes, 2 clarinets, 2 bassoons, 4 horns, 2 trumpets, 3 trombones, timpani, 2 harps, organ, and strings.

First Performance: *Version 1:* 16 January 1888, Church of the Madeleine, Paris; conducted by the composer

Version 2: 28 January 1892; Church of St. Gervais, Paris; Louis Aubert, Louis Ballard, Société Nationale

Editions: Full scores and parts for *Requiem* are available for purchase from Lucks and in a critical edition produced by Hamelle. All materials for the chamber-orchestra version (edited by John Rutter) are available for purchase from Hinshaw. This edition comes with single string parts for which duplication permission is granted.

Autograph: No manuscript of the final symphonic version exists in the archives of either the composer or publisher, which has led Jean-Michel Nectoux to suggest the possibility that this arrangement may have been executed by Fauré's student, Roger Ducasse, who is known to have produced the piano-vocal reduction asdsociated with that edition.[54]

Notes: Version 1 of this work was scored for a minimal orchestra and contained only five movements. Two years after its premiere, Fauré added two movements on texts from the Office of the Dead and expanded the orchestration, which resulted in version 2. In preparation for publication in 1900 an even larger instrumental contingent was employed to satisfy the publisher. This is sometimes referred to as "version 3," but is generally recognized as a revision of version 2, which may or may not reflect the composer's final intentions. Until recently, the larger orchestration appeared only in editions with considerable errors in both the score and parts, but a good edition is now available. The Hinshaw edition utilizes the scoring of the original five-movement work for which the editor, John Rutter, has provided a corresponding orchestration of the movements added in 1889. A subsequent reconstruction has been produced by Roger Delage for the Herreweghe recording listed below.

This work present an individual set of texts as chosen by the composer. The score is organized as follows:

---

[54] Liner notes for "Fauré Requiem, version 1893" Harmonia Mundi: CD HMC 901292.

1. Introit and Kyrie — choir
2. Offertory — baritone solo and choir
3. Sanctus — choir
4. Pie Jesu — soprano solo
5. Agnus Dei — choir
6. Libera me — baritone solo and choir
7. In paradisum — choir

Performance Issues: The choral material is generally homophonic, and although there are some very cosmopolitan harmonies for the singers, traditional part-writing procedures and careful preparation of these events, they pose little challenge even to inexperienced choirs. The choir is clearly supported by the orchestra throughout the score. None of the choral parts presents significant vocal challenges to the singers. The scoring, especially in the chamber-orchestra version, accommodates the use of a small choir. These smaller orchestrations seem to best represent the spirit of the work and also appear to reflect the legitimate intention of the composer were he free of the influence of his publisher. The orchestral parts are all conservatively conceived and practically written so that less experienced players will find them quite accessible. The two horn parts require the most assuredness from the players, but even these are quite practical. Some thought should be applied to the choices of registration for the organ to best complement the orchestration of each movement. **Soloists:** soprano - range: $e^{b'}$-f'', tessitura: f'-f'', this is a simple lyric solo appropriate for a child soloist; baritone - range: d-d', tessitura: d-d', this is a sustained and lyrical solo; **choir:** medium easy; **orchestra:** medium easy.

Selected Discography: Agnès Mellon, Peter Kooy; La Chapelle Royale, Ensemble Musique Oblique; conducted by Philippe Herreweghe. Harmonia Mundi: HMC 901292 or as SACD: HMC 801292.

Selected Bibliography

Robertson, Alec: *Requiem: Music of Mourning and Consolation*, 117-122. New York: Frederick A. Praeger, 1967.

A Life in Letters, translated and edited by J. Barrie Jones, 9, 63, 103, 120-121, 193, 202. London: B. T. Batsford, 1988.

Pahlen, Kurt: *The World of the Oratorio*, translated by Judith Schaefer with additional English-language material by Thurston Dox, 127-128. Portland, OR: Amadeus Press, 1990.

Nectoux, Jean-Michel: *Gabriel Fauré: A Musical Life*, translated by Roger Nichols, 109, 116-124, 127, 167, 175, 177, 258, 260, 271, 301, 428-429, 434, 458, 467, 470, 492, 509-511, 514-515, 517-518, 524, 533, 540-541. Cambridge: Cambridge University Press, 1991.

Berger, Melvin: *Guide to Choral Masterpieces: A Listener's Guide*, 121-124. New York: Anchor Books, 1993.

Messe des pêcheurs de Villerville (1881-1882), composed with André Messager

Duration: ca. 18 minutes

Text: The text is from the Roman Catholic communion liturgy.

Performing Forces: voices: SSA choir; **orchestra:** flute, oboe, clarinet, harmonium, and strings.

First Performance:

version I: 3 September 1881; Villerville, France; Fauré playing harmonium and Messager conducting

version II: 10 September 1882; Villerville, France; Fauré playing harmonium and Messager conducting

Editions: *Messe des pêcheurs de Villerville* is published by Heugel (HE 33 719) in a critical edition prepared by Jean-Michel Nectoux. A full score and piano-vocal score are available for purchase. Orchestral parts are available on rental through Alphonse Leduc.

Autograph: All manuscript materials are in the Bibliothèque nationale de France. The autograph score of the 1882 version, with movements 1-4 in Messager's hand and movement 5 in Fauré's, is Ms. 20302; the autograph score and parts of the 1881 version is Ms. 20301; and the parts of the 1882 version, in a copyist's hand are Vma. Ms. 1191.

Notes: Fauré and Messager vacationed in the village of Villerville on the Normandy coast. There they chose to collaborate on a mass to be sung by the local women as a fund-raiser for the local fishermen's association. The original version was for violin, harmonium, and women's choir. The following year, the two composers orchestrated the work for a second performance. In 1906, under pressure from his publisher, Fauré adapted his portions of this work into the better known, *Messe basse*, for women's choir and organ. This *Messe des pêcheurs de Villerville* comprises five movements as follows:

I.	Kyrie	Messager
II.	Gloria	Fauré
III.	Sanctus	Fauré
IV.	O Salutaris	Messager
V.	Agnus Dei	Fauré

For the 1882 version examined here, Messager orchestrated movements I-IV, and Fauré orchestrated movement V.

Performance Issues: The choral writing is conservative with stepwise motion. Much of the choral material is in unison, and all of it is well supported by the accompaniment. There are divisi for each section. These are minimal with the exception of movement IV, which is in three-part counterpoint throughout. The string writing is very easy and is in unison between all five parts much of the time. The wind parts are slightly more difficult, but still remain within the ability of most amateur players. This is a charming and simple work that should be accessible to all ensembles; however, it is of a quality that should provide musical rewards to all levels; **choir:** easy; **orchestra:** easy.

Selected Discography

Les Petits Chanteurs de Saint-Louis, Ensemble Musique Oblique; conducted by Philippe Herreweghe. Harmonia Mundi: HMC 901292 or as SACD: HMC 801292.

Selected Bibliography

Nectoux, Jean-Michel: *Gabriel Fauré: A Musical Life*, translated by Roger Nichols, 114-115, 257, 260, 274, 303, 364, 369, 507, 517, 536. Cambridge: Cambridge University Press, 1991.

Nectoux, Jean-Michel: "Foreword," to *Messe des pêcheurs de Villerville*. Paris: Heugel: 2000.

Gounod, Charles François (b. St. Cloud, France, 17 June 1818; d. Paris, 18 October 1893)

Life: Gounod's father was an accomplished painter who died while the composer was a child. He was educated by his mother and at the Lycée St. Louis. While studying at the Paris Conservatory, he won the 2nd Prix de Rome, which provided him the opportunity to study in Italy. There he assiduously studied the music of Palestrina. Upon his return to Paris, he became organist of the Missions Étrangères and began studying in preparation for the priesthood; however, after two years, he chose to pursue a career as a composer.

After a number of less successful premieres at the Opéra, Gounod produced his masterpiece, *Faust*. He spent the years of the Franco-Prussian War (1870-1874) in London where he formed and conducted Gounod's Choir for which he composed a number of works including *Gallia*.

Gounod spent the final decade of his life producing a significant number of large sacred compositions. He is best remembered for the operas *Faust* and *Roméo et Juliette*, which have remained in the core repertoire.

Teachers: Fromental Halévy, Jean François LeSueur, Ferdinando Paër

Students: Henri-Paul Büsser

Other Principal Works: opera: *Faust* (1859), *Mireille* (1864), *Roméo et Juliette* (1867); **orchestral:** Symphony No. 1 (1855), Symphony No. 2 (1855), *Marche funèbre d'une marionette* (1873), *Petite Symphony for Wind Instruments* (1888); **choral:** *Messe solenelle* (1849), *Gallia* (1871), *La Rédemption* (1868-1881), *Messe à Ste. Cécile* (1882), *Mors et Vita* (1885), *Te Deum* (1886), *Messe à Jeanne d'Arc* (1887), *Tantum ergo* (1892).

Selected Composer Bibliography

Prudhomme, J-G and A. Dandelot: *Gounod: Sa vie et ses oeuvres*. Paris: Delagrave, 1911.

Büsser, Henri-Paul: *Charles Gounod.* Lyons: Sud-Est, 1961.

Harding, James: *Gounod.* London: Allen and Unwin, 1973.

Rustman, M.: *Lyric Opera: A Study of the Contributions of Charles Gounod.* University of Kansas: dissertation, 1986.

Requiem (1893)

Duration: ca. 36 minutes

Text: The text is from the Roman Catholic liturgy of the Mass for the Dead.

Performing Forces: voices: soprano, alto, tenor, and bass soloists; SATB choir; **orchestra:** clarinet, bassoon, organ, and strings.

First Performance: Holy Week, 1894

Editions: Full scores and parts for are available from Musica Sacra (#98/1) in an edition prepared by József Ács.

Autograph: The location of the composer's manuscript is unknown.

Notes: The score is dedicated to the memory of the composer's grandson, Maurice Gounod. The composer died before the work was orchestrated. The scoring was completed by the composer's pupil, Henri Büsser. The work is organized as follows:

1. Introitus and Kyrie
2. Dies Irae
3. Sanctus
4. Benedictus
5. Pie Jesu
6. Agnus Dei

Performance Issues: The choral writing is mostly homophonic with some a cappella passages. It is a harmonically conservative work with the vocal parts well supported by the accompaniment. The orchestral parts are very simple, and the work lends itself to performance with solo string players. The work is accessible to amateur players; there is one brief florid passage in the violin I part in the

Dies Irae. This is a toucing and gentle work in memory of a child. **Soloists:** soprano - range: f#'-g'', tessitura: a'-f'', this is a lyric and simple solo; alto - range: b-d'', tessitura: d'-a', this is a brief and lyric solo; tenor - range: f-g', tessitura: a-g', this is a lyric and simple solo; bass - range: d-e$^{b'}$, tessitura: g-d', this is a brief and lyric solo; **choir:** easy; **orchestra:** medium easy.

Selected Discography

Eva Buffoni, Irene Friedli, Ruben Amoretti, Alain Clement; Chroale de Brassus, Sine Nomine String Quartet; conducted by Andre Charlet. Claves: 9326.

Selected Bibliography

Wagener, N: "Die Messen Charles Gounod," in *Kirchenmusikalisches Jahrbuch* (1967), volume 51, 145-153.

Liszt, Franz (b. Raiding, Hungary, 22 October 1811; d. Bayreuth, Germany, 31 July 1886)

Life: Liszt's name has become synonymous with virtuoso. He began concertizing at age nine and was touring internationally three years later. He achieved the 19th-century equivalent of superstardom by the time her reached his early 20s. He lived in Paris from 1823 to 1835. During this time, he established close friendships with Berlioz, Chopin, Paganini, Eugène Délacroix, George Sand, and many other notable figures. He applied to the Paris Conservatory, but was rejected by the director Cherubini because he was a foreigner, so he studied composition privately.

Liszt was a lover of women. He never married, but he did have two long-term relationships, the first with Comtesse Marie d'Agoult who bore him three children, including Cosima who later married Hans von Bülow and then Wagner; and Princess Carolyn Sayn Wittgenstein. He took four minor orders in the Roman Catholic Church and received the tonsure, but was never ordained.

Much of Liszt's piano musc was composed to demonstrate his extraordinary talent as a performer, which has led to an undeserved trivialization of his compositions. He was an innovator of keyboard technique, but never at the expense of musical integrity. He also developed the orchestral tone poem, which began an entire genre of programmatic orchestral music. Many of the harmonic revolutions credited to Wagner are actually foreshadowed in the works of Liszt. As a choral composer, he demonstrates an unusual sensitivity for the voice.

Teachers: Anton Reicha, Antonio Salieri

Students: Conrad Ansorge, Jean Paul Ertel, Salomon Jadassohn, Émile Sauer, Giovanni Sgambati

Writings: *De la fondation Goethe à Weimar.* Leipzig: 1851.
Lohengrin et Tannhäuser de Richard Wagner. Leipzig: 1851.
Frederick Chopin. Paris: 1852.
Des bohemiens et de leur musique en Hongrie. Paris: 1859.
Über John Fields Nocture. Leipzig: 1859.

Robert Schumanns musikalisches Haus- und Lebensregeln. Leipzig: 1860.

Other Principal Works: orchestral: *Les Préludes* (1856), *Mazeppa* (1858), *Hamlet* (1859), *Mephisto Waltz* (1860), *A Faust Symphony* (1853-1861); **choral:** *Psalm 13* (1855), *Hungarian Coronation Mass* (1867), *Psalm 116* (1871), *Missa Choralis* (1886); **piano:** *Années de Pèlerinages* (1848-1861), *Études d'exécution Transcendante* (1866), 20 *Hungarian Rhapsodies* (1851-1886), hundreds of other compositions and transcriptions for piano.

Selected Composer Bibliography

Ramann, Lina: *Franz Liszt als Künstler und Mensch*, 3 volumes. Leipzig: Breitkopf and Härtel, 1880-1894.

Woodward, Ralph: *The Large Sacred Choral Works of Franz Liszt.* Doctoral dissertation: University of Illinois, 1964.

Searle, Humphrey: *The Music of Liszt*, revised edition. New York, Dover Books, 1966.

Raabe, Peter: *Franz Liszt*, revised by Felix Raabe, 2 volumes. Tutzing: Hans Schneider, 1968.

Franz Liszt: The Man and His Music, edited by Alan Walker. New York: Tapplinger, 1970.

Perényi, Eleanor: *Liszt: The Artist as Romantic Hero.* Boston: Little, Brown, 1974.

Gut, Serge: *Franz Liszt: Les éléments du language musical.* Paris: Klincksieck, 1975.

Dömling, Wolfgang: *Franz Liszt und seine Zeit.* Laaber: Laaber-Verlag, 1985.

Merrick, Paul: *Revolution and Religion in the Music of Liszt.* London: Cambridge University Press, 1987.

Brookins, John Barton: *Thematic and Motivic Metamorphosis in the Masses and Oratorios of Franz Liszt.* Doctoral dissertation: Southwestern Baptist Theological Seminary, 1988.

Walker, Alan: *Franz Liszt*, Volume I: *The Virtuoso Years, 1811-1847*; Volume II: *The Weimar Years, 1848-1861*, Volume III: *The Final Years, 1861-1886.* London: MacMillan, and New York: Knopf, 1983, 1989, and 1996.

New Light on Liszt and His Music: Essays in Honor of Alan Walker's 65th Birthday, edited by Michael Saffle and James Deaville. Stuyvesant, NY: Pendragon Press, 1997.

The Liszt Companion, edited by Ben Arnold. Westport, CT: Greenwood Press, 2002.

Saffle, Michael: *Franz Liszt: A Guide to Research*, second edition: New York: Routledge, 2004.

Die Legende von der heiligen Elisabeth, S. 2
(1857-1862)

Duration: ca. 120 minutes

Text: The original German text is by Otto Roquette. K. Abranyi prepared a Hungarian singing translation for the premiere.

Performing Forces: voices: Elisabeth (soprano), Sophie (mezzo-soprano), child Ludwig (alto), tenor, adult Ludwig (baritone), Hungarian Magnate (baritone), Seneschall (baritone), and Hermann (bass) soloists; SATB choir; **orchestra:** 3 flutes, 2 oboes, English horn, 2 clarinets, 2 bassoons, 4 horns, 3 trumpets, 3 trombones, tuba, timpani (3 drums), percussion (2 players: snare drum, cymbals, low bell in E), harp, harmonium or organ, and strings.

First Performance: 15 August 1865; Budapest; the First Hungarian Music Festival, conducted by the composer

First German performance: 24 February 1866; Munich; conducted by Hans von Bülow.

For the 800th anniversary of the Wartburg: 28 August 1867; conducted by the composer.

Editions: A critical edition of *Die Legende von der heiligen Elisabeth* is available in the *Neue-Liszt Ausgabe*, series 16. Full scores and parts are available from Kalmus and C. F. Peters.

Autograph: The location of the autograph score is unknown.

Notes: The oratorio is based upon the story of Princess Elisabeth of Hungary (1207-1231) who was canonized in 1235. The score is dedicated to Ludwig II of Bavaria. Liszt was inpired to compose this work when he was examining the frescoes in the Wartburg Castle that portray the principal events in Elisabeth's life. The score incorporates a number of Hungarian folktunes and the Gregorian chant sung on Elisabeth's name day.

Performance Issues: The choral writing is mostly homophonic with divisi in all parts. The work was clearly intended for a large festival choir and symphonic string section. The significant majority of the vocal material is performed by the soloists of whom Elizabeth and the adult Ludwig have the lion's share. The choral material is sometimes vocally demanding due to range and sustained singing in tutti passages. There are two solo lines in the final movement labeled Bishop of Hungary and Bishop of Germany. These may be performed as soli, or by members of the choir. The child Ludwig solo occurs very near the beginning of the work, so a young singer could exit the stage following his one line. The individual orchestral parts are idiomatic and well within the abilities of a good college ensemble. This work is dramatically conceived with a great variety of textures and rubati that require a strong sense of ensemble playing from the orchestra. **Soloists:** Elisabeth (soprano) - range: d'-a'', tessitura: f'-f'', this is a dramatic and sustained role requiring a strong voice; Sophie (mezzo-soprano) - range: $d^{b'}$-$a^{b''}$, tessitura: f'-f'', this is a lyric role that could also be sung by a soprano; child Ludwig (child alto) - range: f'-d'', tessitura: f'-d'', this is a very brief and simple solo; Kaiser Friedrich (bass) - range: A^b-$e^{b'}$, tessitura: c-c', this is a brief declamatory role; adult "Landgraf" Ludwig (baritone) - range: B^b-$f\#'$, tessitura: d-d', this is declamatory and demanding role; Hungarian Magnate (baritone) - range: d-d', tessitura: f-d', this is a brief declamatory role appropriate for a chorister; Seneschall (baritone) - range: d-$e^{b'}$, tessitura: g^b-$d^{b'}$, this is a simple declamatory role; **choir:** medium difficult, **orchestra:** difficult.

Selected Discography: Éva Andor, Erzsébet Komlóssy, Lajos Miller, György Bordás, József Gregor, Kolos Kovács, Turinic Dusan, Eugenia Kraicírova; Czechoslovak Radio Children's Choir at Bratislava, Slovak Philharmonic Choir and Orchestra; conducted by János Ferencsik. Hungaroton: SLPX 11650-52 [LP].

Éva Marton; Hungarian State Orchestra; conducted by Arpád Joó. Hungaroton: HCD 12694-96-2.

Selected Bibliography

Pohl, Richard: "*Die Legende von der heiligen Elisabeth*," in *Franz Liszt: Studien und Erinnerungen*. Gesammelte Schriften über Musik und Musiker, ii, 331-348. Leipzig: Bernhard Schlicke, 1883. This is a review of an early performance.

Woodward, Ralph: *The Large Sacred Choral Works of Franz Liszt*, 218-252. Doctoral dissertation: University of Illinois, 1964.

Palotai, Michael: *Liszt's Concept of Oratorio as Reflected in his Writings and in "Die Legende von der heiligen Elisabeth."* Doctoral dissertation: University of Southern California, 1977.

Reinisch, Frank: "Liszts Oratorium *Die Legende von der heiligen Elisabeth*—ein Gegenentwurf zu *Tannhäuser* und *Lohengrin*," *Liszt-Studien 3* (1986), 128-151.

Walker, Alan: *Franz Liszt, Volume II: The Weimar Years, 1848-1861*, 153, 278, 283, 297, 351, 513, 552. London: MacMillan, and New York: Knopf, 1989.

Pahlen, Kurt: *The World of the Oratorio*, translated by Judith Schaefer with additional English-language material by Thurston Dox, 206-207. Portland, OR: Amadeus Press, 1990.

Legány, Dezsö: "Liszt in Hungary, 1848-1867," in *New Light on Liszt and His Music: Essays in Honor of Alan Walker's 65th Birthday*, edited by Michael Saffle and James Deaville, 3-15. Stuyvesant, NY: Pendragon Press, 1997.

Smither, Howard E.: *A History of the Oratorio, volume 4: The Oratorio in the Nineteenth and Twentieth Centuries*, 203-226. Chapel Hill, NC: The University of North Carolina Press, 2000.

Saffle, Michael: "Sacred Choral Works," in *The Liszt Companion*, edited by Ben Arnold, 335-363. Westport, CT: Greenwood Press, 2002.

Christus, S. 3 (1855-1872)

Duration: ca. 165 minutes[55]

---

[55] Ralph Woodward indicates approximately 210 minutes in *The Large Sacred Choral Works of Franz Liszt*, 254. Doctoral dissertation: University of Illinois, 1964.

Text: The composer compiled the Latin libretto from the Bible, hymns, and Roman Catholic liturgical texts.

Performing Forces: voices: orchestra: 2 piccolos, 2 flutes, 2 oboes, English horn, 2 clarinets, 2 bassoons, 4 horns, 3 trumpets, 3 trombones, tuba, timpani (4 drums), percussion (2 players: cymbals, bass drum), harp, organ,[56] and strings.

First Performance: 29 May 1873; Protestant State Church, Weimar, Germany; conducted by the composer

The first section was performed by the Vienna Society of Friends of Music in 1871 with Bruckner playing the organ and Anton Rubinstein conducting

Editions: A critical edition of *Christus* is available in the *Neue-Liszt Ausgabe*, series 16. Full scores and parts for *Christus* are available for purchase from Kalmus and C. F. Peters.

Autograph: The autograph score is in the British Museum in London, other manuscripts are in the Stiftung Weimarer Klassik, Goethe-Schiller Archive in Weimar, and the Hungarian National Library in Budapest.

Notes: Portions of this work were composed over a span of about 20 years, but the majority of it was completed between 1866 and 1872. It is a telling of the life of Christ, with the baritone soloist assigned to the titular role, in fourteen scenes divided among three larger sections as follows:

Act One: Christmas Oratorio
1. Introduction
2. Angelus ad Pastores ait
3. Stabat Mater speciosa
4. Hirtengesang an der Krippe (orchestra only)
5. Die heiligen drei Könige—March (orchestra only)

Act Two: After Epiphany

---

[56] The 13th movement indicates a harmonium rather than organ.

A Conductor's Guide to 19th-Century Choral-Orchestra Works   189

   6. Beati paupers spiritu
   7. Pater Noster
   8. Tu es Petrus
   9. Das Wunder; Domine salvanos
   10. Der Einzug in Jerusalem; Hosanna

Act Three: Passion and Ressurection
   11. Tristis est anima mea!
   12. Stabat Mater
   13. O Filii et Filliae
   14. Resurrexit

Performance Issues: Much of the choral material is homophonic with two-part divisi occurring intermittently in all choral sections. This includes numerous unaccompanied six-part chorale passages (with allocation of divisi varying by passage) and extended chant-like passages for unison choir. Little of the choral writing is contrapuntal. All of the accompanied choral parts are harmonically well supported by the orchestra. All of the orchestra writing is conservative and idiomatic. None of the individual parts is difficult, although some brass passages are sustained with moderately high tessituras for the first trumpet and horn parts. This score is easily within the abilities of moderately experienced community and college choirs and orchestras. Despite the presence of 11 brass parts, this work is practical for modest-sized string sections. All of the solos are accessible to strong students and amateurs. The third act is by far the most challenging portion of the work. There are substantial solo-quartet passages in the third act that are more vocally demanding than most of the truly solo passages in the previous two acts. **Soloists:** soprano - range: b′-b♭‴, tessitura: g′-e″, this role has very few exposed passages, but does play a critical part in quartet passages so that a chorister with a strong voice could be suitable; mezzo-soprano - range: b-f″, tessitura: f′-d″, this role has the longest exposed solo writing, it is lyrical; tenor - range: f#-g′, tessitura: a-e′, this role has very few exposed passages, but does play a critical part in quartet passages so that a chorister with a strong voice could be suitable; bass - range: G#-e′, tessitura: f-d′, this is a lyric and sustained solo portraying Christ, the majority of the writing is recitative-like with minimal or no accompaniment; **choir:** medium difficult; **orchestra:** medium difficult.

Selected Discography

Veronika Kincses, Klára Takács, János Nagy, Sándor Sólyom-Nagy, László Polgár; Nyiregyhaza Children's Choir, Hungarian Radio and Television Chorus, Hungarian State Orchestra; conducted by Antal Doráti. Hungaroton: HCD 12831-33-2. Originally released on LP as SLPD 12831-34.

Selected Bibliography

Ramann, Lina: *Franz Liszts Oratorium Christus: Eine Studie als Beitrag zur zeit- und musikgeschichtlichen Stellung desselben mit Notenbeispielen und dem Text des Werke*s, third edition. Leipzig: C. F. Kahnt, 1880.
Upton, George: *The Standard Oratorios*, 186-190. Chicago: A. C. McClurg and Company, 1893.
Woodward, Ralph: *The Large Sacred Choral Works of Franz Liszt*, 253-297. Doctoral dissertation: University of Illinois, 1964.
Orr, Nathaniel Leon: *Liszt's "Christus" and Its Significance for Nineteenth-Century Oratorio*. Doctoral dissertation: University of North Carolina at Chapel Hill, 1979.
Orr, Nathaniel Leon: "Liszt, 'Christus,' and the Transormation of the Oratorio," in *Journal of the American Liszt Society 9* (1981), 4-18.
Riedel, Friedrich W.: "Die Bedeutung des 'Christus' von Franz Liszt in der Geschichte des Messias-Oratoriums," in *Liszt-Studien 2* (1981), 153-162.
Knotik, Cornelia: *Musik und Religion im Zeitalter des Historismus: Franz Liszts Wende zum Oratorienschaffen als aesthetisches Problem*, 38-80. Eisenstadt: Burgenländisches Landesmuseum, 1982.
Niemöller, Klaus Wolfgang: "Das Oratorium 'Christus' von Franz Liszt: Ein Beitrag zu seinen konzeptionellen Grundlagen," in *Beträge zur Geschichte des Oratoriums seit Händel: Festschrift Günther Massenkiel zum 60. Geburtstag*, edited by Rainer Cadenbach and Helmut Loos, 329-342. Bonn-Bad Godesberg: Voggenreiter, 1986,
Wagner, Gottfried: "L'éthique Lisztienne: La notion de 'caritas' dans 'Les béatitudes' du 'Christus' (1862-66)," *Revue musicale*, cdv-cdvii (1987), 119-125.
Walker, Alan: *Franz Liszt, Volume II: The Weimar Years, 1848-1861*, 297, 323. London: MacMillan, and New York: Knopf, 1989.

Pahlen, Kurt: *The World of the Oratorio*, translated by Judith Schaefer with additional English-language material by Thurston Dox, 208-211. Portland, OR: Amadeus Press, 1990.

Hamburger, Klára: "Program and Hungarian Idiom in the Sacred Music of Liszt," in *New Light on Liszt and His Music: Essays in Honor of Alan Walker's 65th Birthday*, edited by Michael Saffle and James Deaville, 239-251. Stuyvesant, NY: Pendragon Press, 1997.

Smither, Howard E.: *A History of the Oratorio, volume 4: The Oratorio in the Nineteenth and Twentieth Centuries*, 226-248. Chapel Hill, NC: The University of North Carolina Press, 2000.

Saffle, Michael: "Sacred Choral Works," in *The Liszt Companion*, edited by Ben Arnold, 335-363. Westport, CT: Greenwood Press, 2002.

Mendelssohn-Bartholdy, Felix (b. Hamburg, Germany, 3 February 1809; d. Leipzig, 4 November 1847)

Life: Mendelssohn's grandfather was the Jewish philosopher, Moses Mendelssohn. The composer's father, Abraham, was a prominent banker, who upon converting to Protestantism, added Bartholdy to the family name. Mendelssohn was a prodigy in music, literature, and painting, and his family's largess allowed him to cultivate these gifts through expert tutelage in piano, violin, and composition and social contacts with Goethe who is said to have developed a close friendship with the boy genius 60 years his junior.

Mendelssohn's influence on the course of western art music cannot be overestimated. In 1829, he conducted the first performance of Bach's *St. Matthew Passion* since the composer's death. This concert and many other efforts on Mendelssohn's part led to the revival of Bach's music, and thereby the beginning of the entire 19th-century movement to collect, study, and publish the music of previous generations. In 1835 he was made music director of the Gewandhaus Orchestra where he established an exceptionally high level of performance.

Mendelssohn was also an educational reformer. As the founding director of the Conservatory in Leipzig, he established pedagogies and a curriculum that have become the model for professional music schools throughout the world.

Mendelssohn was an important figure in the development of romanticism in the generation following Beethoven. His music is highly refined and classically proportioned. His works were also significantly shaped by his study of the works of Bach, whose contrapuntal devices he integrated into his own music. Mendelssohn's large choral works became the model for subsequent nineteenth-century oratorios.

Teachers: Carl Friedrich Zelter

Students: Friedrich Marpurg, Gustav Nottebohm, Carl Reinecke, William Rockstro, August Schäffer, Richard Wüerst

Other Principal Works: orchestral: 12 String Symphonies (1821-1823), Symphony No. 1 (1824), Symphony No. 2 (1840), Symphony No. 3 (1830-1842), Symphony No. 4 (1833), Symphony No. 5 (1830-1832), *Hebrides Overture* (1830), *Die erste Walpurgisnacht* (incidental music, 1831), *A Midsummer Night's Dream* (incidental music, overture 1826, remainder 1843), Violin Concerto in E minor (1844) Piano Concerto No. 1 (1832), Piano Concerto No. 2 (1837); **chamber music:** 2 Piano Trios, 6 String Quartets, 3 Qiano quartets, 2 String Quintets, a String Octet, and many works for solo instruments; piano — Caprissio (1825), Lieder ohne Wörte, 8 books (1834-1843) numerous songs and part-songs.

Selected Composer Bibliography

Letters of Felix Mendelssohn Bartholdy from 1833 to 1847, compiled by Julius Rietz, translated by Lady Wallace. Boston: Oliver Ditson and Co., n.d.

Devrient, Eduard: *My Recollections of Felix Mendelssohn Bartholdy, and His Letters to Me*, translated by Natalia MacFarren. London: Richard Bentley, 1869. Reprinted: New York: Vienna House, 1972.

Polko, Elise: *Reminiscences of Felix Mendelssohn Bartholdy: A Social and Artistic Biography*, translated by Lady Wallace. London: Longmans, Green, and Co., 1869.

Kaufman, Schima: *Mendelssohn: A Second Elijah*. New York: Thomas Y. Crowell Co., 1934.

Petitpierre, Jacques: *The Romance of the Mendelssohns*, translated by G. Micholet-Coté. London: Dennis Dobson, 1947.

Werner, Eric: *Mendelssohn: A New Image of the Composer and His Age*, translated by Dika Newlin. London: Free Press of Glencoe, 1963.

Moshansky, Mozelle: *Mendelssohn: His Life and Times*. Neptune City, NJ: Paganiniana Publications, 1982.

Marek, George R.: *Gentle Genius: The Story of Felix Mendelssohn*. New York: Thomas Y. Crowell Co., 1972.

Todd, R. Larry: *Mendelssohn's Musical Education: A Study and Edition of His Exercises in Composition*. Cambridge: Cambridge University Press, 1983.

Köhler, Karl-Heinz: "Mendelssohn" in *The New Grove Early Romantic Masters 2*, 197-301. New York: W. W. Norton, 1985.

Felix Mendelssohn: A Life in Letters, edited by Rudolf Elvers, translated by Craig Tomlinson. New York: Fromm International, 1986.

Mendelssohn and His World, edited by R. Larry Todd. Princeton, NJ: Princeton University Press, 1991.

Schuhmacher, Gerhard: "Felix Mendelssohn Bartholdys Oratorien-Triptychon," *Musik und Kirche*, lxvii (1997), 247-251.

Cooper, John Michael: *Felix Mendelssohn: A Guide to Research*. New York: Routledge, 2001.

Klein, Hans-Günter: *Felix Mendelssohn Bartholdy: Autographe und Abschriften*. Munich: G. Henle, 2003.

Christus, op. 97 (unfinished)

Duration: ca. 21 minutes

Text: The text is by J. F. von Bunsen, based upon the Gospels of Matthew, Luke, and John, and the book of Numbers.

Performing Forces: voices: soprano, tenor, and 2 bass soloists; SATB choir; **orchestra:** 2 flutes, 2 oboes, 2 clarinets (B^b), 2 bassoons, 2 horns (B^b basso, E^b), 2 trumpets (E^b), 3 trombones (alto, tenor, and bass), timpani (2 drums), and strings.

First Performance: 2 November 1854, Leipzig; first U.S. performance: Boston, 7 May 1874

Editions: *Christus* is published in the critical edition: *F. Mendelssohn-Bartholdy: Werke: kritisch durchgesehene Ausgabe*, edited by Julius Rietz, series: 13, volume: 3. Full scores and parts for fragments of Mendelssohn's unfinished oratorio, *Christus*, have been edited by Larry Todd, and are published by Breitkopf and Härtel and Carus-Verlag (edited by R. Larry Todd, 1994).

The first edition was published by Breitkopf and Härtel in full and piano-vocal score, neither with text in 1852. That same year the London publisher, Ewer, issued a piano-vocal score with English text prepared by William Bartholomew. A companion full score followed in 1860.

Autograph: The composer's manuscript fragment is in the Bibliotheka Jagiellonska in Krakau.

Notes: The title of the work, which was left as a fragment of a larger planned oratorio, was applied posthumously by Mendelssohn's friend Ignaz Moscheles. As published in the Rietz edition, it is organized as follows:

1. Da Jesus geboren ward — soprano recitative
2. Wo ist der neugeborne König der Juden? — TBB trio
3. Es wird ein Stern aus Jacob aufgehn — choir
4. Und der ganze Haufe — choir and tenor recitatives
5. Er nimmt auf seinen Rücken — TTBB chorale

Movement 3 incorporates the hymn tune, "Wie schön leuchtet der Morgenstern," which was composed by Philip Nicolai in 1599. It is used in Bach cantatas 1, 36, 37, 49, 61, and 172. Any of these would make an interesting advent-concert pairing with this work if only the first three movements are used.

Performance Issues: The choral writing is primarily syllabic, and it is well set for the voices. The score alternates homophonic passages with fairly complex imitative counterpoint. Most of the vocal material is clearly doubled by the orchestra. It is otherwise harmonically well supported. The instrumental parts are conservatively written and are idiomatic throughout the orchestra. There are two cello parts in movement 2. The string writing is the most challenging, and it is within the ability of most amateur orchestras. This work contains some lovely music, but the lack of textual continuity makes it problematic in concert performance. In some ways the individual movements are more programmable than the whole work. **Soloists:** soprano - range: f#'-d'', tessitura: f#'-d'', this is a brief and simple recitative; tenor - range: f-a', tessitura: g-g', this is a lyric role; bass I - range: d-e', tessitura: f#-d', this is a lyric role that appears only in a brief trio; bass II - range: G-d', tessitura: B-c', this is a lyric role that appears only in a brief trio; **choir:** medium difficult; **orchestra:** medium easy.

Selected Discography

Christoph Pregardien, Johannes Happel, Cornelius Hauptmann; Stuttgart Chamber Choir; Bamberg Symphony Orchestra; conducted by Frieder Bernius. Carus-Verlag: 83.105/00.

Selected Bibliography

Upton, George: *The Standard Oratorios*, 229-233. Chicago: A. C. McClurg and Company, 1893.

Kaufman, Schima: *Mendelssohn: A Second Elijah*, 305. New York: Thomas Y. Crowell Co., 1934.

Köhler, Karl-Heinz: "Mendelssohn" in *The New Grove Early Romantic Masters 2*, 231. New York: W. W. Norton, 1985.

Pahlen, Kurt: *The World of the Oratorio*, translated by Judith Schaefer with additional English-language material by Thurston Dox, 239-240. Portland, OR: Amadeus Press, 1990.

Elijah, op. 70 (1846)

Duration: ca. 131 minutes

Text: The text, based upon *I Kings*, xvii-xix, was written for this work by Julius Schubring. The singing English translation was prepared by William Bartholomew.

Performing Forces: voices: Widow (soprano), Young Boy (soprano), Angel (alto), Ahab (tenor), Obadiah (tenor), Elijah (baritone); Angel trio (SSA), double quartet, SATB choir; **orchestra:** 2 flutes, 2 oboes, 2 clarinets (C, B^b, A), 4 horns (C, D, E^b, E, F, G, A, B^b), 3 trombones (alto, tenor, and bass), ophicleïde,[57] timpani (2 drums), organ, and strings.

First Performance: 26 August 1846, Birmingham, England, conducted by Mendelssohn

Editions: *Elijah* is published in the critical edition: *F. Mendelssohn-Bartholdy: Werke: kritisch durchgesehene Ausgabe*, edited by

---

[57] This may be substituted with a tuba.

Julius Rietz, series: 13, volume: 2. Another scholarly edition prepared by R. Larry Todd (1994) is published by Carus. Full scores and parts for *Elijah* are available for purchase from Breitkopf and Härtel, C. F. Peters, G. Schirmer, and Kalmus.

The first edition was published simultaneously by Simrock and Ewer in 1847, including a piano-vocal score and choral and solo parts.

Autograph: The composer's manuscript is in part 22 of the Mendelssohn Autograph Collection of the Berlin Stadtsbibliothek.

Notes: The score is dated 11 August 1846 on the last page.

The work is organized as follows:

FIRST PART

Prologue Bass Solo: As God the Lord of Israel liveth
Overture
1. Chorus: Help, Lord! Wilt thou quite destroy us?
   Choral Recitative: The deeps afford no water
2. Duet with Chorus: Lord, bow thine ear to our pray'r!
3. Recitative Tenor Solo: Ye people, rend your hearts
4. Aria Tenor Solo: "If with all your hearts ye truly seek me"
5. Chorus: Yet doth the Lord see it not
6. Recitative Alto Solo: Elijah, get thee hence
7. Double Quartet: For He shall give His angels charge
   Recitative Alto Solo: Now Cherith's brook is dried up
8. Recitative Aria and Duet (Soprano and Bass solo): What have I to do with thee
9. Chorus: Blessed are the men who fear Him
10. Recitative with Chorus Bass and Tenor Solo: As God the Lord of Sabaoth liveth
11. Chorus: Baal, we cry to thee
12. Recitative and Chorus Bass Solo: Call him louder! for he is a god
13. Recitative and Chorus: Call him louder! he heareth not
14. Aria Bass Solo: Lord God of Abraham, Isaac and Israel
15. Quartet Soprano Alto Tenor and Bass: Cast thy burden upon the Lord

16. Recitative Bass Solo with Chorus: O Thou, who makest thine Angels
17. Aria Bass Solo: Is not His word like a fire?
18. Arioso Alto Solo: Woe, woe unto them who forsake Him!
19. Recitative with Chorus Soprano, Tenor and Bass Solo: O man of God, help thy people
20. Chorus: Thanks be to God

SECOND PART

21. Aria Soprano Solo: Hear ye, Israel! Hear what the Lord speaketh
22. Chorus: Be not afraid, saith God the Lord
23. Recitative with Chorus Bass and Alto Solo: The Lord hath exalted thee
24. Chorus: Woe to him! He shall perish
25. Recitative Tenor and Bass Solo: Man of God, now let my words
26. Aria Bass Solo: It is enough, O Lord
27. Recitative Tenor Solo: See, now he sleepeth beneath a juniper tree
28. Trio Soprano I, II, and Alto: Lift thine eyes to the mountains
29. Chorus: He, watching over Israel, slumbers not
30. Recitative Alto and Bass Solo: Arise, Elijah
31. Aria Alto Solo: O rest in the Lord, wait patiently for Him
32. Chorus: He that shall endure to the end
33. Recitative Bass and Soprano Solo: Night falleth round me, O Lord!
34. Chorus: Behold, God the Lord passed by
35. Recitative Alto Solo Quartet (Soprano, Alto, Tenor and Bass Solo) with Chorus: Above Him stood the Seraphim; Holy is God the Lord
36. Choral-Recitative and Bass Solo: Go, return upon thy way!
37. Arioso Bass Solo: For the mountains shall depart
38. Chorus: Then did Elijah the prophet break forth
39. Aria Tenor Solo: Then, shall the righteous shine
40. Soprano Solo: Behold, God hath sent Elijah the prophet
41. Chorus: But the Lord, from the north hath raised one
   Quartet (Soprano, Alto, Tenor and Bass Solo): O come ev'ry one that thirsteth

A Conductor's Guide to 19th-Century Choral-Orchestra Works   199

42. Chorus: And then, then shall your light break

Performance Issues: The choral writing is exquisite. It shows Mendelssohn's intense study of the works of Bach. The choral material is well supported by the orchestra. One of the outstanding features of this work is how well it sings in both German and English. Robert Shaw recorded a verion with his own singing English translation as he felt the prosody of the English to be lacking in some sections. This is an eminently well informed, but minority view. The choir is given a wide range of homophonic and imitative textures. There are divisi for all the choral sections. All of the vocal material has an innate lyricism that helps to assure that the singers will not be overly fatigued in spite of the work's significant duration. Solos are labeled with character names and with voice parts. Those labeled with the latter are generally intended to be members of the double quartet although not all of these assignments are clear in the score. There are performances in which some of these sections are assigned to the principal soloists. Also some performances will concentrate all of the solos for four or five singers. Using 15 discrete voices for these parts not only obeys the composer's indications, but it helps to better communicate the drama. Some of these appear only in small ensembles. Only those with exposed solo passages are evaluated below. This also suggests the use of a large choir for contrast. This is also consistent with the oratorio practice of the time. The instrumental writing is fairly conservative, but always effective. As an experienced conductor, Mendelssohn scored this work to support the singers and to be practical. There should be few balance issues between singers and the orchestra. Extra attention to bowing and string articulations will help to dispel the homogeneity of those parts. This is rightfully considered one of the masterworks of the choral-orchestral repertoire. It became the model for many lesser works throughout the 19th century. **Soloists:** Widow (soprano) - range: e'-g'', tessitura: f'-f'', this is a sustained lyric role; Young Boy (soprano) - range: g'-a'', tessitura: g'-g'', this is a brief and simple solo for which a boy should be used; soprano I - range: $d\#'$-$a\#''$, tessitura: f'-f'', this is a lyric and expressive role; soprano II - range: c'-g'', tessitura: e'-e'', this is a simple solo; Angel (alto) - range: b-d'', tessitura: c'-c'', this is a simple declamatory solo; alto - range: b-$f\#''$, tessitura: d'-c'', this is a lyric role with long phrases; Ahab (tenor) - range: g-f'', tessitura: g-f', this is a simple declamatory solo; Obadiah (tenor) - range: d-

$a^{b\prime}$, tessitura: g-g', this is a lyric evangelist-like role; tenor - range: e^b-$a^{b\prime}$, tessitura: g-g', this is a sustained and lyric solo; Elijah (baritone) - range: A-f', tessitura: d-d', this is a dramatic solo role combining declamatory and gently lyric passages; **choir:** difficult; **orchestra:** difficult.

Selected Discography

Helen Donathm Jard van Nes, Donald George, Alastair Miles; Rundfunkchor Leipzig; Israel Philharmonic Orchestra; conducted by Kurt Masur. Teldec: 9031-73131-2.

Christine Schäfer, Cornelia Kallisch, Michael Schade, Wolfgang Schöne; Gächinger Kantorei Stuttgart; Bach-Collegium Stuttgart; conducted by Helmut Rilling, recorded 3-7 July 1994 in the Liederhalle in Stuttgart. Hänssler: CD 98928.

Linda Finney, Rosalind Plowright, Arthur Davies, Willard White; London Symphony Orchestra and Chorus; conducted by Richard Hickox. Chandos: CHAN8774.

Selected Bibliography

Edwards, F. G.: *The History of Mendelssohn's Oratorio "Elijah."* London: Novello, Ewer, and Co., 1896.

Upton, George: *The Standard Oratorios*, 218-229. Chicago: A. C. McClurg and Company, 1893.

Armstrong, Thomas: *Mendelssohn's Elijah*. London: Oxford University Press, 1931.

Mintz, Donald: "Mendelssohn's *Elijah* Reconsidered," *Studies in Romanticism*, iii (1963), 1-9.

Werner, Eric: *Mendelssohn: A New Image of the Composer and His Age*, translated by Dika Newlin, 457-472. London: Free Press of Glencoe, 1963.

Werner, Jack: *Mendelssohn's "Elijah."* London: Chappell, 1965.

Ellison, Ross Wesley: *Overall Unity and Contrast in Mendelssohn's Elijah*. Doctoral dissertation: University of North Carolina at Chapel Hill, 1978.

_____: "Mendelssohn's Elijah: Dramatic Climax of a Creative Career," *American Choral Review*, xx (1980), 3-9.

Felix Mendelssohn: A Life in Letters, edited by Rudolf Elvers, translated by Craig Tomlinson, 277, 283. New York: Fromm International, 1986.

Pahlen, Kurt: *The World of the Oratorio*, translated by Judith Schaefer with additional English-language material by Thurston Dox, 227-239. Portland, OR: Amadeus Press, 1990.

Rothfahl, Wolfgang: "Zu den 'Chorälen' in Mendelssohns *Elias*," *Musik in Gottesdienst*, xliv (1990), 247-251.

Jahn, Otto: "*Elijah*, Johann Sebastian Bach, and the New Covenant: On the Aria 'Es ist genug' in Felix Mendelssohn-Bartholdy's Oratorio *Elijah*," translated by Susan Gillespie in *Mendelssohn and His World*, edited by R. Larry Todd, 121-136. Princeton, NJ: Princeton University Press, 1991.

Staehlin, Martin: "On Felix Mendelssohn-Bartholdy's Oratorio *Elijah*," translated by Susan Gillespie in *Mendelssohn and His World*, edited by R. Larry Todd, 364-381. Princeton, NJ: Princeton University Press, 1991.

Berger, Melvin: *Guide to Choral Masterpieces: A Listener's Guide*, 207-211. New York: Anchor Books, 1993.

Riemer, Erich: "Regenwunder und Witwenszene: Zur Szenengestaltung in Mendelssohns 'Elias,'" *Die Musikforschung*, xlix (1996), 152-171.

Smither, Howard E.: *A History of the Oratorio, volume 4: The Oratorio in the Nineteenth and Twentieth Centuries*, 166-184. Chapel Hill, NC: The University of North Carolina Press, 2000.

Die erste Walpurgisnacht, op. 60 (1830-1831, revised 1842-1843)

Duration: ca. 35 minutes

Text: The text is a poem by Johann Wolfgang von Goethe.

Performing Forces: voices: alto, tenor, baritone, and bass soloists; SATB choir; **orchestra:** 2 flutes, 2 oboes, 2 clarinets (A, B^b, C), 2 bassoons, 2 horns (C, D, E), 2 trumpets (D, E), 3 trombones (alto, tenor, and bass), timpani (2 drums), percussion (2 players — bass drum, cymbals), and strings.

First Performance: 10 January 1833, Berlin; revised version premiered 2 February 1843

Editions: *Die erste Walpurgisnacht* is published in the critical edition: *F. Mendelssohn-Bartholdy: Werke: kritisch durchgesehene Aus-*

gabe, edited by Julius Rietz, series: 15. Full scores and parts are available for purchase from Breitkopf and Härtel, C. F. Peters, G. Schirmer, and Kalmus.

The first edition, consisting of a full score, piano-vocal score, and parts, was published concurrently by Kistner and Ewer in 1844.

Autograph: The composer's manuscript is in part 19 (S. 67) of the Mendelssohn Autograph Collection of the Berlin Stadtsbibliothek.

Notes: The dating of composition varies among sources. Those given above seem the most credible. Schima Kaufman states that the original version was composed in Milan and Paris between 1831 and 1832.[58] The score is organized as follows:

Overture "Das schlechte Wetter"	orchestra
1. Es lacht der Mai!	tenor and SATB choir
2. Könnt ihr so verwegen handeln	alto and women's choir
3. Opfer heut' zu bringen scheut	baritone and men's choir
4. Verteilt euch hier	SATB choir
5. Diese dumpfen Pfaffenchristen	bass and men's choir
6. Kommt mit Zacken und mit Gabeln	SATB choir
7. So weit gebracht	baritone and SATB choir
8. Hilf, ach hilf mir	tenor and SATB choir
9. Die Flamme reignet	baritone and SATB choir

Performance Issues: There are divisi in all of the choral parts. At times the sections of the choir are labeled as particular groups of people (druids, folk, etc.). It is not evident if the composer anticipated different choral groups being used. Likewise, a number of solos are marked "tutti," which appears to mean that they are doubling the corresponding choral parts, but the markings are ambiguous. The choral parts are very clearly supported by the accompaniment. They are nearly entirely syllabic with some very sustained passages and dramatic gestures. There is an appearance of 2/4 and 6/8 in movement 6 that may require some clarification. At the beginning of the movement it appears that the eighth is constant, but later in the movement these meters are concurrent to quarter and

---

[58] Kaufman, Schima: *Mendelssohn: A Second Elijah*, 193. New York: Thomas Y. Crowell Co., 1934.

dotted quarter must be treated as equals between the meters. This is a bright and varied score that uses the orchestra to great effect. The instrumental parts are idiomatic, but require skilled players throughout the orchestra. The string parts are particularly challenging. The variety of contrapuntal textures and varied voicings within the score add challenges for a cohesive performance. In the hands of a good ensemble, this can be a very effective and dramatic work. **Soloists:** alto (Old woman of the People) - range: a-d″, tessitura: c′-c″, this is a declamatory solo; tenor (Druid and a Christian) - range: e-a′, tessitura: a-g′, this is a sustained and lyric role; baritone (unnamed and Priest) - range: B-f′, tessitura: e-e′ this is a lyic and sustained solo; bass (Druid)- range: G-d′, tessitura: A-c′, this is a declamatory solo that must be clear at the bottom of the range; **choir:** medium difficult; **orchestra:** difficult.

Selected Discography

Annelies Burmeister, Eberhard Buchner, Siegfried Lorenz, Siegfried Vogel; Leipzig Radio Chorus, Gewandhaus Orchestra; conducted by Kurt Masur, recorded in 1973. Berlin Classics: 2057.

Selected Bibliography

Werner, Eric: *Mendelssohn: A New Image of the Composer and His Age*, translated by Dika Newlin, 200-205. London: Free Press of Glencoe, 1963.

Szeskus, Reinhard: "*Die erste Walpurgisnacht*, Op. 60, von Felix Mendelssohn Bartholdy," *Beitrage zur Musikwissenschaft*, xvii (1975), 171-180.

Dahlhaus, Carl: "'Hoch symbolisch intoniert': Zu Mendelssohns *Erster Walpurgisnacht*," *Österreichische Musikzeitschrift*, xxxvi (1981), 290-297.

Seaton, Douglass: "The Romantic Mendelssohn: The Composition of *Die erste Walpurgisnacht*." *The Musical Quarterly*, lxviii (1982), 398-410.

Melhorn, Catherine Rose: *Mendelssohn's Die erste Walpurgisnacht*. Doctoral dissertation: University of Illinois at Urbana-Champaign, 1983.

Felix Mendelssohn: A Life in Letters, edited by Rudolf Elvers, translated by Craig Tomlinson, 273, 275. New York: Fromm International, 1986.

Retallack, Diane Johnson: *A Conductor's Study for Performance of Mendelssohn's Die erste Walpurgisnacht*. Doctoral dissertation: Indiana University, 1987.

Pahlen, Kurt: *The World of the Oratorio*, translated by Judith Schaefer with additional English-language material by Thurston Dox, 226. Portland, OR: Amadeus Press, 1990.

Berger, Melvin: *Guide to Choral Masterpieces: A Listener's Guide*, 201-207. New York: Anchor Books, 1993.

Hellmundt, Christoph: "Mendelssohns Arbeit an seiner Kantate *Die erster Walpurgisnacht*: Zu einer bisher wenig beachteten Quelle," in *Felix Mendelssohn Bartholdy: Kongreß-Bericht Berlin 1994*, edited by Christian Mart Schmidt, 76-112. Wiesbaden: Breitkopf and Härtel, 1997.

Hymn, op. 96 (1840)

Duration: ca. 14 minutes

Text: The text is Psalm 13.

Performing Forces: voices: mezzo-soprano soloists, SATB choir; **orchestra:** 2 flutes, 2 oboes, 2 clarinets (B^b), 2 bassoons, 2 horns (E^b), 2 trumpets (E^b), timpani (2 drums), and strings.

First Performance: 5 January 1843, the first three movements were performed with organ accompaniment 12 December 1840

Editions: *Hymn* is published in the critical edition: *F. Mendelssohn-Bartholdy: Werke: kritisch durchgesehene Ausgabe*, edited by Julius Rietz, series: 14, volume: A3 and B.

Autograph: The autograph score is in the British Museum (Add. MS. 31801).

Notes: The score is dated: Leipzig: 14 December 1840, and the final chorus is dated 5 January 1843. The work was composed for Dr. C. Broadley. It is organized in four movements as follows:

1. Lass', o Herr	mezzo and choir
2. Deines Kind's Gebet erhöre (chorale)	mezzo and choir

3. Herr, wir trau'n auf deine Güte   mezzo and choir
4. Lasst sein heilig Lob uns singen (fugue)   choir

Performance Issues: The choral writing is primarily freely contrapuntal, but most of the vocal material is clearly doubled by the orchestra. The soloist and choir generally sing in response to each other. The scoring of movement 2 is unusual. The first verse of this hymn is presented by the soloist, accompanied by 2 clarinets, 2 viola parts, and cello. The orchestral parts are straightforward and well conceived for the instruments. In the final movement the orchestra doubles the choral fugue exclusively. Some of the octave doubling in the orchestra may present intonation problems for less-experienced ensembles. **Soloists:** mezzo-soprano - range: b^b-$e^{b\prime\prime}$, tessitura: d'-d'', this is a sustained lyric role that is prominent throughout the first three movement of the score; **choir:** medium difficult; **orchestra:** medium easy.

Selected Discography

Chamber Choir of Europe, Württembergische Philharmonie Reutlingen; conducted by Nocol Matt. Brilliant Classics: 99997.

Selected Bibliography

Brodbeck, David: "Some Notes on an Anthem by Mendelssohn," in *Mendelssohn and His World*, edited by R. Larry Todd, 43-64. Princeton, NJ: Princeton University Press, 1991.

Lauda Sion, op. 73 (1846)

Duration: ca. 29 minutes

Text: The text, by Thomas Aquinas, is the sequence hymn for the Feast of Corpus Christi. It is in Latin. The score includes a singing German translation as well.

Performing Forces: voices: soprano, alto, tenor, and bass soloists; SATB choir; **orchestra:** 2 flutes, 2 oboes, 2 clarinets (C, B^b), 2 bassoons, 2 horns (C, D, E^b), 2 trumpets (B^b, C, E^b) 3 trombones (alto, tenor, and bass), timpani (2 drums), and strings.

First Performance: 11 June 1846, Church of St. Martin, Liège, France[59]

Editions: *Lauda Sion* is published in the critical edition: *F. Mendelssohn-Bartholdy: Werke: kritisch durchgesehene Ausgabe*, edited by Julius Rietz, series: 14, volume: A3. Another scholarly edition has been prepared by R. Larry Todd (1996) and published by Carus Verlag.

The first edition was published in 1848 in London by Ewer as a piano-vocal score in Latin and English. In 1849, Schott published the work as a piano-vocal score and a full score in two printings, one in German and Latin, the other in German, Latin, and English.

Autograph: The location of this manuscript is unknown.

Notes: The score is dated 10 February 1846. The work is divided into seven movements as follows:

1. Lauda Sion salvatorem   choir

---

[59] The English music critic, Henry Chorley, who accompanied Mendelssohn on the trip that included this premiere, wrote of the performance in his *Modern German Music* (1854): "It is a pity that those who commissioned such a composer to write such a work had so entirely miscalculated their means of presenting it even respectably." Quoted in Upton, George P.: *The Standard Cantatas*, seventh edition, 265. Chicago: A. C. McClurg and Company, 1899.

2. Laudis thema specialis — choir
3. Sit laus plena — soprano and choir
4. In haec mensa novi regis — SATB quartet
5. Docti sacris intitutis — choir
6. Caro cibus, sanguis potus — soprano solo
7. Sumit unus sumunt mille — choir

Performance Issues: The choral material alternates homophonic choral writing with various imitative contrapuntal devices. All of the choral passages are clearly supported by the accompaniment. In the Rietz edition the soprano solo is in soprano clef, and the tenor is in tenor clef, which is to be expected; however, the alto solo is also in soprano clef throughout the work. There is a lovely lyric trio for oboe and two clarinets in movement 6 that will require secure players. The string writing includes some intricate writing, but overall, this is a conservative orchestra score for this composer. The scoring allows the use of a large choral ensemble and full complement of strings, although a moderate-sized group will also work well. **Soloists:** soprano - range: d'-a'', tessitura: a'-f'', this is a declamatory and lyric solo and the most sizeable role; alto - range: b-e'', tessitura: d'-c'', this is a lyric solo role; tenor - range: g-a', tessitura: a-f', this is a lyric solo role; bass - range: G-d', tessitura: c-a, this is a lyric solo role; **choir:** medium difficult; **orchestra:** medium easy.

Selected Discography

Ruth Ziesak, Helene Schneiderman, Jan Kobow, Christoph Pregardien, Gotthold Schwarz, Adolph Seidel; Stuttgart Chamber Choir; Deutsche Kammerphilharmonie Bremen Symphony Orchestra; conducted by Frieder Bernius. Carus-Verlag: 83.202/00.

Nathalie Stutzmann, Guillaume Tourmiaire; Gulbenkian Choir and Orchestra of Lisbon; conducted by Michel Corboz. Apex: 2564-61692-2.

Chamber Choir of Europe, Württembergische Philharmonie Reutlingen; conducted by Nocol Matt. Brilliant Classics: 99997.

Selected Bibliography

Linden, Albert van der: "Un Fragment inédit du 'Lauda Sion" de F. Mendelssohn," *Acta musicologica*, xxvi (1954), 48-64.

_____: "A propos du 'Lauda Sion' de Mendelssohn," *Revue Belge de musicologie*, xvii (1963), 124-125.

Werner, Eric: *Mendelssohn: A New Image of the Composer and His Age*, translated by Dika Newlin, 446-450. London: Free Press of Glencoe, 1963.

Lobgesang, see: Symphony No. 2

St. Paul, op. 36 (1834-1836)

Duration: ca. 130 minutes

Text: The text, based upon *The Acts of the Apostles*, was written for this work by Julius Schubring.

Performing Forces: voices: soprano, alto, tenor, and 2 bass soloists, SATB choir; **orchestra:** 2 flutes, 2 oboes, 2 clarinets (A, B^b, C), 2 bassoons, serpent, 4 horns (B^b basso, C, D, E^b, E, F, G, A, B^b alto), 2 trumpets (C, D, E^b, F, B), 3 trombones (alto, tenor, and bass), timpani (3), organ, and strings.

The score calls for unison "contrafagotto e serpente," part which has been transcribed in the contemporary orchestral sets for 2 players on contrabassoon and tuba respectively.

First Performance: 22 May 1836; Düsseldorf; Rhenish Music Festival, conducted by Mendelssohn

Editions: *St. Paul* is published in the critical edition: *F. Mendelssohn-Bartholdy: Werke: kritisch durchgesehene Ausgabe*, edited by Julius Rietz, series: 13, volume: 1. Another scholarly edition, prepared by R. Larry Todd, has been published by Carus Verlag. Full scores and parts for *St. Paul* are available for purchase from Breitkopf and Härtel, H. W. Gray, C. F. Peters, and Kalmus.

The editions published by Simrock and Novello in 1836 were approved by Mendelssohn, who also prepared the piano-vocal score. The English text for the Novello edition was prepared by W. Ball.

Autograph: The composer's manuscript is in part 19 (S. 1) of the Mendelssohn Autograph Collection of the Berlin Stadtsbibliothek.

Notes: This oratorio uses the following Lutheran chorales: Allein Gott in der Höh' sei Her' und Dank [movement 2], the Lutheran adaptation of "Gloria in excelsis," a plainsong for Easter (1539); Wer nur den lieben Gott [movement 8, on the text: Dir Herr, dir will ich mich ergeben] by Georg Neumark (1640 or 1657); and Wachet auf! Ruft was die stimme [overture and movement 15] by Philipp Nicolai (1599).

Act I is dated 8 April 1836, and Act II is dated 18 April.

St. Paul is organized in two acts as follows:

Overture
Act One
1. choir — Herr, der du bist der Gott
2. chorale — Allein Gott in der Höh' sei Her' und Dank
3. recitative (soprano, basses I and II) — Die Menge der Gläubigen
4. choir — Dieser Mensch hört nicht auf zu reden
5. recitative (soprano/tenor) and choir — Und sie sahen auf ihn Alle
6. aria (soprano) — Jerusalem, die du tödtest die Propheten
7. recitative (tenor) and choir — Sie aber stürmten auf ihn ein
8. recitative (tenor) and chorale — Und sie steinigten ihn
9. recitative (soprano) — Und die Zeugen legten ab
10. choir — Siehe, wir preisen selig
11. recitative and aria (tenor/bass) — Saulus aber zerstörte die Gemeinde
12. recitative and arioso (alto) — Und zog mit einer Schaar gen Damaskus
13. recitative (tenor/bass) and choir — Und als er auf dem Wege war
14. choir — mache dich auf, werde Licht
15. chorale — Wachet auf! Ruft uns die Stimme
16. recitative (tenor) — Die Männer aber die seine Gefährten waren

17. aria (bass) — Gott sei mir gnädig
18. recitative (soprano/tenor) — Es war aber ein Jünger zu Damaskus
19. aria (bass) with choir — Ich danke dir, Herr main Gott
20. recitative (soprano/tenor) — Und Ananias ging hin
21. choir — O welch' eine Tiefe des Reichthums

Act Two
22. choir — Der erdkreis ist nun des Herrn
23. recitative (soprano) — Und Paulus kam zu der Gemeinde
24. duettino (tenor/bass) — So sind wir nun Botschafter
25. choir — Wir lieblich sind die Boten
26. recitative and arioso (soprano) — Und wie sie ausgesandt
27. recitative (tenor) and choir — da aber die Juden ads Volk sah'n
28. choir — Ist das nicht der zu Jerusalem
29. recitative (tenor/bass) — Paulus aber und Barnabas sprachen
30. duet (tenor/bass) — Denn also hat uns der Herr geboten
31. recitative (soprano) — Und es war ein Mann zu Lystra
32. choir — Die Götter sind den Menschen gleich geworden
33. recitative (soprano) — Und nannten Narnabas Jupiter
34. choir — Seid uns gnädig, hohe Götter
35. recitative and aria (tenor/bass) with choir — Da das die Apostel hörten
36. recitative (soprano) — Da ward das Volk erreget wider sie
37. choir — Hier ist des herren Tempel
38. recitative (soprano) — Und sie alle verfolgten Paulus
39. cavatina (tenor) — Sie getreu bis in den Tod
40. recitative (soprano/bass) — Paulus sandte hin und liess fordern
41. choir and recitative (tenor/bass) — Schone doch deiner selbst
42. choir — Sehet, welch' eine Liebe
43. recitative (soprano) — Und wenn er gleich geopfert wird
44. choir — Nicht aber ihm allein

Performance Issues: While most critics attribute much of the style of Mendelssohn's oratorio style to his study of the oratorios of Handel, it is my opinion that this work is as much the fruit of his prolonged study of the choral works of J. S. Bach. The use of chorales, certain instrumental obbliggati, cantus firmus techniques, and recitative writing all betray his affinity for the baroque master. The choral writing is linear, combining homophonic choral exclamations with fugal imitation. All of the choral writing is clearly doubled by the orchestra, and it is sensitively written to accommodate good amateur choirs. None of the parts is particularly vocally taxing, and all of them are musically clear. The choir must be capable of expressing a variety of moods. The organ part does add color to the orchestration, but all its material is covered by the rest of the orchestra if an instrument is not available. There is an extended florid cello solo in movement 39. Throughout the score, the choir and the tenor soloists portray different people, although this is listed in the score, it is not always clear to the ear. This should be considered when preparing the program. This is an eminently practical score. All of the parts are thoughtfully written from the singers' and players' perspectives, so that there are no technical or musical snares in the score. This work is performed far less frequently than *Elijah*, but it is deserving of equal attention. **Soloists:** soprano 1 - range: d'-a'', tessitura: f'-f'', this is a declamatory solo role that functions as a narrator; alto - range: a-d'', tessitura: d'-b', this is a sustained and lyric solo role; tenor (Ananias, Stephen, and Barnabas) - range: d-g#', tessitura: f#-f#', this is a lyric solo with some sustained passages; bass (St. Paul) - range: A-d', tessitura: B-d', this is a sustained and placid solo role. There are two additional bass solo parts (False Witnesses) that can most effectively be assigned to choristers; number 1 - range: e-e', tessitura: e-c'; number 2 - range: d#-c', tessitura: d#-c'; **choir:** medium difficult; **orchestra:** medium difficult.

Selected Discography

Helen Donath, Hanna Schwarz, Werner Hollweg, Dietrich Fischer-Dieskau; Chor des Städtischen Musikvereins zu Düsseldorf; Düsseldorfer Symphoniker; conducted by Rafael Frühbeck de Burgos. EMI: 0077776400525.

Susan Gritton, Jean Rigby, Barry Banks, Peter Coleman-Wright; BBC National Chorus and Orchestra of Wales; conducted by Richard Hickox. Chandos: CHAN9882.

Juliane Banse, Ingeborg Danz, Michael Schade, Adreas Schmidt; Gächinger Kantorei Stuttgart, Prague Chamber Chorus; Czech Philharmonic; conducted by Helmuth Rilling, recorded in November 1994 in Rudolfinum Dvorak Hall, Prague. Hänssler: CD 98926.

Melanie Diener, Annette Markert, James Taylor, Matthias Görne; La Chapelle Royale, Collegium Vocale Ghent; Orchestre des Champs-

Élysées; conducted by Phillippe Herreweghe. Harmonia Mundi: HMC9015584/85.

Selected Bibliography

Jahn, Otto: *Über Felix Mendelssohn Bartholdys Oratorium "Paulus."* Kiel: n.p., 1842. Reprinted in Jahn: *Gesammelte Aufsätze über Musik*, 13-39. Leipzig: Breitkopf and Härtel, 1866.

Upton, George: *The Standard Oratorios*, 208-213. Chicago: A. C. McClurg and Company, 1893.

Kaufman, Schima: *Mendelssohn: A Second Elijah*, 198, 233, 241, 248, 268, 269, 284, 309. New York: Thomas Y. Crowell Co., 1934.

Werner, Eric: *Mendelssohn: A New Image of the Composer and His Age*, translated by Dika Newlin, 287-294. London: Free Press of Glencoe, 1963.

Felix Mendelssohn: A Life in Letters, edited by Rudolf Elvers, translated by Craig Tomlinson, 198, 201, 203, 206, 223, 228, 232, 268. New York: Fromm International, 1986.

Reimer, Erich: "Textanlage und Szenengestaltung in Mendelssohns Paulus." *Archiv für Musikwissenschaft*, xlvi (1989), 42-69.

Pahlen, Kurt: *The World of the Oratorio*, translated by Judith Schaefer with additional English-language material by Thurston Dox, 219-224. Portland, OR: Amadeus Press, 1990.

Reimer, Erich: "Mendelssohns 'edler Gesang': Zur Kompositionsweise der Sologesänge im 'Paulus,'" *Archiv für Musikwissenschaft*, l (1993), 44-70.

Berger, Melvin: *Guide to Choral Masterpieces: A Listener's Guide*, 199-201. New York: Anchor Books, 1993.

Mercer-Taylor, Peter: "Rethinking Mendelssohn's Historicism: A Lesson from *St. Paul*," *Journal of Musicology*, xv (1997), 208-229.

Reichwald, Siegwart: *The Musical Genesis of Felix Mendelssohn's Paulus*. Doctoral dissertation: Florida State University, 1998.

Smither, Howard E.: *A History of the Oratorio, volume 4: The Oratorio in the Nineteenth and Twentieth Centuries*, 152-166. Chapel Hill, NC: The University of North Carolina Press, 2000.

Psalm 42, Wie der Hirsch schreit, op. 42 (1837)

Duration: ca. 21 minutes

Text: The text is from the *Book of Psalms* in the Bible. It is in German.

Performing Forces: **voices:** soprano soloist; SATB choir; **orchestra:** 2 flutes, 2 oboes, 2 clarinets (B^b), 2 bassoons, 4 horns (F), 2 trumpets (C), 3 trombones (alto, tenor, and bass), organ, and strings.

First Performance: 22 December 1837

Editions: *Psalm 42* is published in the critical edition: *F. Mendelssohn-Bartholdy: Werke: kritisch durchgesehene Ausgabe*, edited by Julius Rietz, series: 14, volume: A1. Another scholarly edition has been prepared by Günter Graulich (1980) and published by Carus Verlag.

The first edition of choral parts and a piano-vocal score prepared by the composer was published by Breitkopf and Härtel in German, and by Novello in English in 1838. The full score was published by Breitkopf and Härtel the following year.

Autograph: The composer's manuscript is in part 19 (S. 15) of the Mendelssohn Autograph Collection of the Berlin Stadtsbibliothek.

Notes: The score is dated 22 December 1837. The score is divided into seven movements as follows:

1.	Wie der Hirsch schreit	SATB choir
2.	Meine Seele dürstet nach Gott	soprano aria
3.	Meine Thränen sind meine Speise	soprano recitative
	Denn ich wollte gern	soprano solo and SA choir
4.	Was betrübst du dich	SATB choir
5.	Mein Gott, betrübt	soprano recitative
6.	Der Herr hat es Tages	soprano solo and TTBB quartet
7.	Was betrübst du dich	SATB choir

Performance Issues: The choral writing is practical. Some of it is quite contrapuntal, but there is clear support in the accompaniment.

The text declamation and melodic contours sing very well. The male quartet in movement 6 is entirely appropriate for members of the choir. There are soprano divisi in movement 3. The instrumental writing is very practically conceived for the players. The strings have the most challenging material. The organ part is implied as a continuo instrument. The score indicates when it does and does not play, but there are no figures in the full score. There is an important exposed oboe solo in movement 2 and a cello divisi in movement 6. This is a varied and effective score that takes advantage of contrasting vocal and instrumental sonorities. **Soloists:** soprano - range: $d'-a''$, tessitura: $f'-f''$, this is a significant role that is lyrical with some melismatic writing; **choir:** medium difficult; **orchestra:** medium difficult.

Selected Discography

Ruth Ziesak, Helene Schneiderman, Jan Kobow, Christoph Pregardien, Gotthold Schwarz, Adolph Seidel; Stuttgart Chamber Choir; Deutsche Kammerphilharmonie Bremen Symphony Orchestra; conducted by Frieder Bernius. Carus-Verlag: 83.202/00.

Nathalie Stutzmann, Guillaume Tourmiaire; Gulbenkian Choir and Orchestra of Lisbon; conducted by Michel Corboz. Apex: 2564-61692-2.

Chamber Choir of Europe, Württembergische Philharmonie Reutlingen; conducted by Nocol Matt. Brilliant Classics: 99997.

Selected Bibliography

Robinson, Daniel Vehe: *An Analysis of the Psalms for Chorus and Orchestra by Felix Mendelssohn.* Doctoral dissertation: Stanford University, 1976.

Dinglinger, Wolfgang: *Studien zu den Psalmen mit Orchester von Felix Mendelssohn Bartholdy.* Berlin: Schriftenreihe zur Musikwissenschaft an den Berliner Hochschulen un Universituten, 1993.

Psalm 95, Kommt, laßt uns anbeten, op. 46 (1839, revised 1841)

Duration: ca. 23 minutes

Text: The text is from the *Book of Psalms* in the Bible. It is in German.

Performing Forces: voices: 2 soprano and tenor soloists; SATB choir; **orchestra:** 2 flutes, 2 oboes, 2 clarinets (B^b), 2 bassoons, 2 horns (C, E^b), 2 trumpets (C, E^b), 3 trombones (alto, tenor, and bass), and strings.

First Performance: unknown

Editions: *Psalm 95* is published in the critical edition: *F. Mendelssohn-Bartholdy: Werke: kritisch durchgesehene Ausgabe*, edited by Julius Rietz, series: 14, volume: A1. Another scholarly edition has been prepared by R. Larry Todd (1990) for Carus Verlag.

The first edition full score, piano-vocal score, and parts were published by Kistner in 1842. That same year, Novello published an English version piano-vocal score.

Autograph: The composer's manuscript is in part 19 (S. 36) of the Mendelssohn Autograph Collection of the Berlin Stadtsbibliothek.

Notes: The score is dated 11 April 1839 with a revision dated 3 July 1841. The score is divided into five movements as follows:

1.	Kommt, lasst uns anbeten	tenor and choir
2.	Kommet herzu	soprano and choir
3.	Denn in seiner Hand ist	soprano duet
4.	Denn sein ist das Meer	tenor and choir
5.	Heute, so ihr seine Stimme höret	tenor and choir

Performance Issues: The choral writing is generally syllabic with some sustained passages. The accompaniment provides clear support for the voices, but they are often contrapuntally independent of the instruments. The choral textures integrate imitative counterpoint and homophonic writing. In fact, the contrapuntal sophistication of the choral parts often exceeds that of the orchestra, which is more ostinato driven. The tenor solo in movement 4 is not indicated, but appears unlabeled in the score. The most complex orchestral material is in the final movement, and it is more practical than it first appears. This is an excellent work for a strong choir with limited orchestral resources. **Soloists:** soprano I - range: $e^{b\prime}$-$a^{b\prime\prime}$, tessitura: f'-f'', this is a lyric and articulate role; soprano II - range: $e^{b\prime}$-f'', tessitura: f'-d'', this is a lyric solo appropriate for a soprano or mezzo-soprano; tenor - range: d-f', tessitura: g-d', this is a lyric and sustained role; **choir:** difficult; **orchestra:** medium easy.

Selected Discography

Nathalie Stutzmann, Guillaume Tourmiaire; Gulbenkian Choir and Orchestra of Lisbon; conducted by Michel Corboz. Apex: 2564-61692-2.
Chamber Choir of Europe, Württembergische Philharmonie Reutlingen; conducted by Nocol Matt. Brilliant Classics: 99997.

Selected Bibliography

Robinson, Daniel Vehe: *An Analysis of the Psalms for Chorus and Orchestra by Felix Mendelssohn*. Doctoral dissertation: Stanford University, 1976.
Dinglinger, Wolfgang: "Felix Mendelssohn Bartholdy: Der 95. Psalm op. 46: '...vom dem nur ein Stück mir ans Herz gewachsen war,'" *Mendelssohn-Studien*, vii (1990), 269-286.
Felix Mendelssohn: A Life in Letters, edited by Rudolf Elvers, translated by Craig Tomlinson, 130. New York: Fromm International, 1986.
Dinglinger, Wolfgang: *Studien zu den Psalmen mit Orchester von Felix Mendelssohn Bartholdy*. Berlin: Schriftenreihe zur Musikwissenschaft an den Berliner Hochschulen un Universituten, 1993.

Psalm 98, Singet dem Herrn ein neues Lied, op. 91 (1843)

Duration: ca. 7 minutes

Text: The text is from the *Book of Psalms* in the Bible. It is in German.

Performing Forces: voices: two SATB choirs; **orchestra:** 2 flutes, 2 oboes, 2 clarinets (C), 2 bassoons, 2 horns (D), 2 trumpets (C), 3 trombones (alto, tenor, and bass) timpani (2 drums), harp, organ, and strings.

First Performance: 1 January 1844, Berlin

Editions: *Psalm 98* is published in the critical edition: *F. Mendelssohn-Bartholdy: Werke: kritisch durchgesehene Ausgabe*, edited by Julius Rietz, series: 14, volume: A1. Another scholarly edition, prepared by R. Larry Todd (1990), is published by Carus Verlag.

This work was published posthumously. The first edition, consisting of a full score, piano-vocal score, and parts, was issued by Kistner in 1851. That same year, Novello produced an English version of the piano-vocal score with text by W. Bartholomew.

Autograph: The location of this manuscript is unknown.

Notes: This work was composed for the choir of the Berlin Cathedral. The score is dated 27 December 1843. The score is divided into two movements as follows:

1. Singet dem Herrn	double choir, a cappella
2. Jauchzet dem Herrn	double choir and orchestra

Performance Issues: The choral material combines homophonic and imitative writing. The opening movement alternates call-and-response material between the two choirs with more holistic passages. Some sections are labeled "solo" that are treated like a concertato group. The first movement ends in B minor, and the second movement begins, instruments only, in G major, so a peregrination of pitch center in the a cappella section will not be evident. The orchestral writing is practical and fairly simple. The harp part is important and exposed, and the organ part is fully realized and necessary; **choir:** difficult; **orchestra:** medium easy.

Selected Discography

Nathalie Stutzmann, Guillaume Tourmiaire; Gulbenkian Choir and Orchestra of Lisbon; conducted by Michel Corboz. Apex: 2564-61692-2.

Chamber Choir of Europe, Württembergische Philharmonie Reutlingen; conducted by Nocol Matt. Brilliant Classics: 99997.

Selected Bibliography

Robinson, Daniel Vehe: *An Analysis of the Psalms for Chorus and Orchestra* by Felix Mendelssohn. Doctoral dissertation: Stanford University, 1976.

Dinglinger, Wolfgang: "Ein neues Lied: Der preußische Generalmusikdirektor und eine königliche Auftragskomposition," *Mendelssohn-Studien*, v (1982), 99-111.

_____: *Studien zu den Psalmen mit Orchester von Felix Mendelssohn Bartholdy*. Berlin: Schriftenreihe zur Musikwissenschaft an den Berliner Hochschulen un Universituten, 1993.

Psalm 114, Da Israel aus Aegypten zog op. 51
(1839)

Duration: ca. 13 minutes

Text: The text is from the *Book of Psalms* in the Bible. It is in German.

Performing Forces: voices: SSAATTBB choir; **orchestra:** 2 flutes, 2 oboes, 2 clarinets (C), 2 bassoons, 4 horns (C, G), 2 trumpets (C), 3 trombones (alto, tenor, and bass), timpani (2 drums), and strings.

First Performance: unknown

Editions: *Psalm 114* is published in the critical edition: *F. Mendelssohn-Bartholdy: Werke: kritisch durchgesehene Ausgabe*, edited by Julius Rietz, series: 14, volume: A1. Another scholarly edition, prepared by Oswald Bill (1982), is published by Carus Verlag.

The first edition was produced by Breitkopf and Härtel (piano-vocal score and parts) and Novello (English piano-vocal score) in 1841. In both cases, the piano-vocal score was prepared by the composer.

Autograph: The location of this manuscript is unknown.

Notes: The score is dated Horchheim, 9 August 1839—23 September 1840 and is dedicated to the painter, J. W. Schirmer. The work is organized as a single movement with clearly defined musical subsections.

Performance Issues: The vocal parts integrate homophonic, block-chord sections with complex imitative counterpoint. Much of the choral material is clearly supported by the orchestra, but some passages require choral independence. There are also some brief a cappella passages in eight parts. There is some significant passagework for much of the orchestra, but primarily the bassoons and strings. The brass scoring suggests the use of a full complement of strings and a sizable choral ensemble. There are immediate and dramatic contrasts of tone and dynamics, particularly for the choir. The choir must be a flexible and expressive ensemble capable of navigating some rhythmically articulate passages at a very low dynamic level; **choir:** difficult; **orchestra:** medium difficult.

Selected Discography

Leipzig Gewandhaus Orchestra and Choir; conducted by Riccardo Chailly, recorded live 2-3 September 2005 at the Gewandhaus in Leipzig. DVD — EuroArts: 2054668.
Ruth Ziesak, Helene Schneiderman, Jan Kobow, Christoph Pregardien, Gotthold Schwarz, Adolph Seidel; Stuttgart Chamber Choir; Deutsche Kammerphilharmonie Bremen Symphony Orchestra; conducted by Frieder Bernius. Carus-Verlag: 83.202/00.
Nathalie Stutzmann, Guillaume Tourmiaire; Gulbenkian Choir and Orchestra of Lisbon; conducted by Michel Corboz. Apex: 2564-61692-2.

Chamber Choir of Europe, Württembergische Philharmonie Reutlingen; conducted by Nocol Matt. Brilliant Classics: 99997.

Selected Bibliography

Robinson, Daniel Vehe: *An Analysis of the Psalms for Chorus and Orchestra* by Felix Mendelssohn. Doctoral dissertation: Stanford University, 1976.

Dinglinger, Wolfgang: "'...der letzte Schluß will mir nicht so recht werden': Anmerkungen zum 114. Psalm von Felix Mendelssohn Bartholdy," in *Professor Rudolph Stephan zum 3. April 1985 von seiner Schulern*, 77-80. Berlin: n.p., 1985.

_____: *Studien zu den Psalmen mit Orchester von Felix Mendelssohn Bartholdy*. Berlin: Schriftenreihe zur Musikwissenschaft an den Berliner Hochschulen und Universituten, 1993.

Psalm 115, Non nobis Domine [Nicht unserm namen, Herr], op. 31 (1830)

Duration: ca. 16 minutes

Text: The text is from the *Book of Psalms*; it is set here in German.

Performing Forces: voices: soprano, tenor, and baritone soloists; SSAATTBB choir; **orchestra:** 2 flutes 2 oboes, 2 clarinets (B^b), 2 bassoons, 2 horns (B^b basso, C basso),[60] and strings.

First Performance: 15 November 1830; Frankfurt, Germany

Editions: *Psalm 115* is published in the critical edition: *F. Mendelssohn-Bartholdy: Werke: kritisch durchgesehene Ausgabe*, edited by Julius Rietz, series: 14, volume: A1. Another scholarly edition, prepared by R. Larry Todd (1994), is published by Carus Verlag.

The first edition was published by Simrock. A concurrent edition with English text by W. Bartholomew was published by Hedgley.

---

[60] The score does not indicate basso, but the range certainly suggests it.

Autograph: An early manuscript copy of the score is in the Berlin Stadtsbibliothek (ms. 30372).

Notes: The score is dated 15 November 1830—19 May 1835. It is divided into four movements as follows:

1. Nicht unserm Namen — SATB choir
2. Israel hofft auf dich — ST duet and SATB choir
3. Er segne euch je mehr und mehr — baritone arioso
4. Die Todten werden dich nicht loben — SSAATTBB choir

Performance Issues: The choral material features some complex contrapuntal writing, which includes some intricate melismatic passagework. Movement 4 begins with an eight-part a cappella chorale and moves to a four-part choral texture when the orchestra enters. While the choral material is quite consistently supported harmonically by the orchestra, direct doubling is not as evident as in some of Mendelssohn's other choral-orchestral works. The orchestral writing is idiomatic, but it does include some rhythmically and contrapuntally complex sections that may require attention in rehearsal. **Soloists:** soprano - range: $f'-g''$, tessitura: $g'-f''$, this is a simple lyric solo; tenor - range: $f-g'$, tessitura: $g-f'$, this is a fairly easy lyric solo; baritone - range: $B^b-e^{b'}$, tessitura: $c-d'$, this is a lyric solo with some sustained passages; **choir:** medium difficult; **orchestra:** medium difficult.

Selected Discography

Ruth Ziesak, Sabine Ritterbusch, Christoph Pregardien, Gotthold Schwarz, Michael Volle; Stuttgart Chamber Choir; Stuttgart Chamber Orchestra, Deutsche Kammerphilharmonie Bremen Symphony Orchestra; conducted by Frieder Bernius. Carus-Verlag: 83.204/00.

Nathalie Stutzmann, Guillaume Tourniaire; Gulbenkian Choir and Orchestra of Lisbon; conducted by Michel Corboz. Apex: 2564-61692-2.

Chamber Choir of Europe, Württembergische Philharmonie Reutlingen; conducted by Nocol Matt. Brilliant Classics: 99997.

Selected Bibliography

Werner, Eric: *Mendelssohn: A New Image of the Composer and His Age*, translated by Dika Newlin, 206-208. London: Free Press of Glencoe, 1963.

Robinson, Daniel Vehe: *An Analysis of the Psalms for Chorus and Orchestra* by Felix Mendelssohn. Doctoral dissertation: Stanford University, 1976.

Dinglinger, Wolfgang: *Studien zu den Psalmen mit Orchester von Felix Mendelssohn Bartholdy*. Berlin: Schriftenreihe zur Musikwissenschaft an den Berliner Hochschulen und Universituten, 1993.

Symphony No. 2, Lobgesang ["Song of Praise"], op. 52 (1840)

Duration: Entire work: ca. 70 minutes
Symphonic movements: ca. 26 minutes
Choral portion: ca. 44 minutes
Shortened choral version: ca. 37 minutes

Text: The text is from Martin Luther's translation of the Bible. The English text is a singing translation of that text.

Performing Forces: voices: 2 soprano and tenor soloists; SATB choir; **orchestra:** 2 flutes, 2 oboes, 2 clarinets, 2 bassoons, 4 horns, 2 trumpets, 3 trombones, timpani (2 drums), organ, and strings.

First Performance: 25 June 1840; St. Thomaskirche, Leipzig; conducted by the composer

British premiere: (in English) 23 September 1840; Birmingham; conducted by the composer

Revised version: 3 December 1840, Leipzing, conducted by the composer

Editions: Symphony No. 2 is published in the critical edition: *F. Mendelssohn-Bartholdy: Werke: kritisch durchgesehene Ausgabe*, edited by Julius Rietz, series: 14, volume: A2; additional scholarly editions include one edited by Douglass Seaton (1989), published by Carus Verlag, and another published by Breitkopf and Härtel, edited by Wulf Konold (1998). The opening orchestral symphony movements are published by Breitkopf and Härtel and Kalmus. The Lobgesang cantata is published independently and is available from: Breitkopf and Härtel, G. Schirmer, H. W. Gray, and Kalmus.

The first edition, consisting of a piano-vocal score, full score, and parts, was published by Breitkopf and Härtel and Novello in 1841. The piano-vocal score included a two-piano arrangement of the symphonic portion made by the composer.

Autograph: The composer's manuscript is in part 19 (S. 36) of the Mendelssohn Autograph Collection of the Berlin Stadtsbibliothek.

Notes: This work was composed as part of the quatercentenary celebration of Gutenberg's printing press. There is well-founded supposition that Mendelssohn began the symphony with no intentions of this purpose nor the inclusion of a choral finale, but that when the occasion arose, he built upon a symphony he had begun in 1838.[61] The revised version is dated Leipzig, 27 November 1840. It is dedicated to Frederic Augustus, Duke of Saxony. The score is organized as a symphony followed by a cantata. It may be performed in its entirety, or with either half as a stand-alone work. The complete score is organized as follows:

1. Sinfonia — orchestra alone
   Maestoso con moto — Allegro
   Allegretto un poco agitato
   Adagio religioso
2. Alles was Odem hat — choir
   Lobe denHerrn[62] — soprano and women's choir
3. Saget es…Er zählet unsre Thränen — tenor
4. Sagt, es, die ihr erlöset seid — choir
5. Ich harrete des Herrn — soprano duet and choir
6. Stricke des Todes hatten uns umfangen — tenor
7. Die Nacht ist vergangen — choir
8. Nun danket Alle Gott — choir (hymn)[63]

---

[61] Fiske, Roger, preface to the Eulenberg edition of the score, 1980.

[62] In some editions, this is referred to as movement 2.5.

224　　　　　　　　　The Works

   9. Drum sing' ich mit meinem Leide　　　　soprano and tenor
 10. Ihr Völker! Bringet her dem Herrn　　　　　　　　　　choir

Performance Issues: The choral writing intersperses homophonic and contrapuntal passages. Imitative passages are often quite complex, but logically conceived for effective learning. The choral parts are vocally demanding with long sustained passages and exploitation of the full ranges of the choristers. They are however sensitively written for the singers. Throughout the work, attention will need to be applied to clarity of diction. The nature of the counterpoint and the specific orchestral doubling of the choral parts are inclined to muddy the text. A mature and experienced choir is a necessity. The orchestra provides considerable support of the vocal material, but not all of the choral pitches are directly doubled. The orchestration requires a full complement of strings and large symphonic choral ensemble. The string writing is idiomatic, but contains considerable ornamental passagework. Likewise, there are considerable exposed passages for the brass, some of which are challenging. To ensure effective balance, the brass section must be capable of sensitive dynamic control. The organ part appears only in the choral portion of the work. It is fully notated, and although a performance can be given without organ, its color and reinforcement of certain contrapuntal elements suggests that it is not optional. The score makes considerable use of ostinati, particularly as accompanimental figures. This is an effective and melodically rich score that was once a part of the standard repertoire. It has some quaint features reflective of the tastes of the 19th century, and there are some structural deficiencies related to overall cohesion; however, it is a work that flatters the orchestra and singers that deserves more contemporary performances. **Soloists:** soprano I - range: $e^{b\prime}$-$b^{b\prime\prime}$, tessitura: g'-g'', this is a lyric solo that must be able to penetrate the entire ensemble; soprano II - range: d'-f'', tessitura: f'-f'', this is a declamatory role that appears only in duet; tenor - range: c-$a^{b\prime}$, tessitura: g-g', this is a sustained and lyric solo solo with some long phrases; **choir:** difficult; **orchestra:** difficult.

Selected Discography

---

[63] This hymn by Johann Crüger was published in Leipzig in 1649 as part of his *Geistliche Kirchen-Melodien.*

Elisabeth Connell, Karita Mattila, Hans Peter Blochwitz; London Symphony Orchestra and Chorus; conducted by Claudio Abbado. Deautsche Grammophon: 4231432.

Cynthia Haymon, Alison Hagley, Peter Straka; Leslie Pearson, organ; Philharmonia Chorus and Orchestra; conducted by Walter Weller. Chandos: CHAN10224X.

Anne Schwanewilms, Petra-Maria Schnitzer, Peter Seiffert; Leipzig Gewandhaus Orchestra and Choir; conducted by Riccardo Chailly, recorded live 2-3 September 2005 at the Gewandhaus in Leipzig. DVD — EuroArts: 2054668.

Selected Bibliography

Upton, George: *The Standard Oratorios*, 213-218. Chicago: A. C. McClurg and Company, 1893.

Norris, James Weldon: *Mendelssohn's Lobgesang opus 52: An Analysis for Performance*. Doctoral dissertation: Indiana University, 1974.

Felix Mendelssohn: A Life in Letters, edited by Rudolf Elvers, translated by Craig Tomlinson, 254, 255. New York: Fromm International, 1986.

Kapp, Reinhard: "Lobgesang," in *Neue Musik un Tradition: Festschrift Rudolf Stephan*, edited by Joseh Kuckertz, Helga de la Motte-Haber, Christian Martin Schmidt, and Wilhelm Seidel, 239-249. Laaber: Laaber, 1990.

Pahlen, Kurt: *The World of the Oratorio*, translated by Judith Schaefer with additional English-language material by Thurston Dox, 224-226. Portland, OR: Amadeus Press, 1990.

Town, Stephen: "Mendelssohn's 'Lobgesang': A Fusion of Forms and Textures, " *Choral Journal*, xxxiii (1992), 19-26.

Steinbeck, Wolfram: "Der Idee der Vokalsymphonie: Zu Mendelssohns Lobgesang," *Archiv für Musikwissenschaft*, liii (1996), 222-233.

Tu es Petrus, op. 111 (1827)

Duration: ca. 6 minutes

Text: This Latin text is from the New Testament of the Bible. It is the quote attributed to Jesus, "You are Peter, and upon this rock I shall build my church."

Performing Forces: voices: SSATB choir; **orchestra:** 2 flutes, 2 oboes, 2 horns (D), 2 trumpets (D), 3 trombones (alto, tenor, and bass), timpani (2 drums), and strings.

First Performance: 14 November 1827

Editions: *Tu es Petrus* is published in the critical edition: *F. Mendelssohn-Bartholdy: Werke: kritisch durchgesehene Ausgabe*, edited by Julius Rietz, series: 14, volume: A3. Other scholarly editions those prepared by Brian W. Pritchard (1976) for Harmonia and John Michael Cooper (1996) for Carus Verlag.

Tu es Petrus was published posthumously. The first edition was produced concurrently by Simrock and Ewer as a piano-vocal score in 1868.

Autograph: The composer's manuscript is in part 47 of the Mendelssohn Autograph Collection of the Berlin Stadtsbibliothek.

Notes: The score is dated 14 November 1827—6 December 1827.

Performance Issues: This work is composed in the style of a renaissance polyphonic motet with orchestral accompaniment. The choral parts have some very long, sustained phrases and considerable melismatic writing. The orchestra doubles the choir some of the time, at others, it provides some contrapuntal enrichments or subtle pitch grounding. A smaller string section is entirely suitable for this work. The score is written in 4/2. The frequency of double whole notes in the accompaniment may be distracting to inexperienced players; **choir:** difficult; **orchestra:** medium easy.

Selected Discography

Chamber Choir of Europe, Württembergische Philharmonie Reutlingen; conducted by Nocol Matt. Brilliant Classics: 99997.

Messager, André (b. Montluçon, 30 December 1853; d. Paris, 24 February 1929)

Life: Messager studied at the Paris Conservatory. He was organist at St. Sulpice in Paris and became an important conductor in France. His posts include music director of the Opéra-Comique (1898 to 1903), where he led the premiere of Debussy's *Pelléas et Mélisande*, which is dedicated to him; manager of the Grand Opera Syndicate at Covent Garden (1901-1907); conductor of the Concerts Lamoureux (1905); music director of the Paris Opéra (1907-1914); and conductor of the Société des Concerts du Conservatoire (1908-1919). He also conducted the 1924 season of Diaghilev's Ballets Russes. His music was primarily written for the theater.

Teachers: Gabriel Fauré, Eugène Gigout, Camille Saint-Saëns

Other Principal Works: opera: *Scaramouche* (1891), *Madame Chrysanthème* (1893), *Véronique* (1898), *Béatrice* (1914), *Monsieur Beaucaire* (1919); **ballet:** *Les deux pigeons* (1886), *Le Chevalier aux fleurs* (1897)

Selected Composer Bibliography

Février, Henri: *André Messager, mon Maître, mon ami.* Paris: Amiot-Dumont, 1948.
Augé-Laribé, Michel: *André Messager, musicien de théâtre.* Paris: La Colombe, 1951.

Messe des pêcheurs de Villerville (1881-1882)

See entry under Gabriel Fauré.

Paine, John Knowles (b. Portland, Maine, 9 January 1839; d. Cambridge, Massachusetts, 25 April 1906)

Life: Paine's father owned a music store and conducted the town band. Paine studied in Berlin from 1858 to 1861. Upon his return to the United States he joined the faculty of Harvard University. In 1875, he was appointed Professor of Music at Harvard, becoming the first to hold this title at any American university.

Paine's music is solid and representative of the finest mainstream American concert music of the era, although much of it appears self-consciously serious to modern ears. His best works still have much to offer, but it is as a teacher that he made his most important contributions to American music.

Teachers: Hermann Krotzschmar, Wilhelm Wieprecht

Students: John Alden Carpenter, Frederick Converse, Arthur Foote, Edward Burlingame Hill, Hugo Leichtentritt, Daniel Gregory Mason, Carl Ruggles

Writings: *The History of Music to the Death of Schubert.* Boston: Ditson, 1907.

Other Principal Works: orchestral: Symphony No. 1 (1875), Symphony No. 2 (1879); **choral:** Mass (1865), *St. Peter* (1870-1872), *Centennial Hymn* (1876), *Columbus March and Hymn* (1893), *Hymn of the West* (1903).

Selected Composer Bibliography

Schmidt, John C.: *The Life and Works of John Knowles Paine.* Ann Arbor, MI: UMI Research Press, 1980.

The Nativity, op. 38 (1883)

Duration: ca. 30 minutes

Text: The text is taken from *On the Morning of Christ's Nativity* (1629) by John Milton.

Performing Forces: **voices:** soprano, alto, tenor, and bass soloists; SATB choir; **orchestra:** 2 flutes, 2 oboes, 2 clarinets, 2 bassoons, 4 horns, 3 trumpets, 3 trombones, tuba, timpani, harp, organ, and strings.

First Performance: 2 May 1883; Boston; Emma Thursby, Mathilde Phillipps, George W. Want, Myron W. Whitney; Boston Handel and Haydn Society; conducted by the composer

Editions: *The Nativity* was originally published by Arthur Schmidt in 1883 with a revised edition appearing in 1903. A critical edition, prepared by John C. Schmidt, has been published in *Recent Researches in American Music*, volume 46, by A-R Editions.

Autograph: The composer's manuscript is in the Houghton Library of Harvard University (MS Mus 57.29). This collection also includes the original copyist's score and original parts (fMS Mus 57.30).

Notes: *The Nativity* was composed for the sixth triennial festival of the Boston Handel and Hayden Society. Paine selected 11 of the 27 stanzas of Milton's poem. A comparison of the third movement with the finale of Vaughan Williams's *Hodie*, which is a setting of the same text, is well worth the effort. Paine organized his work into three movements:

1. It Was the Winter Wind (soprano and choir)
2. The Shepherds on the Lawn (quartet and choir)
3. Ring Out, Ye Crystal Spheres (choir)

Performance Issues: The choral writing balances primarily homophonic sections with some pervasive imitation. There are some passages in which individual sections of the choir are treated as solos. All of the choral material is clearly supported by the orchestra and is not vocally difficult. There are significant sections scored for the full ensemble for which a large string section and symphonic choir are needed. The individual instrumental parts are idiomatic and not difficult, but they require good control of quiet tutti playing. The density of scoring and the occasional layering of textures will require attention to guarantee clarity. **Soloists:** soprano - range: e'-b''^{b} (c'''), tessitura: g'-g'', this is a sustained solo with significant sections sung over the entire orchestra and choir; alto - range: c'-$e^{b\prime\prime}$, tessitura: d'-d'', this is a lyric solo with some florid melismatic passages; tenor - range: e^b-$a^{b\prime}$, tessitura: g-f', this is a lyric solo with some florid melismatic passages; bass - range: A^b-$e^{b\prime}$, tessitura: c-c', this is a lyric solo with some florid melismatic passages; **choir:** medium difficult; **orchestra:** medium difficult.

Selected Discography

At the time of this writing, no recordings were available.

Selected Bibliography

Schmidt, John C.: "Introduction" and "Critical Report" from *Recent Researches in American Music*, volume 46, John Knowles Paine: *The Nativity*, Opus 39. Middleton, WI: A-R Editions, Inc., 2004.

Parker, Horatio (Auburndale, Massachusetts, 15 September 1863; d. Cedarhurst, New York, 19 December 1919)

Life: Parker began his musical studies with his mother. After studying with Chadwick and Emery in Boston, he went to Munich to study with Rheinberger. Upon his return to the United States, he settled in New York where he taught in a number of schools including the National Conservatory of Music during the period when it was being led by Dvorak. He served as organist of Trinity Church in Boston from 1893 to 1902.

In 1894, Parker joined the music faculty of Yale University. He became Dean of the School of Music there in 1904 and held that post until his death. He founded the New Haven Symphony Orchestra in 1895 and served as its music director until 1918.

Parker's music is solidly in the German tradition. He was a gifted teacher of technique and structure, and he provided a traditional grounding for his students, many of whom were the most creative of their generation.

Teachers: George Whitefield Chadwick, Stephen Emery, Joseph Rheinberger

Students: Seth Bingham, Charles Ives, Douglas Moore, Quincy Porter, Roger Sessions, David Stanley Smith

Other Principal Works: opera: *Mona* (1912), *Fairyland* (1914); **orchestral:** Symphony in C major (1885), *A Northern Ballad* (1899), Organ Concerto (1902); **choral:** *King Trojan* (1885), *The Holy Child* (1893), *The Legend of St. Christopher* (1897), *Song of the Times* (1911), *Morven and the Grail* (1915).

Selected Composer Bibliography

Chadwick, George: *Horatio Parker.* New Haven: Yale University Press, 1921.
Kearns, W.: *Horatio Parker 1863-1919: A Study of His Life and Music.* University of Illinois: dissertation, 1965.

Hora Novissima, op. 30 (1892)

Duration: ca. 62 minutes

Text: The text is from *De Contemptu Mundi* by Bernard de Morlaix and is in Latin. The composer included a singing English translation prepared by his mother, Isabella G. Parker.

Performing Forces: voices: soprano, alto, tenor, and bass soloists; SATB choir; **orchestra:** 2 flutes, 2 oboes, 2 clarinets (A), 2 bassoons, 4 horns (F), 2 trumpets (D), 3 trombones, tuba, timpani (2 drums), percussion (2 players — bass drum, cymbals), harp, organ, and strings.

First Performance: 3 May 1893; Church of the Holy Trinity, New York; Mrs. Theodore J. Toedt, Miss Ruth Thompson, Mr. S. Fischer Miller, Mr. Ericksson Bushnell; Mr. Will C Macfarlane, organist; Church Choral Society of New York; conducted by the composer

Editions: *Hora Novissima* has been published by H. W. Gray, Novello and Ewer, and Kalmus. Da Capo Press has published a reprint of the 1900 Novello edition with introductory notes by H. Wiley Hitchcock.

Autograph: The composer's manuscript score is in the Library of Congress.

Notes: The full title of the work is *Hora Novissima: The Rhythm of Bernard De Morlaix on the Celestial Country.* It was composed for the Church Choral Society of New York. Of this composition, H. Wiley Hitchcock writes:

> *Hora Novissima* came directly out of Parker's experience, during visits to Britain between 1890 and 1892, of the English choral festivals in such cities as Leeds and Birmingham. However, he also brought to it his solid training in Munich in the 1880s under Josef Rheinberger and his knowledge of works like Dvořák's Stabat Mater and the operas and other works of Rossini and Verdi. The result is a composition of undeniable

eclecticism—but one intergrated by technical devices such as cyclic themes and also by a consistent atmosphere of German-American hymnic grandeur, solidity, and dignity.[64]

The score is organized as follows:

Part One
1.	Hora Novissima	Introduction and choir
2.	Hic breve vivitur	quartet
3.	Spe modo vivitur	bass aria
4.	Pars mea, Rex meus	choir
5.	O bona patria	soprano aria
6.	Tu sine littore	quartet and choir

Part Two
7.	Urbs Syon aurea	tenor aria
8.	Stant syon atria	double choir
9.	Gens duce splendida	alto aria
10.	Urbs Syon unica	a cappella choir
11.	Urbs Syon inclyta	quartet and choir

Performance Issues: The majority of the choral material is homophonic and syllabic. There are some freely contrapuntal sections. The choir is clearly supported by the accompaniment with the exception of the a cappella movement. Some of the harmonic language is interesting in its use of mediant relationships and occasionally provocative chromaticisms; however, the part writing is quite conservative with fairly static melodic motion. The effect is a monumental sound and fairly unmemorable tunes. The sonic quality of the work is consistently appealing if not always inspiring. The choral parts are vocally accessible and easily taught. The a cappella movement betrays a study of Brahms in its integration of renaissance counterpoint and 19th-century harmonic practice. The orchestral writing is idiomatic and solidly arranged. It is a very practically scored composition that will flatter the ensemble. Movement 3 has an extended section of alternating 3/4 and 4/4 measures that were clearly intended to be in 7/4, but lacked the notational practice to write it as such. There is an exposed and im-

---

[64] H. Wiley Hitchcock: "Introduction: to Horatio W. Parker's *Hora Novissima*." New York: Da Capo Press, 1972.

portant cello quintet in movement 7. **Soloists:** soprano - range: c#'-b♭'', tessitura: f'-f'', this is a sustained lyric solo with some very long phrases; alto - range: a-e'', tessitura: c'-c'', this is a very sustained solo with some wide melodic leaps; tenor - range: d-a', tessitura: g-g', this is a sustained and lyric solo; bass - range: A-e', tessitura: c-c', this is a sustained and lyric solo; **choir:** medium difficult; **orchestra:** medium difficult.

Selected Discography: American Recording Society: ARS-0335 [LP], released in 1953.

Desto: D-413-14/DST-6413-14 [LP mono], released in 1965.

Abendmusik Chorus, Nebraska Wesleyan University Choir, Nebraska Chamber Orchestra; conducted by John Levick, recorded in 1994. Albany Records Troy: 125.

Selected Bibliography

"Amusements: The Church Choral Society" [review of the premiere], *New York Times* (4 May 1893). Reprinted in *Source Readings in American Choral Music: Composers' Writings, Interviews, and Reviews*, edited by David P. DeVenney; *Monographs and Bibliographies in American Music*, number 15, 84-86. Missoula, MT: College Music Society, 1995.

Dox, Thurston: *American Oratorios and Cantatas: A Catalogue of Works Written in the United States from Colonial Times to 1985*, volume 1, 144-147. Metuchen, NJ: Scarecrow Press, 1986.

Pahlen, Kurt: *The World of the Oratorio*, translated by Judith Schaefer with additional English-language material by Thurston Dox, 260-262. Portland, OR: Amadeus Press, 1990.

Smither, Howard E.: *A History of the Oratorio, volume 4: The Oratorio in the Nineteenth and Twentieth Centuries*, 493-506. Chapel Hill, NC: The University of North Carolina Press, 2000.

Puccini, Giacomo (b. Lucca, Italy, 22 December 1858; d. Brussels, 29 November 1924)

Life: Puccini was a fifth-generation church-music composer. This family tradition was reflected in his training, but Ponchielli recognized his potential as a composer of theatrical music. His first two operas were unsuccessful, but the faithful patronage of Boito and Ricordi led him to score his first critical success with *Manon Lescaut*. This was followed by a string of works that have become standards of opera houses worldwide.

Puccini is the archetype of the *verismo* style combining the best vocal treatments of the *bel canto* with psychologically compelling characters, rich chromatic harmonies, and exotic orchestrations.

Teachers: Carlo Angeloni, Antonio Bazzini, Fortunato Magi, Amilcare Ponchielli

Writings: *The Letters of Giacomo Puccini*, edited by Giuseppe Adami and translated by Ena Makin. Philadelphia: J.B. Lippincott, 1931.

Other Principal Works: opera: *Le Villi* (1884), *Edgar* (1889), *Manon Lescaut* (1893), *La Bohème* (1896), *Tosca* (1900), *Madama Butterfly* (1904), *La Fanciulla del West* (1910), *La Rondine* (1917), *Il Trittico* (1918), *Turandot* (unfinished, completed by Alfano, 1926); **choral:** *Requiem* (1905).

Selected Composer Bibliography

Carner, Mosco: *Puccini: A Critical Biography.* New York: Alfred Knopf, 1959.
Weaver, William: *Puccini: The Man and His Music.* New York: E. P. Dutton, 1977.
Greenfield, Howard: *Puccini.* London: Robert Hale, 1980.
Puccini, Simonetta and William Weaver: *The Puccini Companion.* New York: W. W. Norton, 1994.
Wilson, Conrad: Giacomo *Puccini.* London: Phaidon Press, 1997.
Budden, Julian: *Puccini: His Life and Works.* Oxford: Oxford University Press, 2002.

Messa a 4 Voci [known as *Messa di Gloria*] (1880)

Duration: ca. 43 minutes

Text: The text is from the Roman Catholic communion liturgy.

Performing Forces: voices: tenor, baritone, and bass soloists; SATB choir; **orchestra:** piccolo, 2 flutes, 2 oboes, 2 clarinets, 2 bassoons, 4 horns, 2 trumpets, 3 trombones, ophicleide,[65] timpani (2 drums), harp, and strings

First Performance: 25 January 1880; Lucca, Italy. The next performance was 12 July 1952 as part of the Grant Park concert series in Chicago with the Swedish Choral Club conducted by Alfredo Antonini. The first 20th-century performance in Europe was 23 December 1952 in Naples performed by the Orchestra e Coro Scarlatti di Napoli.[66]

Editions: Belwin-Mills publishes a piano-vocal score. A newer edition is now published by Ricordi. Carus-Verlag publishes a new edition prepared by Dieter Schickling (Carus 40.645). Full scores and parts are available for rental.

Autograph: The composer's manuscript is in the Museo di Casa Puccini in Torre del Lago Puccini.

Notes: This work was completed as the equivalent of a final examination piece for Puccini's training at the conservatory in Lucca. The score incorporates a motet and Credo composed in 1878. Portions of this mass reappear in the Puccini's opera, *Edgar*. Also, the Agnus Dei reappears as the "Madrigale" in *Manon Lescaut*.[67]

Performance Issues: The "Gloria" is by far the largest movement in this mass, and it is a good litmus test of the overall performability of the entire work. The choral writing combines homophonic and

---

[65] Contemporary performances use tuba.

[66] The first performance dates are conflated in the preface to the piano-vocal score, which indicates the premiere as 12 July 1880.

[67] Preface to the piano-vocal score. Milan: Ricordi, 2006.

polyphonic textures. The counterpoint is a bit stiff obviously complying with the expectations of the composer's teachers. The vocal parts are clearly supported by the orchestra. The tessitura of the sopranos is fairly high. It appears to have been intended for boys. There are some vocally florid passages for the choristers, particularly the tenors. There are extended unison passages for the basses and sopranos. There are some very interesting uses of chromaticism and clever imitative procedures many of which are a bit "Victorian" in sound, but simultaneously show the promise of the distinctive compositional voice to come. There is a tenor/bass duet in the "Agnus Dei" for which either the baritone or bass may be used. If it is the former, the indicated range should be d-$e^{b\prime}$. A single bass soloist is often used. The orchestration is fairly conservative and all of the parts are practically conceived. The timbral palette is less rich than in later works, but it is a sonorously pleasing score. **Soloists:** tenor - range: e^b-$b^{b\prime}$, tessitura: g-g', this is a lyric and sustained solo, it is the largest of the solo roles; baritone - range: e^b-f', tessitura: g-$e^{b\prime}$, this is a light, sustained lyric role that could also be appropriate for a tenor; bass - range: F-$e^{b\prime}$, tessitura: c-c', this is a rhythmic and declamatory solo; **choir:** medium difficult; **orchestra:** medium easy.

Selected Discography

The 23 December 1952 modern European premiere was recorded on LP. It was released as Colosseum: CLPS-1053.

José Carreras, Hermann Prey; Ambrosian Singers, Philharmonia Orchestra, conducted by Claudio Scimone. Erato: 4509-96367-2.

Philippe Huttenlocher, William Johns; Gulbenkian Choir and Orchestra; conducted by Michel Corboz. Erato: 0630-12818-2.

Roberto Alagna, Thomas Hampson; London Symphony Orchestra and Chorus; conducted by Antonio Pappano. EMI: CDC5 57159-2.

Selected Bibliography

Puccini, Simonetta, and William Weaver: *The Puccini Companion*, 55-56, 65-66, 105, 282-284, 296, 336. New York: W. W. Norton, 1994.

Rimsky-Korsakov, Nikolai (b. Tikhvin, Russia, 18 March 1844; d. Liubensk, Russia, 21 June 1908)

Life: Rimsky-Korsakov was born into an affluent family. He embarked on a naval career, but was impressed upon hearing the nationalist compositions of Glinka. He soon established a friendship with Balakirev and began to compose orchestral music ignorant of the fundamental nomenclature of music theory. Despite his technical shortcomings at the time, he was hired as a professor of composition at the St. Petersburg Conservatory in 1871. He served in this capacity with great distinction until his death.

With Balakirev, Borodin, Cui, and Mussorgsky, Rimsky-Korsakov comprised the "Mighty Five." These were the composers who embodied the new Russian nationalist style in music. Rimsky-Korsakov compiled, edited, and even orchestrated works left behind upon Mussorgsky's death. Likewise, he revised Mussorgsky's *Boris Godunov* and completed Borodin's *Prince Igor*.

It is as an orchestrator that Rimsky-Korsakov most distinguished himself. His *Principles of Orchestration* is still regarded as one of the most important treatises on the subject. His works are marked by brilliant use of orchestral colors and an informed practicality from a player's perspective. The rich orchestral palette of 20th-century Russian music is cast in his shadow.

Teachers: primarily self-taught

Students: Anton Arensky, Alexander Glazunov, Mikhail Gnessin, Alexander Gretchaninov, Mikhail Ippolitov-Ivanov, Vasili Kalafati, Nikolai Kazanly, Ivan Kryzhanovsky, Anatoli Liadov, Witold Maliszewski, Nikolai Miaskovsky, Sergei Prokofiev, Ottorino Respighi, Solomon Rosowsky, Mart Saar, Lazare Saminsky, Nikolai Alexandrovich Sokolov, Maximillian Steinberg, Igor Stravinsky, Nikolai Tcherepnin, Joseph Wihtol

Writings: *Principles of Orchestration: With Musical Examples Drawn from His Own Works*, edited by Maximilian Steinberg, translated by Edward Agate, two volumes bound as one. Editions Russe de Musique, 1922; reprinted, New York: Dover, 1964.

A Conductor's Guide to 19th-Century Choral-Orchestra Works 239

Other Principal Works: opera: *May Night* (1878-79), *Snow Maiden* (1880-1881), *Mlada* (1889-1890), *Mozart and Salieri* (1897), *The Tsar's Bride* (1898), *The Legend of Tsar Saltan* (1899-1900), *Tale of the Invisible City of Ktzeh* (1903-1904), *The Golden Cockerel* (1906-1907); **orchestral:** Symphony No. 1 (1861-1865, 1884), Symphony No. 2 (1868), Symphony No. 3 (1873-1874), *Sadko* (1867), *Sheherazade* (1888), *Russian Easter Overture* (1888); **choral:** *Song of Oleg the Wise* (1899), *From Homer* (1901).

Selected Composer Bibliography

Abraham, Gerald: *Rimsky-Korsakov: A Short Biography*. London: AMS Press, 1949.

Seaman, Gerald: *Nikolai Andreevich Rimsky-Korsakov: A Guide for Research*. New York: Garland, 1988.

Alexey, the Man of God [Stikh ob Alexeye Bozh'yem cheloveke] op. 20 (1878)

Duration: ca. 5 minutes

Text: Unknown, perhaps it is by the composer.

Performing Forces: voices: AATTBB choir; **orchestra:** 2 flutes, 2 oboes, 2 clarinets (A), 2 bassoons, 2 horns (D, E), 2 trumpets (E), 3 trombones, timpani, and strings.

First Performance: 22 January 1894, St. Petersburg, conducted by the composer as part of the "Third Russian Symphonic Concert"

Editions: This work was originally published by Beliaiev. It appears in N. A. Rimsky-Korsakov's *Complete Works*, volume 24. Full scores and parts for *Alexey, the Man of God* are available in a pairing with *Slava* from Belwin-Mills (K 5234).

Autograph: The location of the composer's manuscript is unknown.

Notes: This work is an adaptation of a folktune the composer heard while working on the score of the opera, *The Maid of Pskov*, in

1877. It was being sung by pilgrims visiting the Pechersk Monastery.

Performance Issues: The choral writing is homophonic with conservative ranges in all parts. The choral parts are clearly doubled by the orchestra. The orchestral writing is idiomatic and well within the abilities of an amateur ensemble. This is a work that allows less accomplished ensembles to sound their very best; **choir:** medium easy; **orchestra:** medium easy.

Selected Discography

At the time of this writing no commercial recordings appear to be available.

Selected Bibliography

The editor's notes for the *Collected Works* are published in English translation by Olga Browning as a foreword to the Belwin-Mills score.

Slava ["Glory"], op. 21 (1879-1880)

Duration: ca. 5 minutes

Text: The text is taken from a Russian folksong.

Performing Forces: voices: SSATTB choir; **orchestra:** 2 flutes, 2 oboes, 2 clarinets (B^b), 2 bassoons, 4 horns (F), 2 cornets (B^b), 2 trumpets (F), 3 trombones, tuba, timpani (2 drums), and strings.

First Performance: 22 January 1894, St. Petersburg, conducted by the composer as part of the "Third Russian Symphonic Concert"

Editions: This work was first published by A. Bitner and reissued by M.P. Beliaiev. It appears in N. A. Rimsky-Korsakov's *Complete Works*, volume 24. Full scores and parts for *Slava* are available in a pairing with *Alexey, the Man of God* from Belwin-Mills (K 5234).

Autograph: The composer's manuscript is in the M.P. Beliaiev Collection (No. I[3]) in the Saltyon-Shchedrin State Public Library in St. Petersburg.

Notes: The score is an arrangement of a popular Russian folksong. It is dedicated to Ie. S. Azeiev.

Performance Issues: This work juxtaposes flashy, bombastic passages with judiciously conceived choral sections. The choral writing is practical and primarily homophonic and doubled by the orchestra, although there are some a cappella passages. There are some three-part divisi for the sopranos and tenors. All of the writing is practical, and the scoring is masterful. The brass parts require assured players. This is a particularly flattering composition for an orchestra with stronger wind and brass players than the string section. It is well suited to a large choral ensemble; **choir:** medium easy; **orchestra:** medium easy.

Selected Discography

At the time of this writing no commercial recordings appear to be available.

Selected Bibliography

The editor's notes for the *Collected Works* are published in English translation by Olga Browning as a foreword to the Belwin-Mills score.

Rossini, Gioachino (b. Pesaro, Italy, 29 February 1792; d. Paris, 13 November 1868)

Life: Rossini was born into a musical family. His father was a trumpeter, and his mother a singer. He was apprenticed to a blacksmith. His talent was soon recognized, and he became a student the Liceo Musicale in Bologna. He began composing and received a commission for an opera in 1810. Between 1812 and 1829, he composed over 30 operas, many of them great successes.

Rossini had a great dramatic gift that allowed him to bring humor into tragedies and melancholy into comedies. His lyricism and melodic sensitivity were without equal during his career. He received a number of posts in Italy, then Vienna, and finally Paris with an interlude in Bologna. In Paris, he was to receive a series of commissions that were curtailed when the fall of Charles X nullified the contract. He composed no opera during the last forty years of his life, but he lived royaly off of the enormous body of work he had already produced.

Rossini enjoyed the company of the intelligentsia of Europe. He also enjoyed the company and work of the great chefs. To this day, *à la Rossini* refers to a preparation with tomatoes and cream. Rossini is best known to today's audiences through *Il Barbiere Siviglia* and the overtures of many of his other operas. Full productions of his operas reveal his true genius musically and dramatically.

Teachers: Stanislao Mattei

Other Principal Works: opera: *La scala di seta* (1812), *Il Signor Bruschino* (1812), *Tancredi* (1812-1813), *L'Italiana in Algeri* (1813), *Il Turco in Italia* (1814), *Elisabetta, regina d'Inghilterra* (1815), *Il Barbiere Siviglia* (1816), *La Cenerentola* (1816-1817), *La gazza ladra* (1817), *Armida* (1817), *Semiramide* (1822-1823), *Il viaggio a Reims* (1825), *Guillaume Tell* (1828-1829); and a number of cantatas, masses, and chamber music.

Selected Composer Bibliography

Weinstock, Herbert: *Rossini: A Biography*. New York: Alfred Knopf, 1968; reprinted, New York: Limelight Editions, 1987.
Osborne, Richard: Rossini. London: Oxford University Press, 1986.
Kendall, Alan: *Gioachino Rossini: The Reluctant Hero*. London: V. Gollancz, 1992.
Gallo, Denise P.: *Gioachino Rossini: A Guide to Research*. New York: Routledge, 2002.

Petite Messe Solennelle

Duration: ca. 80 minutes

Text: The text is from the Roman Catholic communion liturgy.

Performing Forces: voices: soprano, alto, tenor, and bass soloists; SATB choir; **orchestra:** 2 pianos and harmonium or full orchestra.

First Performance: 12 February 1869; Théâtre Italien, Paris

Editions: A newly edited piano-harmonium score is published by Ricordi. Complete performing materials for all versions are available for rental from Ricordi.

Autograph: The composer's manuscript is in a private collection in Paris.

Notes: The score is organized in to 14 sections as follows:

Part One

1. Kyrie—Christe	soloists and choir
2. Gloria—Laudamus	soloists and choir
3. Gratias	alto—tenor—bass trio
4. Domine Deus	tenor aria
5. Qui tollis	sopran—alto duet
6. Quoniam	bass aria
7. Cum Sancto	soloists and choir

Part Two

8. Credo	soloists and choir
9. Crucifixus	soprano aria
10. Et resurrexit	soloists and choir
11. Preludio religioso	harmonium
12. Sanctus	soloists and choir
13. O Salutari	soprano aria
14. Agnus Dei	alto solo and choir

Performance Issues: The choir is primarily homophonic and well supported by the accompaniment; however, there are some a cappella passages including some with fugal material. There are some divisi in each part. Movement 12 is a cappella, and movement 7 is the most contrapuntally complex for the singers and accompaniment. The second piano part merely reinforces the first part in critical sections. The first piano part has some challenging material and requires a strong player. There are some rhythmically complex sections and extended passages in octaves for the left hand. The harmonium part is less demanding. Rossini uses a series of numerical symbols to indicate the registration of the harmonium. These are not consistent from maker to maker, so some research will need to be undertaken to clarify his intent. **Soloists:** soprano - range: $b-g''$, tessitura: $f'-f''$, this is a sustained and lyric role; alto - range: a^b-d'', tessitura: $b-b'$, this is a sustained role with some rapid coloratura passagework; tenor - range: $e-a'$, tessitura: $g-g'$, this is a lyric role with long phrases; bass - range: $F-e'$ (f'), tessitura: $A-c\#'$, this is a lyric solo role with florid melismatic passages; **choir:** medium easy; **orchestra:** medium difficult.

Selected Discography

Cecilia Gasdia, Bernarda Fink, Vincenzo la Scola, Luciano Sgrizzi, Philippe Corboz and Francesco Ellero d'Artegna; Ensemble Vocal de Lausanne; conducted by Michel Corboz. Erato: 3948-28173-2.

Mirella Freni, Lucia Valentini-Terrani, Luciano Pavarotti, Ruggero Raimondi; Leone Magiera (Piano), Vittoria Rosetta (Harmonium); Milan Teatro alla Scala Chorus; conducted by Romano Gandolfi, recorded December 1970 in Kingsway Hall, London, England. Decca: 455023-2.

A Conductor's Guide to 19th-Century Choral-Orchestra Works   245

Selected Bibliography

Ambros, A. W.: "Die Messe solennelle von Rossini," *Bunte Blätter* (Leipzing, 1872), volume 1, 81-92.

Stabat Mater (1831-1832, final version 1841)

Duration: ca. 61 minutes

Text: The authorship of this text is highly disputed. It has been attributed to Jacopone da Todi who died in 1306. It was removed from sanctioned use at the Council of Trent, and restored to the liturgical canon in 1727. The text addresses the "Seven Sorrows of the Virgin Mary." It is used as the Sequence Hymn on the first Friday after Passion Sunday and on 15 September.[68]

Performing Forces: voices: 2 soprano, tenor, and bass soloists, SATB choir; **orchestra:** 2 flutes, 2 oboes, 2 clarinets (B^b), 2 bassoons, 4 horns (A, G, E^b, E), 2 trumpets in (A, B^b) 3 trombones, timpani, and strings.

First Performance: The original version was premiered in Madrid on Good Friday 1833. The final version was given its first performance 7 January 1842, Salle Ventadour, Théâtre Italien, Paris

Editions: Full scores and parts for *Stabat Mater* are available for purchase from Ricordi, Schott, G. Schirmer, and Kalmus.

Autograph: The composer's manuscripts of the vocal score of the first version and the vocal score and full score of the second verion are in the British Library in London.

Notes: The original score was inscribed "Stabat Mater, composed especially for H. E. Don Francisco Fernandez Varella, Knight of the Grand Cross of the Order of Charles III, Archdeacon of Madrid, General Commissar of the Crusade, dedicated to him by Gioacchino Rossini—Paris 26th March 1832." Rossini had composed

---

[68] Jeffers, Ron: *Translations and Annotations of Choral Repertoire, Volume I: Sacred Latin Texts*, 200-207. Corvallis, OR: Earthsongs, 1988.

the first six movements, leaving the remainder in the hands of Giovanni Tadolini. This is the version premiered in Madrid. Following the death of Varella, the manuscript was sold by his estate to the publisher, Aulagnier. Rossini engaged in a legal battle to allow him to complete the work with his own music and have it published by Troupenas who was paying a commission for the new version of the work. This is the score that was premiered in Paris and remains in the repertoire. Within a year of this premiere, this score had been performed in 29 cities throughout Europe.[69] The score is organized as follows:

1. Introduction: Stabat Mater dolorosa
2. Tenor aria: Cujus animam gementem
3. Soprano I and II duet: Qui est homo qui est fleret
4. Bass aria: Pro peccatis suae gentis vidit Jesum
5. Chorus and bass recitative: Eja, Mater fons amoris
6. Quartet: Sancta Mater, istud agas
7. Soprano II Cavatina: Fac ut portem Christi mortem
8. Soprano I aria and chorus: Inflammatus et accensus
9. Quartet: Quando corpus morietur
10. Finale: Amen

Performance Issues: The choir is scored for soprano I and II, but the voicing is clearly for a traditional SATB choir. Much of the choral material is doubled by the soloists, but the true solo passages are much more demanding, requiring highly skilled singers. The choral parts are quite accessible to inexperienced singers. Movements 5 and 9 are a cappella. The finale is the most demanding movement for the singers. It is more contrapuntally conceived, but the choral parts are well supported by the accompaniment. The orchestral writing is consistent with that of the composer's operas in terms of dramatic effect and technique. It is idiomatically conceived, but quite challenging for the players. Some of the brass writing may prove difficult to balance with modern instruments that are of a larger bore than those in use in Rossini's time. This is an ideal work for a good orchestra and professional soloists to perform with an amateur choral society. The key scheme is built around an assortment of then progressive relationships, especially

---

[69] Tomelleri, Luiano: "Foreword" to *Stabat Mater* by Gioacchino Rossini. London: Ernst Eulenberg, 1957.

thirds. **Soloists:** soprano I - range: c'-c''', tessitura: g'-g'', this is a demanding role with declamatory sections and significant coloratura; soprano II - range: b-g#'', tessitura: d'-e'', this is a demanding role with declamatory sections and significant coloratura; tenor - range: e^b-d$^{b''}$, tessitura: g-g', this is a sustained role requiring odd pitch leaps and the ability to be heard over the full force of the orchestra; bass - range: F-f', tessitura: A-d', this is a lyric role with broad melodic leaps and control and clarity at the extremities of the range; **choir:** medium easy, **orchestra:** difficult.

Selected Discography

Helen Donath, Josef Protschka, Dietrich Fischer-Dieskau; Bayerischen Rundfunks Choir and Symphony Orchestra; conducted by Wolfgang Sawallisch, recorded in 1982 and 1983. EMI Classics: 7243 5 65845 2.

Pilar Lorengar, Yvonne Minton, Luciano Pavarotti, Hans Sotin; London Symphony Chorus and Orchestra; conducted by Istvan Kertesz, recorded March 1971 in Kingsway Hall, London, England. Decca: 455023-2.

Selected Bibliography

Adam, Adolphe: "Rossini: Le Stabat Mater," in *Derniers souvenirs d'un musicien*, 249-275. Paris: Michel Lévy Freres, 1859.

Upton, George: *The Standard Oratorios*, 253-257. Chicago: A. C. McClurg and Company, 1893.

Collita, Carlo: *Il Palazzo dell'Archiginnasio e l'antico studio Bolognese: con il Teatro Anatomico, le Funzioni dell'Anatomia; prima esecuzione dello Stabat Mater di Rossini*. Bologna: Stampa Officina Grafica Bolognese, 1975.

Tomelleri, Luiano: "Foreword" to *Stabat Mater* by Gioacchino Rossini. London: Ernst Eulenberg, 1957.

Burchi, Guido: "Una cadenza inedita per il soprano nello Stabat Mater di Rossini," in *Nuova rivista musicale italiana*, volume 17, number 1 (January-March 1983), 36-42.

Faravelli, Danilo: "Stabat Mater: poesia e musica," *Rivista internazionale di musica sacra*, volume 4, number 1 (January-March 1983), 9-43.

Spada, Marco: "Francesco Rangone e la *Narrazione* sullo Stabat Mater a Bologna con altri documenti," *Bullettino del Centro Rossiniano di Studi*, volume 19 (1989), 5-46.

Pahlen, Kurt: *The World of the Oratorio*, translated by Judith Schaefer with additional English-language material by Thurston Dox, 278-280. Portland, OR: Amadeus Press, 1990.

Kirsch, Winfried: "Gioacchino Rossinis Stabat Mater. Versuch einer Exegese," *Kirchenmusikalisches Jahrbuch*, volume 73 (1990), 71-96.

Berger, Melvin: *Guide to Choral Masterpieces: A Listener's Guide*, 259-260. New York: Anchor Books, 1993.

Collisana, Amalia: "Umorismo di Rossini," *Rivista italiana di musicologia*, volume 33, number 2 (1998), 301-349.

Saint-Saëns, Camille (b. Paris, 9 October 1835; d. Algiers, 16 December 1921)

Life: Saint-Saëns was a child prodigy raised by his great aunt. He began to perform as a pianist when he was five and to compose at six. He studied at the Paris Conservatory. He served as organist at the Madeleine in Paris from 1857 to 1876. He quickly became one of the most influential musicians of his generation. He toured all over the world as a pianist and to conduct his own works.

Saint-Saëns's music is distinguished by its remarkably taut counterpoint and elegant melodies. He combined German technical refinement and French sensibility and harmonic traditions establishing the foundations upon which the next generation would build its music and the walls that the subsequent generation would tear down. His works have never ceased being relevant and popular.

Teachers: Fromental Halévy

Students: Gabriel Fauré, Eugène Gigout, Fromental Halévy, André Messager

Writings: *Harmonie et mélodie*. Paris: 1885.
Problèmes et mystères. Paris: 1894.
Portraits et souvenirs. Paris: 1899.
École buissonnière: Notes et souvenirs. Paris: 1913.
Notice sur Le Timbre d'argent. Brussels: 1914.
On the Execution of Music, and Principally the Ancient Music. San Francisco: 1915.
Au courant de la vie. Paris: 1916.
Les idées de M. Vincent d'Indy. Paris: 1919.

Other Principal Works: opera: *Samson et Dalila* (1877), *Ascanio* (1890), *Déjanir* (1911); **orchestral:** Symphony No. 1 (1853), Symphony No. 2 (1859), Symphony No. 3 (1886), Piano Concerto No. 1 (1858), Piano Concerto No. 2 (1868), Piano Concerto No. 3 (1869), Piano Concerto No. 4 (1875), Piano Concerto No. 5 (1896), *Danse macabre* (1874), *Le Carnaval des animaux* (1886); **choral:** *Le déluge* (1875), *Requiem* (1878), *The Promised Land* (1913).

Selected Composer Bibliography

Baumann, Émile: *Les grandes formess de la musique: L'œuvre de Camille Sanit-Saëns.* Paris: Ollendorff, 1905.

Flynn, Timothy S.: *Camille Saint-Saëns: A Guide to Research.* New York: Routledge, 2003.

Oratorio de Noël (1858), op. 12

Duration: ca. 35 minutes

Text: The text is a telling of the Christmas story in Latin. The G. Schirmer edition only includes a singing English translation by N.H. Dole.[70]

Performing Forces: voices: soprano, mezzo-soprano, alto, tenor, and baritone soloists; SATB choir; **orchestra:** harp, organ, and strings.

First Performance: First performed in 1858 and published in 1863

Editions: Full scores and parts for *Oratorio de Noël* are available for purchase from Durand, G. Schirmer, and Kalmus.

Autograph: The location of the composer's manuscript is unknown.

Notes: The opening page of the score is labeled, "In the style of J. S. Bach." This is not a neo-baroque work, but the composer clearly imagined it as a French spin on Bach's church cantata form, including an overture, varied arrangements of soloists and choir, and a closing chorale.

Performance Issues: The choral writing is homophonic and well doubled by the orchestra. Movement 6 requires the most independence for the singers, but this is very practically composed. The bulk of the score is assigned to the soloists, and their parts are within the abilities of good choristers. The string writing is idiomatic and

---

[70] Although copies of the Schirmer piano-vocal score are plentiful in many American choral libraries, its text does not appear in the Kalmus or Durand full scores, so it will need to be transcribed into those materials if it is used.

generally simple. The more rhythmic passages are in unified rhythm and utilize ostinati. The composer indicates some solo passages for strings, suggesting a full complement; however, with a competent organist, this is a very practical work for a modest church-choir program using a string quintet, an organist, and a secure harpist. The harp writing is practical and well conceived for the instrument. **Soloists:** soprano - range: e'-c''', tessitura: g'-g'', this is lyric role with some coloratura passages; mezzo soprano - range: b-f#'', tessitura: e'-e'', this is a lyric and sustained solo part; alto - range: a-d'', tessitura: c#'-b', this is the simplest of the solo parts, it is lyrical; tenor - range: f-a', tessitura: g-e', this is a declamatory solo part; baritone - range: A-f', tessitura: d-d', this is a lyric solo part with some coloratura writing; **choir:** easy; **orchestra:** medium easy.

Selected Discography

Logumkloster Vocal Ensemble; conducted by Sven-Ingvart Mikkelsen. Classico: 253.

Verena Schweizer, Edith Wiens, Helena Jungwirth, Friedreich Melzer, Kurt Widmer; Mainz Collegium; conducted by Diethard Hellmann, recorded in the Christuskirche in Mainz Germany in 1976. Profil – Edition Günter Hänssler: 5023.

Ute Selbig, Elisabeth Wilke, Annette Markert, Armin Ude, Egbert Junghanns; Dresden Kreuz Choir, Dresden Philharmonic; conducted by Martin Flamig, recorded in 1987. Capriccio: PRSACD 9057.

Selected Bibliography

Upton, George: *The Standard Oratorios*, 269-270. Chicago: A. C. McClurg and Company, 1893.

Vierne, Louis: "La musique religieuse de Saint-Saëns," *Le guide du concert*, volume 3 (1922), 37-39.

Bernier, Conrad: "Emile Baumann et l'œuvre Camille Saint-Saëns," *Georgetown University French Review*, volume 1 (1937), 3-17.

Music, David W.: "Camille Saint-Saëns's Christmas Oratorio: Description, Accessibility, Comparison," in *The Choral Journal* (December 1998), 49-53.

Smither, Howard E.: *A History of the Oratorio, volume 4: The Oratorio in the Nineteenth and Twentieth Centuries*, 565-572. Chapel Hill, NC: The University of North Carolina Press, 2000.

Schubert, Franz (b. Himmelpfortgrund (Vienna), 31 January 1797; d. Vienna, 19 November 1828)

Life: Schubert's father was a poor schoolmaster. Schubert was a boy soprano in the imperial chapel and studied composition with Salieri until his voice changed. He then served as his father's assistant, continuing to write large quantities of music.

In 1817, Schubert quit his teaching position and moved to Vienna. He quickly became part of a circle of musicians and other intellectuals including the poet, Mayrhofer, and the singer, Michael Vogl. The latter became Schubert's principal interpreter, and the group held fairly regular soirées, but Schubert continued to struggle financially. He suffered with health troubles throughout the last five years of his life.

Schubert is credited with establishing the genre of romantic Lieder, to which he contributed over 600 significant works. There are some poems that he set as many as six times. He is perhaps the fastest composer to have lived having completed as many as five songs in a single day. Schubert was truly a master of every genre in which he composed. Late in his short life, he took counterpoint lessons with Sechter. His later works demonstrate the profound effect that these lessons and his friendship with Beethoven had upon his musical style. His final orchestral works and songs serve as a transition between Beethoven and the generation of Schumann and Mendelssohn, and his harmonic inventiveness opened the door for the chromatic explorations of the late 19th century.

Teachers: Antonio Salieri, Simon Sechter

Other Principal Works: opera: *Alfonso und Estrella* (1821-1822), *Fierrabras* (1823); **orchestral:** Symphony No. 1 (1813), Symphony No. 2 (1814-1815), Symphony No. 3 (1815), Symphony No. 4 (1816), Symphony No. 5 (1816), Symphony No. 6 (1818), Symphony No. 7 (1822, unfinished), Symphony No. 9 (1825); **chamber music:** 15 string quartets, Piano Quintet (1819), Arpeggione Sonata (1824); **vocal:** hundreds of songs and part songs.

Selected Composer Bibliography

Deutsch, Otto Erich: *Franz Schubert Thematisches Verzeichnis seiner Werke in chronologischer Folge*. Kassel: Bärenreiter, 1978.

Jaskulsky, Hans: *Die lateinischen Messen Franz Schuberts*. Mainz: Schott 1986.

Jahrmärker, Manuela: "Von der litugischen Funktion zum persönlichen Bekenntnis Die Kirchenmusik," *Schubert Handbuch*, edited by Walther Dürr and Andreas Krause, 345-378. Kassel: Bärenreiter, 1997.

Stanley, Glenn: "Schubert's Religious and Choral Music: Toward a Statement of Faith," in *The Cambridge Companion to Schubert*, edited by Christopher H. Gibbs, 207-223. Cambridge: Cambridge University Press, 1997.

Deutsche Messe, D. 872 (1827)[71]

Duration: ca. 25 minutes

Text: The text is the ordinary of the communion liturgy in a German adaptation. An additional movement is a setting of a sacred poem by Johann Philipp Neumann.

Performing Forces: voices: SATB choir; **orchestra:** 2 oboes, 2 clarinets (B^b), 2 bassoons, 2 horns (E^b, F, G, B^b, C), 2 trumpets (B^b), 3 trombones, and timpani (2 drums).

The score includes an organ reduction for church use without the windband.

First Performance: The first performance of this work is uncertain.

Editions: Full scores and parts for the Deutsche Messe are available from Kalmus, Schott, Carus, and Breitkopf and Härtel. Version A appears in the *Franz Schubert: Neue Ausgabe sämtlicher Werke*, part 1, volume 6. Version B appears in the *Schubert Werke* (re-

---

[71] This date is assumed because Schubert sent a "thank-you" note to the librettist on 16 October 1827 upon the receipt of his part of the commission, which was 100 florins.

printed by Dover) part 13, volume 2, page 325; and in a modern critical edition in the *Franz Schubert: Neue Ausgabe sämtlicher Werke*, part 1, volume 6.

Autograph: The first version with additional materials in the hand of the composer's brother, Ferdinand, including a full set of parts transcribed in 1839, are in the Gesellschaft der Musikfreunde in Vienna.

Notes: The score includes an appended hymn, *Das Gebet des Herrn*, on a text by Neumann. The principal work is organized in seven movements as follows:

1. Zum Eingang (Wohin sol lich mich wenden)
2. Zum Gloria (Ehre, Ehre sei Gott in der Höhe)
3. Zum Evangelium und Credo (Noch lag die Schöpfung formlos da)
4. Zum Offertorium (Du gabst, o Herr, mir Sein und Leben)
5. Zum Sanctus (Heilig, heilig, heilig)
6. Nach der Wandlung (Betrachtend Deine Huld und Güte)
7. Zum Agnus Dei (Mein Heiland, Herr und Meister!)

   Das Gebet des Herrn

Performance Issues: This is a simple and logogenic work. All of the vocal parts are clearly doubled by the winds, and most of the setting is syllabic. All of the vocal ranges are conservative, as are the wind parts. Everything is lyrical, and the score uses folk-like dance rhythms throughout. The pitch material is triadic and scalar with an ear toward congregational use; **choir:** easy, **orchestra:** easy.

Selected Discography

Elmar Schloter (organ); Chor und Symphonie-Orchester des Bayerischen Rundfunks (Josef Schmidhuber, choirmaster); conducted by Wolfgang Sawallisch. EMI: 86011. Previously released as EMI: CDC 7 474072.

Selected Bibliography

Deutsch, Otto: "Über Schuberts sogenannte 'Deutsche Messe,'" in *Musica Divina II*. Vienna, 1914.

Burkhart, Franz: "Franz Schuberts 'Deutsche Messe,'" in *Osterreichische Musikzeitschrift*, volume 31 (1976), 565-573.

Graduale: Benedictus es, Domino, D. 184 (1815)

Duration: ca. 5 minutes

Text: This text is from the Book of Daniel. It is used as an antiphon for Vespers in the Ambrosian tradition and is part of the Proper for the Feast of St. Stephen.

Performing Forces: voices: SATB choir; **orchestra:** 2 oboes, 2 clarinets (C), 2 trumpets (C), 3 trombones (alto, tenor, and bass), timpani (2 drums), strings, and organ.

First Performance: 8 September 1825; Church of St. Ulrich, Vienna

Editions: *Benedictus es Domino* appears in the *Schubert Werke* (reprinted by Dover) part 14, page 29; and in a modern critical edition in the *Franz Schubert: Neue Ausgabe sämtlicher Werke*, part 1, volume 8.

Autograph: The composer's full score is in the Männergesang-Verein in Vienna.

Notes: The score is dated 15 April 1815. It is sometimes listed as op. 150.

Performance Issues: The choral parts are clearly doubled by the orchestra. The score opens with a rhythmic, but purely homophonic, setting of the opening text, which is followed by an extended and highly contrapuntal "Alleluia" that comprises the majority of the work. This alleluia section, which also features thorough doubling of the choir by the instruments, is quite synchopated and frenetically joyful. If the choral parts weren't so well reinforced in the accompaniment, the choral part would be evaluated as "medium difficult," but with the doubling, only the articulation and rhythm present much challenge, as the parts are not very demanding vocally. Likewise, the instrumental parts are all idiomatic and well within the abilities of a good amateur ensemble. The organ plays a continuo part and could be left out; **choir:** medium easy, **orchestra:** medium easy.

Selected Discography

Elmar Schloter (organ); Chor und Symphonie-Orchester des Bayerischen Rundfunks (Josef Schmidhuber, choirmaster); conducted by Wolfgang Sawallisch. EMI: 86011.

Kyrie in D, D. 31 (1812)

Duration: ca. 4 minutes

Text: The text is the first section of the ordinary from the Roman Catholic communion liturgy.

Performing Forces: voices: SATB choir; **orchestra:** flute, 2 oboes, 2 bassoons, 2 trumpets (D), timpani (2 drums), strings, and organ.

First Performance: unknown

Editions: *Kyrie* appears in the *Schubert Werke* (reprinted by Dover) part 14, page 175; and in a modern critical edition in the *Franz Schubert: Neue Ausgabe sämtlicher Werke*, part 1, volume 5.

Autograph: The composer's manuscript is in the Stadtsbibliothek in Vienna (MH 21/c).

Notes: The score is labeled 25 September 1812.

Performance Issues: The choral writing is syllabic and sustained. The choral parts are harmonically well reinforced by the orchestra, but there is little direct doubling. There are considerable melodic leaps for the singers and the tessitura of the women's parts is a bit high. The instrumental parts include some articulate passages, which are mostly in unison between sections of the orchestra. There are some exposed scalar solo passages for the oboe I part. The organ is a continuo part and can be omitted. This is a charming juvenile work that resembles some of the early choral works of Mozart; **choir:** medium easy; **orchestra:** medium easy.

Selected Discography

Lucia Popp, Adolf Dallapozza, Elmar Schloter (organ); Chor und Symphonie-Orchester des Bayerischen Rundfunks (Josef Schmidhuber, choirmaster); conducted by Wolfgang Sawallisch. EMI: 86011.

Selected Bibliography

Stringham, Ronald S.: *The Masses of Franz Schubert*, 148-162. Cornell University: dissertation, 1964.

Kyrie in D, D. 49 (1813)

Duration: ca. 5 minutes

Text: The text is the first section of the ordinary from the Roman Catholic communion liturgy.

Performing Forces: voices SATB choir; **orchestra:** 2 oboes, 2 bassoons, 2 trumpets (D), timpani (2 drums), and strings.

First Performance: unknown

Editions: *Kyrie* appears in the *Schubert Werke* (reprinted by Dover) part 14, page 189; and in a modern critical edition in the *Franz Schubert: Neue Ausgabe sämtlicher Werke*, part 1, volume 5.

Autograph: The composer's manuscript is in the Stadtsbibliothek in Vienna (MH 22/c).

Notes: The manuscript is labeled that the score was completed 15 April 1815.

Performance Issues: The choir and the wind parts are quite simply written with the latter doubling the former throughout. There are intermittent passages for a solo quartet that are entirely appropriate for choristers. These are simple, but do contain the only imitative portions of the score. The string parts are filled with rapid scalar and arpeggiated passages that will require some attention for accuracy and unity of articulation; **choir:** easy; **orchestra:** medium difficult.

Selected Discography

Lucia Popp, Brigitte Fassbaender, Dietrich Fischer-Dieskau; Chor und Symphonie-Orchester des Bayerischen Rundfunks (Josef Schmidhuber, choirmaster); conducted by Wolfgang Sawallisch. EMI: 86011.

Selected Bibliography

Stringham, Ronald S.: *The Masses of Franz Schubert*, 148-162. Cornell University: dissertation, 1964.

Kyrie in F, D. 66 (1813)

Duration: ca. 6 minutes

Text: The text is the first section of the ordinary from the Roman Catholic communion liturgy.

Performing Forces: voices: SATB choir; **orchestra:** 2 oboes, 2 bassoons, 2 trumpets (F), timpani (2 drums), strings, and organ.

First Performance: unknown

Editions: *Kyrie* appears in the *Schubert Werke* (reprinted by Dover) part 14, page 203; and in a modern critical edition in the *Franz Schubert: Neue Ausgabe sämtlicher Werke*, part 1, volume 8.

Autograph: The composer's manuscript is in the Stadtsbibliothek in Vienna (MH 23/c).

Notes: The score is labeled 12 May 1813.

Performance Issues: The choral parts are fairly syllabic and well supported by the accompaniment. There are dramatic dynamic shifts throughout the entire score, but particularly for the singers. The score is in three distinct musical sections that correspond with the three lines of text. In the last of these, there is a sustained fugue for the choral parts, which are doubled by the winds, against which, Schubert has placed an energetic countermelody in the upper strings. This is the section that will require the most attention in rehearsal. The organ is a continuo part and can be omitted. All of the instrumental parts are idiomatic and should be well within the range of experienced amateur players; **choir:** medium easy; **orchestra:** medium easy.

Selected Discography

Elmar Schloter (organ); Chor und Symphonie-Orchester des Bayerischen Rundfunks (Josef Schmidhuber, choirmaster); conducted by Wolfgang Sawallisch. EMI: 86011.

Selected Bibliography

Stringham, Ronald S.: *The Masses of Franz Schubert*, 148-162. Cornell University: dissertation, 1964.

Magnificat, D. 486 (1815)

Duration: ca. 9 minutes

Text: The text from the New Testament: Luke, chapter 1.

Performing Forces: voices: Soprano, alto, tenor, and bass soloists; SATB choir; **orchestra:** 2 oboes, 2 bassoons, 2 trumpets, timpani, organ, and strings.

First Performance: unknown

Editions: *Magnificat* appears in the *Schubert Werke* (reprinted by Dover) part 14, page 77; and in a modern critical edition in the *Franz Schubert: Neue Ausgabe sämtlicher Werke*, part 1, volume 8, in an edition prepared by Marja von Bargen and Salome Reiser. A full score and parts of the latter are published by Carus (70.053/01).

Autograph: The Bargen/Reiser edition is derived from seven manuscript sources. It is believed that the autograph is lost; however, two copies attributed to the composer were recorded to be in private collections prior to World War II. An early manuscript copy is in the Scriptorium in Beverly Hills, California.

Notes: The score is dated 25 September 1815.[72]

Performance Issues: The choral writing is declamatory and syllabic. The vocal parts are well doubled by the winds while the string parts provide a more energized quality to the accompaniment. The choral material is homophonic with some contrasted parts in close imitation. The orchestral parts are idiomatically written and within the abilities of moderately skilled players. The string parts will require rhythmically independent players, but the parts present no significant technical challenges. The soloists appear as a quartet. All of these parts are appropriate for choristers, although the soprano part is more vocally challenging that the others. **Soloists:** soprano - range: c'-$b^{b''}$, tessitura: f'-g'', this is simple declamatory role requiring clarity across the range; alto - range: b-$e^{b''}$, tessitura: c'-c'', this is simple declamatory role; tenor - range: c-$g^{b'}$, tessitura: f-f', this is simple declamatory role; bass - range: A^b-d', tessitura: B^b-b^b, this is simple declamatory role; **choir:** medium easy; **orchestra:** medium easy.

Selected Discography

Sheila Armstrong, Hanna Schaer, Alejandro Ramirez, Philippe Huttenlocher; Ensemble Vocal de Lausanne; Orchestre de Chambre de Lausanne; conducted by Michel Corboz, recorded in Crissier, Switzerland, in November 1978. Erato: 4509-96961-2.

Christiane Oelze, Elisabeth von Magnus, Herbert Lippert, Gerald Finley; Arnold Schoenberg Choir, Concentus musicus Wien; conducted by Nikolaus Harnoncourt. Teldec: 3984-26094-2.

---

[72] Deviations of this date abound due to misreadings of Schubert's handwriting.

Lucia Popp, Brigitte Fassbaender, Adolf Dallapozza, Dietrich Fischer-Dieskau, Elmar Schloter (organ); Chor und Symphonie-Orchester des Bayerischen Rundfunks (Josef Schmidhuber, choirmaster); conducted by Wolfgang Sawallisch. EMI: 86011.

Marietta Zumbült, Elisabeth Graf, Jan Kobow, Albrecht Pohl; Knabenchor Hannover; L'Arco Baroque Orchestra; conducted by Heinz Hennig. Ars Musici: CD-1075.

Selected Bibliography

Reiser, Salome: "Foreword" to *Franz Schubert: Magnificat*. Stuttgart: Carus Verlag, 1996.

Mass No. 1 in F, D. 105 (1814)

Duration: ca. 48 minutes

Text: The text is from the Roman Catholic communion liturgy.

Performing Forces: voices: 2 soprano, alto, 2 tenor, and bass soloists; SATB choir; **orchestra:** 2 oboes, 2 clarinets (B^b, C), 2 bassoons, 2 horns (F, B^b), 2 trumpets (C, F), 3 trombones, timpani (2 drums), organ, and strings.

First Performance: 16 October 1814; for the centenary celebration of the church in Leichtental; Therese Grob was a soprano soloist.

Editions: Full scores and parts for Mass No. 1 in F are available for purchase from Breitkopf and Härtel, H. W. Gray, and Kalmus. It appears in the *Schubert Werke* (reprinted by Dover) part 13, volume 1, page 1; and in a modern critical edition in the *Franz Schubert: Neue Ausgabe sämtlicher Werke*, part 1, volume 1.

Autograph: The composer's manuscript, with some passages in his brother Ferdinand's hand, is in the Stadtsbibliothek in Vienna (MH 13).

Notes: There is an alternate and more elaborate "Dona nobis pacem" movement, which is included in the Breitkopf and Härtel edition and its reprints.

Performance Issues: The choral material is consistently well supported by the orchestra. Most of the choral writing is syllabic and homophonic. The closing section of the "Gloria" has some rapid melismatic passages and some very sustained phrases. This is the most challenging portion of the work for the choir and the orchestra. The soloists have some discrete submovements, but they primarily interject passages as a textural juxtaposition to the full choir. There is an SATB solo quartet with the exception of the "Benedictus," which is scored for SSTT. All of the solos are appropriate for choristers. The orchestration is simple despite some rapid arpeggios and scales throughout the winds and strings. The scoring is suitable for solo strings or a small complement. Likewise a smaller choral ensemble is well suited for this work. The organ part is purely a continuo instrument. **Soloists:** soprano I - range: e'-a'', tessitura: a'-f'', this is a lyric solo; soprano II - range: f'-g'', tessitura: a'-f'', this is a declamatory solo; alto - range: b^b-$b^{b'}$, tessitura: b^b-$b^{b'}$, this is a simple lyric solo; tenor I - range: c-g', tessitura: g-f', this is a simple declamatory solo; tenor II - range: c-g', tessitura: g-f', this is a simple declamatory solo; bass - range: F#-$e^{b'}$, tessitura: B^b-b^b, this is a declamatory role; **choir:** medium difficult; **orchestra:** medium difficult.

Selected Discography

Lucia Popp, Brigitte Fassbaender, Adolf Dallapozza, Dietrich Fischer-Dieskau, Elmar Schloter (organ); Chor und Symphonie-Orchester des Bayerischen Rundfunks (Josef Schmidhuber, choirmaster); conducted by Wolfgang Sawallisch. EMI: 86011.

Selected Bibliography

Prout, Ebenezer: "Franz Schubert's Masses," *Monthly Musical Record*, volume 1, number 1 (1871), 2-6, 13-16.

Stringham, Ronald S.: *The Masses of Franz Schubert*, 162-199. Cornell University: dissertation, 1964.

Mass No. 2 in G, D. 167 (1815)

Duration: ca. 22 minutes

Text: The text is from the Roman Catholic communion liturgy.

Performing Forces: voices: soprano, tenor, and bass soloists; SATB choir; **orchestra:** organ and strings.

First Performance: This mass was first performed in Prague in 1846 at the church of St. Veit under the direction of Robert Führer who attempted to pass the work off as his own.[73]

Editions: Full scores and parts for Mass No. 2 in G are available for purchase from Breitkopf and Härtel; H. W. Gray; Roger Dean, edited by Elmer Thomas (piano-vocal score: CS865, full score: PP199, organ part: PP200, and string parts: PP198); and Kalmus. It appears in the *Schubert Werke* (reprinted by Dover) part 13, volume 1, page 121; and in a modern critical edition in the *Franz Schubert: Neue Ausgabe sämtlicher Werke*, part 1, volume 1.

Autograph: The composer's manuscript, with some materials in his brother Ferdinand's hand, is in the Gesellschaft der Musikfreunde in Vienna (A 203).

Notes: The full score is dated 2 March 1815.

Performance Issues: The choral parts are clearly reinforced by the accompaniment. The choral writing is primarily syllabic and well suited to amateur singers. It is mostly homophonic with some limited imitation in close succession. The mostly vocally complicated section is the "Sanctus." The solo parts are integrated into the choral passages to create textural contrast. The exception is the "Benedictus," which is for solo trio (STB). The string writing is accessible and very practical. This score lends itself well to a solo string quintet and small choir. **Soloists:** soprano - range: d'-a'', tes-

---

[73] Pahlen, Kurt: *The World of the Oratorio*, translated by Judith Schaefer with additional English-language material by Thurston Dox, 291. Portland, OR: Amadeus Press, 1990.

situra: g'-e", this is a sustained and lyrical solo appropriate for a chorister; tenor - range: d-g', tessitura: f-e', this is a simple lyrical solo appropriate for a chorister; bass - range: e-b, tessitura: e-b, this is a simple declamatory solo appropriate for a chorister; **choir:** medium easy; **orchestra:** medium easy.

Selected Discography

Lucia Popp, Adolf Dallapozza, Dietrich Fischer-Dieskau, Elmar Schloter (organ); Chor und Symphonie-Orchester des Bayerischen Rundfunks (Josef Schmidhuber, choirmaster); conducted by Wolfgang Sawallisch. EMI: 86011. Previously released as EMI: CDC 7 474072.

Barbara Bonney, Jorge Pita, Andreas Schmidt; Vienna State Opera Concert Chorus; Chamber Orchestra of Europe; conducted by Claudio Abbado, recorded in the Grosser Saal, Musikverein in Vienna in 1990. Deutsche Grammophon: 435486-2.

Selected Bibliography

Prout, Ebenezer: "Franz Schubert's Masses," *Monthly Musical Record*, volume 1, number 2 (1871), 26-29.

Spiro, Friedrich: "Zu Schubert's G-dur-Messe," in *Zeitschrift der International Musikgeschichten*, volume 5 (1903/1904), 51-54.

Stringham, Ronald S.: *The Masses of Franz Schubert*, 200-220. Cornell University: dissertation, 1964.

Berger, Melvin: *Guide to Choral Masterpieces: A Listener's Guide*, 270-271. New York: Anchor Books, 1993.

Mass No. 3 in B^b, D. 324 (1815)

Duration: ca. 30 minutes

Text: The text is from the Roman Catholic communion liturgy.

Performing Forces: voices: soprano, alto, tenor, and bass soloists; SATB choir; **orchestra:** 2 oboes, 2 bassoons, 2 trumpets (B^b), timpani (2 drums), organ, and strings.

First Performance: unknown

Editions: Full scores and parts for Mass No. 3 in B^b are available for purchase from Breitkopf and Härtel, H. W. Gray, and Kalmus. It appears in the *Schubert Werke* (reprinted by Dover) part 13, volume 1, page 157; and in a modern critical edition in the *Franz Schubert: Neue Ausgabe sämtlicher Werke*, part 1, volume 2.

Autograph: An incomplete manuscript with portions in two unknown hands is in the Perabo Collection of the British Library in London (Ms 41632).

Notes: The score is dated 11 November 1815. It is sometimes listed as op. 141.

Performance Issues: The choral material is primarily syllabic and all of the vocal parts are well supported by the accompaniment. The orchestration is light, and the use of solo strings or a small section is advisable. There are some rapid figurations in the violin parts that are very practical, but may present some intonation challenges when these parts are in octaves. A smaller choral ensemble is also appropriate. The organ serves only as a continuo instrument. The solos generally appear as interjections within the choral material. These parts are within the abilities of good choristers. This is an excellent work for a good church choir with limited instrumental resources. **Soloists:** soprano - range: e'-a'', tessitura: g-e$^{b''}$, this is a sustained and lyric solo; alto - range: d$^{b'}$-e'', tessitura: f'-c'', this is a declamatory solo role best suited to a mezzo-soprano; tenor - range: f-a'(b$^{b'}$), tessitura: g-f', this is a sustained and lyric solo; bass - range: A^b-e', tessitura: c-c', this is a declamatory solo; **choir:** medium easy; **orchestra:** medium easy.

Selected Discography

Lucia Popp, Brigitte Fassbaender, Adolf Dallapozza, Dietrich Fischer-Dieskau, Elmar Schloter (organ); Chor und Symphonie-Orchester des Bayerischen Rundfunks (Josef Schmidhuber, choirmaster); conducted by Wolfgang Sawallisch. EMI: 86011.

Selected Bibliography

Prout, Ebenezer: "Franz Schubert's Masses," *Monthly Musical Record*, volume 1, number 3 (1871), 39-43.

Stringham, Ronald S.: *The Masses of Franz Schubert*, 220-236. Cornell University: dissertation, 1964.

Mass No. 4 in C, D. 452 (1816)

Duration: ca. 26 minutes

Text: The text is from the Roman Catholic communion liturgy.

Performing Forces: voices: soprano, alto, tenor, and bass soloists; SATB choir; **orchestra:** 2 oboes or clarinets (C), 2 trumpets (C), timpani (2 drums), organ, and strings (without violas).[74]

First Performance: 8 September 1823; the church in Lichtenthal

Editions: Full scores and parts for Mass No. 4 in C are available for purchase from Breitkopf and Härtel, G. Schirmer, and Kalmus. It appears in the *Schubert Werke* (reprinted by Dover) part 13, volume 1, page 209; and in a modern critical edition in the *Franz Schubert: Neue Ausgabe sämtlicher Werke*, part 1, volume 2.

Autograph: The autograph score is in the Whittall Collection of the Library of Congress in Washington, D.C. A portion of the Benedictus is lost.

Notes: This is the only mass of Schubert's to be published during his lifetime. The score is dedicated to the composer's friend, Michael Holzer. Holzer was the choirmaster of the Lichtenthal Church and is believed to effected the work's publication.[75] There is a second setting of the "Benedictus" that requires the use of the wind parts and is somewhat more complicated than the first setting.

Performance Issues: This is a very simple seting of the mass that is practical for most church choirs. The use of two violins and continuo as the sole accompaniment is completely serviceable, as is

---

[74] The score indicates that the oboe, clarinet, trumpet, and timpani parts are all optional.

[75] Hilmar, Ernst: *Franz Schubert in his Time*, 110. Portland, OR: Amadeus Press, 1988.

the use of solo singers throughout. The organ is a continuo part, but the *ad libitum* wind and timpani are rhythmicized realizations of the figured bass. If they are not used, the organist may want to mimick their rhythms and voicing. The vocal writing is nearly all syllabic and vocally conservative. This is an attractive work that would be an excellent choice of repertoire for a less experienced choir wishing to incorporate a small instrumental ensemble into its programming. **Soloists:** soprano - range: e'-$b^{b''}$, tessitura: g'-g'', this is a lyric solo; alto - range: b^b-$e^{b''}$, tessitura: d'-d'', this is a declamatory solo best suited to a mezzo-soprano; tenor - range: d-a', tessitura: g-f', this is a simple lyric solo; bass - range: F-d', tessitura: B^b-b^b, this is a declamatory solo requiring clarity at the bottom of the range; **choir:** easy; **orchestra:** easy.

Selected Discography

Lucia Popp, Brigitte Fassbaender, Adolf Dallapozza, Dietrich Fischer-Dieskau, Elmar Schloter (organ); Chor und Symphonie-Orchester des Bayerischen Rundfunks (Josef Schmidhuber, choirmaster); conducted by Wolfgang Sawallisch. EMI: 86011.
Teresa Seidl, Liliana Bizineche, Algirdas Janutas, Benno Schollum; Kauna State Choir (Nomeda Kazlauskaite, choirmaster), Lithuanian Chamber Orchestra; conducted by Yehudi Menuhin. Apex: 2564-60304-2.

Selected Bibliography

Prout, Ebenezer: "Franz Schubert's Masses," *Monthly Musical Record*, volume 1, number 4 (1871), 69-72, 84-87.
Stringham, Ronald S.: *The Masses of Franz Schubert*, 236-245. Cornell University: dissertation, 1964.

Mass No. 5 in A^b, "Missa Solemnis," D. 678 (1819-1822)

Duration: ca. 48 minutes

Text: The text is from the Roman Catholic communion liturgy.

Performing Forces: voices: soprano, alto, tenor, and bass soloists; SATB choir; **orchestra: flute,** 2 oboes, 2 clarinets (A, B^b, C), 2 bassoons, 2 horns (C, E^b, E, F), 2 trumpets (B^b, C, E), 3 trombones, timpani (2 drums), organ, and strings.

First Performance: unknown

Editions: Full scores and parts for Mass No. 5 in A^b are available for purchase from Breitkopf and Härtel, H. W. Gray, and Kalmus. Version A appears in a modern critical edition in the *Franz Schubert: Neue Ausgabe sämtlicher Werke*, part 1, volume 3. Version B appears in the *Schubert Werke* (reprinted by Dover) part 13, volume 2, page 1; and in a modern critical edition in the *Franz Schubert: Neue Ausgabe sämtlicher Werke*, part 1, volume 3.

Autograph: There is an assortment of manuscript materials of this work, including sketches and the first version in the Gesellschaft der Musikfreunde in Vienna (A 204). Additional materials are in the Stadtsbibliothek in Vienna (MH 24/c). It appears that most of the manuscript materials of the second version have been lost.

Notes: There are alternate versions of the "Cum sancto Spirito" and "Osanna." One of the many remarkable features of this work is Schubert's radical exploitation of key relationships between movements:

1.	Kyrie	A^b major
2.	Gloria	E major
3.	Credo	C major
4.	Sanctus	F major
5.	Benedictus	A^b major to F major
6.	Agnus Dei	F minor to A^b major

Performance Issues: There are divisi in all of the choral parts. The choral writing incorporates homophonic and freely imitative passages. All of the choral material, which is primarily syllabic, is clearly supported by the accompaniment. Solo passages are integrated into the ensemble movements to provide textural contrast. In the "Benedictus," the solo quartet actually sings in opposition to the choir, requiring soloists capable of balancing with the ensemble. Unlike the earlier masses, this work is not suitable for solo strings. In fact, this mass requires, at minimum, a medium-sized string section and choir. There are exposed passages for all of the wind parts, some of which are at minimal dynamics. The vocal and instrumental writing is idiomatic, but the intermittent use of some instruments for orchestrational color makes their entrances less intuitive than in Schubert's earlier works. The organ is treated as a continuo part. Some of the contrapuntal writing is quite complex, and in certain passages quite densely voiced requiring extra attention to the clarity of the individual parts as well as for diction. This is a challenging and dramatic work. There are some extreme dynamic shifts that will provide great effect if followed with accuracy and control. Extra attention to textural clarity in the choral rehearsals is of great importance. Marking the instrumental parts to correspond with the natural text stresses of the vocal lines they double will help to integrate the couterpoint between the voices and instruments. **Soloists:** soprano - range: $f\#'-a''$, tessitura: $a'-g''$, this is a lyric solo with some sustained passages; alto - range: b^b-e'', tessitura: $e'-c''$, this is a lyric solo; tenor - range: $e^b-a^{b'}$, tessitura: $g-g'$, this is a lyric and sustain solo; bass - range: $F\#-d'$, tessitura: B-b, this is a sustained solo role; **choir:** difficult; **orchestra:** medium difficult.

Selected Discography

Marietta Zumbült, Elisabeth Graf, Jan Kobow, Albrecht Pohl; Knabenchor Hannover; L'Arco Baroque Orchestra; conducted by Heinz Hennig. Ars Musici: CD-1075.

Teresa Seidl, Liliana Bizineche, Algirdas Janutas, Benno Schollum; Kauna State Choir (Nomeda Kazlauskaite, choirmaster), Lithuanian Chamber Orchestra; conducted by Yehudi Menuhin. Apex: 2564-60304-2.

Helen Donath, Brigitte Fassbaender, Francisco Araiza, Dietrich Fischer-Dieskau; Chor und Symphonie-Orchester des Bayerischen Rundfunks (Josef Schmidhuber, choirmaster); conducted by Wolfgang Sawallisch. EMI: 86011.

Donna Brown, Monica Groop, James Taylor, Michael Volle; Oregon Bach Festival Choir and Chamber Orchestra; conducted by Helmuth Rilling. Hänssler: CD98120.

A Conductor's Guide to 19th-Century Choral-Orchestra Works   271

Selected Bibliography

Prout, Ebenezer: "Franz Schubert's Masses," *Monthly Musical Record*, volume 1, number 5 (1871), 53-57.

Stringham, Ronald S.: *The Masses of Franz Schubert*, 246-287. Cornell University: dissertation, 1964.

Berger, Melvin: *Guide to Choral Masterpieces: A Listener's Guide*, 272-274. New York: Anchor Books, 1993.

Mass No. 6 in E^b, D. 950 (1828)

Duration: ca. 58 minutes

Text: The text is from the Roman Catholic communion liturgy.

Performing Forces: voices: soprano, alto, 2 tenor, and bass soloists; SATB choir; **orchestra:** 2 oboes, 2 clarinets (B^b), 2 bassoons, 2 horns (E^b), 2 trumpets (C, E^b), 3 trombones, timpani (2 drums), and strings.

First Performance: 4 October 1829; Holy Trinity Church in Alser (a suburb of Vienna), conducted by the composer's brother, Ferdinand.

Editions: Full scores and parts for Mass No. 6 in E^b are available for purchase from Breitkopf and Härtel, H. W. Gray, C. F. Peters, and Kalmus. It appears in the *Schubert Werke* (reprinted by Dover) part 13, volume 2, page 167; and in a modern critical edition in the *Franz Schubert: Neue Ausgabe sämtlicher Werke*, part 1, volume 4.

Autograph: The composer's finished score is in the Stadtsbibliothek in Vienna (MH 174/c). There are manuscript sketches in the Stadtsbibliothek in Berlin (Ms. Schubert 5).

Notes: Some musicological sources indicate the presence of paraphrases of the music of J. S. Bach, especially the C-minor fugue from the first book of the *Well-Tempered Clavier*, as signs of heightened introspection on the part of the composer. While such self-reflection may or may not be a contributing factor in this work, Schubert was engaged in lessons with Simon Sechter with whom he was exploring assorted contrapuntal processes. There is an intensification of imitative devices in Schubert's music at the end of his life, which is a clear reflection of these new studies. Such an undertaking probably also led him to a renewed examination of emblematic works of Bach.

Performance Issues: The choral parts are clearly supported by the accompaniment, but there are more additional accompanimental figures appearing concurrently. The choristers have many articulate and rapid text declamations on sustained pitches, as well as long melismatic passages. There are a number of passages in which the instruments articulate a repeated pitch in rapid succession. Schubert also utilizes a significant number of ostinato figures throughout the score. Of Schubert's masses, this is the only one that does not call for an organ part. The soloists appear less frequently in this work than in the other masses. These passages are quite appropriate for choristers. The orchestral writing is idiomatic. Some of the orchestral parts foreshadow choral entrances by a few beats. Although the actual choral parts are doubled by other instruments, these melodic anticipations may prompt some false starts. This score utilizes extreme dynamic contrasts that require seasoned players and a choral ensemble capable of confident control at extremes of range and volume. The choral parts are actually more vocally demanding than the solo passages. The density of the wind scoring suggests the use of a full complement of strings and a sizable choral ensemble. This score is significantly marked with accents and other articulation symbols. It is a clever amalgamation of early 18th-century contrapuntal devices and early romantic harmonic language and orchestration. **Soloists:** soprano - range: $e^{b\prime}$-g'' ($b^{b\prime\prime}$), tessitura: g'-f'', this is a simple declamatory solo, the optional high note is really critical to match the melodic contour of other imitating parts; alto - range: b^b-$e^{b\prime\prime}$, tessitura: d'-c'', this is a sustained lyric solo; tenor I - range: e^b-$a^{b\prime}$, tessitura: g-f', this is a sustained lyric solo; tenor II - range: e-$g^{b\prime}$, tessitura: f-f', this is a brief declamatory solo; bass - range: F-b^b, tessitura: B^b-a^b, this is a simple declamatory role; **choir:** difficult; **orchestra:** medium difficult.

Selected Discography

Helen Donath, Brigitte Fassbaender, Francisco Araiza, Dietrich Fischer-Dieskau; Chor und Symphonie-Orchester des Bayerischen Rundfunks (Josef Schmidhuber, choirmaster); conducted by Wolfgang Sawallisch. EMI: 86011.
Luba Orgonasova, Birgit Remmert, Deon van der Walt, Wolfgang Holzmair; Arnold Schoenberg Choir, Chamber Orchestra of Europe; conducted by Nikolaus Harnoncourt. Teldec: 0630-13163-2.
Audrey Michael, Brigitte Balleys, Aldo Baldin, Christophe Homberger, Michel Brodard; Chœur de Chambre Romand, Chœur Pro Arte de Lausanne (André Charlet, director), Orchestre de la Suisse Romande; conducted by Armin Jordan. Recorded in May 1987 in Victoria Hall, Geneva. Erato: ECD 75387.
Karita Mattila, Mariana Lipovsek, Jerry Hadley, Robert Holl; Vienna State Opera Concert Chorus, Vienna Philharmonic; conducted by Claudio Abbado. Deutsche Grammophon: 423088-2.

Selected Bibliography

Pfannhauser, Karl: "Zur Es-Dur-Messe von Franz Schubert," *Neue Zeitschrift für Musik*, volume 119 (1958), 435.
Stringham, Ronald S.: *The Masses of Franz Schubert*, 288-366. Cornell University: dissertation, 1964.
Berger, Melvin: *Guide to Choral Masterpieces: A Listener's Guide*, 274-276. New York: Anchor Books, 1993.

Offertorium: Intende voci in B^b, D. 963 (1828)

Duration: ca. 4 minutes

Text: Psalm 5, 3-4a, which is the offertory for the Friday of the third Passion Sunday.

Performing Forces: voices: tenor soloist; SATB choir; **orchestra:** oboe, 2 clarinets (B^b), 2 bassoons, 2 horns (B^b), 3 trombones (alto, tenor, and bass), and strings.

First Performance: 19 June 1890; Stadttheater, Eisenach

Editions: *Intende voci* appears in the *Schubert Werke* (reprinted by Dover) part 21, page 277; and in a modern critical edition in the *Franz Schubert: Neue Ausgabe sämtlicher Werke*, part 1, volume 8.

Autograph: The composer's manuscript is in the Stadtsbibliothek in Berlin (Ms. Schubert 14). A second version is in the Osterreichische Nationalbibliothek in Vienna (MHs. 19488).

Performance Issues: The choral material is harmonically supported by the orchestra. The vocal parts are all well conceived for the singers and present no vocal challenges. The orchestration is conservative and all of the parts with the exception of the oboe are quite easy. There is a significant oboe solo throughout this work that requires lyrical and sustained playing. **Soloist:** tenor — range: d-g', tessitura: g-f', this is a very sustained solo; **choir:** medium easy; **orchestra:** medium easy.

Selected Discography

Peter Schreier; Chor und Symphonie-Orchester des Bayerischen Rundfunks (Josef Schmidhuber, choirmaster); conducted by Wolfgang Sawallisch. EMI: 86011.

Offertorium: Tres sunt, D. 181 (1815)

Duration: ca. 4 minutes

Text: The text is from John I, 5:7-8.

Performing Forces: voices: SATB choir; **orchestra:** 2 oboes, 2 clarinets (C), 2 bassoons, 3 trombones (alto, tenor, and bass), strings, and organ.

First Performance: unknown

Editions: *Tres sunt* appears in the *Schubert Werke* (reprinted by Dover) part 14, page 23; and in a modern critical edition in the *Franz Schubert: Neue Ausgabe sämtlicher Werke*, part 1, volume 8.

Autograph: The manuscript score is in Conservatory Collection of the Bibliotheque Nationale in Paris (Ms. 274).

Notes: The score is labeled 10 April 1815.

Performance Issues: The choral parts are principally syllabic. Most of the vocal writing is homophonic or in close imitation, and all of the vocal material is clearly doubled by the orchestra. There is a little echo figure in the opening line that becomes a repeated motive throughout the work. Care should be given to highlight this syncopated figure as it propels the work forward. The organ is a continuo part with figures in the score. The orchestra parts are all easy. This is a good score for a small orchestra and choir as an introduction to the concerted choral genre; **choir:** medium easy; **orchestra:** easy.

Selected Discography

Elmar Schloter (organ); Chor und Symphonie-Orchester des Bayerischen Rundfunks (Josef Schmidhuber, choirmaster); conducted by Wolfgang Sawallisch. EMI: 86011.

Ensemble Vocal de Lausanne; Orchestre de Chambre de Lausanne; conducted by Michel Corboz, recorded in Crissier, Switzerland, in November 1978. Erato: 4509-96961-2.

Stabat Mater in G minor ["The Little"], D. 175
(1815)

Duration: ca. 7 minutes

Text: The authorship of this text is highly disputed. It has been attributed to Jacopone da Todi who died in 1306. It was removed from sanctioned use at the Council of Trent, and restored to the liturgical canon in 1727. The text addresses the "Seven Sorrows of the Virgin Mary." It is used as the Sequence Hymn on the first Friday after Passion Sunday and on 15 September.[76]

---

[76] Jeffers, Ron: *Translations and Annotations of Choral Repertoire, Volume I: Sacred Latin Texts*, 200-207. Corvallis, OR: Earthsongs, 1988.

Performing Forces: voices: SATB choir; **orchestra:** 2 oboes, 2 clarinets (B♭), 2 bassoons, 3 trombones, organ, and strings.

First Performance: unknown

Editions: Full scores and parts for *Stabat Mater* in G minor are available for purchase from Breitkopf and Härtel and Kalmus. It appears in the *Schubert Werke* (reprinted by Dover) part 14, page 101; and in a modern critical edition in the *Franz Schubert: Neue Ausgabe sämtlicher Werke*, part 1, volume 8.

Autograph: The manuscript score is in the Stadtsbibliothek in Vienna (MH 15/c).

Notes: The score is dated 4 April 1815. It is a setting of only the first stanza of the poem.

Performance Issues: This is a brief, simple, and very practical setting of the Stabat Mater. The choral writing is homophonic and syllabic. The vocal parts are generally doubled by the instruments. In the few passages where this doubling is not absolute, there is still thorough harmonic support in the accompaniment. The vocal parts are clearly conceived to be within the abilities of small provincial church choirs. The orchestral parts are all accessible to less experienced players with none having any technical passagework. The organ part is continuo only, and it could be eliminated if necessary. This work is well suited for a small choral ensemble and a one-on-a-part orchestra; **choir:** easy; **orchestra:** easy.

Selected Discography

Elmar Schloter (organ); Chor und Symphonie-Orchester des Bayerischen Rundfunks (Josef Schmidhuber, choirmaster); conducted by Wolfgang Sawallisch. EMI: 86011. Previously released as EMI Classics: 7243 5 65845 2.

Stabat Mater in F, D. 383 (1816)

Duration: ca. 38 minutes

Text: This is a setting of F. G. Klopstock's German translation of the traditional Latin sequence hymn.

Performing Forces: voices: soprano, tenor, and bass soloists; SATB choir; **orchestra:** 2 flutes, 2 oboes, 2 bassoons, 2 horns (E^b, F, G), 3 trombones, and strings.

First Performance: 24 March 1833; Vienna

Editions: Full scores and parts for *Stabat Mater* in F minor are available for purchase from Breitkopf and Härtel and Kalmus. It appears in the *Schubert Werke* (reprinted by Dover) part 14, page 109; and in a modern critical edition in the *Franz Schubert: Neue Ausgabe sämtlicher Werke*, part 1, volume 7.

Autograph: The manuscript score is in the Stadtsbibliothek in Vienna (MH 16/c).

Notes: This setting of the Klopstock translation is broken into 12 movements in the model of some earlier settings of the original Latin, such as the Pergolesi. The work is organized as follows:

1.	Jesus Christus schwebt am Kreuze	choir
2.	Bei des Mittlers Kreuze standen	soprano
3.	Liebend neiget ersein Antlitz	choir
4.	Engel freuten sich jener Wonner	tenor/soprano duet
5.	Wer wird Zähren sanften	choir
6.	Ach, was hätten wir empfunden	tenor
7.	Erben sollen sie am Throne	choir
8.	Sohn des Vaters	bass
9.	O du herrlicher Vollender	choir
10.	Erdenfreuden und ihr Elend	soprano/tenor/bass trio
11.	Das dereinst wir, wenn im Tode	trio and choir
12.	Amen	choir

The score is dated 28 February 1816.

Performance Issues: The vocal writing is generally syllabic and the choral textures are primarily homophonic and well supported by the orchestra. Movements 7 and 12 are complex four-voice fugues in which the choral parts are doubled colla parte by the oboe and trombones, much in the manner of many of Bach's cantatas. These two movements are considerably more challenging for the choir than the rest of the composition. All of the parts are vocally conservative and quite easily learned with the exception of the two movements mentioned above. The instrumental writing is fairly simple and very idiomatic. There is exposed melodic material in all of the principal wind parts. There are some active accompanimental figures in the violins and some rhythmically delicate passages for the orchestra that will require some attention in rehearsal A smaller string section and choir will work well in this piece if desired. **Soloists:** soprano - range: $f'-b^{b''}$, tessitura: $g'-g''$, this is a lyric solo with sustained passages at the top of the range; tenor - range: $d-a'$, tessitura: $f-f'$, this is a lyric solo; bass - range: $G-e'$, tessitura: $d-d'$, this is a lyric solo with some coloratura and sustained passages at the bottom of the range; **choir:** medium difficult; **orchestra:** medium easy.

Selected Discography

Sheila Armstrong, Alejandro Ramirez, Philippe Huttenlocher; Ensemble Vocal de Lausanne; Orchestre de Chambre de Lausanne; conducted by Michel Corboz, recorded in Crissier, Switzerland, in November 1978. Erato: 4509-96961-2.

Helen Donath, Josef Protschka, Dietrich Fischer-Dieskau; Chor und Symphonie-Orchester des Bayerischen Rundfunks (Josef Schmidhuber, choirmaster); conducted by Wolfgang Sawallisch. EMI: 86011. Previously released as EMI Classics: 7243 5 65845 2.

Selected Bibliography

Hirschberg, L.: "Franz Schuberts deutsches 'Stabat Mater,'" *Deutsches Musikerzeitung*, volume 59 (1928), 388-390.

Tantum Ergo in C, D. 460 (1816)

Duration: ca. 2 minutes

Text: This text is a portion of the *Pange lingua* hymn by Thomas Aquinas, which was written c. 1264 at the request of Pope Urban IV for use in the newly established Feast of Corpus Christi.[77]

Performing Forces: voices: soprano soloist; SATB choir; **orchestra:** 2 oboes, 2 trumpets (C), timpani (2 drums), organ, and strings (no violas).

First Performance: unknown

Editions: *Tantum Ergo* appears in the *Schubert Werke* (reprinted by Dover) part 14, page 39; and in a modern critical edition in the *Franz Schubert: Neue Ausgabe sämtlicher Werke*, part 1, volume 8.

Autograph: The composer's manuscript score is in the Whittall Collection of the Library of Congress in Washington, D.C.

Notes: The score is labeled August 1816 and is dedicated to Michael Holzer, the choirmaster of the Lichtenthal Church. He is also the dedicatee of Schubert's Mass in C (D. 452) of the same year.

Performance Issues: The choral writing is homophonic and syllabic. All of the vocal material is clearly doubled by the instruments. It is entirely appropriate for a small church choir of limited experience. Solo string parts will work well. The violin parts contain a lot of 16th-note figurations in parallel thirds and sixths. These are idiomatic, but will require precise ensemble playing. The wind and brass parts are quite conservative, remaining within the abilities of most amateur players. The organ part is continuo only, but should not be excluded given the light orchestration of this work. **Soloist:** soprano - range: g'-g'', tessitura: g'-g'', this is a simple four-measure solo for a chorister; **choir:** very easy; **orchestra:** easy.

---

[77] Jeffers, Ron: *Translations and Annotations of Choral Repertoire, Volume I: Sacred Latin Texts,* 213-214. Corvallis, OR: Earthsongs, 1988.

Selected Discography

Erika Rüggeberg, Elmar Schloter (organ); Chor und Symphonie-Orchester des Bayerischen Rundfunks (Josef Schmidhuber, choirmaster); conducted by Wolfgang Sawallisch. EMI: 86011.

Tantum Ergo in C, op. 45, D. 739 (1814)

Duration: ca. 5 minutes

Text: This text is a portion of the *Pange lingua* hymn by Thomas Aquinas, which was written c. 1264 at the request of Pope Urban IV for use in the newly established Feast of Corpus Christi.[78]

Performing Forces: voices: SATB choir; **orchestra:** 2 oboes or 2 clarinets (C), 2 trumpets (C), timpani (2 drums), organ, and strings (no violas).

First Performance: 8 September 1825; Church of St. Ulrich, Vienna

Editions: *Tantum Ergo* appears in the *Schubert Werke* (reprinted by Dover) part 14, page 37; and in a modern critical edition in the *Franz Schubert: Neue Ausgabe sämtlicher Werke*, part 1, volume 8.

Autograph: The composer's manuscript has been lost.

Performance Issues: The choral writing is homophonic and syllabic. All of the vocal material is reinforced by the accompaniment. The opening phrase is accompanied by continuo only, which necessitates the use of the organ. This is a good work for a small choir of limited experience, and the use of solo strings is quite appropriate. This is a lovely and expressive miniature setting of this text in which all of the parts are quite simple; **choir:** very easy; **orchestra:** very easy.

---

[78] Jeffers, Ron: *Translations and Annotations of Choral Repertoire, Volume I: Sacred Latin Texts*, 213-214. Corvallis, OR: Earthsongs, 1988.

Selected Discography

Elmar Schloter (organ); Chor und Symphonie-Orchester des Bayerischen Rundfunks (Josef Schmidhuber, choirmaster); conducted by Wolfgang Sawallisch. EMI: 86011.

Tantum Ergo in D, D. 750 (1822)

Duration: ca. 4 minutes

Text: This text is a portion of the *Pange lingua* hymn by Thomas Aquinas, which was written c. 1264 at the request of Pope Urban IV for use in the newly established Feast of Corpus Christi.[79]

Performing Forces: voices: SATB choir; **orchestra:** 2 flutes, 2 oboes, 2 bassoons, 2 trumpets (D), 2 trombones, timpani (2 drums), organ, and strings.

First Performance: unknown

Editions: *Tantum Ergo* appears in the *Schubert Werke* (reprinted by Dover) part 14, page 43; and in a modern critical edition in the *Franz Schubert: Neue Ausgabe sämtlicher Werke*, part 1, volume 5.

Autograph: The first draft of the manuscript is in the Conservatory Collection of the Bibliothek Nationale in Paris (Ms. 301).

Notes: The score is labeled 20 March 1822. It divides the text in half, treating it as a two-verse strophic work.

Performance Issues: The choral material is entirely syllabic and homophonic. It is harmonically supported by the orchestra, but is less clearly doubled than in Schubert's two other settings of this text. The choir has some fairly rapid text declamations and precise rhythmic figures. The orchestration calls for multiple string players, and the score has a significant number of rhythmic complexi-

---

[79] Jeffers, Ron: *Translations and Annotations of Choral Repertoire, Volume I: Sacred Latin Texts*, 213-214. Corvallis, OR: Earthsongs, 1988.

ties including off-beat playing and concurrent dotting at differing beat values that will require some attention in rehearsal. The organ is a continuo part and can be left out if necessary. This is an attractive and energetic work that would be a fine short work to fill out a concert program; **choir:** medium easy; **orchestra:** medium difficult.

Selected Discography

Elmar Schloter (organ); Chor und Symphonie-Orchester des Bayerischen Rundfunks (Josef Schmidhuber, choirmaster); conducted by Wolfgang Sawallisch. EMI: 86011.

Tantum Ergo in E^b, D. 962 (1828)

Duration: ca. 6 minutes

Text: This text is a portion of the *Pange lingua* hymn by Thomas Aquinas, which was written c. 1264 at the request of Pope Urban IV for use in the newly established Feast of Corpus Christi.[80]

Performing Forces: voices: SATB quartet, SATB choir; **orchestra:** 2 oboes, 2 clarinets (B^b), 2 bassoons, 2 horns (E^b), 2 trumpets [clarini] (E^b) 3 trombones (alto, tenor, and bass), timpani (2 drums) and strings.

First Performance: 19 June 1890; Stadttheater, Eisenach

Editions: *Tantum Ergo* appears as a sketch in the *Schubert Werke* (reprinted by Dover) part 14, page 227. A complete score appears in the 1897 supplement: part 21, page 269. It is also published in a modern critical edition in the *Franz Schubert: Neue Ausgabe sämtlicher Werke*, part 1, volume 8.

Autograph: A draft manuscript is in the Stadtsbibliothek in Vienna (MH 178/c). A second version manuscript is in the Österreichesches National Bibliothek in Vienna (MHs. 19488).

---

[80] Jeffers, Ron: *Translations and Annotations of Choral Repertoire, Volume I: Sacred Latin Texts*, 213-214. Corvallis, OR: Earthsongs, 1988.

Notes: Like the previous setting, this one also divides the text in half, treating it as a two-verse strophic work.

Performance Issues: The score alternates sections of solo quartet and full choir. In each case the vocal writing is in a homophonic four-part chorale texture. The vocal material is harmonically well supported by the orchestra, which utilizes ostinato accompanimental figures throughout much of the string writing. All of the winds have leading melodic material. The instrumental parts are idiomatic and conservatively rendered. The orchestration suggests a medium to large choir and a full complement of strings. This is a harmonically progressive composition that uses some unusual third relationships that may be less intuitively read by most singers. These harmonic experiments are accomplished through conservative part writing, so it is not difficult to learn. The score features independent doublebass parts that include numerous low E^bs; **choir:** medium easy; **orchestra:** medium difficult.

Selected Discography

Lucia Popp, Brigitte Fassbaender, Adolf Dallapozza, Dietrich Fischer-Dieskau; Chor und Symphonie-Orchester des Bayerischen Rundfunks (Josef Schmidhuber, choirmaster); conducted by Wolfgang Sawallisch. EMI: 86011.

Barbara Bonney, Dalia Schaechter, Jorge Pita, Andreas Schmidt; Vienna State Opera Concert Chorus; Chamber Orchestra of Europe; conducted by Claudio Abbado, recorded in the Grosser Saal, Musikverein in Vienna in 1990. Deutsche Grammophon: 435486-2.

Schumann, Robert (b. Zwickau, Germany, 8 June 1810; d. Endenich, Germany, 29 July 1856)

Life: Schumann studied law at the Universities of Leipzig and Heidelberg. He met the celebrated piano virtuoso, Clara Wieck, and soon after, became a pupil of her father, living in their home. He permanently injured his hand with a stretching device of his own design. He wrote music criticism eventually founding the *Neue Zeitschrift für Musik*, which he edited for a decade. He wrote under the names of Florestan and Eusebius, allowing these voices to disagree with each other in print. He also established an intellectual circle called the *Davidsbündler*, which included Mendelssohn in its membership. Mendelssohn hired Schumann for the faculty of the Leipzig Conservatory in 1843.

Clara and Robert were married in 1840 over the objections of her father. The first year of their marriage yielded an exceptional outpouring of new music. Schumann suffered from insomnia, depression, and he heard things that weren't there. His mental health began to deteriorate rapidly in 1850, and in 1854, he threw himself into the Rhine. He voluntarily committed himself to a sanitorium where he spent his final years.

Schumann was a critical figure in the development of romanticism in music. His orchestral music has been unduly criticized for being ineffectively scored for successful balance, but when played with period small-bore brass instruments, these works are innately functional. Schumann was one of the most imaginative artists of his era, and he produced a body of exceptionally expressive and original music.

Clara edited a critical edition of his complete works, which were published in 34 volumes by Breitkopf and Härtel with a supplementary volume prepared by Johannes Brahms, one of Schumann's closest friends and steadfast pupil.

Teachers: Heinrich Dorn, Friedrich Wieck

Students: Johannes Brahms, Gustav Nottebohm, Carl Reinecke

Writings: Schumann's article in the *Neue Zeitschrift für Musik* were collected in 4 volumes as *Gesammelte Schriften über Musik und Musiker.* Leipzig: Breitkopf and Härtel, 1854.

Other Principal Works: orchestral: Symphony No. 1 (1841), Symphony No. 2 (1845-1846), Symphony No. 3 (1850), Symphony No. 4 (1841), *Manfred* (incidental music, 1848-1849), Piano Concerto (1845), Concertstücke for 4 horns (1849), Cello Concerto (1850); **chamber music:** 3 string quartets, piano quintet, 3 piano trios, 2 violin sonatas; **piano:** *Papillons* (1829-1831), *Carnaval* (1834-1835), *Davidsbündlertänze* (1837), *Kinderscenen* (1838), *Albumblätter* (1832-1845); **vocal:** *Liederkreis* (1840), *Dichterliebe* (1840), *Frauenliebe und Leben* (1840), many others.

Selected Composer Bibliography

Abraham, Gerald, editor: *Schumann: A Symposium.* London: Oxford University Press, 1952.

Walker, Alan, editor: *Robert Schumann: The Man and His Music.* London: Barry and Jenkins, 1972.

McCorkle, Margit: *Robert Schumann: Thematic-Bibliographical Catalogue of the Works.* Mainz: Schott, 2003.

Das Paradies und die Peri, op. 50 (1843)

Duration: ca. 105 minutes

Text: The text is "Lalla Rookh" by Thomas Moore, which was translated into German by Emil Flechsig.

Performing Forces: voices: Peri (soprano), mezzo soprano, alto, tenor I, tenor II (Jüngling), and baritone (Gazna) soloists; SATB choir; **orchestra:** piccolo, 2 flutes, 2 oboes, 2 clarinets, 2 bassoons, 4 horns, 2 trumpets, 3 trombones, ophicleide, timpani, percussion (2 players: triangle, cymbals, bass drum), and strings.

First Performance: 4 December 1843; Gewandhaus in Leipzig; conducted by the composer

Editions: *Das Paradies und die Peri* was published in *Robert Schumann: Werke*, edited by Clara Schumann and Johannes Brahms, series 9, volume 1. Edwin Kalmus published a study score of that edition (468). It also appears in a new critical edition, *Robert Schumann: Neue Ausgabe sämtlicher Werke* published by the Robert-Schumann-Gesellschaft in Düsseldorf, series 4, volume 2, part 1.

Autograph: The composer's manuscript is in the Prussian Collection of the Stadtsbibliothek in Berlin (Ms auto, Schumann 2).

Notes: This is a large oratorio in three acts, organized as follows:

Act I

1. Vor Eden's Thor imMorgenprangen (alto)
2. Wie glücklich sie wandeln (Peri)
3. Der hehre Engel, der die Pforte (tenor and Angel)
4. Wo find' ich sie? (Peri)
5. So sann sie nach (tenor)
   O süsses Land! (solo quartet)
6. Doch seine Ströme sind jetzt roth (choir)
7. Und einsam steht ein Jüngling (tenor I, Jüngling, Gazna)
8. Weh', weh', er fehlte das Ziel (choir)
9. Die Peri sah das Mal der Wunde (tenor and Peri)

Act II

10. Die Peri tritt mit schüchterner Geberde (tenor, alto, choir)
11. Ihr erstes Himmelshoffen schwand (tenor)
    Hervor aus den Wässern (choir of the Genies of the Nile)
12. Fort streit von hier das Kind der Lüfte (tenor and Peri)
13. Die Peri weint (tenor)
    Denn in der Thrän' ist Zaubermacht (solo quartet)
14. Im Waldesgrün am stillen See (alto and Jüngling)
15. Verlassener Jüngling (mezzo soprano, tenor I, Jüngling)
16. O lass mich von der Luft durchdringen (soprano and tenor)
17. Schlaf' nun und ruhe in Träumen voll Duft (Peri and choir)

Act III

18. Schmücket die Stufen zu Allah's Thron (choir of prostitutes)
19. Dem Sang von ferne lauchsend (tenor and Angel)
20. Verstossen! Verschlossen auf's neu' (Peri)
21. Jetzt sank des Abends gold'ner Schein (baritone)
22. Peri, ist's wahr? (solo quartet)
23. Hinab zu jenem Sonnentempel (Peri, tenor, mezzo soprano, Der Mann)
24. O heil'ge Thränen inn'ger Reue (solo quartet and choir)
25. Es fällt ein Tropfen (Peri, tenor, and choir)
26. Freud', ew'ge Freude, mein Werk ist gethan (Peri and choir)

Performance Issues: There is a brief solo quartet from the choir. There are divisi in all choral parts, as well as some semi-choirs identified as groups of characters including a number of SSAA sections. Likewise, the soloists are labeled with proper names in some movements and by voice type in others; however, there is nothing in the score to indicate if these should in fact be different singers with the exception of the Jüngling, which is labeled "tenor II." The choral writing is mostly homophonic and all of the choral material is clearly reinforced by the orchestra. The orchestration is inconsistent. Intonation and balance will present some difficulties, as will the balance between the choir and instruments. Small-bore instruments were intended at the time, and this may lead to control issues on modern instruments. The individual parts include some very challenging passages. The ophicleide part should be played by tuba. The piccolo appears in only a brief section of the work, but it requires an independent player as both flutes appear with it. **Soloists:** soprano (Peri) - range: $c\#'-c'''$, tessitura: $f'-a''$, this is a difficult solo requiring a powerful voice with some very sustained passages at the very top of the range; mezzo soprano - range: $b-g''$, tessitura: $e'-e''$, this is a lyric role; alto (Angel) - range: $c\#'-f''$, tessitura: $e'-d''$, this is a simple lyric solo; tenor I - range: $c-a'$, tessitura: $f-f'$, this is a challenging declamatory role; tenor II (Jüngling) - range: $d\#-g^{b'}$, tessitura: $f-f'$, this is a simple lyric solo; baritone (Gazna and Der Mann) - range: $A-e'$, tessitura: $c-c'$, this is a fairly simple declamatory role; **choir:** medium difficult; **orchestra:** difficult.

Selected Discography

Edda Moser, Regina Marheineke, Brigitte Fassbaender, Nicolai Gedda, Alva Tripp, Günter Wewel; Chor des Städtischen Musikvereins Düsseldorf (Hartmut Schmidt, choirmaster), Düsseldorf Symphoniker; conducted by Henryk Czyz, recorded 20-23 August 1973 in the Rheinhalle in Düsseldorf. EMI: 1C 193—30 187/88Q [LP].

Constanze Backes, Barbara Bonney, Alexandra Coku, Donna Deam, Bernarda Fink, Jacqueline Connell, Christoph Prégardien, William Dazeley, Gerald Finley, Carnelius Hauptmann; Monteverdi Choir, Hanover Boys' Choir; Orchestre Révolutionnaire et Romantique; conducted by John Eliot Gardiner. Archiv: 028945766027.

Simone Kermes, Kathaina Wollitz, Almut Cechova, Melinda Paulsen, Julio Fernandez, Thomas Dewald, Eike Wilm Schulte; Sing-Akademie zu Berlin, Pforzheim Wind Ensemble; conducted by Joshard Daus, recorded live 15 February 2001 in Die Glocke, Bremen, Arte Nova: 878170.

Selected Bibliography

Upton, George: *The Standard Oratorios*, 273-279. Chicago: A. C. McClurg and Company, 1893.

Horton, John: "The Choral Works," in *Schumann: A Symposium*, edited by Gerald Abraham, 283-286. London: Oxford University Press, 1952.

Dohm, Jürgen: "Robert Schumann: Das Paradies und die Peri," English translations by Geoffrey Watkins, liner notes to the recording above.

Halsey, Louis: "The Choral Music," in *Robert Schumann: The Man and His Music*, edited by Alan Walker, 28, 149, 325, 351, 372-377. London: Barry and Jenkins, 1972.

Pahlen, Kurt: *The World of the Oratorio*, translated by Judith Schaefer with additional English-language material by Thurston Dox, 297-300. Portland, OR: Amadeus Press, 1990.

Smither, Howard E.: *A History of the Oratorio, volume 4: The Oratorio in the Nineteenth and Twentieth Centuries*, 184-199. Chapel Hill, NC: The University of North Carolina Press, 2000.

Szenen aus Goethes Faust, WoO 3 (1844-53)[81]

Duration: ca. 104 minutes

Text: The text is from Johann Wolfgang von Goethe's *Faust*.

Performing Forces: voices: Gretchen (soprano), Sorge (soprano), Marthe (alto), Ariel (tenor), Pater Ecstaticus (tenor), Dr. Marianus (tenor or baritone), Faust (baritone), Böse Geist (bass), Mephistofeles (bass), Pater Profundis (bass), and Pater Seraphicus (bass) soloists; SATB choir; **orchestra:** 2 flutes, 2 oboes, 2 clarinets (B^b), 2 bassoons, 4 horns (2 valved and 2 Waldhorns), 2 trumpets, 3 trombones, timpani, harp, and strings.

First Performance: The third section, "Fausts Verklärung" was performed separately in 1849 in Dresden, Leipzig, and Weimar. Franz Liszt conducted the third of these concerts.

Complete work: 13 January 1862, Cologne, Germany

Editions: *Szenen aus Goethes Faust* was published in *Robert Schumann: Werke*, edited by Clara Schumann and Johannes Brahms, series 9, volume 7. Performance materials for the overture are available from the Fleischer Collection.[82] Edwin F. Kalmus publishes a study score (476). It also appears in a new critical edition, *Robert Schumann: Neue Ausgabe sämtlicher Werke* published by the Robert-Schumann-Gesellschaft in Düsseldorf, series 4, volume 2, part 3.

Autograph: The composer's manuscript is in the Prussian Collection of the Stadtsbibliothek in Berlin (Ms. Auto. Schumann 3,1 and 3,2).

Notes: The score is a concert drama in which Schumann has created a virtual opera without staging. This may present some challenges in

---

[81] The oratorio was composed between 1847 and 1850. The overture was composed in 1853.

[82] David Daniels: *Orchestral Music: A Handbook*, third edition, 371. Lanham, MD: Scarecrow Press, 1996.

proffering a meaningful performance for audiences not aware of which character is speaking at any given time. For this reason a full libretto is advised as part of the concert program. It is organized as follows:

Overture

Act I
1. Scene im Garten
2. Gretchen vor dem Bild der Mater dolorosa
3. Scene in Dom

Act II
4. Sonnenaufgang
5. Mitternact
6. Faust's Tod
7. Faust's Verklärung

Act III
1. Choir: Waldung, sie schwankt heran
2. Tenor: Ewiger Wonnebrand, glühendes Liebesband
3. Bass: Wie Felsen-Abgrund mir zu Füssen
4. Choir: Gerettet ist das edle Glied
5. Bass: Hier ist die Aussicht frei
6. Bass and choir: Dir, der Unberührbaren
7. Mystic choir: Alles Vergängliche ist nur ein Gleichniss

Performance Issues: The score indicates placement of characters relative to one another on the stage. Although the logistics of each venue may limit adherence to these suggestions, they do provide some clarity to the drama. Also, throughout the work, some semichoirs are labeled as specific groups including a choir of heavenly boys. If a small musically secure children's choir were available, this would also help to keep the drama on track. The choral writing in Acts I and II is conservative and accessible to less experienced singers. Much of the choral material is conspicuously doubled by the orchestra. None of these parts is vocally demanding. The choir is a more integral part of Act III. The final chorus is scored for two SATB choirs and a solo SSATB quintet. For this, Schumann does not indicate which soloists are assigned to each part. Movement 4 includes a sextet from the choir, which is juxtaposed against the

A Conductor's Guide to 19th-Century Choral-Orchestra Works   291

remaining choir. There are two soprano solos in Act III, movement 4 that may be sung by Gretchen and either Sorge or Marthe. Additional solos presumably from the choir appear throughout the final Act representing assorted characters in the afterlife. The roles of the Profundis, Seraphicus and the Böse Geist could be sung by the same soloist as Mephistofeles. The same can be done with Ariel and Ecstaticus, although the effect of separate characters is desirable. Faust and Mephistofeles must be sung by different soloists as they have dialogue in one scene. The orchestral writing is imaginative and colorful, but will require attention to achieve balance. Some of the voicings of sustained harmonies in the winds and brass may also prove troublesome for accurate intonation. **Soloists:** Gretchen (soprano) - range: d'-$b^{b''}$, tessitura: f'-f'', this is a prominent lyric and expressive role; Sorge (soprano) - range: $d^{b'}$-$a^{b''}$, tessitura: f'-f'', this is a lyric role; Marthe (alto) - range: g'-c'', tessitura: g'-c'', this is a minor lyric role appropriate for a chorister; Ariel (tenor) - range: f-$b^{b'}$, tessitura: g-g', this is a declamatory role with crisp melodic leaps; Pater Ecstaticus (tenor) - range: f-a', tessitura: g-g', this is a lyric and sustained role; Dr. Marianus (tenor or baritone) - range: A-g', tessitura: d-d', this is a declamatory role; Faust (baritone) - range: $F\#$-g', tessitura: f-f', this is a demanding role with wide melodic leaps and sustained passages that are best suited to a "Verdi" baritone; Mephistofeles (bass) - range: A^b-f', tessitura: c-d', this is a small role requiring a powerful voice; Böse Geist (bass) - range: A-f', tessitura: d-d', this is a declamatory but not overly challenging role; Pater Profundis (bass) - range: B^b-$e^{b'}$, tessitura: d-d', this is a sustained and simple role; Pater Seraphicus (bass) - range: B^b-$e^{b'}$, tessitura: d-d', this is a sustained and simple role; **choir:** difficult; **orchestra:** difficult

Selected Discography

Edith Mathis, Lou Ann Wyckoff, Charlotte Barthold, Brigitte Fassbaender, Norma Procter, Werner Krenn, Hermann Prey, Franz Crass; Bavarian Radio Symphony Orchestra and Choir; conducted by Erich Leinsdorf, recorded live on 21 May 1971 in Hercules Hall, Munich, Germany. Released on CD 1 May 2002. Melodram: 40054.

Edith Mathis, Elisabeth Robinson, Frances Gregory, Ameral Gunson, Lesley Reid, Anne Collins, Stuart Burrows, Dietrich Fischer-

Dieskau, Brian Rayner Cook, Gwynne Howell, Richard Van Allan; BBC Symphony Orchestra and Chorus; conducted by Pierre Boulez, recorded live in London on 7 March 1973. Released on CD in 2005. Opera d'Oro: 1427.

Karita Mattila, Barbara Bonney, Brigitte Poschner-Klebel, Susan Graham, Iris Vermillion, Endrik Wottrich, Hans-Peter Blochwitz, Bryn Terfel, Jan-Hendrik Rootering, Harry Peeters; Berlin Philharmonic Orchestra and Chorus; conducted by Claudio Abbado. Sony: CD 66 308 2.

Selected Bibliography

Pahlen, Kurt: *The World of the Oratorio*, translated by Judith Schaefer with additional English-language material by Thurston Dox, 302-304. Portland, OR: Amadeus Press, 1990.

Requiem für Mignon, op. 98b (1849)

Duration: ca. 12 minutes

Text: The text is taken from Johann Wolfgang von Goethe's novel, *Wilhelm Meister*. It is a poem on the death of the character Mignon.

Performing Forces: voices: 2 soprano, 2 alto, and baritone soloists; SATTBB choir; **orchestra:** 2 flutes, 2 oboes, 2 clarinets (B^b), 2 bassoons, 2 horns (E - valved parts), 2 trumpets (F), 3 trombones, timpani, harp, and strings.

First Performance: 21 November 1850; Düsseldorf

Editions: *Requiem für Mignon* was published in *Robert Schumann: Werke*, edited by Clara Schumann and Johannes Brahms, series 9, volume 3. Full scores and parts are available for purchase from Breitkopf and Härtel and Kalmus. Kalmus also produces a study score (#1126), which also contains *Nachtlied*, op. 108. It also appears in a new critical edition, *Robert Schumann: Neue Ausgabe sämtlicher Werke* published by the Robert-Schumann-Gesellschaft in Düsseldorf, series 4, volume 2, part 4.

Autograph: The composer's manuscript is in the Universitätsbibliothek in Bonn. Additional materials are in private collections.

Notes: Version A of this composition utilizes piano accompaniment. This work is through composed in six brief sections as follows:

1. Choir: Wen bringt ihr uns zur stillen Gesellschaft?
2. SA: Ach wie ungern brachten wir ihn her!
3. Choir: Seht die mächtigen Flügel doch an!
4. Choir: In euch lebe die bilden der Kraft
5. SSAAB: Kinder, kehret ins Leben zurück!
6. Choir: Kinder, eilet ins leben hinan!

Performance Issues: The choral writing is homophonic and chordal throughout. The choral parts are thoroughly doubled by the orchestra. The solos are fully interpolated into the choir. The orchestration is conservative in that the individual parts are not difficult; however, transparency in the scoring may present challenges for balance and pitch within the orchestra. This same feature ensures that the choir will not be overpowered by the orchestra. **Soloists:** soprano I - range: $f'-f''$, tessitura: $g'-f''$, this is an easy and lyric solo role; soprano II - range: $d^{b'}-f''$, tessitura: $f'-e^{b''}$, this is a simple part that appears in ensemble only; alto I - range: $b-a'$, tessitura: $d'-a'$, this is an easy and lyric solo role; alto II - range: $b-a'$, tessitura: $d'-a'$, this is a simple part that appears in ensemble only; baritone - range: $d-e'$, tessitura: $d-e'$, this is a simple part that appears in ensemble only; **choir:** medium easy; **orchestra:** medium difficult.

Selected Discography

Brigitte Poschner-Klebel, Barbara Bonney, Margaretha Hintermeier, Dalia Schaechter, Jorge Pita, Andreas Schmidt; Vienna State Opera Concert Chorus; Chamber Orchestra of Europe; conducted by Claudio Abbado, recorded in the Grosser Saal, Musikverein in Vienna in 1990. Deutsche Grammophon: 435486-2.

Brigitte Lindner, Andrea Andonian, Mechthild Georg, Monika Weichhold, Dietrich Fischer-Dieskau; Düsseldorf Städtischer Musikvereins Chorus, Düsseldorf Symphony Orchestra; conducted by Bernhard Klee, recorded in July 1983 in the Tonhalle in Düsseldorf, re-released on CD in 2006 as EMI 50900.

Selected Bibliography

Horton, John: "The Choral Works," in *Schumann: A Symposium*, edited by Gerald Abraham, 297. London: Oxford University Press, 1952.

Halsey, Louis: "The Choral Music," in *Robert Schumann: The Man and His Music*, edited by Alan Walker, 379-383. London: Barry and Jenkins, 1972.

Nachtlied, op. 108 (1849)

Duration: ca. 9 minutes

Text: The text is by Friedrich Hebbel.

Performing Forces: voices: SSAATTBB choir; **orchestra:** 2 flutes, 2 oboes, 2 clarinets (B^b), 2 bassoons, 2 horns (D), 2 trumpets (D), bass trombone, timpani (2 drums), and strings (with 2 cello parts).

First Performance: 13 March 1851; Düsseldorf

Editions: *Nachtlied* was published in *Robert Schumann: Werke*, edited by Clara Schumann and Johannes Brahms, series 9, volume 3. Full scores and parts are available for purchase from Breitkopf and Härtel and Kalmus. Kalmus also produces a study score (#1126), which also contains *Requiem für Mignon*, op. 98b. It also appears in a new critical edition, *Robert Schumann: Neue Ausgabe sämtlicher Werke* published by the Robert-Schumann-Gesellschaft in Düsseldorf, series 4, volume 2, part 4.

Autograph: The composer's manuscript is in the Bibliothèque Nationale in Paris (Ms. 323).

Notes: This is a brief, but dramatically effective secular romantic composition that would be effective as a complement to works like Brahms's *Nänie* or *Schicksalslied*.

Performance Issues: The eight-part choral writing implies the use of a larger ensemble. The orchestra harmonically supports the choir throughout the score, but this is not accomplished through clear direct doubling. The orchestral writing is very sustained with gradual shifts of orchestrational color, but little rhythmic drive. The rhythmic clarity of the work must be generated by the choir on top of a field of instrumental sound; **choir:** medium difficult; **orchestra:** medium difficult.

Selected Discography

Monteverdi Choir; Orchestre Révolutionnaire et Romantique; conducted by John Eliot Gardiner. Released in 1999. Archiv: 028945766027.

Selected Bibliography

Horton, John: "The Choral Works," in *Schumann: A Symposium*, edited by Gerald Abraham, 297-299. London: Oxford University Press, 1952.

Halsey, Louis: "The Choral Music," in *Robert Schumann: The Man and His Music*, edited by Alan Walker, 383-385. London: Barry and Jenkins, 1972.

Mass, op. 147 (1852-1853)

Duration: ca. 42 minutes

Text: The text is from the Roman Catholic communion liturgy.

Performing Forces: voices: soprano and bass soloists; SATB choir; **orchestra:** 2 flutes, 2 oboes, 2 clarinets (B^b), 2 bassoons, 2 horns (C, E^b), 2 trumpets (C, E^b), 3 trombones (alto, tenor, and bass), timpani, organ, and strings.

First Performance: 3 March 1853; Geislerschen Saal, Düsseldorf; Allgemeinen Musikvereins; conducted by the composer, as part of a Schumann benefit concert

Editions: *Mass* was published in *Robert Schumann: Werke*, edited by Clara Schumann and Johannes Brahms, series 9, volume 9. Full scores and parts are available for purchase from Breitkopf and Härtel and Kalmus. Kalmus produces a miniature score (#474). It also appears in a new critical edition, *Robert Schumann: Neue*

Ausgabe sämtlicher Werke published by the Robert-Schumann-Gesellschaft in Düsseldorf, series 4, volume 3, part 2.

Autograph: The composer's manuscript is in the Prussian Collection of the Stadtsbibliothek in Berlin (Ms. Auto. Schumann 6).

Performance Issues: Some of the choral writing is contrapuntally complex. There are extended passages of pervasive imitation. Much of this choral material is directly doubled by the orchestra. The density of the scoring suggests the use of a large choral ensemble. The Gloria is rhythmically detailed, requiring an articulate and flexible choir. The orchestration is often thickly scored. There are extended passages wherein the brass and winds are quite sustained. This is a melodically attractive work that is particularly well conceived from a vocal perspective. Some attention will need to be applied to establish good balances between the choir and orchestra and between sections of the orchestra. **Soloists:** soprano - range: $d'-f''$, tessitura: $f'-e^{b''}$, this is a lyric role within the abilities of a good student soloist; bass - range: $f-d'$, tessitura: $f-d'$, this is a brief and simple solo part; **choir:** medium difficult; **orchestra:** medium difficult.

Selected Discography

Mitsuko Shirai, Peter Seiffert, Jan-Hendrick Rootering; Dusseldorf Städtischer Musikvereins Chorus, Berlin Philharmonic; conducted by Wolfgang Sawallisch, recorded in the Philharmonie in Berlin in September 1987 and re-released on CD in 2004 as EMI: 85819 and in 2006 as EMI: 50900.

Selected Bibliography

Horton, John: "The Choral Works," in *Schumann: A Symposium*, edited by Gerald Abraham, 294-295. London: Oxford University Press, 1952.

Requiem, op. 148 (1852)

Duration: ca. 43 minutes

Text: The text is from the Roman Catholic liturgy of the Mass for the Dead.

Performing Forces: voices: soprano, alto, tenor, and bass soloists, SATB choir; **orchestra:** 2 flutes, 2 oboes, 2 clarinets, 2 bassoons, 2 horns (E^b, F) 2 trumpets (F), 3 trombones, timpani, and strings.

First Performance: 19 November 1864; Domkirche in Königsberg; Musikalischen Akademie; conducted by Heinrich Laudien

Editions: *Requiem* was published in *Robert Schumann: Werke*, edited by Clara Schumann and Johannes Brahms, series 9, volume 9. Full scores and parts are available for purchase from Breitkopf and Härtel and Kalmus. A study score is published by Kalmus (475). It also appears in a new critical edition, *Robert Schumann: Neue Ausgabe sämtlicher Werke* published by the Robert-Schumann-Gesellschaft in Düsseldorf, series 4, volume 3, part 3.

Autograph: The composer's manuscript is in the Prussian Collection of the Stadtsbibliothek in Berlin (Ms. Auto. Schumann 5).

Notes: This is a wonderful and underperformed setting of the Requiem Mass.[83] The harmonic language is rich and expressive and the vocal writing is delicate and very effective. It is somewhat unconventionally organized into nine succinct movements as follows:

1. Requiem in aeternam
2. Te decet hymnus
3. Dies irae
4. Liber scriptus

---

[83] Kurt Pahlen states that "At the time of its composition, Schumann was no longer capable of sustained concentration, so passages of great nobility are placed next to banalities." in *The World of the Oratorio*, translated by Judith Schaefer with additional English-language material by Thurston Dox, 305. Portland, OR: Amadeus Press, 1990.

5. Qui Mariam absolvisti
6. Domine Jesu Christe! Rex gloriae!
7. Hostias et preces tibi, Domine
8. Sanctus
9. Benedictus

Performance Issues: The choral writing is very practical combining homophonic and imitative passages, all of which are well supported by the orchestra. The most complex choral writing appears in the sixth movement, which has more extended pervasive imitation and varied articulation between parts. All of the solo parts should be well within the abilities of strong choristers. The ranges of each solo part are more conservative than the parallel choral part. The orchestral writing is idiomatic for all instruments. Care will need to be taken to assure good balance within the orchestra as well as between the instruments and voices. The composer has judiciously used light scoring for all solo vocal passages. The brass and wind writing suggests the use of a large string section and choir. **Soloists:** soprano - range: $d^{b\prime}$-g'', tessitura: e'-e'', this is a lyric solo with some sustained passages; alto - range: b^b-e'', tessitura: e'-b', this is a lyric and sometimes declamatory role; tenor - range: e^b-$f\#'$, tessitura: a-e', this is a simple role that appears only in the context of the solo quartet; bass - range: G^b-b, tessitura: A-a, this is a simple role that appears only in the context of the solo quartet; **choir:** medium difficult, **orchestra:** medium difficult.

Selected Discography

Helen Donath, Doris Soffel, Nicolai Gedda, Dietrich Fischer-Dieskau; Düsseldorf Städtischer Musikvereins Chorus, Düsseldorf Symphony Orchestra; conducted by Bernhard Klee, recorded in July 1983 in the Tonhalle in Düsseldorf, re-released on CD in 2004 as EMI: 85819; and 2006 as EMI 50900.

Selected Bibliography

Horton, John: "The Choral Works," in *Schumann: A Symposium*, edited by Gerald Abraham, 295. London: Oxford University Press, 1952.

Scriabin, Alexander (b. Moscow, 6 January 1872; d. Moscow, 27 April 1915)

Life: Scriabin's father was a lawyer and his mother was a very fine pianist who died when he was a baby. Scriabin was raised by his aunt. He attended the Moscow Conservatory graduating with a gold medal in piano, but never completing the diploma in composition because he failed a required exam in fugue.

Scriabin toured as a performer of his own compositions sometimes in duo-piano concerts with his wife, Vera Isakovich. One of his early champions was Serge Koussevitsky; another was Modeste Altschuler.

Scriabin's music is exciting, colorful, and an historic anomaly. He developed a remarkably rich harmonic language using 4ths and 2nds in a manner that had no forebears, nor any disciples. His most celebrated harmonic device was his "mystery chord: C, F#, B^b, E, A, and D.

Teachers: Anton Arensky, Sergei Taneyev

Other Principal Works: orchestral: Symphony No. 1 (1890-1891), Symphony No. 2 (1897-1903), Symphony No. 3, *Divine Poem* (1903), Symphony No. 4, *Poem of Ecstasy* (1907-1908), Symphony No. 5, *Prometheus—Poem of Fire* (1909-1910), Piano Concerto (1897-1898); **piano:** 10 sonatas, 24 Études, 85 Préludes.

Selected Composer Bibliography

Bowers, Faubion: *Scriabin: A Biography of the Russian Composer, 1871-1915*, two volumes. Tokyo annd Palo Alto: Kondasha International, 1969.
Vordi, Luigi: *Alexander Scriabin: Bibliography.* New York: The Scriabin Society of America, n.d.
Sato, Taiichi and Farhan Malik: *Alexander Scriabin: Discography.* New York: The Scriabin Society of America, 1996.

Symphony No. 1, op. 26 (1899-1900)

Duration: ca. 51 minutes

Text: The text, in praise of art, is by the composer.

Performing Forces: voices: mezzosoprano and tenor soloists; SATB choir; **orchestra:** 3 flutes, 2 oboes, 3 clarinets (B^b, A), 2 bassoons, 4 horns (F), 3 trumpets (B^b), 3 trombones, tuba, timpani, harp, and strings.

First Performance: 29 March 1901, Moscow

Editions: Full scores and parts for Symphony No. 1 are available for purchase from M. P. Belaieff and Kalmus. The vocal portion has singing texts in Russian, French, and German.

Notes: The text that Scriabin wrote for this symphony calls for all to bow down to the greatness of art.

Performance Issues: The singers appear in only the sixth (final) movement, and the choral portion is only about four or five minutes of music. The choral material begins as SSATBB, but with the exception of 12 measures it is scored for SATB. The choral parts are fairly simple and clearly doubled by the orchestra. The bass part must be able to clearly project at the bottom of the staff. The orchestral parts are quite accessible to moderately experienced players. Despite Scriabin's progressive harmonic practices, the orchestration is surprisingly conservative with extensive passages using all of the instruments in block choirs. Some of the voicings may require attention to intonation. The winds and brass scoring is suggestive of a large string contingent. This is reinforced by the occurrence of string divisi at the end of the first movement for four first-violin, three second-violin, 3 viola, and 2 cello parts. This is an interesting and attractive composition that has such a limited choral component that one may wish to program a more extensive choral work for the same program. **Soloists:** mezzosoprano - range: b-g#", tessitura: d'-d", this is a declamatory role with considerable passages in parallel with the tenor; tenor - range: c#-b', tessitura: f#-f#', this is a lyric solo that may be sung with only a high g#'; **choir:** medium easy; **orchestra:** medium difficult.

Selected Discography

Stefania Toczyska, Michael Myers; Westminster Choir, Philadelphia Orchestra; conducted by Riccardo Muti. Brilliant Classics: 92744.

Ludmila Legostayeva, Anatoly Orfenov; USSR Radio Large Symphony Orchestra; conducted by Nikolay Golovanov. Boheme Music: CDBMR 907081.

Brigitte Balleys, Sergei Larin; Berlin Radio Symphony Orchestra and Chorus; conducted by Vladimir Ashkenazy. Decca: 460299-2.

Selected Bibliography

Bowers, Faubion: *Scriabin: A Biography of the Russian Composer, 1871-1915*, volume one, 267-275. Tokyo annd Palo Alto: Kondasha International, 1969.

Symphony No. 5, Prométhée, le poème du feu,
op. 60 ["Prometheus, The Poem of Fire"] (1908-1910)

Duration: ca. 21 minutes

Text: The choir is given a series of nonsense syllables.

Performing Forces: voices: SATB choir; **orchestra:** piccolo, 3 flutes, 3 oboes, English horn, 3 clarinets (B^b), bass clarinet (B^b), 3 bassoons, contra bassoon, 8 horns (F), 5 trumpets (B^b), 3 trombones, tuba, timpani (3 drums), percussion (4 players — bass drum, triangle, cymbals, tam-tam, glockenspiel, chimes), celesta, 2 harps, piano, and strings.

First Performance: 15 March 1911; Moscow; composer as pianist; conducted by Serge Koussevitsky

Editions: This work was originally published by Edition Russe de Musique in 1911. Full scores and parts are available for purchase from Boosey and Hawkes and Kalmus. A study score is also available from Dover.

Notes: This score has the unusual feature of a "color organ" part, which can be left out. This was a device constructed by Alexander Moser that would project colored lights in synchrony with the musical score. This "keyboard" part appears at the top of the score. The first performance of this work with lights was a concert of the Russian Symphony Society of New York, conducted by Modest Altschuler in Carnegie Hall.[84]

Performance Issues: The choir appears in a brief section near the end of the score. The part is static, sustained, and quite easy. The choral parts are doubled in the orchestra. The original score indicated that the glockenspiel [campanelli] part sounds an octave higher than written. While it is true that traditional glockenspiel parts sound two octaves above written, this part is should be read an octave lower. The part actually requires two players. The score has a "campane" for which the composer intended chimes. The two parts are integrated on a grand staff and the bass-clef portions are the chimes part. A number of octave decisions will need to be made prior to rehearsal as neither part corresponds to the ranges of the instruments. Likewise, there is a part labeled "cassa," which must mean bass drum. The piano part is virtuosic and important. The player must be very strong and have a broad reach. To balance appropriately, the string section must be large. There are a number of string divisi. A moderate-sized choir will be sufficient as it is used for color and appears in a subdued passage for the orchestra; **choir:** easy; **orchestra:** very difficult.

Selected Discography

Dmitri Alexeev, piano; Choral Arts Society of Philadelphia (Sean Deibler, chorusmaster), Philadelphia Orchestra; conducted by Riccardo Muti, recorded in 1990. Aquarius: AQVR 145-2.

Anatol Ugorski, piano; Chicago Symphony Orchestra and Chorus; conducted by Pierre Boulez. Deutsche Grammophon: 437 850-2.

Alexander Toradze, piano; Kirov Orchestra and Chorus; conducted by Valery Gergiev. Philips: 446715-2.

---

[84] A description of the concepts behind the use of this device and Scriabin's theories of synesthesia appears in Faubion Bowers's preface to the Dover score.

Selected Bibliography

Bowers, Faubion: *Scriabin: A Biography of the Russian Composer, 1871-1915*, volume two, 211-231. Tokyo annd Palo Alto: Kondasha International, 1969.

Strauss, Richard (b. Munich, Germany, 11 June 1864; d. Garmisch-Partenkirchen, Germany, 8 September 1949)

Life: Strauss was the son of the celebrated hornist and composer, Franz Strauss for whom he composed his first horn concerto, which the father never performed. A child prodigy, Strauss did not attend music school. By the time he was 20, he had secured a professional conducting post and had received performances of his orchestral music in Munich and New York.

Strauss was introduced to the music and ideas of Wagner and Liszt by the poet Alexander Ritter. He began to composer tone poems in the tradition of Liszt and quickly established himself as the leading composer of his generation. He produced his first opera in 1894, and had become chief conductor of the Munich Court Theater by 1896. He established a partnership with librettist Hugo Hofmannsthal that resulted in a series of musically and psychologically remarkable operas. Strauss was appointed to the conducting staff of Berlin Royal Opera in 1898, becoming general director in 1908, a post he left in 1918 to become co-director with Franz Schalk of the Vienna Stadstoper from 1919 to 1924. He also played an important role in establishing the Salzburg Festival. The Nazis appointed him president of the newly formed Reichsmusikkammer in 1933 from which he resigned in 1935. By establishing a working relationship with Stefan Zweig, he entered into a conflict with the party. He was officially cleared of any collaborations in 1948. He completed his final composition, *Vier letzte Lieder*, that year.

Strauss possessed a remarkable orchestral technique and a natural dramatic sense. His tone poems brought the form to its zenith at the turn of the 20th century. His operas while maintaining vocal lyricism explored the Freudian depths of their subject matter whether in the symbolic implications of Salome's necrophilia or the portrayal of incidents in the composer's own marriage, as in *Intermezzo*. Like Mahler, Strauss was an international celebrity as both composer and conductor, particularly leading performances of his own works of which a number of recordings survive.

Writings: Strauss edited and revised Berlioz's *Grande Traité d'Instrumentation et d'orchestration modernes* to reflect changes in instruments during the 19th century. A number of compilations of his correspondence with colleagues including Hoffmansthal, Zweig, Romain Rolland, Clemens Krauss, and others have been published.

Other Principal Works: opera: *Salome* (1903-1905), *Elektra* (1906-1908), *Der Rosenkavalier* (1909-1910), *Ariadne auf Naxos* (1911-1912), *Die Fraue ohne Schatten* (1914-1918), *Intermezzo* (1918-1923), *Arabella* (1929-1932), *Die schweigsame Frau* (1933-1934), *Capriccio* (1940-1941); **orchestral:** Horn Concerto No. 1 (1882-1883), *Burleske* (1885-1886), *Macbeth* (1886-1888), *Don Juan* (1888-1889), *Tod und Verklärung* (1888-1889), *Till Eulenspiegels lustige Streiche* (1894-1895), *Also sprach Zarathustra* (1895-1896), *Don Quixote* (1896-1897), *Ein Heldenleben* (1897-1898), *Symphonia domestica* (1902-1903), *Eine Alpensinfonie* (1911-1915), Horn Concerto No. 2 (1942), *Metamorphosen* (1945), Oboe Concerto (1945-1946).

Selected Composer Bibliography

Del Mar, Norman: *Richard Strauss*, in three volumes. Philadelphia: Chilton Book Company; 1962, 1969, and 1972.
Kennedy, Michael: *Richard Strauss*, second edition. London: Oxford University Press, 1983.
Wilhelm, Kurt: *Richard Strauss persönlich*. Hamburg: Kindler Verlag, 1984. Published in English, translated by Mary Whittall, as *Richard Straus: An Intimate Portrait*. London: Thames and Hudson, 1989.

Wanderers Sturmlied ["Wanderer's Storm Song"] (1884)

Duration: ca. 16 minutes

Text: The text is a German poem by Johann Wolfgang von Goethe.

Performing Forces: voices: SSATBB choir; **orchestra:** piccolo, 2 flutes, 2 oboes, 2 clarinets (B^b), 2 bassoons, contrabassoon, 4 horns (F), 2 trumpets (D), 3 trombones, timpani, and strings.

First Performance: 8 March 1887; Cologne; conducted by the composer

Editions: Full scores and parts for *Wanderers Sturmlied* are available for purchase from Kalmus and Universal Edition. A critical edition appears on page 1 in volume 30 of the *Richard Strauss Edition* published by Verlag Dr. Richard Strauss.

Autograph: The composer's manuscript is in the Prussian Library of the Stadtsbibliothek in Berlin (Ms. Auto. R. Strauss 9). Another autograph score is in the British Library in London (49/7). Additional manuscript materials can be found in the Bayerischen Stadtsbibliothek in Munich. The London score is dated and the Berlin is not, which may suggest that the British copy is the original.

Notes: The score is dated 22 May 1885 in Munich. It is dedicated to "Herrn Professor Dr. Franz Wüllner in Verehrung und Dankbarkeit."

Performance Issues: This score presents an interesting mixture of rich late 19th-century orchestration and harmonic practices with significant elements of imitative counterpoint. Strauss uses fugal procedures and pervasive imitation in a manner clearly influenced by Brahms and, to a lesser extent, Bruckner. The choral writing is primarily syllabic, and the choral parts are fairly consistently doubled by the orchestra. The passages that are a cappella or lacking in rhythmic doubling are all homophonic. The thickness of the orchestration and the complexity of the counterpoint may make it difficult for the singers to identify their own parts as being doubled, but the support is there. Because of the imitative nature of the score, the soprano parts frequently cross, and parts should be assigned to accommodate equal tessituras. The tessitura of the bass I part is quite high, and all of the vocal parts are physically demanding. The orchestral writing is already masterful at this early point in Strauss's career. He does call for pianissimo dynamics from the entire ensemble, which will require seasoned players. The voicing of the brass and winds suggests a large symphonic choir and substantial string section. The parts are quite idiomatically written, but require an expert orchestra. There are particularly tricky passages for the violas and cellos. Although demanding of the choir and orchestra, this is an impressive and exciting work that deserves more performances; **choir:** difficult **orchestra:** difficult.

Selected Discography

Wiener Akademie-Kammerchor, Wiener Symphoniker; conducted by Henry Swoboda. Westminster WN 18075 [LP].
Dresdener Philharmonic Chorus and Orchestra; conducted by Michel Plasson. EMI (7243 56572 2).
Münchner Motettenchor; Münchner Symphoniker; conducted by Hayko Siemens. ARTE NOVA Classics 74321 72107 2.

Selected Bibliography

Del Mar, Norman: *Richard Strauss*, in three volumes, I: 31-35, II: 46, 352, 360, 370. Philadelphia: Chilton Book Company; 1962, 1969, and 1972.

Taillefer, op. 52 (1903)

Duration: ca. 16 minutes

Text: The text is a ballad by Johann Ludwig Uhland.

Performing Forces: voices: Williams's sister (soprano), Taillefer (tenor), and William the Conqueror (baritone) soloists; SSAATTBB choir; **orchestra:** 2 piccolos, 4 flutes, 4 oboes, 2 English horns, 2 clarinets (in D), 4 clarinets (A, B^b), bass clarinet (B^b), 4 bassoons, contrabassoon, 8 horns (D^b, D, E, F), 6 trumpets (B^b, D^b, D, E^b, E, F), 4 trombones, 2 tubas, timpani (4 drums), percussion (6 players — 2 small snare drums [military], 2 large snare drums [rühr], bass drum, triangle, cymbals, glockenspiel), and strings (24, 24, 16, 14, 12)

First Performance: 26 October 1903; Emma Rückbeil-Hiller, Emil Pinks, Rudolf von Milde; conducted by Richard Strauss

Editions: Full scores and parts for *Taillefer* were published by Fürstner in 1903. A critical edition appears on page 57 in volume 30 of the *Richard Strauss Edition* published by Verlag Dr. Richard Strauss.

This new edition includes an English singing translation by Paul England.

Autograph: The composer's manuscript is in the Richard Strauss Archive in the Bayerischen Stadtsbibliothek in Munich.

Notes: *Taillefer* is a musical portrayal of the Battle of Hastings and William the Conqueror's compatriot, the warrior and trouvère, Taillefer. The score is dedicated to the Philosophy Faculty of the University of Heidelberg. It was completed in Charlotenburg, 2 May 1903.

Performance Issues: The title character should be pronounced in the French manner [tie-uh-fay] to properly serve the rhyme. The choral writing is generally syllabic and homophonic. The majority of the score uses four-part choral writing, divisi are harmonic rather than contrapuntal. There is very little direct doubling of the choir by the orchestra, but the choral parts are not musically difficult, and the often more melodic orchestral material does provide clear harmonic support. There are some brief three-part divisi in all parts but the basses. The choral tessituras are fairly high, and the vocal writing for the choir is quite operatic. A very large choral ensemble is required to balance the exceptionally large orchestra. The orchestral parts are all challenging with rapid passagework, demanding ranges, and rhythmic complexity. The orchestration is quite heavy-handed, which may present some balance issues with the singers. The soloists' parts are not difficult, but singers must be selected to carry over the orchestra. This is an orchestral tour de force that requires 143 instrumentalists if one follows the string indications in the score, which are reasonable in balance with the other parts. This is a much briefer work that uses its forces in the manner of Schoenberg's *Gurrelieder*. **Soloists:** William's sister (soprano) - range: a'-$g\#''$, tessitura: a'-$g\#'$, this is a simple, declamatory role; Taillefer (tenor) - range: e-$b^{b'}$, tessitura: g-g', this is a sustained and lyrical role; William the Conqueror (baritone) - range: B-f', tessitura: d-d', this is a declamatory and straightforward solo role; **choir:** medium difficult; **orchestra:** very difficult.

Selected Discography

Maria Cebotari, Walter Ludwig, Hans Hotter, The Rudolf Lamy Choir, Symphony Orchestra of Radio Berlin; conducted by Arthur Rother, recorded in 1944. Released on LP by Urania (UR 7042) and reissued on on CD, Preisser 90222.

Johan Botha, Michael Volle; Dresdener Philharmonic Chorus and Orchestra; conducted by Michel Plasson. EMI (7243 56572 2).

Elisabeth-Maria Wachutka, Gerhard Siegel, Hans-Peter Scheidegger; Münchner Motetten Chor; Münchner Symphoniker; conducted by Hayko Siemens. ARTE NOVA Classics 74321 72107 2.

Selected Bibliography

Del Mar, Norman: *Richard Strauss*, in three volumes, I: 182, 183; II: 363-366, 368, 375; III: 250, 338, 348. Philadelphia: Chilton Book Company; 1962, 1969, and 1972.

Tchaikovsky, Piotr Ilyich (b. Votkinsk, Russia, 7 May 1840; d. St. Petersburg, 6 November 1893)

Life: Tchaikovsky initially studied law and then attended the St. Petersburg Conservatory. He later joined the faculty of the Moscow Conservatory. In 1877 he married one of his pupils from whom he separated after only nine weeks. This was surely the result of his homosexuality, but it led him to a near mental breakdown. He received significant patronage from Nadezhda von Meck, who was also the principal patroness of the Moscow Conservatory, which allowed him to live comfortably and dedicate all of his energies to composition. This arrangement was suddenly ended in 1890, which significantly hurt Tchaikovsky, but he was quite fiscally independent as his career had flourished under her sponsorship.

Tchaikovsky traveled extensively as a composer and conductor. He led the inaugural concert in Carnegie hall as part of his one trip to the United States.

Tchaikovsky's music is marked by an exceptional melodic gift. He is matched only by Mozart, and perhaps Gershwin, in his ability to produce important music filled with memorable tunes that have become part of our everyday musical vocabulary. While his music is distinctly Russian to modern listeners, those composers at the center of the nationalist movement perceived his music to be cosmopolitan and even Germanic. The technical refinement of his works led them to be the most performed of all Russian composers during his lifetime, and their lyricism and melodic fluency has kept them at the heart of the standard repertory.

Teachers: Anton Rubinstein, Nikolai Zaremba

Students: Nikolai Klenovsky, Sergei Taneyev

Writings: Tchaikovsky did not publish prose, but a number of diaries and correspondence have been published in English translations. Some of these are listed below under "Composer Bibliography."

Other Principal Works: opera: *Eugene Onegin* (1877-1878), *Queen of Spades* (1890); **ballet:** *Swan Lake* (1875-1876), *Sleeping Beauty* (1888-1889), *Nutcracker* (1891-1892); **orchestral:** Symphony No.

1 (1866), Symphony No. 2 (1872), Symphony No. 3 (1875), Symphony No. 4 (1877-1878), Symphony No. 5 (1888), Symphony No. 6 (1893), Piano Concerto No. 1 (1874-1875), Piano Concerto No. 2 (1879-1880), Violin Concerto (1878), *Romeo and Juliet* (1869), *1812 Overture* (1880), Serenade (1880), *Manfred Symphony* (1885), *Hamlet* (1888).

Tchaikovsky's complete works were published in a critical edition overseen by Boris Asafiev. This set was reprinted by Edwin F. Kalmus. This edition contains a number of significant textual changes reflecting Soviet will. A new authoritative monument has been begun by Muzyka and Schott, which will be more true to the composer's original; however, only the first few scores of this project have yet come to print.

Selected Composer Bibliography

Tchaikovsky, Piotr Ilyich: *The Diaries of Tchaikovsky*, translated and annotated by Wladimir Lakond. New York: W. W. Norton, 1945.
_____: *Letters to His Family: An Autobiography*, published in an English translation by Galina von Meck. London: 1981; reprinted, New York: Cooper Square Press, 2000.
Abraham, Gerald, editor: *The Music of Tchaikovsky*. New York: W. W. Norton, 1946.
Warrack, John: *Tchaikovsky*. New York: Charles Scribner's Sons, 1973.
Orlova, Alexandra: *Tchaikovsky: A Self Portrait*. Oxford: Oxford University Press, 1990.
Brown, David: *Tchaikovsky: A Biographical and Critical Study*, 4 volumes. New York: W. W. Norton, 1978-1991.
Poznansky, Alexander: *Tchaikovsky: The Quest for the Inner Man*. New York: Schirmer Books, 1991.
Kearney, Leslie: *Tchaikovsky and His World*. Princeton: Princeton University Press, 1998.
Poznansky, Alexander: *Tchaikovsky Through Others' Eyes*. Bloomington: Indiana University Press, 1999.
_____, and Brett Langston: *The Tchaikovsky Handbook: A Guide to the Man and His Music*, 2 volumes. Bloomington: Indiana University Press, 2002.
Brown, David: *Tchaikovsky: The Man and His Music*. London: Pegasus Books, 2007.

www.tchaikovsky-research.net provides a thorough and up-to-date discography and well-annotated notes on all of Tchaikovsky's works including English translation of notes from important Russian sources.

K radosti ["Ode to Joy"], TH 66 (1865)

Duration: ca. 28 minutes

Text: The text is Friedrich Schiller's "An die Freude," used in Beethoven's Symphony No. 9, translated into Russian by Konstantin Axakov and others.

Performing Forces: voices: soprano, alto, tenor, and bass soloists; SATB choir; **orchestra:** piccolo, 2 flutes, 2 oboes, 2 clarinets (B^b, A), 2 bassoons, 4 horns (E, F, G), 2 trumpets (C, E^b, E), 3 trombones, tuba, timpani (2 drums), percussion (3 players — bass drum, triangle, cymbals), and strings.

First Performance: 10 January 1866;[85] St. Petersburg; possibly conducted by Anton Rubinstein

Editions: A critical edition of *K radosti* is published in *Piotr Ilyich Tchaikovsky: Polnoye sobraniye sichiyeni*, volume 27, page 3. A new critical edition. *P.I. Chaykovsky: Nonoye polnoye sobraniye sochineniy*, volume 33, page 3 is published by Muzyka and Schott.

Notes: This work was composed as a graduation exercise. Plagued by nerves, Tchaikovsky did not attend the premiere, which was negatively reviewed by Cesar Cui who represented "the Five." In spite of the mixed reception of this work, Tchaikovsky was granted a silver medal upon his graduation.

Performance Issues: The choral writing combines homophonic textures and close imitation, Some of the choral material is clearly doubled by the orchestra, but there are some extended a cappella passages and additional sections wherein the accompaniment and

---

[85] Some sources will indicate 24 April, which is the old-Russian calendar system.

vocal parts are quite independent. All of the vocal material is practically written, so it is easily taught and presents no significant vocal challenges to the choir or the soloists. There are divisi for all sections of the choir. The brass scoring requires the use of a symphonic chorus and a full complement of strings. There is significant doubling of the choir by the full brass section, which may present some challenges to good balance. This is a student work, and it betrays this in a number of ways including less varied and imaginative orchestration than one would expect from Tchaikovsky and a number of "stiff" contrapuntal exercises. All of the instrumental parts are practical and idiomatic, but balance will be the primary challenge throughout the orchestra. It is nonetheless an attractive and beautifully melodic composition. Later is his life Tchaikovsky expressed concern that this work not be published for fear of comparisons with Beethoven's setting of the same text. While it is not a work in the same league as the Beethoven, it is an attractive and practical composition that would be a good showpiece for a large choir. **Soloists:** soprano - range: $d'-a^{b''}$, tessitura: $b'-f\#''$, this is a simple lyric solo; alto - range: a^b-d'', tessitura: $d'-b'$, this is a sustained lyric role; tenor - range: $g-a'$, tessitura: $a-f'$, this is a lyric role, it is the largest of the solo, but not considerably; bass - range: $G-e^{b'}$, tessitura: $B-c'$, this is a declamatory solo part; **choir:** medium difficult; **orchestra:** medium easy.

Selected Discography

Alia Arkadov, Ludmila Shemechuk, Aleksandr Nauomenko, Dmitri Kharitonov; Geoffrey Mitchell Chorus, London Symphony Orchestra; conducted by Derek Gleason, recorded in 1993. Pickwick: 30366 00122.

Ludmila Belobragina, Ludmila Simonova, Yuri Elnikov, Evgenii Vladimirov; USSR Radio and Television Symphony Orchestra and Chorus; conducted by Yuri Simonov, recorded in 1979. Citadel: CDT 88138.

Selected Bibliography

Abraham, Gerald: "Religious and Other Choral Music," in *The Music of Tchaikovsky*, edited by the author, 230-231. New York: W. W. Norton, 1946.

Warrack, John: *Tchaikovsky*, 44, 45. New York: Charles Scribner's Sons, 1973.

Orlova, Alexandra: *Tchaikovsky: A Self Portrait*, 13. Oxford: Oxford University Press, 1990.

Brown, David: *Tchaikovsky: A Biographical and Critical Study*, 4 volumes; I: 83-86, 89, 95, 127, 130, 146, 169 250-251; II: 52; III: 215. New York: W. W. Norton, 1978-1991.

Cantata for the Opening of the Polytechnic Exhibition, TH 67 (1872)

Duration: ca. 32 minutes

Text: The text is by Yakov Petrovich Polonsky.

Performing Forces: voices: tenor soloist; SATB choir; **orchestra:** piccolo, 2 flutes, 2 oboes, 2 clarinets (B^b, A), 2 bassoons, 4 horns (F), 2 trumpets (D, E), 3 trombones, tuba, timpani (3 drums), percussion (4 players[86] — snare drum, bass drum, triangle, and cymbals), and strings.

First Performance: 12 June 1872;[87] Moscow; as the opening of the Polytechnic Exhibition; Aleksandr Dodonov, tenor; conducted by Karl Davydov

Editions: A critical edition of this cantata under the title, *Cantata to Commemorate the Bicentenary of the Birth of Peter the Great*, is published in *Piotr Ilyich Tchaikovsky: Polnoye sobraniye sichiyeni*, volume 27, page 189. A new critical edition. *P.I. Chaykovsky: Nonoye polnoye sobraniye sochineniy*, volume 33, page 85, is being published by Muzyka and Schott. Edwin F. Kalmus publishes full scores (no. 586) and parts for this work under the title, *Cantata for the Opening of the Moscow Poytichnic Exposition*.

---

[86] Three players should be sufficient. There is one measure just after rehearsal number 56 that presents an awkward switch to cymbals for one of the other players.

[87] Some sources will indicate 31 May, which is the old-Russian calendar system.

Notes: Soviet editions of this worked called it "Cantata to Commemorate the Bicentenary of the Birth of Peter the Great."

Performance Issues: The choral writing is primarily homophonic, although there are some very interesting sections utilizing a variety of imitative procedures reminiscent of the works of Mendelssohn. There are some divisi throughout the choir and some sustained fortissimo sections. The choral material is generally clearly doubled by the orchestra, but there are some a cappella passages. All of the winds have some challenging material. There are particularly exposed and extended passages with intricate passagework for the flutes and clarinet I. The brass and string writing is idiomatic and very playable. There are some rapidly articulate fanfares for the brass that may require attention to unify articulations. This is a colorfully orchestrated work that is generally sensitive to issues of balance for the soloist, but there are some significant bombastic sections with full brass and percussion that demand a large choir and full string section, which is reflective of the venue for which it was composed. This is a powerful and impressive celebratory work for a vocally athletic choir and skilled orchestra. **Soloists:** tenor - range: e-a', tessitura: f-f', this is a substantial lyric role with long sustained phrases; **choir:** medium difficult; **orchestra:** medium difficult.

Selected Discography

Lev Kuznetsov; USSR Radio and Television Symphony Orchestra and Chorus; conducted by V. Kozhukar, recorded in 1982. Regis: 1182.

Selected Bibliography

Orlova, Alexandra: *Tchaikovsky: A Self Portrait*, 158. Oxford: Oxford University Press, 1990.
Brown, David: *Tchaikovsky: A Biographical and Critical Study*, 4 volumes; I: 248, 250-251, 253; II: 46, 52; III: 215. New York: W. W. Norton, 1978-1991.

Cantata in Celebration of the Golden Jubilee of Osip Petrov, TH 68 (1875)

Duration: ca. 4 minutes

Text: The text is by Nikolai Nekrasov.

Performing Forces: voices: tenor soloist,[88] SATB choir; **orchestra:** piccolo, 2 flutes, 2 oboes, 2 clarinets (A), 2 bassoons, 4 horns (F), 2 trumpets (D), 3 trombones, tuba, timpani (2 drums), and strings.

First Performance: 6 May 1876,[89] St. Petersburg Conservatory; conducted by Karl Davydov

Editions: A critical edition of this cantata is published in *Piotr Ilyich Tchaikovsky: Polnoye sobraniye sichiyeni*, volume 27, page 341. A new critical edition. *P.I. Chaykovsky: Nonoye polnoye sobraniye sochineniy*, volume 33, page 151, is published by Muzyka and Schott.

Notes: Osip Afanasevich Petrov was a celebrated bass in the Marinskii Opera. This work was commissioned by the Russian Music Society to celebrate his 50th year as a performer.

Performance Issues: The choral writing is mostly homophonic and quite simple. The orchestration is quite playable and fairly static. This is a practical and cheerful work that could be a good concert opener for a large choir and community orchestra. **Soloists:** tenor - range: e-f#', tessitura: a-f#', this is a lyric role for powerful voice; **choir:** easy, **orchestra:** medium easy.

---

[88] According to the critical edition, the autograph indicates that a soprano may be substituted for the soloist.

[89] Some sources will indicate 24 April, which is the old-Russian calendar system.

Selected Discography

At the time of this writing no commercial recordings appear to be available.

Selected Bibliography

Brown, David: *Tchaikovsky: A Biographical annd Critical Study*, 4 volumes; II: 52. New York: W. W. Norton, 1978-1991.

Moskva ["Moscow" or "Coronation Cantata"], TH 69 (1883)

Duration: ca. 22 minutes

Text: Apollon N. Maikov

Performing Forces: voices: mezzo-soprano and baritone soloists, SATB choir; **orchestra:** 3 flutes, 2 oboes, 2 clarinets (A), 2 bassoons, 4 horns (F), 2 trumpets (D), 3 trombones, tuba, timpani (3 drums), harp, and strings.

First Performance: 27 May 1883;[90] Moscow in the Granovitskii Palace; Elizaveta Lavrovskaia, Ivan Mel'nikov; conducted by Eduard Nápravnik

Editions: A critical edition of *Moskva* is published in *Piotr Ilyich Tchaikovsky: Polnoye sobraniye sichiyeni*, volume 27, page 361. A new critical edition. *P.I. Chaykovsky: Nonoye polnoye sobraniye sochineniy*, volume 33, page 161, is published by Muzyka and Schott.

Notes: This work was commissioned as part of the coronation festivities for Alexander III. It is organized as follows:

1. Chorus
2. Arioso   mezzo-soprano
3. Chorus

---

[90] Some sources will indicate 15 May, which is the old-Russian calendar system.

4. Monologue and Chorus baritone
5. Arioso mezzo-soprano
6. Finale tutti

Performance Issues: The choral writing is almost entirely homophonic and quite simple, although much of it is loosely accompanied. There are divisi throughout the choir. The orchestral writing is quite challenging. There are rapid and complex passages throughout the orchestra. The brass writing is more judicious than in Tchaikovsky's earlier cantatas, but the most fully orchestrated passages still require a large choral group. This is an excellent work for a large community choir and a strong professional orchestra. Contemporary performance might benefit from a new text. **Soloists:** mezzo-soprano - range: a^b-g'', tessitura: $e^{b'}$-$e^{b''}$, this is lyric role with a folk-like vocal line; baritone - range: B-f#', tessitura: B-b, this is a declamatory role functioning as a narrator with recitative-like parts; **choir:** medium easy; **orchestra:** difficult.

Selected Discography

Nina Derbina, Alexander Polyakov; USSR Radio and Television Symphony Orchestra and Chorus; conducted by Gennadi Cherkassov. Recorded in 1982. Regis: 1182.

Svetlana Furdui, Vassily Gerelo; Dallas Symphony Orchestra and Chorus; conducted by Andrew Litton, recorded in 1995. Delos: DE 3196.

Olga Teriuchkova, Boris Statsenko; Berlin Radio Symphony Orchestra and Chorus; conducted by Mikhail Jurowski, recorded in 1997. Koch Schwann: 3 6553-2.

Malin Fritz, Jung-Hack Seo; Russian Chamber Chorus of New York, American Symphony Orchestra; conducted by Leon Botstein, recorded live in 1997. Town Hall: THCD 53.

Selected Bibliography

Davidova and Protopopov: *Muzikal'noye naslediye Chaykovskovo*, 347-349. Moscow: 1958.

Orlova, Alexandra: *Tchaikovsky: A Self Portrait*, 246-247, 250-251, 258. Oxford: Oxford University Press, 1990.

Brown, David: *Tchaikovsky: A Biographical annd Critical Study*, 4 volumes; III: 175, 214-218, 223, 266; IV: 267. New York: W. W. Norton, 1978-1991.

Verdi, Giuseppe (b. Le Roncole, Italy, 9 October 1813; d. Milan, 27 January 1901)

Life: Verdi's father ran a tavern. He had uneven early musical training. A local patron, Antonio Barezzi, sent him to Milan for formal study, but he was unable to pass the entrance exam to the conservatory. He undertook private instruction with Vincenzo Lavigna, and in a few years passed the exam to hold the post of *maestro di musica* in Busseto. In 1836, he married his patron's daughter. They lost two children in infancy, and she died in 1840. Pouring himself into his work, he scored his first operatic success with *Nabucco*. This was followed by a string of successful operas, and Verdi quickly became the most celebrated Italian opera composer of his generation.

Verdi was a strong believer in Italian independence from Austria, and many of his works can be seen as a metaphorical commentary on the politics of the time. He was frequently embroiled with the censors over the subtext of his libretti. Likewise, Verdi lived with the singer Giuseppina Strepponi for a decade before they were married, and *La traviata* is the composer's response to social critics of that relationship. Verdi became an important national figure in the founding of unified Italy and was even nominated to the Italian senate.

Verdi's works are filled with memorable tunes, but of equal importance they are eminently singable. He possessed a remarkable theatrical sense for communicating directly to his audiences. Some critics have unduly described his accompaniments as simplistic. He was a master of supporting his singers without making them compete with their accompaniments. His later works demonstrate that he remained in touch with the harmonic developments of the late 19th century.

Teacher: Vincenzo Lavigna

Other Principal Works: opera: *Nabucco* (1841), *I Lombardi* (1842), *Ernani* (1843), *Macbeth* (1846-1847), *Luisa Miller* (1849), *Stiffelio* (1950), *Rigoletto* (1850-1851), *Il trovatore* (1851-1852), *La traviata* (1853), *Les Vêpres siciliennes* (1854), *Simone Boccanegra* (1856-1857), *Un ballo in maschera* (1857-1858), *La forza del des-*

tino (1861), *Don Carlos* (1866), *Aida* (1870), *Otello* (1884-1886), *Falstaff* (1889-1893).

Selected Composer Bibliography

Weaver, William: *Verdi: A Documentary Study.* London: Thames and Hudson, 1977.

Budden, Julian: *Verdi.* London: J. M. Dent and Sons, 1985. Reprinted under same title in the *Master Musicians* series, New York: Vintage, 1987.

Osborne, Charles: *Verdi: A Life in the Theatre.* London: George Wiedenfeld and Nicolson, 1987. Reprinted, New York: Fromm International Publishing Corporation, 1989.

Phillips-Matz, Mary Jane: *Verdi: A Biography.* Oxford: Oxford University Press, 1993.

Messa da Requiem (1873-1874)

Duration: ca. 84 minutes

Text: The text is from the Roman Catholic liturgy of the Mass for the Dead.

Performing Forces: voices: soprano, mezzo-soprano, tenor, and bass soloists; SATB choir; **orchestra:** 3 flutes (flute III doubling piccolo), 2 oboes, 3 clarinets (A, B^b, C), 4 bassoons, 4 horns (C, E^b, E, F, A^b, A, B^b), 4 trumpets (C, E^b), 3 trombones, tuba, timpani (3 drums), percussion (1 player — bass drum), and strings.

An additional group of 4 off-stage trumpets (E^b) is required.

First Performance: 22 May 1874; San Marco, Milan to commemorate the first anniversary of the death of Alessandro Manzoni; Teresa Stolz, Maria Waldmann, Giuseppe Capponi, Ormondo Maini; conducted by the composer

Final version: 12 May 1875; Royal Albert Hall, London

Editions: A critical edition of *Messa da Requiem* is published by Ricordi and the University of Chicago as part of *The Works of Giuseppe Verdi*, series III, volume 1. Full scores and parts are available for purchase from Ricordi, Kalmus, C. F. Peters, and G. Schirmer. There is a facsimile edition of the manuscript as well.

Autograph: The composer's manuscript full score is in the Museo Teatrale alla Scala in Milan. Additional manuscript materials are in the archives of Villa Verdi in Busseto, Italy.

Notes: When Gioacchino Rossini died in 1868, Verdi initiated a Requiem project for which a different composer would compose each section. Although the work was completed in time, rancor among the contributors and conductor prevented the proposed concert. The "Libera me" movement was composed in 1869 as Verdi's contribution to this composition by committee. Four years later, Alessandro Manzoni, the great Italian poet and national hero died. Verdi had idolized Manzoni and embarked on this work as a memorial tribute to him. He utilized his earlier "Libera me" movement. The premier was probably Verdi's first appearance as a conductor. He led another performance a few days later in the Teatro alla Scala. The mezzosoprano solo in the "Liber scriptus" section was added shortly after the premiere. This version was premiered the following year, and that has remained the definitive version since.[91]

Performance Issues: The choral material is generally well supported by the orchestra. There are some a cappella passages. All of the choral writing demonstrates a keen awareness of the singing voice. Much of the score is expectedly operatic, but very singable even by ambitious amateur ensembles. Some of the tenor and soprano passages will present vocal challenges to such ensembles. There are divisi for all of the choral parts. The tunefulness and logic of the counterpoint make this remarkably easy to teach to choirs allowing for more time to rehearse timbre and pacing. There are some passages where it is nearly impossible to effectively balance the choir and orchestra. A large symphonic chorus is necessary, and clever

---

[91] Pahlen, Kurt: *The World of the Oratorio*, translated by Judith Schaefer with additional English-language material by Thurston Dox, 320-321. Portland, OR: Amadeus Press, 1990.

pacement of the singers with respect to the orchestra may alleviate some of these challenges. The "Sanctus" is scored for a double chorus, which may further affect placement decisions. There is one passage in which the piccolo exceeds the bottom of the standard range of the instrument, which reflects Verdi's familiarity with the instruments of an Italian maker whose products had an extened foot. These notes can just be left out with no detrimental effect. The general orchestral writing is dramatic and practical. Great care must be given to adhere to the dynamics indicated in the score. The brass parts may be troublesome to balance. The use of small-bore trombones will help in this regard. There is some florid passagework for each of the principal winds. All of the solo parts are vocally difficult. The women have some significant pairings, so the selection of soloists should include a consideration of how these two voices complement each other. **Soloists:** soprano - range: b-c''', tessitura: g'-g'', this is a sustained and lyric role that must me able to balance against the full ensemble and sing the top of the range at a very low dynamic; mezzo-soprano - range: g-a$^{b'''}$, tessitura: f'-f'', this is a dramatic and sustained role; tenor - range: c-b$^{b'}$, tessitura: g-g', this is a lyric solo role; bass - range: G-e', tessitura: c-c', this is a powerful declamatory solo; **choir:** difficult; **orchestra:** difficult.

Selected Discography

Maud Cunitz, Elisabeth Hongen, Walther Ludwig, Josef Greindl; Bavarian Radio Orchestra and Chorus; conducted by Eugen Jochum, recorded in 1950. Re-released on CD as Orfeo d'Or: 195892.

Herva Nelli, Fedora Barbieri, Giuseppe di Stefano, Cesare Siepi; Robert Shaw Chorale, NBC Symphony; conducted by Arturo Toscanini. Live broadcast, 27 January 1951, Carnegie Hall, New York. Re-released on CD as RCA: 60299-2-RG.

Leonie Rysanek, Christa Ludwig, Giuseppe Zampieri, Cesare Siepi; Singverein der Gesellschaft der Musikfreunde; Vienna Philharmonic Orchestra; conducted by Herbert von Karajan. EMI: 0724356688025.

Leontyne Price, Janet Baker, Veriano Luchetti, José Van Dam; Chicago Symphony Orchestar and Chorus; conducted by Georg Solti. RCA: 62318.

Susan Dunn, Diane Curry, Jerry Hadley, Paul Plishka; Atlanta Symphony Orchestra and Chorus; conducted by Robert Shaw; recorded in 1987. Telarc: 80152.

Selected Bibliography

Upton, George: *The Standard Oratorios*, 303-308. Chicago: A. C. McClurg and Company, 1893.
Tovey, Francis: "Requiem in Memory of Manzoni," in *Essays in Musical Analysis*, volume 5, 195-209. London: Oxford University Press, 1937.
Robertson, Alec: *Requiem: Music of Mourning and Consolation*, 96-110. New York: Frederick A. Praeger, 1967.
Rosen, David: "Verdi's 'Liber scriptus' Rewritten," in *Musical Quarterly*, volume 55 (1969), 151-169.
Greene, David B.: "Giuseppe Verdi's *Dies irae*," in *Response in Worship, Music, the Arts*, volume 11 (1971), 77-88.
Rosen, David: *The Genesis of Verdi's Requiem*, Doctoral dissertation: University of California at Berkeley, 1976.
Martin, George: "Verdi, Manzoni, and the *Requiem*," in *Aspects of Verdi*, 31-58. New York: Limelight Editions, 1988.
Rosen, David: "The Operatic Origins of Verdi's 'Lacrymosa,'" in *Studi verdiani*, volume 5 (1988-1989), 65-84.
Pahlen, Kurt: *The World of the Oratorio*, translated by Judith Schaefer with additional English-language material by Thurston Dox, 320-325. Portland, OR: Amadeus Press, 1990.
Rosen, David: "Critical Commentary" for *Messa da Requiem* in *The Works of Giuseppe Verdi*, series III, volume 1. Chicago: University of Chicago Press, 1990.
Roeder, John: "Pitch and Rhythmic Dramaturgy in Verdi's Lux æterna," in *19th Century Music*, volume 14, number 2 (1990), 169-185.
Berger, Melvin: *Guide to Choral Masterpieces: A Listener's Guide*, 325-328. New York: Anchor Books, 1993.
Phillips-Matz, Mary Jane: *Verdi: A Biography*, 601-615, 622, 624-625, 648-649. Oxford: Oxford University Press, 1993.
Rosen, David: *Verdi: Requiem* [from the series, *Cambridge Music Handbooks*]. Cambridge: Cambridge University Press, 1995.
_____: "Reprise as Resolution in Verdi's *Messa da Requiem*," in *Theory and Practice*, volume 19 (1994).

Roeder, John: "Formal Functions of Hypermeter in the 'Dies irae' of Verdi's *Requiem*," in *Theory and Practice*, volume 19 (1994).

Stabat Mater (1895-1897)

Duration: ca. 12 minutes

Text: The authorship of this text is highly disputed. It was removed from sanctioned use at the Council of Trent, and restored to the liturgical canon in 1727. The text addresses the "Seven Sorrows of the Virgin Mary." It is used as the Sequence Hymn on the first Friday after Passion Sunday and on 15 September.[92]

Performing Forces: voices: SATB choir; **orchestra:** 3 flutes, 2 oboes, 2 clarinets (B^b), 4 bassoons, 4 horns (C), 3 trumpets (C), 4 trombones, timpani (2 drums), percussion (1 player — bass drum), harp, and strings.

First Performance: 7 April 1898; Paris Opéra; Société des Concerts, conducted by Paul Taffenel

First complete performance of *Quattro Pezzi Sacri*: 26 May 1898; Turin; conducted by Arturo Toscanini

Editions: Full scores and parts for *Stabat Mater* are available for purchase from Ricordi, Kalmus, and C. F. Peters.

Notes: This is the second of the *Quattro Pezzi Sacri*:

1. *Ave Maria* — SATB, unaccompanied (1889)
2. *Stabat Mater* — SSAA, orchestra (1897)
3. *Laudi alla Vergine Maria* — SSAA, unaccompanied (1887)
4. *Te Deum* — double SATB, orchestra (1896)

These pieces, while composed independently and using different performing forces utilize some common melodic material. They are frequently presented as a group in concerts. Each functions

---

[92] Jeffers, Ron: *Translations and Annotations of Choral Repertoire, Volume I: Sacred Latin Texts*, 200-207. Corvallis, OR: Earthsongs, 1988.

well as a free-standing composition. The *Ave Maria* and *Laudi alla Vergine Maria* are not discussed in detail here because they are unaccompanied. In preparation for the premiere of the complete set, Toscanini met with the composer. Accounts of that meeting indicate that the composer recommended a choir of 120 rather than the 200 originally planned for the concert. [93]

Performance Issues: The choral writing is generally homophonic with occasional imitative passages. The choral material is well supported by the orchestra. There are a number of unison passages for the choir or for a section of the choir. For the latter, soloists could be used. There are divisi for all choral sections except the sopranos. There are complex and rapid passages for all of the instruments, and the choir and orchestra are expected to span a broad dynamic range. The score demands a choir of mature voices capable of powerful sustained singing interjected with *sotto voce* passages at the extremes of traditional ranges. The entire ensemble must be flexible and expressive. This is a dramatic and very effective brief setting of this text that deserves more performances from first-rate ensembles; **choir:** difficult; **orchestra:** difficult.

Selected Discography

Helen Donath, Josef Protschka, Dietrich Fischer-Dieskau; Bayerischen Rundfunks Choir and Symphony Orchestra; conducted by Wolfgang Sawallisch, recorded in 1982 and 1983. EMI Classics: 7243 5 65845 2.

Selected Bibliography

Berger, Melvin: *Guide to Choral Masterpieces: A Listener's Guide*, 328-332. New York: Anchor Books, 1993.
Phillips-Matz, Mary Jane: *Verdi: A Biography*, 737-738. Oxford: Oxford University Press, 1993.

---

[93] Phillips-Matz, Mary Jane: *Verdi: A Biography*, 747. Oxford: Oxford University Press, 1993.

Te Deum (1895-1897)

Duration: ca. 15 minutes

Text: This is an anonymous hymn of thanksgiving in church use since the sixth century. It is usually sung during the Matins service. The apocryphal source of its genesis is that it was spontaneously sung by Ss. Ambrose and Augustine on the evening when Augustine was baptized.[94]

Performing Forces: voices: soprano soloist; double SATB choir; **orchestra:** 3 flutes, 2 oboes, English horn, 2 clarinets (B^b), bass clarinet (B^b), 4 bassoons, 4 horns (E^b), 3 trumpets (E^b), 4 trombones, timpani (2 drums), percussion (1 player — bass drum), harp, and strings.

First Performance: 7 April 1898; Paris Opéra; Société des Concerts, conducted by Paul Taffenel

Editions: Full scores and parts for *Te Deum* are available for purchase from Ricordi, Kalmus, and C. F. Peters.

Notes: See notes above for Verdi's *Stabat Mater*.

Performance Issues: The score begins with an a cappella section that includes an incipit of chant. There are additional unaccompanied passages for eight-part choir. Much of the choral material is freely contrapuntal and often quite independent of the accompaniment. The choral writing is vocally demanding for the entire choir, but especially the sopranos and tenors who maintain high tessituras. There are challenging passages for much of the orchestra as well. The scoring requires a large choir and full string section. This is an impressive setting, which might in fact make an effective companion to the Bruckner setting of the same text. It is an excellent showpiece for a skilled choir and strong orchestra. **Soloists:** soprano - range: e'-b'', tessitura: e''-b'', this is a very brief, simple

---

[94] Jeffers, Ron: *Translations and Annotations of Choral Repertoire, Volume I: Sacred Latin Texts*, 218. Corvallis, OR: Earthsongs, 1988.

solo for a chorister, all but the e″ is in unison with the section; **choir:** difficult; **orchestra:** difficult.

Selected Discography

Robert Shaw Chorale, NBC Symphony; conducted by Arturo Toscanini. Live broadcast, 14 March 1954, Carnegie Hall, New York. Re-released on CD as RCA: 60299-2-RG.

Selected Bibliography

Berger, Melvin: *Guide to Choral Masterpieces: A Listener's Guide*, 328-332. New York: Anchor Books, 1993.

Phillips-Matz, Mary Jane: *Verdi: A Biography*, 733-735. Oxford: Oxford University Press, 1993.

TEXT SOURCES

Abranyi, Kornel von (1822-1903) was a composer, pianist, and a very successful writer about music. He was an avid follower of Wagner and Liszt, becoming a friend of the latter. He also produced some Hungarian translations of Italian operas. Found in Liszt: *Die Legende von der heiligen Elisabeth.*

Acworth, Harry was a British ciil servant in India. He served as the President of the Bombay Anthropological Society and published English translations of a number of Indian poems, particularly from Marathi. In retirement, he was neighbors with Edward Elgar for whom he provided libretti. Found in Elgar: *Caractacus.*

Aquinas, Thomas (1225-1274) was an Italian philosopher and theologian. Against the wishes of his family he entered the Dominican order. He studied under Albertus Magnus. His work combined Aristotelian philosophy with Christian doctrine. His magnum opus, *Summa Theologica* (1266-1273) remained unfinished at his death. Found in Mendelssohn: *Lauda Sion*; Schubert: *Tantum Ergo in C* (D. 460), *Tantum Ergo in C* (D. 739), *Tantum Ergo in D* (D. 750), *Tantum Ergo in E^b* (D. 962).

Barbier, Henri-Auguste (1805-1889) was a Paris-born poet and satirist. Found in Berlioz: *Vox Populi.*

Bartholomew, William was an English chemist and vioinist who provided English translation for many of Mendelssohn's compositions. Found in Mendelssohn: *Elijah.*

Belloc, Louise (1796-1881) is also cited as Lousie Swanton-Belloc. She was an Irish-born writer who translated numerous English texts into French. Found in Berlioz: *Tristria.*

Béranger, Pierre-Jean de (1780-1857) was a popular Parisian poet whose works were politically charged enough to land him in prison twice in the 1820s. Found in Berlioz: *Le Cinq Mai.*

Bible Found in Beach: *Festival Jubilate* (Psalm 100); Brahms: *Eine deutsches Requiem, Psalm 13, Triumphlied*; Bruch: *Moses*; Bruckner: *Psalm 112, Psalm 146, Psalm 150*; Dvorak: *Psalm 149*;

Elgar: *The Light of Life*, Liszt: *Christus*; Mendelssohn: *Christus, Elijah, Hymn* (Psalm 13), *Psalm 42, Psalm 95, Psalm 98, Psalm 114, Psalm 115, St. Paul, Symphony No. 2, Tu es Petrus*; Schubert: *Graduale: Benedictus es, Domino, Offertorium: Intende voci in B^b, Offertorium: Tres sunt.*

Bulthaupt, Heinrich (1849-1905) was a librarian in Bremen. He produced opera and oratorio libretti and produced a multi-volume work on dramaturgy. Found in Bruch: *Achilleus, Das Feuerkreuz.*

Bunsen, J.F. von was a baron and theological writer. Found in Mendelssohn: *Christus.*

Capel-Cure, Edward was a fellow at Merton College, Oxford and Rector of the Church of St. George in Bloomsbury. He published sermons and other religious writings. Found in: Elgar: *The Light of Life.*

Cüppers, J. see Hellmuth, Friedrich.

Deschamps, Emile (1791-1871) was a French poet born in Bourges. He founded the journal, *La Muse Moraliste* with Victor Hugo. Found in Berlioz: *Romeo et Juliette.*

Erben, Karel Jaromir (1811-1870) was a Czech poet, writer, and historian. He wrote many poems and song lyrics based upon Czech folklore. Found in Dvorak: *Svatební kosile.*

Ferrand, Humbert was a lawyer and a devout Roman Catholic. He was a friend of Berlioz for whom he provided poetry. Found in Berlioz: *La révolution grecque, scène héroïque.*

Francis of Assisi (1181-1226) was born to a wealthy family with the given name of Giovane Bernadone. He renounced his fortune and dedicated himself to the service of the poor. He established the Franciscan monastic order and its female counterpart, the Porr Clares. Found in Beach: *Canticle of the Sun.*

Gandonnière, Almire worked with Berlioz to adapt Nerval's French translation of Goethe's *Faust*. Found in Berlioz: *La Damnation de Faust.*

Geibel, Emanuel (1815-1884) was a German poet. He produced many German translations of Greek, Italian, and Spanish poems. He was a founder of the Munich School. Found in Bruch: *Schön Ellen.*

Goethe, Johann Wolfgang von (1749-1832) was one of the most important figures in German literature. He was a prolific poet, author, natural scientist, and a figure at court. His numerous works include: *Leiden des jungen Werthers* (1774), *Egmont* (1788), *Wilhelm Meisters Lehrjahre* (1796), and *Faust* (1808 and 1832). Found in Beethoven: *Meerestille und Gluckliche Fahrt*; Berlioz:

La Damnation de Faust, Huit scènes du Faust, Lélio ou le Retour à la vie; Brahms: *Alto Rhapsody, Gesang der Parzen, Rinaldo*; Mendelssohn: *Die erste Walpurgisnacht*; Schumann: *Requiem für Mignon, Szenen von Goethes Faust*, Strauss: *Wanderers Sturmlied.*

Graff, Wilhelm Paul (1845-1904) was a German poet and book vendor. Found in Bruch: *Odysseus.*

Hackenburg, Albert (1852-1912) was German theologian. He was the leader of the Evangelical Church in Germany from 1908 to 1912. Found in Bruch: *Gustav Adolf.*

Hebbel, Friedrich (1813-1863) was a German playwright. He is best known for his *Nibelungen* trilogy (1855-1860). Found in Schumann: *Nachtlied.*

Hellmuth, Friedrich (1879-1919) was a German writer. He used the pseudonym J. Küppers (sometimes printed as Cüppers). Found in Bruch: *Arminius.*

Hölderlin, Friedrich (1770-1843) was a great German poet. His philosophy teachers included Hegel and Schelling. He was encouraged by Klopstock and Schiller. He established his reputation with the novel, *Hyperion* (1799). He was debilitated by mental illness throughout the second half of his life. Found in Brahms: *Schicksalslied.*

Holmes, Oliver Wendell (1841-1935) was an American jurist. His great legal work was *The Common Law* (1881). He served as associate justice of the U.S. Supreme Court for 30 years. Found in Beach: *The Chambered Nautilus.*

Homer (8th century BCE) was a blind epic poet to whom authorship of the *Iliad* and the *Odyssey* is attributed. Found in Bruch: *Achilleus* and *Odysseus.*

Huber, Franz Xavier (1760-1810) was a Viennese poet and librettist. Found in Beethoven: *Chistus am Oelberge.*

Kotzebue, August von (1761-1819), born in Weimar he was a playwright and poet. After 1811, he lived in Estonia. He was assassinated in Mannheim. Found in Beethoven: *Die Ruinen von Athen, König Stephan*

Kuffner, Christoph, This name is sometimes given as the possible author of the text of Beethoven's Choral Fantasy; however, no confident attribution can be made. Found in Beethoven: *Fantasia in C minor.*

Küppers, J. see Hellmuth, Friedrich.

Lafont, Pierre-Chéri (1797-1873) abandoned a naval career as a physician's assistant to pursue acting and singing. He worked primarily in Vaudeville as a performer and director. Found in Berlioz: *L'Imperiale*.

Legouvé, Ernest (1807-1903) was a prolific French dramatist. He was the son of the poet, Gariel Legouvé. He was a leading figure in the Académie Français and received the highest level of the Legion d'Honneur. Found in Berlioz: *Tristria*.

Lingg, Hermann (1820-1905) was a German poet and playwright. Found in Bruch: *Salamis*.

Liturgical texts: These various texts are connected with regular liturgical practice, or are relevant to a specific day or season within the church year.

Ave Maria — This is found in Brahms: *Ave Maria*.

Mass — This refers to the Ordinary of the Roman Catholic Communion Service comprising the following sections:

>Kyrie eleison
>Gloria in excelsis
>Credo
>Sanctus and Benedictus
>Agnus Dei

The mass is found in Beach: *Mass in E^b*; Beethoven: *Mass in C*, *Missa Solemnis*; Berlioz: Messe *solonnelle*; Bruckner: *Missa Solemnis in B^b minor*; *Mass No. 1 in D minor*, *Mass No. 2 in E minor*, *Mass No. 3 in F minor*; Delibes: *Messe Brève*; Fauré: *Messe des pêcheurs de Villeville*; Messager: *Messe des pêcheurs de Villeville* [see under Fauré]; Puccini: *Messa a 4 Voci (Messa di Gloria)*; Rossini: *Petite messe solonnelle*; Schubert: *Kyrie in D* (D. 31), *Kyrie in D* (D. 49), *Kyrie in F* (D. 66), *Magnificat, Mass No. 1 in F*, *Mass No. 2 in G*, *Mass No. 3 in B^b*, *Mass No. 4 in C*, *Mass No. 5 in A^b*, *Mass No. 6 in E^b*, *Deutsche Messe* (in German translation); Schumann: *Mass*.

Pater Noster — Literally "Our Father," it is the Lord's Prayer in Latin. Found in: Liszt: *Christus*.

Requiem — Also known as the Missa pro Defunctis, or Mass for the Dead, this service went through centuries of evolution and was sanctioned in its final form at the Council of Trent. It is organized in the following sections:

Introit	Requiem æternam
Kyrie	Kyrie eleison
Gradual	Requiem æternam
Tract	Absolve, Domine
Sequence	Dies irae
Offertory	Domine Jesu Christe
Sanctus	Sanctus, Santus, Sanctus
Benedictus	Benedictus qui venit
Agnus Dei	Agnus Dei
Communion	Lux æterna
Responsory	Libera me, Domine
Antiphon	In paradisum

The Requiem is found in: Berlioz *Grande messe des morts*; Bruckner: *Requiem in D minor*; Cherubini: *Requiem Mass in D minor*; Dvorak: *Requiem Mass*; Fauré: *Messe de Requiem*; Gounod: *Requiem*; Schumann: *Requiem*; Verdi: *Messa da Requiem*.

Stabat Mater — The text addresses the "Seven Sorrows of the Virgin Mary." Found in: Dvorak: *Stabat Mater*; Liszt: *Christus*; Rossini: *Stabat Mater*; Schubert: *Stabat Mater in G minor, Stabat Mater in F*; Verdi: *Stabat Mater*.

Te Deum — This is an anonymous hymn of thanksgiving in church use since the sixth century. It is usually sung during the Matins service. The apochryphal source of its genesis is that it was spontaneously sung by Ss. Ambrose and Augustine on the evening when Augustine was baptized.[95] Found in Berlioz: *Te Deum*; Bruckner: *Te Deum*; Dvorak: *Te Deum*; *Te Deum*.

Tu es Petrus — This is found in Liszt: *Christus*; Mendelssohn: *Tu es Petrus*.

---

[95] Jeffers, Ron: *Translations and Annotations of Choral Repertoire, Volume I: Sacred Latin Texts*, 218. Corvallis, OR: Earthsongs, 1988.

Longfellow, Henry Wadsworth (1807-1882) was a popular American lyric poet. His best known works include: *Ballads* (1841), *Evangeline* (1847), *The Golden Legend* (1851), *Hiawatha* (1855), *The Courtship of Miles Standish* (1858), and *Tales of a Wayside Inn* (1863). Found in Coleridge-Taylor: *The Song of Hiawatha*.

Maikov, Apollon N. (1821-1897) was a painter and sculptor who turned to a career in poetry. He also worked as a censor for the czar. Found in Tchaikovsky: *Moskva*.

Milton, John (1608-1674) was an influential poet and the son of a stark church-music composer. He is the author of numerous religious and political pamphlets. His poetical works include: *Paradise Lost* (1665), *Paradise Regained* (1671), and *Samson Agonistes* (1671). Found in Paine: *The Nativity*.

Mischka, Caroline was a little-known Victorian-Americn poet from Buffalo, New York. Found in Beach: *The Rose of Avon-town*.

Missa pro Defunctis — see Requiem under Liturgical Texts.

Mohnike, Gottlieb (1781-1841) was a German theologian, linguist, and translator. Found in Bruch: *Frithjof*.

Montesquiou, Count Robert de (1855-1921) was a poet and art collector. He is thought to have been the inspiration for the character of Baron de Charlus in Proust's *Rememberance of Things Past*. Found in Fauré: *Pavane*

Moore, Thomas (1779-1852) was a an Irish poet. His works include: *Irish Melodies* (1807-1834), and *Lalla Rookh* (1817). Found in Berlioz: *Tristia*; Schumann: *Das Paradies und die Peri*.

Morlaix, Bernard de (12th century) was a monk in the order of Cluny who produced many Latin hymns and other poetry. Found in Parker: *Hora Novissima*.

Nekrasov, Nikolai (1821-1878) was a Russian journalist, critic and poet. He is associated with the Realistic school.Found in Tchaikovsky: *Cantata in celebration of the golden jubilee of Osip Petrov*

Nerval, Gérard de (1808-1855) was a French author who produced a French translation of Goethe's *Faust* when he was 20-year-old. He led a tragic life, which ended in suicide. Found in Berlioz: *La Damnation de Faust, Huit scènes du Faust*.

Neumann, Johann Philipp (1774-1849) was an Austrian physicist, poet, and librarian. He served as the librarian and a professor of the Polytechnic Institute in Vienna for thirty years. Found in Schubert: *Deutsche Messe*.

Pater Noster — see under Liturgical Texts

Polonsky, Yakov Petrovich (1819-1898) was a Russian poet born into a noble family. He was trained at Moscow University and wrote in a romantic style. Found in Tchaikovsky: *Cantata for the Opening of the Polytechnic Exhibition*.

Psalms — This is a biblical book of poetry attributed to King David. Found in: Beach: *Festival Jubilate* (Psalm 100); Brahms: *Psalm 13*, Bruckner: *Psalm 112, Psalm 146, Psalm 150*; Dvorak: *Psalm 149*; Mendelssohn: *Hymn* (Psalm 13), *Psalm 42, Psalm 95, Psalm 98, Psalm 114, Psalm 115*; Schubert: *Offertorium: Intende voci in B^b* (Psalm 5).

Roman Catholic Mass — see under Liturgical Texts

Roquette, Otto (1824-1896) studied languages in Heidelberg, Berlin and Halle. He became a professor at the Darmstadt Polytechnikum. Found in: Liszt: *Die Legende von der heiligen Elisabeth*.

Schiller, Friedrich (1759-1805) was a great German poet, historian, and playwright. He was a leader of the Sturm und Drang style. His works include: *Über naive und sentimentalische Dichtung* (1795-1796), *Wallenstein* (1797-1798), *Das Lied von der Glocke* (1799), *Maria Stuart* (1800), and *Wilhelm Tell* (1804). Found in Beach: *The Minstrel and the King*; Beethoven: Symphony No. 9, Brahms: *Nänie*; Bruch: *Das Lied von der Glocke*, Tchaikovsky: *K radosti*.

Schubring, Julius (1806-1889) was a Lutheran pastor in Dessau and a childhood friend of Mendelssohn. Found in Mendelssohn: *St. Paul*.

Scott, Sir Walter (1771-1832) was a successful Scottish poet and novelist. His works include: *The Lady of the Lake* (1810), *The Bride of Lammermoor* (1819), *Ivanhoe* (1820), *The Talisman* (1825), and *Woodstock* (1826). Found in Bruch: *Feuerkreuz*.

Shakespeare, William (1564-1616) is the pre-eminent playwright and poet of Elizabethan England. His work form the very foundation of the English theatrical repertoire. Found in Berlioz: *Romeo et Juliette, Tristria*.

Silberstein, August (1827-1900) was an Austrian author. His satirical articles in the German publication, *Leuchtkugeln*, resulted in a prison sentence. He favored rustic scenes in his poetry, which was set by Strauss and Bruckner. Found in Bruckner: *Helgoland*.

Spitta, Ludwig (1801-1859) was a theologian and poet from Hanover. His brother, Philipp was the renowned Bach biographer. Found in Bruch: *Moses*.

Stabat Mater — see under Liturgical Texts.

Te Deum — see under Liturgical Texts.

Tegner, Esaias (1782-1846) was Bishop of Wexiö, Sweden. He was a successful poet and a professor of Greek at Lund. He is primarily remembered for his *Frithof's Saga* (1825). Found in Bruch: *Frithjof.*

Tennyson, Alfred First Baron Tenyson (1809-1892) was a immensely popular English poet. He succeeded Wordsworth in 1850 as Poet Laureate. His works include: *Poems* (1842) and *In Memoriam* (1850). Found in Beach: *The Sea-fairies.*

Tu es Petrus — see under Liturgical Texts.

Uhland, Johann Ludwig (1787-1862) was born in Tübingen, Germany. He was a successful poet and held a number of minor governmental posts. Found in Strauss: *Taillefer.*

Vrchlicky, Jaroslav is the pseudonym of Emil Frida (1853-1912). A pupil of Victor Hugo, he wrote much Czech poetry as well as Czech translation of classical texts. Found in Dvorak: *Svata Ludmila.*

Weisse, Michael (1488-1534) was a Franciscan monk and the author of many hymns. He joined the Moravian Brothers and edited the first Moravian hymnal, *Ein New Gesengbuchlin* (1531). Found in Brahms: *Begräbnisgesang.*

Weissenbach, Alois (1766-1821) was a deaf surgeon who met Beethoven in Vienna and ingratiated himself to the composer leading to their collaboration on *Der glorreiches Augenblick.* Found in Beethoven: *Der glorreiches Augenblick.*

About the Author

Composer and conductor, **Jonathan D. Green**, is dean of the college and vice president for Academic Affairs at Sweet Briar College.

As a composer, he has received awards from ASCAP, the North Carolina Arts Council, and the Virginia Center for the Creative Arts. His works include numerous songs, choral works, three piano concertos, and seven symphonies.

Dr. Green is the author of five other music-reference books: *A Conductor's Guide to Choral-Orchestral Works: The Twentieth Century*, parts I and II, *A Bio-Bibliography of Carl Ruggles*, *A Conductor's Guide to the Choral-Orchestral Works of J. S. Bach*, and *A Conductor's Guide to the Choral-Orchestral Works of the Classical Period, Part I: Mozart and Haydn*.

He is a member of ASCAP, the College Music Society, the Conductors Guild (board member), and Phi Mu Alpha Sinfonia. He presently resides at Sweet Briar with his wife, Lynn Buck.